D0836785

Higher Education Law

# Higher Education Law
*The Faculty*

STEVEN G. POSKANZER

**VCTC Library**
**Hartness Library**
Vermont Technical College
Randolph Center, VT 05061

The Johns Hopkins University Press
*Baltimore and London*

© 2002 The Johns Hopkins University Press
All rights reserved. Published 2002
Printed in the United States of America on acid-free paper
9 8 7 6 5 4 3 2 1

The Johns Hopkins University Press
2715 North Charles Street
Baltimore, Maryland 21218-4363
www.press.jhu.edu


Library of Congress Cataloging-in-Publication Data

Poskanzer, Steven G.
    Higher education law: the faculty / Steven G. Poskanzer.
        p.    cm.
Includes bibliographical references and index.
    ISBN 0-8018-6748-7 (hardcover : alk. paper) — ISBN
0-8018-6749-5 (pbk. : alk. paper)
    1. Education, Higher—Law and legislation—United States. 2. College
teachers—Legal status, laws, etc.—United States. I. Title.
    KF4225.P67 2001
    344.73'074—dc21                                                    00-012805

A catalog record for this book is available from the British Library.

George Keller, Consulting Editor

*To Janie—for teaching me what really matters and endures*

# Contents

Acknowledgments    ix

Introduction    1

1  The Lay of the Land    5
Constitutional, Statutory, and Regulatory Requirements  5 /
Case Law  9  /  State Action  11  /  First Amendment Principles  16 /
Contractual Obligations  19  /  Immunity from Suit  22

2  Scholarship    25
Selection of Research Topics  25  /  Obtaining Support for
Scholarship  30  /  Ownership and Exploitation of Scholarly
Work  34  /  Dissemination of and Access to Scholarly Work  46 /
Conflicts of Interest and Conflicts of Commitment  55 /
Concluding Thoughts  60

3  In the Classroom    63
Foundations of Academic Freedom  64  /  External Attacks on
Faculty Classroom Autonomy  69  /  Intra-University Disputes about
Faculty Teaching  71  /  Copyright and Teaching Materials  94 /
Concluding Thoughts  102

4  Faculty as Institutional Citizens    104
Faculty Involvement in Institutional Governance and
Operations  105  /  Conferences and Symposia  117  /  Academic
Freedom at Religiously Affiliated Colleges and Universities  120 /
Concluding Thoughts  125

5   Faculty as Public Citizens   127
Faculty Extramural Speech  127  /  Faculty Membership in
Controversial Organizations  139  /  Concluding Thoughts  140

6   Faculty as Employees   143
Hiring, Promotion, and Job Security  143  /  The Overlay of
Nondiscrimination Law  158  /  Terms of Employment  182  /
Faculty Discipline  200  /  Concluding Thoughts  249

Final Observations on Faculty Law   253
The Risk of Personal Liability  254  /  Basic Sources of Legal
Tension  256  /  Assessing the Law's Impact  258

Notes   261

Index   339

# Acknowledgments

It turns out that it's really hard to write a book. Like a student submitting a late term paper, I always had a plausible excuse for the extra time this effort was taking: my son was born; I was teaching; I'd moved and started a new job; the case law kept changing. Eventually, however, the overriding need to bring this effort to conclusion prevailed. Suffice it to say that you hold in your hands the product of countless late evenings, lost weekends, and forgone vacations since 1994.

It is, of course, customary for authors to take responsibility for any errors or omissions in their work (which I freely do here) while sharing credit with peers and friends who helped bring a project to fruition. Since this book has undergone such a long gestational period, I now have a great many persons to thank.

That list must begin with two former colleagues at the University of Pennsylvania. George Keller, then head of the Higher Education Program in Penn's Graduate School of Education, would have earned my lifetime gratitude for giving me my first opportunity to teach. But he went much further by suggesting that I write a book on college and university law and putting me in contact with the Johns Hopkins University Press. George's inspiration and kindness reinforced an earlier conversation with Bob Zemsky, the Director of Penn's Institute on Research on Higher Education, who urged a certain lawyer-turned-academic-administrator to write an "important book" on colleges and universities. Only time and the critics will tell whether I have succeeded in crafting a volume of genuine significance, but I have certainly tried to follow Bob's injunction by pouring my soul into this manuscript.

My career peregrinations from Penn to Princeton to Penn to Chicago to SUNY have left me with a wide trail of individuals to acknowledge. Hugo Sonnenschein, with whom I took several of those career steps, has been the finest personal and professional mentor I could ever have wished for, and he continues to be my role model. Geof Stone, Provost at the University of Chicago, has unflaggingly supported my teaching and scholarship and showed incredible generosity of time and spirit (not to mention a searing intellect) in reviewing this book. Douglas Baird, as Dean of Chicago's Law School, gave me a chance to test my ideas with first-rate students.

I also owe much to colleagues and friends among the ranks of university attorneys. My former boss at Penn, Shelley Green, lived up to her reputation as a spectacular editor, kindly tearing my manuscript apart and putting it back together in tighter and sharper form. Two other Penn colleagues, Frank Roth and Neil Hamburg, regularly answered questions about disparate topics and offered guidance—and specific case cites. Frank's assistance also included commenting on the finished manuscript—a task undertaken as well by Richard Zansitis at Rice, whose trenchant insights particularly strengthened the sections on employment discrimination and labor law.

More specific gaps were filled with the help of colleagues across the academic landscape, including Joe DeFilippo, Joyce Villa, and Martianne Ellerman at SUNY System Administration; Bob Spitzer of SUNY Cortland; Shirley Egan and Pat McClary at Cornell; and David Foster. Beth Bringsjord, Georgianne Crabill, and Ginette Chambers provided key support (the latter two were even pressed into service to produce printed versions); Marianna O'Dwyer was a source of constant encouragement (at one point loaning me her house in which to write!); and my current boss, SUNY Provost Peter Salins, has been deeply supportive of my scholarship and an excellent model of an intellectually engaged administrator. Indeed, all my SUNY colleagues deserve thanks for indulgently bearing with me through each stage of the book-writing process.

That process, of course, has been brilliantly shepherded by Jackie Wehmueller, my editor at the Johns Hopkins University Press. I shall always be indebted to Jackie for her extraordinary patience in dealing with a first-time (and perhaps despairingly slow) author, for never losing faith in this project, and for repeatedly offering sound advice on critical subjects and their presentation. Indeed, if not for Jackie's idea to focus my initially envisioned (and much longer) volume covering all of higher education law into a book on the law pertaining to faculty, I might still be at work on this manuscript. Now, thanks to her, I have a second book to look forward to! Thanks are also owed to the readers who critiqued—and improved—the book, and to the copyediting and production staff at Hopkins, especially Lois Crum and Carol Zimmerman.

Finally, I owe what are obviously my deepest thanks to my family: my father, Charles Poskanzer, whose teaching, research, and service at SUNY Cortland epitomize faculty at their best; my mother, Joan Poskanzer, whose college service is equally an exemplar; my in-laws, George and Anne Nofer, for letting me do research and write in seclusion at their home; my wife, Jane, who let me devote to a book massive chunks of time that I could have spent with her—and who, on countless occasions, endured my requests to read "just one more section"; and Jill and Craig, the best kids I'll ever know—who will now see a lot more of their dad.

Higher Education Law

# Introduction

"Do we need to talk to our lawyers about this?"

"What do the attorneys say?"

"Why didn't you get the lawyers involved before now?"

Just about every department chair and dean, certainly every president and provost, and an ever-increasing number of faculty find themselves asking—or being asked—such questions. Lawyers, legal requirements, and lawsuits have become established parts of the apparatus of American higher education. In many respects this is a positive development. Most faculty would agree, for example, that laws mandating safer laboratories and judicial opinions articulating stronger protection for the academic freedom (and job security) of scholars have considerable value. At the same time, in some respects the growth of college and university law has been an unwelcome, if not downright unfortunate, occurrence. One thinks here of governmental or administrative efforts to chill scholarly discussion of legitimate academic topics, of cumbersome and ineffective procedural requirements for faculty discipline cases, and of faculty who are hesitant to offer candid evaluations of students or colleagues for fear of being drawn into legal disputes.[1]

Boon, bane, or something in between, legal considerations now exert an enormous impact on the day-to-day work of colleges and universities.[2] And this impact is likely to grow. Thus, it is essential that faculty and administrators have a solid understanding of the most important legal concepts and rules applicable to American higher education. Hence this book.

This book describes the central legal principles governing the activities of faculty and the regular academic affairs of colleges and universities. It explains, in general terms and in an accessible manner, the range of legal action available to such individuals and their institutions (i.e., both the constraints imposed by the law and the protections and rights that it affords), the kinds of legal traps to watch for, and how best to ensure that the academic, disciplinary, and employment decisions involving faculty that are made by college and university representatives are proper and legally defensible. In providing a guide to this area of higher education law, this volume also attempts to identify areas of heightened legal tension (e.g., between claims of individual and institutional academic freedom) and areas where the law is particularly unsettled.

Faculty sometimes find it necessary to remind administrators that the institution's ultimate strength and distinction derives from the quality of its faculty. They are right to stress this point. More than any other factor, it is the presence of an outstanding faculty that enables a college or university to attract the most talented undergraduate, graduate, and professional students and to recruit the new faculty who are the key to its future.

The words and actions of faculty—in performing their regular duties of scholarship, teaching, and service; in their sometime capacity as institutional representatives; and in their everyday role as private citizens—give rise to a host of legal questions, which are the focus of this volume. We live in a litigious age, one in which faculty conduct (or misconduct) is increasingly likely to be challenged by students or colleagues, perhaps to become the subject of institutional discipline. Extra-institutional actors, such as the press, the government, and interested citizens, also subject faculty behavior to heightened scrutiny. At the same time, faculty themselves are more willing to turn to the courts to assert claims and zealously to protect their rights. All of this means that there is a special urgency to understanding how the law both limits and facilitates the efforts of college and university faculty.

The chapters of this book address in turn the legal aspects of the various facets of a faculty member's work and life: conducting research in the library or the laboratory, preparing to teach and then providing instruction in the classroom, attending committee meetings, and participating in public events both on and off campus.[3] This will, of course, also involve discussion of a faculty member's status as an institutional employee.

One recurrent theme of the book must also be identified and drawn out a bit at the start. If our colleges and universities are to fulfill the great tasks we set for them, such as discovering and sharing knowledge, equipping students with the information and skills needed to lead meaningful lives, and (at institutions whose mission includes public service) bringing knowledge to bear on pressing issues, the college and university faculty who will take the lead in accomplishing these tasks will require enormous intellectual and didactic latitude—what is commonly termed *academic freedom*.

The justifications for and proper scope of academic freedom are considered in more detail throughout this volume. But even at the beginning of our discussion of the law pertaining to faculty, it is essential to stress that, as a general rule, externally imposed law or internal rules with the force of law that restrict the faculty's range of intellectual action harm not only the faculty members in question but also the institution itself and society at large. Judges, legislators, regulators—and above all college and university administrators—who deal with faculty must always keep this in mind.

This book is aimed at faculty and administrators who do not have formal legal training but who periodically confront issues with legal implications: department chairs and deans making renewal and promotion decisions, researchers concerned about the financial and intellectual consequences of corporate sponsorship, faculty concerned about teaching controversial subjects, administrators charged with disciplining professors for nonperformance of assigned duties. It should help administrators and faculty to understand better when they need to seek legal advice (in my experience, quite often at an earlier point in the decision-making process than actually occurs) and to assist them in evaluating it. Furthermore, by educating these key users of legal advice about the basic legal environment in which their institutions operate, it may also be possible to avoid some fundamental substantive or procedural errors that could result in disputes and litigation. In other words, this is a book that will help avoid legal land mines.

My hope is that readers will use the information and analysis contained in this volume to act in legally thoughtful and appropriate ways as a matter of course (this being preventive law) and to be sophisticated consumers of legal services. Knowledge of the law pertaining to faculty and its underlying rationale should also result in better and fairer academic and administrative decisions, not just more easily defensible ones. Furthermore, because this book examines currently operative legal principles and extant patterns in the case law, points out inconsistencies and gaps in the law, and identifies emerging issues and possible new directions for courts to follow or commentators to pursue, it is likely to hold genuine interest for scholars, students, and practitioners of higher education law.

In explaining what this book seeks to be and to achieve, it may also be helpful to speak briefly about what it is not. This volume is not intended as a digest or encyclopedia of college and university law for use by practicing attorneys. It does not comprehensively describe all of the legal principles and rules applicable to higher education. Rather, it self-consciously selects

particular topics—those that are likely to be of greatest interest and importance to faculty and administrators—and describes the status of the law in
those areas, with special emphasis on the law's practical effect on such
individuals and their institutions.

Nor should this book be viewed as a substitute for formal legal advice on
particular factual questions. Putting completely aside the author's desire to
maintain the goodwill of his fellow university attorneys, this is not a reference volume to consult instead of your institution's lawyer (nor does any
such magical tome exist). However, it is my hope that the information and
analysis contained herein will make the reader a considerably more discriminating user of legal advice.

Two final caveats. First, American colleges and universities are a diverse
multitude,[4] and different types of institutions—public and private, proprietary and nonprofit—face markedly different legal requirements. For example, a critical distinction is made throughout this book between institutions that are state-supported and those that are not. When geography is
thrown into the mix, our ability to make broad generalizations about what
"the law" requires is reduced even further. Federal law is a constant, but
state and local codes vary widely. And as we shall see, state law, which
governs contracts and property rights, is particularly important for colleges and universities. One therefore cannot assume that the legal result
obtained by another institution in similar (or even identical) circumstances
would follow at one's own college or university. However, there are enough
nationwide laws and regulations, common statutory language, similar case
law, and judicial reliance upon precedent from other jurisdictions to allow
us to speak with reasonable certainty and authority about what the law
requires of faculty, administrators, and institutions in important situations.

Last, it is crucial to remember that the law is not static. Legislatures and
public officials continually promulgate new statutes and regulations, and
judicial opinions relevant to colleges and universities are issued almost
daily. Attempting to fix definitively the meaning and import of "the law of
higher education" is rather like, in the memorable phrase, "trying to nail
gelatin to the wall." However, the basic doctrines of higher education law
are by now relatively well established and enduring. College and university
law will continue to evolve, mostly by accretion, but its central concepts—
which are the focus of this book—are unlikely to change dramatically. In
any event, this volume is certainly an accurate depiction of the state of law
affecting faculty and institutions as of early 2001.

# 1 The Lay of the Land

Our discussion and analysis of higher education law must start with a brief overview of the various sources of law applicable to colleges and universities, including some mention of how these sources relate to and affect one another, and a few observations on the structure and operation of our judicial system.

## Constitutional, Statutory, and Regulatory Requirements

Colleges and universities face a thicket of constitutional, statutory, regulatory, judicial, and quasi-judicial directives that, depending on your perspective, either limit institutional behavior or establish and safeguard individual and group rights.[1] The ultimate source of law applicable to American higher education is, of course, the U.S. Constitution. The Constitution is primarily concerned with the organization and operation of the federal government, the relationship between the federal government and state governments, dealings among the various states, and the relationship between both the federal and state governments and the general populace. While the Constitution does not apply to or limit the actions of private educational institutions (a central theme of this book),[2] it *is* directly applicable to the actions of public colleges and universities and their authorized representatives. For constitutional purposes, public institutions are *state actors* analogous to the federal, state, or municipal government. Thus, just as FBI agents and local police must comply with constitutional limits in conducting searches or detaining citizens, so too must law enforcement officials at public colleges and universities meet constitutional requirements when investigating charges of misconduct by faculty or students.

The Constitution has a broad impact on public higher education. The First Amendment guarantees of freedom of speech, freedom of the press, and the right to assemble protect (for the most part) from institutional censorship or punishment the scholarly investigations of faculty, the in-class remarks of professors and students, and the extracurricular orations of faculty or student firebrands/gadflies and campus newspapers.[3] The Fifth and Fourteenth Amendments ensure that the state—in this case, the state university—may not take away your property (which includes intangible but essential rights such as continued employment) without prior notice, an opportunity to present your side of the story, and the other procedural and substantive safeguards that constitute "due process of law." The Four-teenth Amendment's command that states may not deny any person the "equal protection of the laws" has resulted in lawsuits alleging unlawful discrimination on the basis of race, sex, and other characteristics as well as comprehensive efforts to desegregate state systems of higher education.[4]

Using the powers vested in it by the Constitution, the Congress has passed numerous statutes that directly and indirectly affect American higher education. Such statutes may regulate the activities of both public and private colleges and universities. Much of this legislation has been enacted in the last fifty years, beginning with the G.I. Bill and government sponsor-ship of research after World War II. Prominent examples of federal laws applicable to colleges and universities today include civil rights statutes banning various forms of discrimination in employment, antitrust laws (which have been used to investigate allegedly collusive admissions and financial aid practices), and workplace legislation such as the Occupational Safety and Health Act. Again, it is important to understand that these stat-ues may be crafted in ways that allow the federal government to direct the conduct of private, as well publicly owned, institutions. Sometimes this is accomplished through the Congress's broad power to regulate "interstate commerce" (a term that has been read in a sweeping fashion by the courts); more frequently, it is achieved by linking statutory compliance with the receipt of federal funds. The "dollar hook" has enabled the federal govern-ment to exercise considerable influence over the internal affairs of colleges and universities. Thus, the provisions of Title IX of the Education Amend-ments of 1972 outlawing discrimination on the basis of sex—which have caused much upheaval in the realm of intercollegiate athletics—apply to any public or private educational institution that receives federal funds, including funds (such as student aid moneys) that are used for purposes far afield from the locus of the alleged discrimination.

In order to implement and enforce congressional statutes, federal agen-cies have promulgated many volumes of regulations that are applicable to colleges and universities. As long as these regulations are consistent with the language and intent of the underlying statutes, they are equally binding on institutions. Continuing with our Title IX example, while the wording of the actual statute is quite general ("No person . . . shall, on the basis of sex, be excluded from participation in, be denied the benefits of, or be subjected to discrimination under any educational program or activity receiving federal financial assistance"),[5] the Title IX regulations issued by the Department of Education specify in great detail what constitutes unlawful discrimination and how enforcement proceedings will be conducted.[6] These regulations address everything from admissions to housing to course registration to student services and medical benefits. In the area of athletics, the regulations enumerate criteria for evaluating whether an institution is providing equal opportunities for men and women (e.g., are the interests of both sexes being effectively accommodated? are locker rooms and practice facilities equivalent?).[7] Notwithstanding politicians' rhetoric about reducing regulatory burdens, new regulations are constantly being issued and colleges and universities must spend enormous amounts of time reviewing such rules and ensuring compliance.[8]

Because the federal Constitution and the statutes enacted pursuant to it are the "supreme law of the land,"[9] superseding all other sources of law, federal statutes must be consistent with the dictates of the Constitution, federal regulations must be consistent with the Constitution *and* the provisions of the statute they are intended to implement, and so on down through the various levels of state and local law.

Even with the deepening federal involvement in higher education described above, the states remain the primary shapers of higher education law. This reflects the historical and cultural fact that in America, education is viewed as a matter of state, if not local, concern—and thus control. It is no coincidence that the United States has no national university.

The federal constitutional, statutory, and regulatory apparatus applicable to the activities of colleges and universities is mirrored at the state level. Each state has its own constitution, which defines the rights of its citizens and establishes governmental structures (including, in many instances, state universities).[10] State constitutions may be quite comprehensive, delving into areas and extending protections well beyond those of the U.S. Constitution. For instance, the California constitution grants citizens an express right to privacy, which has no federal counterpart.[11]

State statutes are the most significant source of college and university law. A few examples quickly demonstrate their ubiquitous nature. Each year, state legislatures pass appropriations bills providing operating funds to public (and sometimes private) educational institutions.[12] State legislation creates higher education coordinating boards, and state nonprofit corporation law typically sets the organization framework of private colleges and universities, including the actions of their boards of trustees. State civil service laws apply to the personnel decisions of many public institutions, state antihazing laws protect fraternity pledges, state drug and alcohol laws apply to student behavior within the jurisdiction, and state law may even seek to ensure the free exchange of ideas on campus or to dictate the number of hours professors must spend in classroom instruction.[13]

Like federal laws, state statutes are given effect through detailed regulations. These regulations, promulgated by state agencies, cover an equally wide gamut of college and university activities. Examples would include environmental regulations for the transport and disposal of hazardous wastes generated in laboratories or teaching hospitals, rules establishing (or permitting an institution to challenge) the eligibility of former employees for unemployment compensation, and licensure requirements for academic programs or graduates entering certain professions such as pharmacy or psychology.[14] As is apparent from several of these examples, some state regulations that are not specifically directed at colleges and universities nonetheless cover them along with other industries or activities.

Below this layer of state law lies a dense thatch of local (county and municipal) law directly applicable to institutions of higher education.[15] Among the central concerns of local law are property taxation and land use. Thus, decisions about whether real estate taxes are payable on a particular piece of college or university land—say, the president's house or an athletic/events center—are typically made by local authorities interpreting local tax codes. Local zoning ordinances determine what use institutions may make of their lands, and building and fire safety codes greatly influence the shape and scope of campus development. This legal aspect of town-gown relations can generate real controversy—witness Ithaca, New York, where city officials, citing Cornell University's noncompliance with an applicable (but clearly outdated) zoning ordinance, refused to issue building permits to Cornell in an attempt to gain leverage in a long-running dispute over payments in lieu of taxes.[16] Localities also frequently establish legal rights or obligations that extend beyond the sweep of federal and state law. Many large cities, for example, have banned discrimination on the basis of sexual orientation, even though this is not a protected classification under federal law.[17]

## Case Law

The preceding sketch of the formal, written legal standards (constitutional, statutory, and regulatory) applicable to colleges and universities at the federal, state, and local levels covers only part of the relevant legal landscape. These formal rules are interpreted, supplemented—and occasionally supplanted—by the decisions of adjudicatory, especially judicial, entities at each level, forming a body of law known as case law.

Much case law involves the application of formal legal rules in various contexts. For example, does Title IX's prohibition against discrimination on the basis of sex require the Virginia Military Institute, a state institution, to admit women applicants? Case law also involves the interpretation (and perhaps the development) of legal principles formulated in the first instance by judges or courts themselves. These "common law" principles include hoary doctrines of contract and tort (personal injury) law, such as what constitutes an offer to make a legally binding contract or whether you are liable if your guests are injured on your property, as well as modern theories of product liability law and the use of economic analyses to determine legal responsibilities and damages.

The final judgment in any dispute is, of course, directly binding on the litigants. For them, it becomes a legal requirement with the same force as a statute. In addition, the holding in the case serves as a precedent available to the same or other decision makers in subsequent cases. It thus becomes a potential source of law for present and future actors. The body of case law is massive, and it grows each day, in courtrooms and offices of adjudicatory authorities across the nation. It is worth emphasizing here that federal, state, and local judges are by no means the sole or even the largest source of case law. Quasi-judicial officials and bodies, such as hearing examiners, zoning boards, arbitrators, and Equal Employment Opportunity Commission investigators regularly make findings of fact and determinations that have the full force of law (even if they may be appealed in a formal judicial setting) and which merit that appellation.

A few brief words on the organization and operation of federal and state judicial systems. Jurisdictions across the United States (almost) uniformly employ the same trilevel structure: disputes are first heard in a *trial* court, before a single decision maker (e.g., a judge or a magistrate) or a jury, which carries out a detailed examination of the facts and the relevant law; the controversy next proceeds to an *appellate* court, before a panel of judges, which ascertains whether an error of law has been made at the trial level; it may then move to a *supreme* court, again before a panel of judges, for a final review.[18] While appeals from the trial to the appellate court level are usually "of right"—that is to say, either party's appeal will automatically be heard—there is typically no right to have one's case heard by the supreme court of the jurisdiction, which customarily chooses to hear only cases of considerable import. Most disputes, of course, never go to trial in the first place because the parties settle before litigation is filed or after filing but before proceeding to an expensive and uncertain trial; many decisions are not appealed; and most appeals are unsuccessful.

Readers should also appreciate that beneath the supreme court level, when the federal or state judiciary is split into geographically distinct appellate and trial-level districts, a decision made by a court in one of these districts is not the controlling law in others. Taking an example from the federal judiciary (which includes twelve regional appellate circuit courts), a decision by the Fifth Circuit,[19] which covers Texas, Louisiana, and Mississippi, is officially binding only in those three states. (Given the inevitable differences of legal interpretation between circuit courts, the U.S. Supreme Court frequently hears cases to resolve such "splits.") In the absence of other binding legal authority, courts in one jurisdiction will of course readily turn to precedent from other jurisdictions (state or federal) for guidance in adjudicating disputes. Obviously, though, the larger the jurisdiction and influence of the court issuing the precedent, the greater value it will have. An opinion from the Second Circuit is thus likely to carry more weight with the Michigan Supreme Court than one from Essex County Court in New Jersey.

Further general discussion of this sort would run the risk of turning this volume into a civics textbook.[20] Therefore, let us now discuss in more detail a series of critical features of the college and university legal environment that will frame and shape all subsequent analysis and discussion.

## State Action

The federal Constitution, the ultimate source of law in the United States, exerts a powerful and pervasive influence throughout our society. The value of and the need for constitutional protections (e.g., the right of free speech) are so deeply ingrained in popular consciousness that it is commonplace for citizens and noncitizens alike to invoke their "constitutional rights" in a wide variety of contexts. But in fact, the Constitution does not apply to dealings between private parties. It has no direct impact on the vast majority of what transpires in homes and workplaces. Parents can search their teenagers' rooms with impunity (and without a warrant), private employers can forbid their employees from discussing politics while on the job, and—no matter how morally objectionable it may be—private individuals may blatantly discriminate against minorities in almost all social and many business settings. The Constitution is concerned instead with relations between the government (at any level: federal, state, and political subdivisions of states) and the populace, as well as with relations among different parts of the government itself.

For higher education law, this means that a crucial distinction exists between public and private universities and colleges. Institutions that are deemed part of the state or local government—in legal parlance, *state actors*—are bound by the dictates of the Constitution in all their activities, from employment decisions to faculty and student discipline. Private institutions do not have to meet constitutional requirements, and thus they enjoy considerably more leeway in setting their own standards for institutional and individual conduct. It therefore becomes absolutely essential for administrators and faculty to know whether their particular institution will be deemed a state actor or a private party for constitutional law purposes.

In some cases, the answer is clear. Colleges or universities established, governed, funded, and maintained by the state will almost certainly be state actors. Ohio State University and the State University of New York (SUNY) fall into this category. Such obviously public institutions are part and parcel of their respective state governments, subject to the same constitutional restraints as the Ohio or New York legislatures or the cities of Cleveland or Syracuse. There is likewise a large group of private, especially denominational, institutions whose status as non–state actors is beyond question (e.g., Georgetown University or Swarthmore College). But a murky middle ground lies in between. In unusual circumstances, even an institution that would nominally seem to fall on the private side of the divide may in fact be subject to constitutional strictures. What is the status, say, of the University of Pennsylvania, a private institution that has its own considerable endowment but also receives a substantial yearly appropriation from the Commonwealth of Pennsylvania for its Veterinary School and has four state-appointed trustees on its approximately sixty-member board?[21]

The courts recognize the difficulty of determining whether a given actor is a *state* actor and the futility of making broad generalizations about which entities will fall under this rubric.[22] It is ultimately and "necessarily [a] fact-bound inquiry,"[23] which turns upon the specific circumstances of an institution's history and its current organization and activities. However, courts have developed a number of tests to help them sift through the facts germane to any potential state actor—educational institutions, businesses, individuals—and decide whether that actor must follow the same standards of conduct and restraint as the government.

One such test calls on the court to ascertain whether "there is a sufficiently *close nexus* between the State and the challenged action . . . so that the action . . . may be fairly treated as that of the State itself."[24] This "close nexus" test focuses on whether the state is responsible for the *specific conduct* or *behavior* that is being challenged.[25] If the state has "exercised coercive power or has provided such significant encouragement, either overt or covert, that the choice must in law be deemed to be that of the State,"[26] conduct that might otherwise appear private will be equivalent to the direct act of the government, and the actor in question will be a state actor. For example, in *Coleman v. Wagner College,*[27] the court considered whether a privately supported college's expulsion of students who had participated in a sit-in constituted state action. In 1969, at the height of student protests over the Vietnam War, New York passed legislation requiring colleges to adopt rules for maintaining public order on their campuses.[28] Pursuant to this statute, Wagner College promulgated rules that later became the basis for the expulsions. When the former students sued, claiming a denial of their constitutional right to due process of law, the Second Circuit refused to dismiss their case and demanded further inquiry into whether the New York law was in fact "intended to coerce colleges to adopt disciplinary codes embodying a 'hard-line' attitude towards student protesters."[29] If such coercion were present—for instance, if state officials interpreted the statute as requiring colleges to consider stiffer penalties, such as suspensions or expulsions, for protests—Wagner College's action would have constituted state action under what is now recognized as the "close nexus" test.[30]

A second common test for state action is whether the purported state actor is carrying out a function that is "traditionally the exclusive prerogative of the state."[31] However, it is extremely unlikely that any college or university will be found to be a state actor under this "public function" test. In the United States, education—especially higher education—has never been regarded as solely or even primarily a governmental responsibility.[32] From its very inception, American higher education has been characterized by a vibrant private sector.

The third major test for determining whether an entity is a state actor is the "symbiotic relationship" test. Here, courts examine whether the state has "so far insinuated itself into a position of interdependence with [an otherwise private party] that it must be recognized as a joint participant in the challenged activity."[33] If the state and the private party are closely linked in ways that are mutually beneficial, state action will be found. Unlike the "close nexus" test, which focuses on the state's involvement in a specific behavior or activity, the "symbiotic relationship" test is concerned with the *overall relationship* between the state and the ostensibly private entity.[34]

Courts have sometimes interpreted "symbiotic relationship" very broadly in order to find state action and thus to extend the reach of constitutional safeguards. This is especially so when they confront blatant acts of racial or sexual discrimination. Consider the case of *Burton v. Wilmington Parking Authority*,[35] in which a coffee shop's refusal to serve black customers was found to be state action. The shop leased space in a public parking garage, and the rent it paid helped to support the parking facility. The U.S. Supreme Court held that a symbiotic relationship existed here because the state profited from the restaurant's discriminatory conduct.

In recent years, however, the trend has been for judicial authorities to adopt a narrower view of what satisfies the "symbiotic relationship" test and what constitutes state action generally.[36] In 1982 the Supreme Court decided a series of state-action cases that helped clarify this area. In *Rendell-Baker v. Kohn*,[37] the Court declared that a privately operated high school for students with behavioral problems was not a state actor, even though more than 90 percent of the school's operating budget came from public funds and almost all of its students had been referred to it by local or state authorities. The Court found no symbiotic relationship, reasoning instead that the school resembled a government contractor that depended upon renewed contracts.[38] And in *Blum v. Yaretsky*,[39] it found that neither extensive state regulation of private nursing homes nor the fact that Medicaid paid for almost all of the homes' patient expenses turned such entities into state actors. No close nexus or symbiotic relationship was present here.

But even after *Rendell-Baker* and *Blum*, there is plenty of legal authority for the proposition that a college or university may be so closely intertwined with the state as to make it a state actor under the "symbiotic relationship" test. In *Schier v. Temple University*,[40] a federal district court clearly demonstrated why Temple should be regarded as such an actor. In 1965 the Commonwealth of Pennsylvania's desire to expand its system of higher education in a cost-effective way and pressing financial difficulties at Temple combined to produce legislation "establishing Temple University as an instrumentality of the Commonwealth to serve as a State-related institution in the Commonwealth system of higher education."[41] Under this statute, the formerly private Temple changed its name (to Temple University of the Commonwealth System of Higher Education), and state officials or appointees filled fifteen slots on the university's thirty-nine-member board of trustees. Pennsylvania set the tuition and fees Temple charged to students, reviewed the university's budget, audited its finances, and required its president to file an annual report on all university activities with the board for transmittal to the state. In return, Temple received substantial annual appropriations (by the early 1970s, over 62% of Temple's unrestricted revenue came from the commonwealth). These funds were to be used for specified purposes and kept in a specific account. Temple could participate in state capital development programs on the same terms as land-grant universities, and its bonds were exempt from state income tax. This web of connections led the court to conclude that Temple was as much a state actor as Penn State University or the Pennsylvania Department of Transportation.[42]

However, while Temple was declared to be a state actor, its cross-town sister medical institution, the "state-aided" Hahnemann University, was not—even though, among other state ties, Hahnemann had received annual appropriations from the commonwealth for seventy years, it had "tilted" its admissions decisions in favor of Pennsylvania students partly to strengthen its claim to state financial support, it had participated in state programs to finance the construction of new facilities, and it too was subject to a host of state licensing, programmatic, and financial reporting requirements.[43] Yet compared to Temple, Hahnemann's state appropriation represented a much smaller percentage of its budget; even more important, Hahnemann was not subject to "comprehensive and affirmative legislative enactments accepting responsibility for [it]."[44] Hahnemann retained its independent board of trustees (without state representatives) and "the autonomy of a private institution operating in a state-regulated field."[45]

State action typically arises as a threshold question in suits against colleges or universities: only if the institution is a state actor can the plaintiff's constitutional claims be considered. For example, in *Stone v. Dartmouth College*,[46] the court never reached the underlying question of whether Dartmouth's student discipline process was constitutionally flawed because the college was found not to be a state actor. There was no close nexus with the state because Dartmouth's decision to punish the student plaintiffs (for tearing down shanties erected to protest the college's ties to South Africa) was not compelled or influenced by the state. Likewise, the provision of college-level education was not an exclusively public function. Nor, finally, was there any symbiotic relationship with New Hampshire or the Town of Hanover. The plaintiffs argued that Dartmouth's intracollege discipline substituted for a criminal prosecution. But the court found that Dartmouth's code of student conduct did not replace state laws or relieve New Hampshire of its responsibility to enforce those statutes. It also flatly rejected the argument that the existence of an on-campus security force allowed Hanover to save money that it would otherwise have to spend on law enforcement.

It bears repeating that the particular circumstances of each college and university will determine its state-actor status. The fine calibrations drawn by courts under the various tests mean that a decision as to which side of the state-action line a given institution falls on (or, to be more accurate, where it falls under certain conditions) will offer scant guidance in other contexts and to other institutions.[47] If there are prior judicial rulings about one's home institution, these should already be familiar to the central administration and the faculty leadership. If this question has never been formally addressed by the courts, college or university counsel should develop an interpretation. And an important corollary follows from an institution's state-action status: a college or university that is legally a private entity should be careful not to jeopardize that position unintentionally. Any strengthened tie with state or local government—funding agreements, granting ex officio or other board memberships, scholarship commitments, formal and regularized consultations—may be enough to tilt the balance. This is not to say that entering into such arrangements is unwise, but rather that they may have serious consequences for institutional autonomy that merit consideration.

It is also important to remember that while non–state actors are exempt from federal constitutional requirements, *state* constitutions may impose similar or more stringent obligations even upon private parties. As a private educational institution, Princeton University is not bound to extend First Amendment protections to campus visitors. However, in *State v. Schmid*,[48] the New Jersey Supreme Court held that the state constitution required all public *and* private landowners in New Jersey, including universities, to recognize and safeguard to some extent the expressional rights of persons invited onto their property.

And of course, even though private colleges and universities are not bound to follow constitutional requirements, nothing prevents them from voluntarily choosing to extend equivalent substantive and procedural protections to community members. This in fact occurs quite frequently. The commitment to open inquiry and free expression that lies at the very heart of the academic enterprise leads even private institutions to adopt formal policies ensuring that faculty, students, and staff are free to explore ideas leading in any direction and to share their opinions with others.[49] Free speech on private campuses, then, is typically guaranteed by institutional rather than constitutional means. And considerations of fundamental fairness (as well as a time-honored vision of the campus, and especially the faculty, as a close-knit community of scholars) lead institutions to develop detailed procedural schemes for faculty and student discipline. The protections established here—formal notice of charges, hearings before impartial panels, appeals, sometimes even counsel—often approximate those required of state actors under the Constitution. This is further evidence of the influence of constitutional standards throughout our society, and of the necessity of understanding what the law actually requires of both private parties and state actors.[50]

## First Amendment Principles

Of course, this volume is not a treatise on constitutional law or the First Amendment. But throughout the following chapters, discussions of academic freedom and faculty rights at public, state-actor institutions will so frequently turn on First Amendment jurisprudence that readers will benefit from having at least a rudimentary understanding of the basic legal principles and approaches that courts will follow in analyzing disputes over faculty speech and expression.[51]

The First Amendment declares simply that "Congress shall make no law respecting an establishment of religion, or prohibiting the free exercise thereof; or abridging the freedom of speech, or of the press; or the right of the people peaceably to assemble, and to petition the Government for a redress of grievances."[52] This constitutional provision, as interpreted and enforced by the courts over the last two hundred plus years, enshrines the free exchange of ideas as being fundamental to the preservation and health of our democracy. There are also obvious parallels and ties between the open discourse that supports democratic governance and the free exchange of ideas that advances the discovery of new knowledge and promotes learning. As the Supreme Court stated in *Keyishian v. Board of Regents,* in which it identified academic freedom as a "special concern of the First Amendment,"[53] the "nation's future depends upon leaders trained through wide exposure to that robust exchange of ideas which discovers truth 'out of a multitude of tongues, [rather] than through any kind of authoritative selection.'"[54]

A prominent and recurrent question in higher education law is whether a particular instance of government regulation of speech—which at state-actor colleges and universities includes administratively imposed limits or sanctions on faculty (and student) expression—is constitutionally permissible. A key analytic concept that courts employ in resolving such disputes is a distinction between content-*neutral* and content-*based* restrictions on speech. In the words of one treatise:

> Content-based restrictions restrict communication because of the message conveyed. Laws prohibiting the publication of "confidential" information, forbidding the hiring of teachers who advocate the violent overthrow of government, or banning the display of the swastika in certain neighborhoods illustrate this type of restriction. Content-neutral restrictions, on the other hand, restrict communication without regard to the message conveyed. Laws prohibiting noisy speeches near a hospital, banning the erection of billboards in residential communities, or requiring the disclosure of the names of all leafleteers are examples.[55]

Federal courts—which under the First Amendment must regard any government limits on speech warily—have tended to look more favorably on content-neutral regulations. Such restrictions have been upheld in a variety of contexts, classic examples being rules governing the time, place, and manner of lawful expression. Thus, in *Kovacs v. Cooper,* the Supreme Court upheld a city ordinance banning sound trucks or other loud or noisy instruments on public streets;[56] in *Grayned v. Rockford* it upheld an ordinance prohibiting protests adjacent to school buildings that disturbed the peace or good order of such schools;[57] and in *Clark v. Community for Creative Non-Violence* the Court let stand a National Park Service regulation against "camping" in a park across the street from the White House or on the Mall in Washington, D.C.[58] Content-*based* restrictions on speech, however, are often legally vulnerable and have been characterized by the Supreme Court as "presumptively invalid."[59] Yet even content-based rules may be used to limit or control specific categories of "low" value speech—such as obscene expression, commercial advertising, "fighting words" that provoke a hostile reaction from hearers, and defamation—that are accorded little or no protection under the First Amendment. (These examples of "low" value speech are distinct from "high" value speech, such as the kind of classic political discourse animating the First Amendment, which typically would be protected.)[60]

A second major analytic construct in First Amendment law is the distinction between *subject matter*-based and *viewpoint*-based restrictions on speech. When considering both of these subsets of (always suspect) content-based regulation, courts will be especially reluctant to uphold rules that censor or promote speakers' underlying ideas and perspectives. As a starting point, readers should understand that there are indeed circumstances in which courts allow limits on speech about particular topics. For example, in *Greer v. Spock,* the Supreme Court upheld a regulation that prohibited speeches or demonstrations of a partisan political nature on a military base. Such a ban was consistent with having a politically neutral military.[61] But in sharp contrast, courts will regard *viewpoint* discrimination as "an egregious form of content discrimination."[62] In *Rosenberger v. Rector and Visitors of University of Virginia,* the Court struck down an institutional policy prohibiting the use of student fees to support religious activities (in the case at bar, the university had refused to pay for printing a student journal because it promoted a particular religious doctrine). According to a majority of the justices, UVa had excluded neither the general topic of religion nor the specific issues that were addressed from a "Christian perspective" in the disputed publication (e.g., homosexuality, racism) from student (and student-fee-supported) discourse. But the university had engaged in unconstitutional viewpoint discrimination when it singled out for "disfavored treatment those student journalistic efforts with religious editorial viewpoints. . . . The prohibited perspective, not the general subject matter, resulted in the refusal [to pay for the printing]."[63] Note that the more specific the subject matter on which speech is restricted, the more such limitation will resemble (or indeed operate as) a constitutionally infirm viewpoint-based restriction. In any event, faculty and administrators at state-actor institutions should guard against efforts to restrict speech because of the ideas it expresses.

Another principle of First Amendment jurisprudence deserving brief mention here is the distinction between limits on speech imposed by the government in its capacity as a *regulator* and limits on speech that arise from the government's *subsidization* of (or even direct participation in) discourse. Put simply, the government has much greater latitude to shape or control the content of speech when it is the speaker or is paying for such speech. Thus, in *Rust v. Sullivan,* the Supreme Court held that the U.S. government could prohibit federally funded family planning projects from providing counseling about abortion.[64] As the Court articulated in a later opinion, "when the government appropriates public funds to promote a particular policy of its own it is entitled to say what it wishes. . . . [and] When the government disburses public funds to private entities to convey a governmental message, it may take legitimate and appropriate steps to ensure that its message is neither garbled nor distorted by the grantee."[65] In contrast, when the government is not engaging in either direct or indirect speech itself, but rather is promulgating rules applicable to other parties' speech or expression, courts and analysts will turn back to standard First Amendment axioms, including those discussed above.

In closing this introduction to First Amendment principles, it is critical to recall that the amendment (and the legal rules flowing from it) do not apply to private colleges and universities. However, as I previously explained, those institutions may be bound by local policies that ensure faculty freedom of speech to the same extent (or even more broadly) than the constitutional guarantees in force at state-actor schools.

## Contractual Obligations

Another key feature of the college and university legal environment is the growing importance of contract law in establishing the rights and obligations of both institutions and individuals.[66] Colleges and universities have always been liable for contracts they make in commercial settings, and they could in turn sue for breach of those agreements. But courts have become increasingly willing to recognize and enforce contractual relationships within the academy itself: between the institution and its faculty and between the institution and potential, current, and former students.[67] These contractual relationships exist even in the absence of the formal signed documents that most of us think of as contracts. And the various strands of obligation that comprise such intra-institutional contracts are found in a variety of places, some obvious, others less so.

The guts of the contractual relationship between a college or university and its faculty are the terms under which faculty are appointed and promoted, the conditions (including the kinds and levels of support) under which they will perform their academic duties, and the institution's expectations about professors' teaching, research, and service. Of course, when faculty and the institution engage in collective bargaining, much of this is meticulously spelled out in a written agreement. But other documents and patterns of behavior will typically supplement or substitute for such agreements. Faculty appointment letters and notices of salary increases establish terms of employment and thus are integral parts of the contract with individual faculty. So too are faculty handbooks containing college or university policies (these policies may be aimed directly at faculty [consulting, conflicts of interest] or be institution-wide in scope [campus protests, sexual harassment]). Board of trustee resolutions and official statements by top-level administrators may create binding commitments, as may a regular course of conduct, such as a college practice of always appointing retiring faculty to emeritus status. Finally, courts will look to general custom and usage within the broader academic community to flesh out the terms of the institution-faculty contract.[68] It should be emphasized that most of the essential features of this contract can be set by the college or university and its faculty without any external involvement. Whatever the original source of the contract terms, an institution should be prepared to observe them scrupulously and may insist upon similar conformance by its faculty. For example, a university that has included detailed procedural requirements for faculty promotions in a handbook (thereby elevating such rules to contractual status) will be expected to comply with them.

The primary elements of the university-*student* contract are how students are admitted, what they must do to earn academic credit, what standards of behavior they are expected to observe, and what they may expect in return for their tuition dollars. Here too, the content of the contract lies largely within the control of the contracting parties. The terms of this contract may typically be found in admissions materials (which create an obligation on the part of the institution to review an applicant's file and to make a decision on the basis of articulated standards), catalogs, registration materials, student handbooks, institutional policy manuals, the institution's past dealings with students, and, once again, general custom in the higher education community.

The significance of written institutional rules or policies—and, in their absence, *unwritten* institutional custom and practice—in defining the legal rights and duties of members of the academic community cannot be overestimated. Although federal and state laws are sometimes intrusive, the bulk of the day-to-day activities of colleges and universities remain unfettered by statutory and regulatory requirements. No externally generated legal rule, for instance, requires that faculty be granted sabbatical or research leaves, or on what conditions. Accordingly, when an institution explicitly or implicitly regularizes how it will conduct its basic activities (e.g., approving new majors, setting teaching loads, establishing research and lab safety protocols) or how it will approach particular decisions or problems (e.g., distribution of royalties from faculty inventions, selection of department chairs, conduct of faculty discipline hearings), such "standards" fill a legal gap and acquire both intrinsic value and contractual import. We shall see throughout this book how individual administrators, institutional review panels, and courts must regularly interpret and assess locally enacted (or locally embraced) policies to resolve disputes involving faculty. Thus, in *Johnson v. Bd. of Regents*, a federal court upheld faculty layoffs at the University of Wisconsin that were necessitated by budget cuts and carried out pursuant to written guidelines.[69] And in *Riggin v. Bd. of Trustees of Ball St. Univ.*, an Indiana court affirmed a professor's discharge for violating the broad and precatory language of a handbook, as fleshed out by unwritten local and national expectations about proper faculty behavior.[70]

Recognition of college or university custom in interpreting contracts may also be part of a broader pattern of legal deference to academic decisions made by experts. Courts and juries are frequently reluctant to question, much less overturn, the specialized knowledge of professors about appropriate scholarly standards and whether they have been (or how they should be) met. For instance, as the Second Circuit observed in rejecting a sex discrimination claim by a terminated faculty member, "Of all fields, which the federal courts should hesitate to invade and take over, education and faculty appointments at a University level are probably the least suited for federal court supervision."[71] Such deference constitutes the legal system's recognition and endorsement of the concept that scholars commonly term *academic freedom.*[72]

Given the growing prominence of contract law in dealings between institutions and their faculty and students, college and university administrators should take particular care to avoid creating unwanted contractual liability through publications, pronouncements, or official actions. Likewise, faculty and students should recognize that they enjoy a variety of contract-based rights in their dealings with their respective institutions and that they are equally bound to follow the terms of those contracts.

## Immunity from Suit

Lest readers conclude that private institutions always occupy a more favorable legal position than state actors, some mention should be made of the doctrine of immunity, which redounds primarily to the advantage of public institutions.

Grants of immunity stem from the ancient legal principle that the state (originally, this meant the king) cannot be sued without its consent.[73] Today, state governments continue to invoke this principle successfully to avoid various kinds of liability—usually for breach of contract or personal injury. Put simply, sovereign immunity blocks suits against a state government in its own courts.[74] Public colleges and universities, as "agents or instrumentalities of the state in the performance of [their public educational] function,"[75] also frequently assert that they are entitled to institutional immunity from suit because they fall under the broader umbrella of state government. For example, in *Leadbetter v. Rose,* a University of North Dakota student claimed that that institution had failed to investigate her complaint of sexual assault and to provide her with a safe environment in which to pursue her education. The North Dakota Supreme Court declared that the university was an arm of the state, thwarting this litigation under the doctrine of sovereign immunity.[76]

State-actor colleges and universities also have a genuine—and perhaps growing—measure of immunity to suit in *federal* court. The Eleventh

Amendment bars such courts from entertaining suits brought against a state by one of its citizens.[77] Just within the last few years, the Supreme Court has given new bite to this provision by invoking it in a series of cases shielding public entities (including universities) from suits—most significantly, from suits for alleged violations of civil rights.[78] Thus, in *Kimel v. Florida Board of Regents* the Court decreed that individual faculty members could not sue their public-university employer for damages under the Age Discrimination in Employment Act (ADEA) because of the immunity bar raised by the Eleventh Amendment.[79] And in 2001, the Court's reasoning in *Kimel* was extended to block lawsuits by employees against public universities for discrimination on the basis of disability.[80] However, even the most robust interpretation of the Eleventh Amendment would not prevent (1) discrimination suits by the federal *government* against state universities (litigation being a key enforcement tool of U.S. civil rights agencies); (2) suits by private persons when a public university has *waived* its immunity; or (3) suits against *private* colleges and universities (even for violations of statutes like the ADEA under which public institutions are now immune from suit).[81]

Immunity may also be granted to public college or university officials who are being sued in their *individual* capacities. The arguments for such personal immunity rest largely upon public policy grounds: immunity avoids the danger that officials' performance will be influenced by the threat of litigation; without immunity, citizens might be reluctant to enter public service; immunity reduces the time and resources wasted in unnecessary lawsuits; it is unfair to subject officials to personal liability for the acts of their subordinates; and elections and removal procedures are better means of dealing with official misconduct.[82]

Successful invocations of immunity can provide real protection to public institutions and their officers. But it would be foolhardy for a college or university or its representatives to assume that claims of immunity will always be enforced. Courts have been ingenious in circumventing the immunity doctrine in order to make sure that injured parties have some form of redress and that genuine justice is done. The scope of the sovereign immunity available to institutions can be sharply limited, for example, by a holding that immunity applies to the college or university only in its *governmental* capacity and not when it engages in commercial activities.[83] Or a court may find that sovereign immunity bars a suit against a state university for breach of contract but that it does not bar a suit for the wrongful taking of property (such as stripping someone of the right to a continuing academic appointment).[84]

Grants of immunity to individual college or university officials can also be restricted in various ways. Thus, immunity might extend to officials making discretionary judgments but not to the same or other officials carrying out purely routine or ministerial tasks.[85] Even within the realm of discretionary action, immunity may apply only to conduct that "does not violate clearly established statutory or constitutional rights of which a reasonable person would have known."[86] (This requires public officials to be conversant with relevant evolving case law.) Furthermore, immunity would almost never shield individuals who intentionally cause injury to others. And of course, a court can find that although immunity technically applies to an institution or an individual, it has been waived by state law or by a particular pattern of conduct.[87]

In short, administrators and faculty at public institutions should recognize the continuing validity of the doctrine of immunity, understand that it may operate to block certain lawsuits, and appreciate that it is not a guaranteed safe harbor.

Having acquired a firmer grasp of the basic legal context in which colleges and universities operate, we can now turn our attention to a more detailed exploration of how the law affects the day-to-day work and life of institutions and their faculty.

# 2 Scholarship

Scholarship, including the dissemination of properly verified and peer-reviewed research findings, is central to faculty life at almost all universities and many colleges. To be a faculty member at such institutions means to be actively engaged with the development and testing of ideas. Professional status, salary and perquisites, and opportunities for sabbatical or other leave typically turn on one's productivity and impact as a scholar. At the same time, as scholars from Socrates to Galileo to the targets of the 1950s red scares can attest (and as the AAUP's Committee A on Academic Freedom and Tenure will confirm), scholars' ideas may put faculty in conflict with colleagues, administrators, trustees, or the broader community. Faculty will insist that the principle of academic freedom permits them to explore whatever lines of thought they choose and to propound whatever theories or explanations they develop. Do they in fact enjoy such protection?

For all practical purposes, the answer is yes. Faculty are basically free to select whatever topics they want for research, to draw and defend their own conclusions, and to publish their findings when and where they see fit.[1] This freedom would apply with equal force across the entire institution, there being no tenable distinction between a scholar working in the library and a scholar working in a laboratory.

## Selection of Research Topics

The broad protection afforded faculty research stems from a powerful confluence of personal, institutional, and intellectual interests. To be sure, freedom in conducting research helps professors advance their own careers. And colleges and universities seeking to hire and retain the most distinguished scholars will find it prudent to accord faculty the widest possible latitude in their research, especially since faculty discoveries bring with them considerable reflected glory. But beyond these rather self-serving justifications, faculty freedom in research directly promotes student learning. Advanced graduate students are trained as a next generation of scholars by doing cutting-edge research in close collaboration with today's leading scholars. Active researchers are also better equipped to share fresh developments in their fields with undergraduates. Moreover, if the didactic process works as it should, the act of explaining current disciplinary thinking to bright and questioning undergraduates can help faculty put their specialized learning in a broader perspective and test their ability to demonstrate the importance of their work to an informed citizenry. Most importantly, though, leaving faculty free to pursue ideas of their own choosing has repeatedly led to advances in human knowledge and understanding.

Consensus among faculty, students, and administrators on the importance of faculty freedom in research has solidly entrenched scholars' ability to pursue their own research agendas.[2] For many faculty, freedom in the selection of research topics is by now a straightforward matter of contract law. Collective bargaining agreements with faculty unions often include express provisions ensuring that faculty members will have enormous discretion in conducting research.[3] Equivalent contractual safeguards are also found in a nonunion context. If a college or university has a written policy affirming the faculty's academic freedom in research, and that policy is made an explicit term of employment by reference in an appointment letter or by incorporation in a faculty handbook, faculty can properly argue that any restrictions on their choice of research subjects would constitute a breach of their employment contract. And even if an institutional policy on academic freedom is not a formal written part of their employment contract, faculty members may still claim that their institution has a long-standing practice of noninterference with faculty scholarship, which should be elevated to the status of contractual right.

Because no employment contract can possibly address every detail and condition of a working relationship, courts regularly treat local "custom and usage" as a necessary subtext in fleshing out the full meaning of a contract. Courts are especially willing to assume that an unwritten local practice was intended by the parties to be a part of their contract when such local custom and usage is consistent with a wider national (or even international) "industry standard." Thus, the fact that the freedom of faculty to select and pursue research agendas without interference from institutional or external authorities is commonly accepted in the academic community reinforces the belief that this freedom should exist on any particular campus, especially on campuses where such freedom has been accorded— or not challenged—in the past.[4]

These days, extra-institutional attacks on the content of faculty scholarship are extremely unusual and most unlikely to succeed. Thus, a lawsuit brought by tobacco interests against a University of California cardiologist (and frequent industry critic) alleging politically motivated research and the misuse of public funds was dismissed as having no legal basis.[5] Furthermore, given the wide agreement within the modern academy that scholars should be able to examine and develop whatever ideas they choose, disputes (much less judicial opinions) involving formal institutional efforts to limit or direct a faculty member's research are equally rare. When such efforts do occur, they are often difficult to distinguish from other controversies about the quality of a faculty member's performance. For example, in 1994 the Board of Regents of the University of Colorado at Boulder initially refused to approve the promotion to full professor of a scholar whose research specialty was the use of erotica in literature.[6] Though this decision was ostensibly justified by questions about the faculty member's credentials (he lacked a Ph.D.) and his overall academic record, according to press accounts one regent who opposed promotion—and who admitted that he had not read the professor's work—believed that Coloradans "would not approve of [his] focus on erotic literature. 'The people that put me in office would not think that his specialty is very essential to liberal-arts education.'"[7] Predictably, the regents' actions gave rise to a firestorm of criticism from the university's chancellor and other defenders of academic freedom. The board ultimately reversed itself,[8] but whether this incident might have a chilling effect on other faculty scholarship at Boulder and elsewhere is less certain.

For another example of how entrenched the right of faculty to conduct research on topics of their choosing is, consider what occurred when the Idaho Board of Education sought to block the award of a research grant to an Idaho State University professor to study the history of gay communities in the Pacific Northwest. The executive director of the board argued that this study, which had previously been endorsed by a panel of scholars overseeing the grant program, was "out of sync" with Idaho taxpayers. The professor brought suit in federal court, and the board quickly settled the case for an amount equivalent to the contested grant (and the professor's legal costs).[9]

Much more common than administrative or trustee frontal assaults on the selection of research topics is the application of peer pressure. This might include anything from department chairs or senior faculty "suggesting" interesting areas of inquiry to junior colleagues to organized efforts by faculty or students, or both, to shame or embarrass a faculty member into abandoning a particular research agenda. This latter technique has been used at a variety of institutions against faculty who conduct research on animals or who work in consultation with the military or intelligence agencies.[10] At Texas A&M University, a chemistry professor whose experiments sought to turn mercury into gold was pilloried by his fellow faculty for engaging in alchemy. Members of his own department publicly called on him to resign to avoid further harm to the university's reputation; other scholars asked the university's provost to strip him of his title of distinguished professor.[11] But as foolish as such a project seems, the faculty member probably did have the right to engage in such research. For if sanctions can be imposed for pursuing such unconventional experiments, how can other paradigm-busting researchers feel secure in their work?

Some commentators would argue that a chemist taking alchemy seriously (or a mathematician asserting that $2 + 2 = 5$) is so ludicrous and self-contradictory that the "scholar" in question should not be hired—or could be disciplined—purely on the basis of such beliefs.[12] I would agree that in appropriate circumstances a lack of (or breakdown in) objectivity should constitute grounds for sanction. And of course, as I discuss later, even a tenured faculty member may lose his or her position for incompetence or research fraud.[13] But if the right of faculty to select and follow their own research agendas is to have any real teeth, institutions (and their hiring and promotion committees) should tread very carefully here. Both as a matter of law and as wise academic policy, the alchemist professor has the right to pursue even this long-discredited theory. (His ability to proceed down such a lonely scholarly path, though, will be buttressed if he attempts to transform base metals through rigorous and carefully documented experiments, as opposed to making bald declarations of correctness.) However, while this professor must be allowed to delve into alchemy, he should not expect to earn tenure, to be promoted, to be awarded big raises, to receive research funds, or to garner the respect of his disciplinary colleagues unless his research proves sound and significant (should that ever occur).

With limited funds and faculty positions at their disposal, institutions must also make distinctions among scholars on the basis of perceived quality.[14] But even the wisest and fairest of scholars may fail to recognize the power of a new theory or the significance of research findings.[15] And more venal considerations may also intervene: "reluctance to admit professional error, careerist jealousy, political differences, and simple personal animosity may lead committees of faculty peers to misjudge the professional work of individual colleagues."[16] Therefore, in evaluating a fellow scholar's work, the "assessor must exercise due care and must make his or her assessment on scholarly grounds, without excessive love for his or her own commitments" (i.e., without overinvestment in the intellectual framework that underlies one's own work and through which one must initially view the work of others, and attempting to correct for possible biases).[17]

The contours of faculty freedom in research become especially murky when a scholar's heterodoxy extends past the rejection of conventional research techniques and standard interpretations to a direct attack on the most basic theoretical constructs of a discipline.[18] Would a biology department be justified in not hiring or promoting a faculty member who refused to employ the scientific method? I would say yes, because this individual is not engaged in "science" as we know it, which involves the formulation and testing of propositions with evidence, under conditions that are replicable by other researchers. Much less is this person engaging in good science. What of a fundamentalist biologist who explains that his research results are preordained by God's will (or who rejects evidence of evolution solely with the assertion that such findings are contrary to revealed truth in the Bible)? For the same reasons—this person is not conducting science, much less top-quality science—an institution could penalize this biologist for his choice and conduct of research. But an entirely different case is presented by the deeply religious biologist who rejects Darwin and sets about to prove, by rigorous scientific experiment, that the creation of life is accurately depicted in Genesis. Atheistic colleagues may be convinced that our biologist will never succeed in this endeavor, but he should—and legally would—be given the opportunity to prove them wrong. Of course, should he fail to make a persuasive case, he should not expect to receive tenure or other accolades for his work.

A social science analogue to our creationist biologist would be a Marxist economist or political scientist. Although being a Marxist (or belonging to the Communist Party) also implicates faculty associational rights that are addressed later in this volume,[19] the law is fairly settled that a scholar may not be denied an academic appointment merely because of his or her political views (which in this case equal intellectual views). Thus, in *Ollman v. Toll,* an unsuccessful candidate for a department chair at the University of Maryland could not prevail against the university once Maryland demonstrated that its hiring decision was premised on grounds other than the plaintiff's ideology, such as his relative lack of administrative experience and his modest stature in the discipline.[20]

But is it really possible for faculty on recruitment committees or peer review panels to confine their assessment to the quality—as opposed to the content—of a current or prospective colleague's work? Many would argue that the political and cultural underpinnings of all scholarship and thought make such objectivity impossible. Others would assert that while objectivity is difficult to attain (and may even be flawed in ways we do not realize), it must still be pursued. With no clear answer, scholar-evaluators should at the very least be circumspect and aware of their own intellectual prejudices when reviewing others' novel or paradigm-shattering work. The fact that discussions of scholarly merit typically take place in the open in group meetings, and the use of multiple peer reviews—particularly from external referees with no prior links to the scholar whose work is under scrutiny—also provide critical checks against bias. Still, we undeniably place great trust in faculty and institutions (and ask for a high level of integrity) by expecting them to self-police for intellectual quality.

## Obtaining Support for Scholarship

For most faculty the selection of a research topic leads almost immediately into the pursuit of financial and other support necessary to conduct that research. The provision of such resources has the potential—though largely unrealized up till now—to engender legal disputes between institutions and faculty, which may have sharply divergent notions of the adequacy and appropriateness of particular funding arrangements. As we shall see, basic principles of contract law govern this area.

Historically, resources furnished by one's own institution (paid leaves of absence, graduate student stipends, libraries, laboratories, etc.) sufficed to meet the research needs of most faculty—although scholars doing sophisticated experimental work in the physical and biological sciences have long had to rely upon external, especially federal, funding.[21] Of course, this is not to say that scholars—or for that matter institutions—have ever been close to satisfied with the available level of resources! Faculty demand customized research support all the time, especially when they are being recruited to or lured away from an institution. As with any other condition of employment, support for research is a legitimate subject of negotiation between parties, and institutional commitments to fund research are just as binding as salary obligations. Thus, in *Nardi v. Stevens Institute of Technology*,[22] a research professor could sue the institute when it canceled a multiyear federal grant that supported the plaintiff's work and forced him to vacate his lab space to accommodate shifting institutional research priorities. In rejecting the institute's motion for a summary judgment in its favor, the court correctly held that the aggrieved professor had a plausible breach-of-contract claim against his employer for violating an implied promise that he would be permitted to conduct research for all the years of the grant.

At colleges and universities where research is an expected part of a faculty member's duties, the institution has an implied contractual obligation to provide faculty with at least a minimal level of research support (e.g., access to a library or a laboratory, some hours during the week free from scheduled classes and meetings). In theory, then, a disgruntled faculty member might claim that his institution had breached his employment contract by failing to provide him with appropriate and necessary support. However, absent reasonably definite agreements about the type and level of such assistance, it would be very difficult for a faculty plaintiff to prevail in such a suit. Courts will be extremely reluctant to question institutional evaluations of scholarly need and their allocations of always-limited resources. For example, in the context of a tenure denial, the court in *McElearney v. Univ. of Illinois* rejected the notion that the university was obligated to underwrite a scholar's future work, noting in passing that "the First Amendment does not require . . . the University, to provide [the plaintiff] with facilities and financing for his research" and that "academic freedom does not empower a professor to dictate to the University what research will be done using the school's facilities."[23] Complaints about the general quality of institutional research support, then, may be folded into broader lawsuits alleging discrimination or infringement of free speech, but a free-standing claim of a failure to provide an appropriate level of support would be most unusual.

Given limited institutional funds and ever-growing needs, scholars from all disciplines have increasingly sought external support for their research. Fortunately from the faculty perspective, the law imposes almost no extra-institutional limits on the sources and magnitude of such outside funding. With rare exceptions (typically having to do with the dictates of American foreign policy), faculty and their home institutions are free to solicit and accept research support from any source, including repressive governments and unpopular, even reprehensible, organizations and individuals.[24] While such linkages may cause embarrassment to the institution and make both it and the faculty member(s) in question a target of controversy, neither federal nor state law prohibits funding arrangements freely entered into by competent and duly authorized parties.

However, consistent with the foregoing discussion about the challenges of conducting and evaluating highly unconventional scholarship, faculty whose research is deemed overly provocative or downright bizarre will have a hard time attracting external support. For example, a biologist who argued that AIDS was caused by recreational drug use and by the drug AZT used contributions from friends to keep his lab operating after he had filed twenty unsuccessful grant applications with the National Institutes of Health and private foundations.[25] This sort of "problem" though, may simply reflect the fact that peer review of scholarship is effective in spotting and promoting quality research.

I would argue that the only meaningful limits on faculty pursuit of external research support come from *institutional* rules and policies that are legally binding on faculty as a matter of contract law. For example, some colleges and universities refuse to perform classified military research for the government.[26] This is an institutional choice that is not compelled by external legal authority. However, once such a policy is formally and properly adopted (assuming also that the faculty receive adequate notice of it, such as by inclusion in an employee handbook), it governs faculty behavior just as surely as any statute.[27] Faculty who take objection to such policies must seek to have them modified or overturned by their institution.

Institutions and their faculty will differ from time to time on how to balance corporate interests and individual scholars' need for more and better research funding. In these inevitable disputes, each side may invoke the doctrine of academic freedom to buttress its position. Institutions will assert that they must be free to accept external funding only on terms that promote the discovery and sharing of knowledge and do not compromise their autonomy or integrity.[28] Scholars will respond that limitations on external research funding may be tantamount to prohibiting research in a given area. It may strike readers as inconsistent and wrong that a professor would be free to conduct research on any topic of his or her choice but must comply with local restrictions on sources of support for that research. However, the pursuit of research funding—particularly if the funding flows through university channels on its way to individual investigators—adds broad institutional goals and concerns as factors to be weighed in evaluating claims of academic propriety and freedom. Such values may take precedence over short-term financial benefits to a given professor. For example, in order to facilitate the exchange of ideas (and thereby improve lives), a university might legitimately refuse support from a pharmaceutical company that insists on maintaining the secrecy of research findings until it begins marketing a drug based on such work (as opposed to waiting only until a patent application is filed), even overruling some of its own faculty in the process.

Restrictions on an individual professor's external funding are most clearly justified in order to preserve other (including future) scholars' autonomy and scope of inquiry. Universities may therefore reject sponsor-imposed limits on the conduct and especially the dissemination of research. Funding restrictions are more objectionable (but may still be warranted) when they primarily serve institution-centric goals such as avoiding bad publicity. Recognizing this tension, most colleges and universities do not seriously constrain the faculty's pursuit of external support. A university would thus be unlikely to bar its faculty from accepting grants from tobacco companies for research that might rebut evidence on the dangers of smoking or identify potential benefits of tobacco use.[29] However, if college or university policy did prohibit sponsored research by tobacco companies, as a matter of contract law a faculty member would have to abide by such institutional rules unless he or she (1) changed the policy, (2) negotiated an exception, or (3) entered into a private individual funding agreement (i.e., independent of university duties and sponsorship) with such a firm. Also bear in mind that faculty who generate external research support still hold the ultimate trump card: they can take their extant and prospective grants and go elsewhere.

This discussion raises the question of who exactly enters into funding agreements. It is certainly possible for individual faculty to contract directly with sponsors (such arrangements would resemble the private consulting agreements discussed later). But it is far more common for external research funds to be run through the institution before they reach particular scholars.[30] This structure is desirable from the sponsor's perspective because legal responsibility for performance is placed on a more established and solvent party, even though the actual research will still be carried out by the designated researchers. It is attractive to researchers because they receive earmarked funds with no direct contractual liability to the sponsor. And from the standpoint of the college or university, such an arrangement can facilitate institutional monitoring and control of external funding, including ensuring compliance with institutional policies. More aggressive institutions may insist on appropriating a portion of any funds received from sponsors to defray the costs of negotiating and administering sponsored research agreements. It is worth stressing that, as the usual contracting party, the college or university has considerable power to shape the content of external funding agreements. If the institution refuses to approve a proposed agreement with a sponsor, the affected faculty member would typically have no legal recourse (although he or she would of course be able to express displeasure in other ways, such as by leaving the institution).

## Ownership and Exploitation of Scholarly Work

Institutional and judicial recognition that faculty are free to develop their own research agendas does not necessarily translate into the freedom to do whatever they want with the fruits of their research. To understand why requires a brief foray into the field of intellectual property (in particular copyright and patent) law, which defines the legitimate uses and users of faculty scholarship.

Our starting point must be a fundamental principle that underlies all intellectual property law in this democratic society: namely, that no one can own or control an idea, a theory, an explanation of naturally occurring phenomena, or particular facts or features discovered about our world.[31] As the Supreme Court explained in *Diamond v. Chakrabarty*,[32] "The laws of nature, physical phenomena, and abstract ideas have been held not patentable. . . . Thus, a new mineral discovered in the earth or a new plant found in the wild is not patentable subject matter. Likewise, Einstein could not patent his celebrated law that $E = MC^2$; nor could Newton have patented the law of gravity. Such discoveries are 'manifestations of . . . nature, free to all men and reserved exclusively to none.'"[33] Such untrammeled access to new knowledge clearly advances the goals of the academy as well as the ideal of self-government.

But while safeguarding access to ideas and basic information, American intellectual property law also affirmatively seeks to tap the creative energies of artists, authors, inventors, and thinkers for the benefit of larger society. It does this through a most powerful incentive: allowing these individuals, under certain circumstances, to reap the financial rewards that flow from their labors.[34] Thus, under our intellectual property regime, an idea or an observable fact may not belong to anyone, but the way in which that idea is *expressed* or that knowledge is *applied*—acts that often require at least as much blinding insight and creativity as the development of the idea or the uncovering of the fact in the first place—*may* become the exclusive property of the person whose genius and tenacity gave shape and expanded meaning to such knowledge. Thus, the idea of star-crossed lovers caught between rival factions belongs to no one, but the expression of that theme in, say, *Romeo and Juliet* or *West Side Story* can become the property of the playwright.

Our system of intellectual property law is also highly categorical, drawing critical distinctions among various classes of property. While some commentators regard this taxonomy as artificial and unnecessarily confusing,[35] it is by now deeply entrenched and unlikely to be overhauled. Under this system, the intellectual property rights that attach to any given scholarly creation depend first and foremost on whether the work in question is protected by copyright or patent.[36]

Copyright protects original works of authorship, including literary and other texts, music, drama, choreography, the fine arts, motion picture and audiovisual productions, sound recordings, and architecture.[37] It thus encompasses much of what is traditionally regarded as faculty scholarship, such as monographs and articles in scholarly journals. In order for a creative or thoughtful work of one's mind to receive federal copyright protection, however, the work must be "fixed in a tangible medium of expression,"[38] such as the printed page, a computer disk, audio or visual tape, canvas, marble, or film. In other words, it must be put into a form capable of being perceived by and communicated to others.[39]

Patent law establishes property rights in new or improved and useful processes, machines, manufactures, or compositions of matter.[40] It thus applies to a wide array of faculty-driven advances in the physical and natural sciences and engineering, such as new ceramics, improved cheese-making techniques, and the creation of transgenic species.[41] However, the fruits of faculty scholarship that can be patented, while typically just as much the product of abstract theory and experimentation as scholarly work that is protected by copyright, do tend to have a more instrumental or practical cast. Some copyrightable works generate considerable financial returns (e.g., a best-selling novel), but it is much more common for patented intellectual property to have obvious commercial value.[42]

The border between faculty scholarship covered by copyright and scholarship covered by patent occasionally blurs. Consider computer software.[43] On the one hand, software programs use computer language (fixed on a disk or tape) to convey ideas, instructions, and images to computers and users. They therefore would seem to fit rather neatly under the rubric of copyright, especially since stand-alone mathematical formulas and algorithms are unpatentable.[44] On the other hand, the U.S. Patent and Trademark Office has issued patents on new, computer-implemented inventions at the core of which lie specially tailored software.[45] Again, the classification of software is important because of different customs within the academy about the treatment accorded various kinds of intellectual property, and most of all because of the different statutory enforcement schema. Generally speaking, patent law provides more aggressive remedies, including treble damages for willful infringement.[46]

In order to draw any conclusions about faculty ownership and control of scholarship, then, it is first necessary to consider, for each potentially copyrightable or patentable work, what the applicable statutes and case law—if operating in isolation, as a kind of baseline—would provide. But as we shall see, a growing number of colleges and universities have adopted their own institutional copyright and patent policies that must be layered onto this baseline. Such policies, if carefully drafted and enforced, can create contractual relationships with faculty that dramatically alter the results that would otherwise obtain. Our inquiry must therefore include an examination of the scope and effect of these policies.

## Copyright

As a general principle, the author (the individual who actually created the work) is the owner of the copyright.[47] As such, the author/copyright holder has the exclusive right, during the term of the copyright,[48] to reproduce or sell the work, to perform or display it (if applicable), and to use it to make derivative works, such as a screenplay drawn from a book.[49] There is, however, one important circumstance relevant to faculty where the creator is not regarded as the "author" and thus does not hold the copyright: when the work is created by an employee within the scope of his or her employment and the employer takes ownership of the work as a "work made for hire."[50] The theory here is that some works of authorship only come about through the instigation and insistence (not to mention the resources) of the employer. In circumstances in which employees are expressly hired to take pen or brush (or computer keyboard) in hand to produce a particular result, it has seemed fair to courts that the employer control the disposition of the finished work.

Whether faculty scholarship is work made for hire (with the copyright belonging to the institutional employer) is currently an open question.[51] This controversy erupted after the Copyright Act was substantially revised in 1976. The new federal statute cast doubt on the continuing validity of older, typically state-based, case law that had apparently established a professorial exception to the work-made-for-hire doctrine.[52] The commentators are split on this issue,[53] offering different rationales to support faculty or institutional ownership.

Colleges and universities can make a fairly powerful case that they are the lawful copyright holders. Faculty are legally institutional employees. They are hired to teach in a particular field, which entails producing written, copyrightable materials such as syllabi, lecture notes, and exams. Faculty at research universities are also expected to be actively engaged in scholarship and to produce and publish regularly articles and books in their areas of expertise.[54] Teaching loads are frequently adjusted to accommodate research agendas, and many faculty receive paid leaves of absence or sabbaticals to help progress in their research. Institutional employers carefully monitor the quality of faculty scholarship, particularly at promotion and salary review time. And finally, it is the institution that bears most of the costs associated with the production of scholarship. Colleges and universities provide faculty with libraries (often granting them unlimited borrowing privileges), access to electronic databases, secretarial support, office space and supplies, graduate or undergraduate students to serve as research assistants (these students' salaries are often paid by the institution or they may receive academic credit for such work), photocopying and postage, travel funds, computers—and, for experimental work in the biological and physical sciences—sophisticated research instruments that may cost many thousands of dollars.[55] All this might reasonably lead a court to conclude that faculty scholarship is created under institutional control and supervision, at institutional insistence and expense.

However, we can also construct a compelling argument why faculty schol-arship should not be considered work made for hire. To begin with, faculty are not directed to research or write on particular subjects the way a news-paper reporter is assigned to cover a story. Faculty set their own scholarly agendas and select their own topics.[56] To assert otherwise would raise seri-ous questions of academic freedom. Faculty scholarship is created for its own sake and not for the use of institutional employers.[57] Unlike tradi-tional employees, faculty do not work set hours or even in a set location. They may produce much of their scholarship at home or at sites far distant from the direction or control of institutional authorities.[58] Furthermore, and perhaps most importantly, treating colleges and universities as the owners of faculty scholarship would wreak havoc with established and widely shared expectations within the academy. At most institutions, faculty have long been treated as the unquestioned owners of their research.[59] Faculty make their own arrangements for publishing their scholarly work (i.e., iden-tifying and negotiating with appropriate journals or university presses) and have traditionally been allowed to keep any royalties generated by such publication.[60]

What little case law has developed since the revision of the Copyright Act on whether faculty scholarship is work made for hire somewhat am-biguously supports faculty ownership. In two opinions the Seventh Circuit Court of Appeals observed that the new law could be interpreted as vest-ing copyright in the institutional employer.[61] But in both of those cases the court was clearly uncomfortable with such an interpretation and reached for ways to provide for continued faculty title to copyright. In *Weinstein v. University of Illinois* (a case involving a pathetic dispute among coauthors about the order of listing their names on an article), the court dodged the statutory work-for-hire issue by declaring that under the university's own copyright policy the coauthors were co-owners of the work.[62] In *Hays v. Sony Corporation of America* (which involved high school teachers' copy-right claims to a word processing manual), the court even went so far as to say that given the "lack of fit between the policy of the work-for-hire doc-trine and the conditions of academic production . . . we might, *if forced to decide the issue,* conclude that the [teacher] exception had survived the enactment of the 1976 Act."[63] Therefore, while I think that the federal work-made-for-hire doctrine should not ordinarily be applied to faculty scholarship, at present we have only tantalizing hints (but still no definitive guidance) on whether courts would invoke that doctrine to settle the ownership of scholarly work.

To date, though, the murky status of copyright in scholarly works under the statute has proved to be less of a problem than one might expect, for two major reasons. First, as previously noted, it has not been the custom for colleges and universities to claim ownership of faculty writings. Even after the purported demise of the professorial exception to the work-made-for-hire doctrine, the potentially interested parties (institutions, faculty, publishers) have tended to assume that faculty own such work. The absence of case law reflects a conscious institutional passivity in claiming copyright (a politically prudent stance) and reinforces faculty expectations of ownership. Second, the "baseline scenario," in which copyright ownership is determined solely by relevant statute and judicial opinion, does not always obtain. Many colleges and universities have promulgated internal copyright policies that clarify the rights of the various parties.[64] Because the Copyright Act provides for the assignment of copyrights,[65] these policies, if expressly made a part of the faculty member's employment contract, can lawfully shift ownership from scholar to institution or vice versa.[66]

It is difficult to generalize about copyright policies since they can be structured to meet a variety of institutional objectives.[67] Frequently these policies provide for institutional ownership of works created with the use (or substantial use) of college or university resources.[68] But copyright policies need not expand institutional property rights at the expense of faculty. Some institutions have chosen to reaffirm faculty copyright in conventional fruits of scholarship,[69] and almost all policies seek to accommodate faculty concerns through "statements of support for academic freedom, provisions for professors to receive a share of royalties, and provisions giving some limited degree of control over the copyright to the professor."[70] Given the lack of controversy they have engendered, copyright policies may not be overly aggressive in content—or at the very least, they have not been aggressively enforced.

However, such institutional passivity appears to be changing, as the ownership and use of copyrightable research and teaching material has gone from being a quiet backwater of higher education law and policy to one of its "hot spots." This shift is explained by the burgeoning opportunities to distribute intellectual wares via the Internet and other technologies and the huge gains that many anticipate will be reaped from distance learning.

In short, intellectual property has new meaning—and perhaps much more value—in the digital era, and universities and their faculty are a prime source of the "content" or "authenticated knowledge" desired by multimedia conglomerates, dot.com start-up companies, and, ultimately, consumers.

A host of synchronous and asynchronous distance learning options are being explored, from full-scale degree programs, to nondegree certificates, to focused training classes, to the simple provision of information or data. Some universities are directly involved in commercial activities: Cornell is creating a for-profit subsidiary, tentatively named e-Cornell, to develop and market on-line distance learning courses;[71] New York University has its own for-profit arm;[72] and Columbia has entered into a new venture with a set of other academic centers.[73] Other colleges and universities have joined the fray under the banner of corporate partners: a company known as UNext.com now offers on-line business courses drawing on content provided by the University of Chicago, Columbia, Carnegie-Mellon, Stanford, and the London School of Economics and Political Science. Students who take these courses (which will be taught by adjunct faculty hired by UNext, not faculty at the partner universities) will receive credit and degrees from a UNext subsidiary named Cardean University.[74] Both wholly owned subsidiaries and corporate partnerships have advantages and disadvantages. For example, working with (or under the rubric of) a corporate partner gives colleges or universities less control over products and marketing. But going solo may make it harder to find financial backing—and venture capitalists who bankroll a university-owned subsidiary will exercise great influence over the development of projects.

To many faculty, these initiatives seem unprecedented, disconcerting, and even threatening. Some professors fear that institutions will mandate the use of distance learning to increase teaching loads, or, conversely, that embracing such technology will lead to the elimination of faculty jobs. Others worry that electronic learning will turn a class of professors into the academic equivalent of free-agent athletes who sell their talents to the highest bidder (and perhaps play on more than one university "team"),[75] further weakening an already-diminished sense of campus community. Of course, other faculty enthusiastically welcome such opportunities—and it is undeniable that superstars already command great market power even without distance learning.[76]

Viewed from a more sanguine perspective, electronic instruction is simply the latest form of the extension or outreach activities in which many colleges and universities have long been engaged—the modern-day equivalent of correspondence courses, lyceum programs, and remedial and continuing education. While investments in commercial distance learning undoubtedly raise important questions about institutional priorities and the likely effect on existing or proposed programs, colleges and universities face similar concerns and opportunity costs with all new academic ventures. Furthermore, the concept of intellectual property—and intellectual property law—have successfully adapted to many new technologies (e.g., radio, motion pictures, television), and there is every reason to believe that they will be flexible enough to accommodate the digital era too.

Some of the current frenzied activity is defensive in nature, with institutions trying to block other parties (including other colleges and universities) from hiring their faculty away to produce instructional materials, and seeking to preserve claims to profits derived from their professors' work. This pointedly raises again the question of who owns such work. University claims of ownership here are strengthened by the fact that typically the employer institution gives faculty more help in developing on-line courses (in the form of computer equipment, software, and tech support) than in preparing traditional classroom lectures or scholarly monographs. Faculty counterclaims will reprise all the arguments made above and, in addition, the charge that a college or university's insistence on ownership might act as a disincentive for faculty to develop on-line courses.[77]

To date, there has been much more abstract debate over appropriate distance learning goals and policies than directly applicable legal precedent. One public controversy arose when Harvard Law School professor Arthur Miller provided videotaped course lectures for the on-line Concord University School of Law without the permission of Harvard administrators. Miller argued that he was not "teaching" at Concord: he did not meet or interact with students, did not test or grade them, but merely provided material as if he were giving a televised lecture—something he had done many times in the past without seeking approval.[78] (Of course, Miller's previous television viewers had not been law students who paid tuition.) However, I do not think it is possible to draw a meaningful distinction between the "provision of course material" and "teaching." Miller's behavior is almost identical to that of a professor who only gives twice-weekly lectures from a podium to a large introductory course, leaving teaching assistants to conduct discussion sections, prepare and administer exams, and award grades (an all-to-common situation, perhaps, but one that all parties have regarded as "teaching"). Instead, I view the Miller dispute as a relatively straightforward conflict of interest or commitment, with Harvard's efforts to limit this electronic moonlighting as analogous to enforcing regulations that bar faculty from simultaneously holding tenure at another university.[79] In the wake of this quarrel, Harvard is moving to adopt clearer rules that forbid faculty from teaching on-line courses for other institutions without prior authorization.[80]

As with the Harvard dispute, the quickest and cleanest way to clarify the limits of faculty entrepreneurship in the digital age and to regularize the development and marketing of electronic instruction will be carefully drawn copyright and conflict-of-interest or conflict-of-commitment policies. As far as the law is concerned, the ownership of such intellectual property and the distribution of any royalties derived therefrom are entirely negotiable. For example, the parties might agree that faculty will hold the copyright but that the employer university will have a no-cost, long-term license to use such materials, the ability to direct the marketing and distributing of such products, and a hefty share of any profits. Alternatively (as with most patent policies), the parties might agree that the university will hold the copyright and direct all commercialization efforts, but that faculty authors will receive a large slice of the revenues. The ultimate distribution of profits, of course, should ideally reflect how much value is added to the intellectual product by the university's reputation (or "brand") and marketing skill, as opposed to the stature and effort of the individual scholar.

Institution-wide policies can be shaped in any direction. A 1999 University of Chicago policy affirms institutional ownership of intellectual property created under university auspices or with university resources but declares that income generated "from the use of new information technologies in teaching and research" will belong to faculty until it becomes "substantial"—at which point the appropriate faculty share must be determined with greater precision.[81] In this rapidly changing environment, Chicago felt it was "too soon to set down fixed rules and formalities" to govern the distribution of electronic profits.[82] Across the country, Duke University is poised to take a sophisticated approach that separates ownership (faculty would own what they have created) from compliance with conflict-of-interest rules (faculty would be restricted in teaching on-line courses that compete with Duke's conventional or electronic offerings).[83] In the absence of general institutional policies, individual negotiations will be needed to clarify the parties' respective rights.

New information technologies will also give rise to new disputes about the need to identify (or to refrain from identifying) institutional affiliations. Colleges and universities have a deep and legally protectible property interest in the use of their names. The wider the potential dissemination of information, the greater the harm of an inaccurately implied or omitted sponsorship.

Perhaps the anticipated profits will never materialize, and efforts to capitalize on Internet-based learning will be a flash in the pan. But if, as seems more likely, distance learning becomes a prominent feature of higher education across the globe, we can expect more fierce debate about the control and use of Web-based educational materials and further evolution of the law resolving such disputes.

## Patent

Patents are granted to inventors, that is, the person(s) who actually conceptualize or discover the patentable machine, process, or other item.[84] In contrast to the situation under federal copyright law, under federal patent law inventors who happen to be employees are almost always entitled to claim patent rights for themselves.[85] In those special circumstances in which an employer has hired an employee to make a particular invention, the employer would be granted the resulting patent. But if an employee is hired to make one invention but makes another, or if an employee is hired to conduct general research (rather than to make patentable discoveries) but such inventions nevertheless occur, the inventor-employee would be entitled to claim the ensuing patents.[86] A typical faculty member—who is expected to do scholarship but is given minimal (if any) direction about which areas to pursue or how to pursue them—would not qualify as someone "hired to invent."[87] The case of *Kaplan v. Johnson* is instructive.[88] In *Kaplan,* the chief of nuclear medicine at a Veterans Administration hospital had invented a camera system for whole-body imaging. The hospital claimed that it owned this invention because conducting research was one of the physician's job responsibilities. The court rejected this argument, recognizing a distinction between "employment calling for general research work and employment with the specific objective of invention."[89]

The standard recompense for an employer whose employee makes a patentable invention or discovery on company time or with company resources is a "shop right": a nonexclusive, royalty-free, irrevocable license to use the invention or discovery in the employer's business. Under a "baseline patent scenario," then, a typical faculty member would hold the patents on his or her own inventions and the institutional employer would acquire a shop right on the basis of the financial and material support that made such research breakthroughs possible.[90]

As with copyright, however, patents that would ordinarily belong to an employee can be assigned to an employer as an explicit condition of employment. The ultimate distribution of patent rights within a college or university thus becomes a matter of contract law. Here, too, a growing number of institutions have patent policies that are carefully incorporated into faculty employment agreements or are even signed as independent documents.[91] For a variety of reasons, institutions have been more assertive in claiming ownership of patentable than of copyrightable research. Leading this list, of course, is the hope of vast financial rewards, which is spurred by examples of peer institutions that have reaped substantial returns from faculty discoveries. For example, Stanford and the University of California system have shared multimillion-dollar payments on patents for gene-splicing techniques, and the University of Florida collects 20 percent of the income from sales of Gatorade sports drink, which was invented by university faculty for the school's football team.[92] Colleges and universities may also believe that their ownership helps ensure that new (especially biomedical) discoveries are more quickly turned into useful products. Institutional ownership received yet another boost by the 1980 passage of a federal statute permitting college and university recipients of research grants to obtain any patents resulting from such federally funded research.[93] Indeed, shortly after this law was enacted, many institutions adopted patent policies for the first time or overhauled extant policies to make them stronger.[94]

As might be expected, college and university patent policies run the gamut,[95] but they ordinarily provide for institutional ownership of at least some faculty inventions and in return give faculty a slice of the royalties flowing from their discoveries. The policy's scope depends most of all on how bold the institution wants to be—or believes it is politic to be. Some colleges and universities claim ownership of any faculty inventions made with significant use of university resources; others claim as well inventions made in the course of a faculty member's employment; still others expansively claim all inventions made by faculty employees, period.[96]

Faculty opponents of institutional patent policies have questioned not only their enforceability but also their basic rationale. Thus, one hears that a policy is overly vague (what, after all, is a "significant" use of university resources?), that faculty lack adequate notice that the policy is in effect (especially when it has been unilaterally revised), or that faculty have not executed a legally binding document transferring their ownership rights to the institution (indeed, appointment letters are often signed just by chairs or deans and may simply refer to "relevant policies").[97] At a deeper level, opponents claim that policies vesting ownership in college or university employers can subtly pervert institutional academic priorities and judgments,[98] can reduce faculty incentives to invent,[99] and can even drive researchers out of the academy.[100] Faculty ownership, it is argued, is also necessary to "ensure the invention's proper development from an abstract idea to its practical application . . . [because faculty] best understand the fundamental nature as well as the intricate nuances of the discovery."[101] Of course, faculty may also stand to benefit financially by eliminating university claims of ownership or royalty rights.

Regardless of the theoretical merits or demerits of patent policies, such policies are by now an established feature of academic life. I maintain that this is perfectly acceptable, for what matters most in unleashing faculty creative energies is not the ultimate designation of ownership (remember that faculty have for years freely assigned copyrights to third-party publishers), but rather the perceived fairness of the revenue split under the institution's patent policy. The possibility of vast gains is so small, and most faculty (as well as institutions) are sufficiently motivated by the altruistic pursuit of knowledge (or the less noble desire for recognition), that it makes little sense for scholars or institutions to spend energy fighting over marginal variations in hypothetical royalties. Recognizing this, institutions have chosen to be rather generous in sharing "their" patent royalties with faculty inventors. Faculty slices of 25–50 percent of net revenues are not uncommon. For example, Stanford (which claims title to inventions conceived or first reduced to practice in whole or in part in the course of university responsibilities or with more than incidental use of university resources) gives faculty inventors one-third of net royalty income.[102]

There is, however, one large gap in many intellectual property policies (both patent and copyright). The usual focus on physical control and financial exploitation of the fruits of scholarship obscures intellectual issues that subsequently arise from that research. Within the academy the most important rights associated with scholarship may be those such as the authority to determine whether an invention or a written work is ready to be shared with colleagues or the broader public; the ability to accept or reject proposed revisions to one's work and to decide who should make any necessary changes; the right to conclude whether further developments in a field have rendered one's work obsolete and if so, whether that obsolescence requires amendment or scrapping of an earlier effort (for example, when is a second edition of a text appropriate?); and the ability to determine how a work should be distributed or performed.[103] These more purely intellectual matters are peculiarly within the province of faculty and thus are likely to be left to their discretion, but most patent and copyright policies do not distinguish them from other incidents of ownership. Regardless of who holds formal title and who cashes the royalty checks, institutions should refine their policies to make sure that faculty have an appropriate level of control over how their scholarship is developed and shared. This brings us back squarely to the question of how faculty research is disseminated.

## Dissemination of and Access to Scholarly Work

From both a legal and a practical standpoint, faculty have enormous discretion in determining whether and how their research findings are made public. Since no copyright can even exist in scholarly work until it is fixed in a tangible medium of expression, it is faculty who decide whether to turn their research into an article or book in the first place and what form such a work might take. And as we have seen, many faculty do in fact hold the copyright in their scholarly writings (by operation of law, formal institutional policy, or institutional custom).[104] They are therefore free to submit manuscripts to the journal or press of their choice, on their own timetable. Even institutions that claim copyright ownership in faculty works are not usually so bold as to tread on these long-established faculty prerogatives. It is simpler for such institutions just to claim a share of the royalties.

Publishers will ordinarily demand an assignment of copyright to them before printing a manuscript.[105] This presents no problem when the faculty member is the copyright holder, but it raises a dilemma if the employer institution claims copyright but has not been involved in the publication process. Publishers often attempt to shift legal responsibility for such problems to the author. They may require the author to formally warrant that he or she is the copyright owner and to agree to hold the publisher harmless from any expenses or damages incurred in a subsequent dispute over ownership.

Successful research often depends upon access to the data or scholarship of others. Here too, the right to use such materials turns in the first instance on who holds copyright to such works (or who owns raw data not yet fixed in copyrightable form). Faculty would ordinarily need the permission of the copyright holder to use his or her work. Fortunately, since scholarly norms include the free exchange of information, such permission is usually easily obtained. Faculty seeking access to others' works may also be able to rely upon a doctrine of copyright law known as "fair use." This doctrine protects unauthorized but socially beneficial uses of copyrighted materials in circumstances that do not materially detract from the interests of authors or discourage them from producing further works. The federal Copyright Act provides that "fair use of a copyrighted work . . . for purposes such as criticism, comment . . . teaching . . . scholarship, or research, is not an infringement of copyright."[106] Whether a particular use qualifies as fair calls for a fact-specific inquiry involving a variety of factors, including (1) the purpose and character of the use (nonprofit educational uses are treated favorably); (2) the nature of the copyrighted work (the more noncommercial its character, the more likely the use will be found to be fair); (3) the amount and substantiality of the portion used in relation to the copyrighted work as a whole (smaller, of course, is better); and (4) the effect of the use upon the potential market for or value of the copyrighted work (again, the smaller the unfavorable impact, the more likely a given use will be deemed "fair").[107] Disputes over fair use are common when faculty seek to use copyrighted works as in-class handouts or as assigned readings in course packs,[108] but they can also arise in the research context.

In *American Geophysical Union v. Texaco Inc.*, a federal appellate court held that the copying of scientific journal articles by Texaco scientists for "archival" purposes (i.e., keeping a copy readily available in case it becomes relevant to a particular line of research an individual scientist is pursuing) did not qualify as fair use.[109] Like many faculty, the scientists had simply made complete copies of articles that interested them, without requesting permission from journal publishers/copyright holders. The court, however, found that this practice harmed the copyright holder's ability to license the use of such articles and possibly damaged the market for journal subscriptions as well. Notwithstanding the observation that Texaco's systematic photocopying program for its hundreds of corporate scientists was a defining characteristic of the dispute at bar, and the judges' express avowal that they were not deciding the case of "a professor or an independent scientist engaged in copying and creating files for independent research," this holding is disquieting to faculty who seek easy access to the raw materials of scholarship.[110] As photocopying—and now digital copying—technology evolves, such access paradoxically becomes both physically easier and legally more complicated. Copyright holders anxious to preserve the value of their property may place new procedural and financial hurdles on faculty work.

At the same time, the growth in research conducted by teams of scientists (especially in the physical and biological sciences), possibly even at different institutions, has inevitably given rise to arguments—often petty but impassioned—between former colleagues over access to data. Both individual institutions and federal agencies that sponsor research have begun to craft policies to address such conflicts. As one might expect from institutions dedicated to discovery, most colleges and universities that have grappled with this issue have come out strongly in favor of ensuring that "when a collaborative team splits up, each member . . . should have continuing access to the data and . . . materials with which he or she had been working."[111]

The flip side of a scholar's ability to obtain access to source materials is the right to control others' access to one's own research and supporting documentation. As we have seen, academic custom and special accommodations for scholars under copyright law work in tandem to limit a faculty member's power to prevent other scholars from examining, citing, building upon, or criticizing one's published or otherwise distributed work. However, faculty may elect for a variety of reasons to withhold works in progress or even finished works from wider scrutiny—for example, if key experimental results have not yet been replicated. Such decisions typically are respected by fellow scholars. In some instances, even after their research has been made public, faculty may insist on retaining absolute control over the underlying data or primary sources. They are legally entitled to take this position if they own the materials in question, and other researchers would have to abide by such a decision, contrary though it may be to scholarly norms and expectations.

Faculty also occasionally face demands that they disclose the results of (or supporting bases for) their research to third parties for *nonacademic* purposes. When called to resolve such disputes, courts balance the academic benefit of scholars' controlling how their research is shared against countervailing social interests, such as the basic principle of our legal system that all persons must share relevant evidence in their possession. Two factors carry special weight in this balance: (1) the anticipated harm to the scholar's research agenda from disclosure (in particular, whether the fruits of his or her research have already been published or shared with others in some fashion) and (2) whether the data in question are sought in connection with a criminal proceeding.[112]

Judicial authorities are for the most part genuinely appreciative of the years of effort required for successful scholarship and recognize the potential damage to individual careers and to the broader goal of discovering knowledge that may result from the unwanted or premature disclosure of research findings. Faculty resistance to such compelled dissemination—often under the banner of academic freedom—has therefore received a modest measure of legal protection. In *Dow Chemical Co. v. Allen*,[113] the plaintiff corporation subpoenaed all reports, notes, drafts, working papers, experimental protocols, lab notebooks, and raw data from two University of Wisconsin scientists' studies (still incomplete and unpublished) of the toxic effect on animals of ingesting a particular chemical compound.[114] Dow had been using this compound in herbicides it manufactured. When the Environmental Protection Agency suspended the use of these products, Dow sought access to these research materials in order to bolster its case that they were in fact safe. A federal appeals court granted the scientists' request to quash these subpoenas, concluding that enforcement would impose unreasonable burdens upon the researchers. The court was very sympathetic to the scholars' claims that "public access to the research data would make the studies an unacceptable basis for scientific papers . . . ; that peer review and publication of the studies was crucial to the researchers' credibility and careers and would be precluded by whole or partial public disclosure of the information; [and] that loss of the opportunity to publish would severely decrease the researchers' professional opportunities in the future."[115]

In addition to concerns about the effect of compelled disclosure on the careers of these particular scientists, the *Dow* court recognized potentially chilling effects on the very process of faculty scholarship at Wisconsin and other institutions. Stating that scholars must be free to carry out their research without government interference, the court concluded that forced, broad, and intrusive access to faculty research could quickly sap the ardor and fearlessness of scholars. "Enforcement of the subpoenas," the court opined, "would leave the researchers with the knowledge . . . that the fruits of their labors had been appropriated by and were being scrutinized by a not-unbiased third party whose interests were arguably antithetical to theirs. It is not difficult to imagine that that realization might well be both unnerving and discouraging."[116] *Dow Chemical* then, is strong precedent for the proposition that at state-actor colleges and universities, faculty scholarship (here in the aspect of faculty controlling access to and use of their research findings) "comes within the First Amendment's protection of academic freedom."[117]

In early 1998, a professor of labor relations at Cornell University whose research focused on antiunion tactics used by management was sued for defamation by a nursing home company. The plaintiff company alleged that the professor made false public statements about its compliance with labor laws. It claimed, in effect, that the professor had turned from an objective scholar into a union propagandist. In connection with the suit, the company sought access to the researcher's database of confidential information about union organizing strategies. Not surprisingly, faculty across the nation rallied to the Cornell professor's defense, fearful of the chilling effect this suit could have on scholarly independence and the integrity of data collection. The suit was dismissed and the unpublished and confidential data remained secure.[118]

Later that same year, federal courts refused to give Microsoft Corporation access to the raw research materials of a Harvard and an MIT professor for use in its defense against antitrust charges. These materials (including notes and tape-recorded interviews with executives of one of Microsoft's competitors) had been obtained under assurances of confidentiality and formed the backbone of an as-yet-unpublished book on the struggle for control of the Internet browser market. In rejecting Microsoft's request for such items, the First Circuit held that "academicians engaged in prepublication research should be accorded protection commensurate to that which the law provides for journalists."[119] Like reporters, "scholars too are information gatherers and disseminators. . . . a drying up of sources would sharply curtail the information available to academic researchers and thus would restrict their output."[120] Having weighed the company's need for this information (which it could have obtained by other means) against the professors' interest in maintaining confidentiality and the potential harm resulting from disclosure, the court determined that enforcing Microsoft's subpoenas would "hamstring not only the respondents' future research efforts but also those of other similarly situated scholars. This loss of theoretical insight into the business world is of concern in and of itself. Even more important, compelling the disclosure of such research materials would infrigidate the free flow of information to the public, thus denigrating a fundamental First Amendment value."[121] The fact that the professors were in no way connected to the underlying antitrust litigation, of course, made their position especially sympathetic.

However, unlike the researchers in the *Dow,* Cornell, and Microsoft cases, faculty who have already *published* their findings have a much harder time preventing judicially compelled disclosure of supporting data. Thus, in 1982 a federal district court ordered a University of Michigan professor to furnish the Jeep Corporation with research materials that formed the basis of his published study on the crash-worthiness of utility vehicles.[122] Jeep expected this study would be used against it by the plaintiff in a personal-injury suit. The court rejected both the scholar's claim of an "academic privilege" that excused him from testifying or handing over such information (analogous to a physician's right to refuse to testify about the treatment of a patient) and his assertion that disclosure would infringe his First Amendment rights as a researcher and writer. It held instead that faculty, like all other persons, are expected to share or produce information they possess. "Balancing the minimal chance that compelling [the scholar] to testify or produce his underlying data would cause him to abandon research and writing as against the needs of the justice system to use basic research information," the latter interests were clearly paramount—especially since the professor had already placed the results of his research in the "public domain" by publishing them.[123]

More recently, in *In re Mt. Sinai School of Medicine v. American Tobacco Co.,*[124] three cigarette manufacturers sought to obtain the underlying data for journal articles arguing that smokers who are exposed to asbestos at their jobs have a geometrically increased risk of developing cancer. This research formed the crux of a series of product-liability claims against the companies. The faculty author refused to comply with the companies' subpoenas, in part because he had assured his research subjects that the information they provided would be confidential. After a state court refused to enforce a sweeping demand for background information, the companies submitted a more limited and specific request, which was deemed appropriate and enforceable by federal courts. Both the trial and the appellate courts declined to recognize a scholars' privilege exempting faculty from the general obligation to produce evidence. The appeals court was also unmoved by claims that scientific research could be chilled by such compelled disclosure, observing that since the data in question formed the basis of previously published articles, there was no risk of "preemptive or predatory publication by others."[125]

Even more troubling from a faculty perspective, the *Mt. Sinai* court noted that "publication of [a researcher's] findings and conclusions invites use by persons whom the findings favor and invites reliance by the finders of fact."[126] Carried to its logical conclusion, such reasoning would make scientists' data in controversial areas (environmental hazards, gene therapy, birth control) fair game for all manner of litigants in all kinds of judicial forums. Indeed, the more significant the research, the more likely that it will have such undesired consequences.

In *Deitchmann v. E.R. Squibb & Sons, Inc.*,[127] an author of groundbreaking studies linking prenatal exposure to DES to the subsequent development of cancer was served with an intrusive discovery request by the drug's manufacturer. The scholar, by then a department chair at the University of Chicago, had for many years been compiling a registry of women who contracted particular kinds of cancer associated with DES. Data from this registry was continually being used as the basis of academic publications. The scientist opposed the discovery of such data on the grounds that any breach of the confidentiality promised patients would destroy the usefulness of the registry as a research tool and impede other epidemiological scholarship. He also argued that disclosure of his research findings would infringe his academic freedom to "divulge to the public the results of his studies only in his own time and way."[128] The Seventh Circuit Court of Appeals refused to leave the drug company without access to information that was clearly essential for cross-examining plaintiffs' expert witnesses in ongoing liability suits. But in remanding the case to the District Court to fashion a remedy that avoided breaches of confidentiality and preserved the registry for further research, the appellate court approved giving additional protection to works in progress. It held that "no discovery should be allowed of any material reflecting development of [the physician's] ideas or stating his or others conclusions *not yet published*."[129]

It is easy to imagine how the prospect of compelled disclosure of research data might curb a scholar's enthusiasm or subtly influence his choice of topics, notwithstanding assurances that scientists themselves would not have to prepare data submissions or that the cost of production would be borne by the parties seeking access to the data. In the final analysis, though, the developing case law in this area correctly recognizes that the loss of some time that could otherwise be devoted to research and the imposition of minor burdens (such as amending protocols to avoid making unenforceable promises of confidentiality) do not put one's research at risk to the same degree as disclosure of unpublished research.[130]

In addition to ordering the release of data that supports published scholarship, courts have consistently allowed third-party access to faculty research materials when such information is sought in connection with a criminal investigation or trial. Cries that faculty research must be inviolate tend to fall upon deaf ears when that research is needed by prosecutors deciding whether to bring charges and juries deciding whether to convict. The recent case of *Scarce v. United States*[131] is instructive. Rik Scarce was a doctoral student in sociology at Washington State University researching the radical environmental movement. After animal rights activists vandalized a Washington State laboratory, a federal grand jury subpoenaed Scarce to testify about his conversations with a break-in suspect who had been house-sitting for Scarce at the time of the incident. Scarce refused to answer the prosecutor's questions, relying upon a purported First Amendment and common law "scholar's privilege" to withhold "confidential information which he had gathered in the course of his sociological research."[132] He argued that both news reporters and scholars had the legal authority, if not the obligation, to protect the confidentiality of sources (and that such behavior was in fact required under the code of ethics of his discipline's professional association). Indeed, in Scarce's view, all scholars should have the right "to pursue their research unhindered by governmental interference."[133] The courts flatly rejected the existence of any "scholar's privilege" and further denied that reporters enjoyed such blanket protection. Not only was the subpoena valid, but Scarce was jailed for contempt of court for over five months when he continued to refuse to testify.[134]

The holding in *Scarce* is consistent with the federal appeals court's decision in *In re Grand Jury Subpoena*.[135] There, too, a sociology graduate student was ordered to share information he had gleaned while conducting research (in this case, observations made during fieldwork as a waiter at a restaurant where a suspicious fire occurred). The student, who was not a suspect in the incident, had testified before a grand jury but balked at handing over his journal containing field notes for a dissertation titled "The Sociology of the American Restaurant." The lower court had found a limited federal common law privilege against disclosure, analogizing serious scholars to journalists.[136] But the appellate court reversed, stating that it was improper to recognize such a privilege without a much more rigorous showing "of the nature and seriousness of the scholarly study in question, of the methodology employed, of the need for assurances of confidentiality to various sources to conduct the study, and of the fact that disclosure . . . will seriously impinge upon that confidentiality."[137] While not ruling out the possibility of circumstances meeting these requirements, the court was most inhospitable to claims of what it termed "virtually an unqualified and indeterminate immunity attaching generally to all academically related inquiries upon the bald assertion that someone was promised confidentiality in connection with the study."[138]

The potential harm from the compelled disclosure of supporting data or information is undoubtedly greater when the scholarship premised on such materials has not yet been published. From an investigator's perspective, the type and amount of current data or the overall state of a work in progress may be woefully inadequate. If disclosure is ordered before the research has been vetted by reviewers to identify gaps or errors, the early release of a flawed work will confuse, if not set back, the course of scholarship in the field—and will certainly damage the reputation of the scholar who is "responsible" for any inaccuracies. In addition, compelled disclosure strips the researcher of the ability to set his or her work in an appropriate context, explaining what assumptions or preconditions are necessary for the findings and what further propositions ought to be derived from the results.[139] Court-ordered release also ignores that the manner and location of a work's presentation may be important to the author and disciplinary peers. And forced *prepublication* disclosure of a scholar's work will lead to the same kinds of problems caused by postpublication release (e.g., new hurdles in proceeding with further investigations; damage to a scholar's credibility and stature when promises of confidentiality are broken). The magnitude of the preceding harms, of course, will grow in concert with the publicity (or notoriety) accorded to the disclosed research.

For all of these reasons, judges have been (correctly, in my view) very cautious in ordering the prepublication disclosure of a professor's work or its underlying bases. But given the overriding need for courts to have the best and most complete evidence before them in deciding legal—especially criminal—disputes, even prepublication status has not proved (and will not be) an absolute bar to disclosure. There is no "academic privilege" protecting scholarly works or underlying data from disclosure, and promises of absolute confidentiality to sources are unenforceable.

## Conflicts of Interest and Conflicts of Commitment

Our discussion of the legal principles applicable to faculty as researchers would be incomplete without brief mention of these two common snares that scholars should seek to avoid. In the words of the former president of Rensselaer Polytechnic Institute:

> Conflicts of *interest* arise when . . . faculty members . . . have financial or other interests in a business or organization that militate against their making impartial decisions. . . . Conflicts of *commitments* are those situations wherein members of the university community become so involved in a commercial [or other outside] endeavor that they can no longer do justice to their academic responsibilities, either in terms of time, or in terms of the free, open, and complete sharing of scientific information and discovery.[140]

Either type of conflict—and sometimes even perceived conflicts—can create legal disputes between faculty and their institutions and do serious harm to both.

Within a research setting, conflicts of interest arise most frequently in connection with (1) external funding arrangements and (2) efforts by individuals and institutions to exploit faculty scholarship for commercial gain.[141] For example, classic conflicts of interest may be presented when a company sponsors faculty research in areas directly related to its products or if faculty members have direct financial interests in companies that fund their work (e.g., owning a substantial block of stock, holding a position as a director or a part-time employee). Of course, the more controversial the sponsor or the field being studied, or the greater the financial rewards at stake, the more likely that such relationships will be questioned. Even relatively mundane scholarship is vulnerable to conflicts of interest, however. Efforts to develop fluffier popcorn that are funded by a grain company should demand the same scrutiny as research on the efficacy of gun control laws that is funded by a firearms manufacturer.

The pursuit of research support and commercial profit also create other temptations properly labeled as conflicts of interest. Is it appropriate for faculty to assign their graduate students or postdocs to research projects from which the advisor expects to reap financial rewards, either in the form of future funding streams or higher stock values? What about using university facilities to conduct scholarship that benefits third parties or faculty in their "nonuniversity" capacity? One could argue persuasively that both of these are equivalent to (and present just as much of a conflict as) a researcher receiving a more generous level of corporate sponsorship. Faculty who are asked to review other scholars' work for possible publication or on peer review panels selecting grant recipients face yet another variety of conflict of interest. If the reviewer has a direct or indirect financial stake in the review's outcome (for example, if publicizing a research breakthrough might drive down the value of his own start-up company) perhaps additional safeguards (disclosure, recusal) are called for.

The underlying fear with any of these conflicts of interest is that financial links between scholars and sponsors or between scholars and for-profit businesses will warp faculty members' research and teaching.[142] The pursuit of more funding or higher royalties could subtly influence the selection of research topics. At the extreme, research subjects might even be chosen on the basis of marketability. It is, after all, much easier and quicker to measure market demand than to gauge true intellectual significance. Conflicts of interest also threaten the integrity of faculty research. Might not a scholar with a conflict of interest keep following an unproductive avenue for longer than necessary (perhaps without even recognizing this) because, if fruitful, it stands to make him and his sponsor wealthy? Faculty with conflicts of interest may seek to soft-pedal their conclusions to avoid unnecessarily antagonizing a funding source. Even more perniciously, they may be tempted to delay or withhold findings that are inconsistent with their own and their sponsors' financial interests. Fortunately, both educational institutions and individual scholars are vitally concerned with research integrity. This is why many conflict-of-interest policies include powerful affirmations of the need for rigor and openness in conducting research.[143]

It is important to reiterate here that faculty are not alone in trying to avoid or minimize conflicts of interest. Since research funds and royalties from technology licenses regularly flow through—and in part to—institutions, as corporate entities colleges and universities face similar risks of allowing financial arrangements with third parties to subvert the achievement of their missions. The promise of external funding or future profit can affect decisions about new programs, the number of faculty slots, salaries, and promotions just as it can shape a scholar's choice of topics. Sometimes institutional conflicts of interest are layered on top of individual ones— as when a university and members of its faculty each own part of a company formed to exploit those scholars' research. If the employer and employee share the conflict of interest, ordinary safeguards against biased or flawed decisions (e.g., the decision to reappoint an assistant professor whose scholarship is undistinguished but whose work is of great value to the jointly owned firm) may be ineffective.

In recent years federal agencies have also become very concerned about conflicts of interest involving government-funded research. Both the National Science Foundation and the Public Health Service now require all institutions receiving federal funds to have in place written financial conflict-of-interest policies and enforcement procedures meeting detailed criteria, such as obligatory disclosures by "investigators" (the definition of which includes the employee's spouse and dependent children); the designation of institutional officials responsible for collecting and reviewing faculty disclosure statements and determining whether conflicts exist; the specification of actions the college or university will take to manage, reduce, or eliminate conflicts; comprehensive record-keeping requirements; and provisions for agency access to such institutional records.[144] Given tight federal funding for science and the government's understandable desire to account fully for all expenditures, it is safe to assume that federal efforts to avoid conflicts of interest in sponsored research will escalate.

Beyond the direct harm done to the work of individual scholars and institutions by financial conflicts of interest, the potential damage from the mere *appearance* of impropriety must also be noted. As highly visible (and inevitably controversial) charitable institutions, colleges, universities, and their denizens must pay careful attention to public perceptions of their activities. Even if no monetary gain actually results from a conflict situation, external audiences will all too readily assume that funding sources or the lure of commercial opportunities improperly influenced academic decisions. The end result may not be much different than if something untoward had really occurred. Unrealized conflicts are nevertheless damning because they demonstrate that the institution and the faculty member in question failed to consider (or worse, didn't care enough to protect) their reputation.

As distinguished from conflicts of interest, conflicts of commitment have less to do with financial ties than with the appropriate use of one's time and the need to maintain scholarly focus. Conflicts of commitment arise most frequently in connection with faculty members' consulting work in the area of their academic expertise (though conflicts are also created by extensive government service, significant leadership posts in professional societies, journal editorships, and even moonlighting in an unrelated business). Colleges and universities try to resist conflicts of commitment because of a conviction—which has by now become an honored tradition—that faculty owe their primary allegiance to their home institutions and should carry out the bulk of their professional efforts under its auspices. Quite understandably, institutions want to get a full salary's worth of time and effort from their faculty employees.[145]

Institutions typically regulate both conflicts of interest and conflicts of commitment by promulgating official policies, which then become part of the employment contract with individual faculty. (Recall here that some minimal legal formalities, such as referring to these policies in an appointment letter, inclusion of the policies in a faculty handbook, and notice of any changes in the policies, must be observed in order to make them clearly binding upon faculty.)[146] Faculty who violate such policies can be disciplined (even dismissed) or sued for breach of contract. Conflict-of-commitment policies, for example, ordinarily prevent faculty from simultaneously holding tenured (or otherwise inconsistent) positions at two different colleges or universities.[147]

Courts have unambiguously upheld conflict-of-commitment policies as appropriate and enforceable provisions of faculty employment contracts. In *Kaufman v. Board of Trustees*,[148] a federal trial court upheld a rule prohibiting full-time faculty at the City Colleges of Chicago from holding concurrent full-time positions with other employers. The court opined that such a rule was a rational and legitimate means of ensuring that faculty "devote their primary loyalty and attention to their duties as employees of the City Colleges."[149] In *Marks v. New York Univ.*,[150] a clinical professor of business at NYU was lawfully discharged when, in direct contravention of that university's conflict-of-commitment/external-employment policies, she began working full-time at Fordham University. And in *Gross v. University of Tennessee*, a federal appellate court agreed that the university's College of Medicine could, in an effort to "limit the faculty's outside private practice and thus to foster greater devotion to teaching responsibilities," require faculty to sign written agreements turning over to the institution external earnings above a certain threshold.[151] Properly adopted and reasonably understandable conflict-of-interest policies would be accorded similar deference by judicial authorities.

Although conflict-of-interest and conflict-of-commitment policies will of course vary in scope and content across institutions, it is possible to identify some broad themes that characterize such rules. One definite trend is for colleges and universities to require faculty to *disclose* (to their department chair or even dean) any external relationships or obligations that might give rise to either kind of conflict. Indeed, well-crafted policies will urge faculty to make such disclosure whenever they are uncertain about the propriety of their behavior. In the words of the University of Chicago's policy, "Disclosure is a key factor in protecting one's reputation and career from potentially embarrassing or harmful allegations."[152]

Conflict-of-commitment policies typically affirm in sweeping language the benefits to individual scholars and their institutions of outside work. These would include opportunities for intellectual regeneration, identifying new research topics, exposure to "real-world" issues that can improve teaching, and connections that may lead to jobs for students, in addition to more obvious financial rewards. At the same time, however, most conflict-of-commitment policies set clear and unequivocal limits on how much time faculty can spend consulting. One day in seven (i.e., no more than one day per week) is the traditional industry standard.[153]

In contrast, overt restrictions on conflicts of interest are much less common. Under many if not most policies, conflict-fraught activities may still proceed with the prior approval of disinterested superiors.[154] This makes sense because the value to society of the research or other activity in question may far exceed the dangers associated with the conflict. Once aware of a conflict, institutional authorities can also minimize its impact—for example, by publicly disclosing information that might be controversial.[155] Only the most egregious conflicts (e.g., a faculty member who is conducting clinical trials on a drug also owns stock in the company that manufactures it) would automatically invoke extra safeguards or possibly be banned outright.[156] However, institutions have imposed dollar limits on financial conflicts to minimize both the temptation to make (and the appearance of having made) improperly motivated decisions. Along these lines, a highly publicized sponsored biomedical research agreement between Washington University and the Monsanto Corporation provided that yearly funding from the company could not exceed 7 percent of the medical school's total research budget.[157] Finally, an increasingly common response to conflicts of interest is the use of independent institutional (or even external) oversight committees to ensure research integrity. Many conflict policies now explicitly provide for the appointment of such panels at the discretion of relevant college or university authorities.[158]

## Concluding Thoughts

A central theme that emerges in our study of how law protects and affects scholarship is that this is a sphere of professional activity in which faculty require—and in fact enjoy—the intellectual latitude conducive to the discovery of knowledge. The law helps carve out this broad zone of independence and also establishes meaningful faculty direction over the dissemination, use, and possible exploitation of the fruits of scholarship. As is often the case in higher education, the law structures faculty members' rights to carry out and to benefit from scholarship principally by contract: that is, employment agreements with professors (including policies and custom on research-related matters like academic freedom, intellectual property, and conflicts of interest and commitment) and research agreements with funding agencies and sponsors. Readers should understand that while colleges and universities have the legal right to demand compliance with institutional rules as a condition of employment, faculty need not work on unpalatable terms. Consequently, fair and mutually acceptable compromises usually ensue.

Perhaps somewhat surprisingly (but also reassuringly), little litigation has arisen to date over faculty research. This reflects commonly shared views among scholars, administrators, and sponsors that faculty should drive the content of research while these other actors work to enable such inquiry. Relative harmony has also obtained because conducting research is typically a quiet and isolated activity, because most scholarship is only of interest to other academics, and because most university research was deemed to have little or no pecuniary value. As this last assumption is now regularly called into question, the law pertaining to faculty scholarship will surely become more important and more often contested.

One area of potential legal controversy involving scholarship arises from the heightened specialization—and sometimes politicization—of knowledge. We have seen how critical, yet how difficult, it is for faculty to review the work of peers without falling prey to intellectual bias or sloppiness. With academic disciplines proliferating and subdividing, and with some fields roiled by internecine strife over what constitutes "quality" work or what is "true," the prospect of poorly made (and subsequently litigated) hiring, tenure, and promotion decisions grows. This is a long-standing legal risk, but it is becoming more acute.

In the future, increasingly entrepreneurial faculty and academic institutions are also likely to find themselves in conflict over the commercialization of scholarly work. While faculty have the actual ideas and do the actual labor, scholarship generally cannot occur without space, equipment, library collections, data, time for reflection, colleagues (both peers and graduate student assistants), and the intellectually stimulating atmosphere furnished by the employer institution (or perhaps by an external sponsor). I would posit that with carefully crafted copyright and patent policies, the ownership of research will become less contentious than the distribution of the royalty stream. And on this latter point, brute market power will prove decisive. Faculty who can command a higher price, a larger cut, or a special deal will do so aggressively (threatening to take their ideas and themselves elsewhere if their demands are not met); employer colleges and universities will insist upon general rules that secure a healthy slice of profits for the institution (thus supporting research across the entire entity); and corporate sponsors will try to squeeze the combined academic share as small as possible.

Over the course of the requisite negotiations (and inevitable disputes), egos will be bruised and alliances (perhaps unholy) will be formed: for example, individual researchers in league with businesses to perform research outside of university auspices, or universities "locking up" sponsors and faculty through agreements that cover whole research units or departments. I therefore expect that we shall see universities trying to unwind— or to discipline professors for—too-close collaborations with industrial patrons (e.g., accepting an equity position in a start-up company for which the professor conducts research; consulting arrangements that subsume the professor's intellect and time) as well as litigation by faculty challenging institutional restrictions on the pursuit or the terms of outside funding. In my estimation, biotechnology and computer science are the most likely arenas of legal combat, followed by electronic distance learning (on this latter subject, intellectual property law, especially copyright, must develop to accommodate owners' rights and users' needs).[159]

I explained earlier that the great danger with efforts to secure external research funding, to capture the rewards flowing from research, and to pursue academic profit more generally is that faculty and institutions will become so business-oriented that fundamental academic values are compromised. There is nothing inherently wrong with close university-industry ties; indeed, scholarship that benefits the business community can be an important form of service. Recall that an explicit purpose of founding land-grant institutions was to promote state agriculture, industry, and commerce.[160] And, given their pressing financial needs, colleges and universities understandably seek support from a wide variety of corporate sponsors. But if individual research agendas or institutional intellectual priorities are shaped with an eye towards the bottom line or satisfying business partners, universities may lose a slice of the hard-won independence and skeptical detachment that they need—just as much as money—to accomplish their mission, part of which involves social and intellectual criticism. This is not a new dilemma. Early in the last century Thorstein Veblen warned of universities torn between "the claims of science and scholarship on the one hand and those of business principles and pecuniary gain on the other hand."[161] But in times like the present, when the prospects for large gains seem so inviting, faculty and institutions should exercise special care in evaluating and entering into profit-making ventures linked to scholarship.

# 3 In the Classroom

Teaching is the common thread running through the work of faculty at all institutions, from new or experimental colleges or schools to the most staid or venerable of universities. Indeed, a key reason why college and university faculty became faculty in the first place was their excitement at the prospect of sharing their knowledge and skills with others, helping them to learn and grow. The primary purpose of all two- and four-year colleges, of course, is undergraduate instruction. But even research universities, whose missions prominently include the creation of new knowledge, are commonly judged by alumni, government officials, and the general public on the quality of the undergraduate, graduate, and professional instruction they provide.[1] (This to the sometimes legitimate consternation of those institutions and their faculty.) If, as I have argued before, scholarship is a central feature of much faculty life, teaching lies at its very core.

One obvious (and, as we shall see, legally significant) way that teaching differs from scholarship is the public nature of the former. Scholarship is essentially a private, often solitary, activity. Decisions about research agendas and the content and distribution of articles are made quietly by individual scholars or teams; most published work has a limited readership and attracts little attention. By definition, however, teaching involves the presentation of unfamiliar ideas to others and the encouragement of thoughtful reactions to those ideas. Because teaching takes place in the open and good teaching asks students to stretch their minds (sometimes in uncomfortable ways), students, parents, faculty colleagues, college or university administrators, government authorities, alumni, and interested citizens have ample opportunity to hear about and evaluate what is being taught, to what end, and how the teaching is being done. The faculty teacher, of course, has his or her own views on these matters. When the expressed views—and underlying interests—of these various parties conflict, legal controversy can erupt. Faculty teaching has therefore given rise to much more legal posturing and litigation than has faculty research.

In a research context, the interests of faculty in selecting their own topics and the interests of an institution in giving its faculty free rein to pursue those topics are closely aligned. Generally speaking, scholarship is its own end, and neither faculty nor institutions seek research results intended to satisfy particular constituencies. In a teaching context, however, colleges and universities are frequently torn among (1) their own assessment of how best to meet the educational needs of students; (2) the prudent inclination to defer to the course instructor's judgments about content and delivery (after all, he or she is the expert in the field); and (3) the desire to cater to the legitimate expectations of students, who, in a very real sense, are the paying customers. To the extent that tuition bills are paid by students' parents, their voices must be added to this mix. Challenges to faculty teaching thus come from both inside the institution (chairs, deans, students) and from outside the campus gates (parents, legislators). Typically, in disputes about the propriety of research, the various constituencies within the institution close ranks, especially against external challenge. But in disputes over teaching, it is much more likely that those groups will be at war with each other. When this occurs, each of the warring parties will almost certainly invoke "academic freedom" to justify its actions. Institutions will claim that academic freedom allows them to set and enforce curricular requirements upon faculty and students. Teachers will claim that academic freedom allows them to determine what transpires in their classrooms. Students may even claim that *they* should be free to learn what they want on their own terms. What does academic freedom mean—legally? And who has it?

## Foundations of Academic Freedom

Violations of "academic freedom" are ubiquitously (some might say indiscriminately) alleged at colleges and universities and its prospective infringement is routinely inveighed against. Faculty rely upon "academic freedom" to shield them both from the intrusions of the outside world (being asked to take government loyalty oaths, or being scrutinized for alleged discrimination) and the depredations of college or university administrators (being punished for on-campus speech). At the same time, institutions assert for themselves a version of "academic freedom" necessary to perform key administrative and educational tasks (e.g., making faculty personnel decisions). Given these conflicting views, academic freedom resists easy legal definition.[2] I believe however, that it should be thought of as conscious *deference* by judicial or other governmental authorities to a college or university (or to individual faculty) on decisions that are fundamentally academic in content.

One key justification for such deference is surely the expertise of the relevant academic actors (and, conversely, the limited knowledge of external authorities in such matters). Following this line of reasoning, just as external legal authorities may choose to defer to institutions and faculty under the rubric of academic freedom, so too do authorities at those institutions regularly defer to faculty judgments about academic matters. But—as is developed further in the following pages—academic freedom also rests on deeper intellectual and cultural footings than mere deference to specialized knowledge. For if local expertise alone warranted intra- and extra-institutional deference, we should grant an equal measure of autonomy and respect to the decisions of police, prison officials, military leaders, and maybe even businessmen.[3] A second and more instrumental justification for academic freedom posits that deference to the academic judgments of faculty and institutions is necessary to nourish an environment—unique to colleges and universities—that facilitates society's goal of discovering new knowledge and transmitting both old and new understandings to students and the general public. Working backwards towards the achievement of this goal, a healthy university must have a local culture of skepticism (or at least the suspension of certainty); of insistence by faculty, students, and staff upon rigor and honesty in thought and argument; and of placing the highest priority on the pursuit of learning.[4] External authorities and internal administrators must therefore defer to properly made academic decisions to inculcate and maintain these defining values.

The nature and consequences of academic freedom have long been popular topics of scholarly discourse.[5] Fierce debates rage among commentators about its meaning.[6] This is hardly surprising, given its direct impact on faculty work and careers. The Fifth Circuit Court of Appeals observed in *Hillis v. Stephen F. Austin University* that "'academic freedom is an amorphous field about which a great deal has been said in esoteric law journal articles and academic publications, but little determined in explicit, concrete judicial opinions.' . . . Its perimeters are ill-defined and the case law defining it is inconsistent."[7]

At *public* (i.e., state-actor) colleges and universities, academic freedom is largely rooted in federal constitutional law. As you might expect, a constitutional underpinning for academic freedom also exerts a powerful influence in support of such freedom at *private* institutions not bound by constitutional strictures. Furthermore, at *both* public and private institutions, academic freedom is also grounded in contract law, because explicit or implicit guarantees of such freedom are typically part of the college or university's contract with its faculty and students. It is striking, however, that the vast majority of academic freedom cases that wend their way to the courts come from public institutions. Therefore, it is appropriate for us to touch briefly on possible justifications for academic freedom under the First Amendment's guarantee of freedom of expression.

This turns out not to be a simple matter. When academic freedom is invoked to protect the right of faculty to make independent scholarly decisions, it is often tied to the importance of discovering and exchanging ideas in a free society. Developing new knowledge and sharing knowledge with students and the public are key steps in building a stronger polity. But why should university faculty—as opposed to other public employees whose speech also helps find the truth and strengthen democracy—be afforded special treatment under the First Amendment? If you're hired as a public prosecutor, you do not have a constitutional right to make arguments in court that intentionally favor the defendant. If the government hires you to wear a sandwich board on Election Day that says "Vote!" you have no First Amendment right to change that sign to read "Don't Vote!" Why shouldn't the government therefore expect professors to perform their teaching duties in ways that institutional authorities believe are wise and accurate (as with prosecutors or our sandwich-board man)?

One might claim instead that a *university classroom* is a forum where professorial (and student) speech should be particularly freewheeling. But there are gaps in this argument too. First, it might afford more academic freedom to faculty as teachers than as scholars, which flies in the face of experience and expectations. Second, it fails to recognize that teaching occurs beyond the classroom. Our justification for academic freedom should not distinguish between (1) what is taught in a lecture, (2) what is taught as a professor converses with students leaving the lecture hall, (3) what is taught in a laboratory where faculty and graduate students collaborate on research, and (4) what students learn from each other over dinner in the dining hall. Third, by this logic, why wouldn't we treat elementary and secondary school classrooms the same way?

Perhaps the strongest argument, alluded to earlier, is that colleges and universities should be treated as sui generis for First Amendment purposes: as unique societal entities blending the search for new knowledge, the preservation of old knowledge, the dissemination of *all* knowledge through instruction and publication, and various public service obligations. Such an amalgam of critical functions, one could claim, merits special constitutional protection. Compared to alternative rationales, this argument justifies institutional claims of academic freedom. It also helps explain why faculty at the university level might require more deference than secondary school teachers. But it opens the door to similar special pleading by other institutions (e.g., the media).[8]

The primary point that readers should take from this discussion is that academic freedom can be linked to the federal Constitution in various ways (or even not at all),[9] but that the fit will never be airtight because academic freedom, which is loaded with different meanings and encrusted with tradition, began as a nonlegal, non-American, and nonconstitutional notion.

## A Conceptual Framework

In trying to make sense of the hodgepodge of claims of academic freedom and the tangled case law arising from them, it is useful to ask the following questions whenever one encounters the assertion that an activity is protected by "academic freedom." The answers help predict and explain the likely judicial response:

1. Is the matter with regard to which academic freedom is claimed central to the mission of a college or university, or does it relate to interests or activities far removed from core academic functions? The farther from such core activities, the less deference will be accorded.
2. Do the various groups comprising the college or university community (faculty, students, administrators, trustees) all support the claim? If these internal constituencies agree that academic freedom is implicated and that the questioned activity deserves protection, courts will be inclined to tread lightly.
3. Who stands to benefit from a particular claim of academic freedom? This question properly draws attention to the likely *impact* of judicial or administrative deference to the academic judgment of the party or parties asserting such freedom.

As an example of how these questions can help clarify the amount of deference accorded academic decisions, consider the ability of faculty to develop and pursue their own research agendas.[10] Faculty conduct of research is absolutely central to the academic enterprise. Along with teaching, it lies at the very core of a university's mission. Moreover, there is broad consensus among the various constituencies that make up a college or university that faculty self-determination of research agendas is genuinely valuable and deserves protection.[11] Given such unequivocal answers to our first two questions, we should expect that legal authorities would tend to be very deferential to faculty claims of independence in this area— and, as we have seen, that is in fact the case. Who benefits from recognizing academic freedom in faculty selection of research topics? In the first instance, the scholars themselves. But I would argue that institutions, students, and even broader society also gain much from the knowledge acquired through such freedom. With such a wide group of potential beneficiaries, a claim of academic freedom here will find widespread support.

What of academic freedom in the selection of course materials (a topic that is discussed in more detail later)? Determinations of exactly what books or articles students should read and discuss are also central to the mission of a college or university. Sharing information with students is at the heart of the teaching process. But there is likely to be much less consensus on whether faculty should have the authority to make such determinations. Student notions about what they think they need to know (or what they find interesting), administrative opinions about what the award of a degree (or of course credit) from the institution signifies, and alumni and parental views of what students should be learning all combine to muddy the waters. Thus, legal authorities have been considerably less clear about the degree of deference that should be accorded faculty decisions on course materials—though I would assert that faculty still have considerable leeway here. Again, who stands to benefit from recognizing the faculty's academic freedom in designating course materials? Primarily the faculty. Only this time there may be a clearer set of "losers": for example, students who do not get to read (or administrators or parents who cannot require that students read) the course materials they themselves would have selected.[12]

With this construct in mind—in particular its focus on the centrality of questioned activities and the consensus generated in their favor across the university community—we can examine how much freedom faculty actually have in their classrooms. What we shall find is that, with limited exceptions, faculty remain the principal arbiters of what is taught, how it is taught, and how student learning is evaluated in their courses. The limits that do exist on faculty conduct within the classroom are primarily related to non-controversial administrative requirements for the orderly and efficient delivery of quality education to students.

## External Attacks on Faculty Classroom Autonomy

A key consideration in appraising the deference that will be accorded a faculty member's in-class actions is whether such conduct is being questioned by a party external to the college or university (e.g., the local government or concerned citizens) or by another segment of the university community (e.g., students or administrators). Faculty and institutions have been very successful at fending off external attacks on teaching practices. Courts have been very deferential to faculty behavior in such cases, consistently recognizing academic freedom in the classroom. While it may seem counterintuitive that courts would be more willing to become involved in intra-institutional disputes about faculty conduct, this can be explained (returning once more to our framework questions) by the consensus within the academy about the value of deferring to faculty judgments on teaching matters, especially when those judgments are being questioned by outsiders. College and university communities may wage bitter internal battles but will reliably unite against an external threat.

The most famous example of judicial deference to faculty classroom conduct in the face of an external attack is the case of *Sweezy v. New Hampshire*.[13] In 1954, in connection with a New Hampshire investigation of "subversive persons," the state's attorney general asked the Marxist economist Paul Sweezy to answer several questions about the substance of a guest lecture Sweezy had given in a humanities class at the University of New Hampshire. Sweezy refused and was held in contempt of court.[14] His appeal ultimately wound its way to the U.S. Supreme Court, which overturned his conviction in a plurality opinion that is generally supportive of faculty autonomy in the classroom. A concurring opinion by (former law professor) Felix Frankfurter is even bolder in supporting faculty independence from external constraint, arguing for "the exclusion of governmental intervention in the intellectual life of a university"[15] and delineating the "four essential freedoms" of a university (which should not be subjected to external interference): "to determine for itself on academic grounds who may teach, what may be taught, how it shall be taught, and who may be admitted to study."[16] Two of Frankfurter's four freedoms are exclusively classroom-based, reflecting the centrality of faculty independence in this venue.

Other cases since *Sweezy* also support faculty decisions about course content and teaching style and defend them from external scrutiny or challenge. In *White v. Davis*,[17] a history professor at UCLA sought to enjoin the Los Angeles Police Department's on-campus surveillance, which allegedly included, among other activities, undercover officers registering as students, attending classes, and submitting reports to their superiors about in-class discussions. A more direct interference with university teaching would be hard to envision, and as one might expect, the California Supreme Court unequivocally rejected such practices. According to the court, "Because the identity of such police officers is unknown, no professor or student can be confident that whatever opinion he may express in class will not find its way into a police file. If the after-the-fact inquiry conducted in *Sweezy* threatened to cast a pall of orthodoxy over classroom debates, the covert presence of government agents within the classroom itself must cast a deeper shadow."[18]

Likewise, in another dispute stemming from campus unrest of the early 1970s, a federal court in Ohio ordered the destruction of a special grand jury report investigating the circumstances preceding the shooting of Kent State students by National Guardsmen.[19] Portions of that report sharply criticized some Kent State faculty for "an over-emphasis on dissent" in their classrooms, "devot[ing] their entire class periods to urging their students to openly oppose our institutions of government."[20] The court agreed that the compilation and distribution of a report evaluating the classroom practices of university faculty was an unlawful restriction of faculty speech. The report was "dulling classroom discussion and . . . upsetting the teaching atmosphere."[21] Such external attacks on the ability of faculty to run their classes as they saw fit could not be countenanced.

This line of cases shows that faculty have little to fear from extra-institutional challenges to their teaching. Thus, advocacy groups seeking to block college courses on controversial topics such as human sexuality or revisionist versions of world history are unlikely to meet with success. But our analysis of faculty prerogatives in teaching becomes more complicated when an intra-institutional controversy erupts about course requirements or in-class behavior.

## Intra-University Disputes about Faculty Teaching

This is where claims of institutional and individual academic freedom most often collide. While the case law is not crystal clear or particularly consistent,[22] I believe that the best guide is to consider whether the institutional limits or sanctions being imposed on faculty (often in response to student concerns or needs) encroach upon academic decisions about what ideas students should be exposed to and how they are presented. If such academic decisions are being impeded, courts will be more inclined to uphold a faculty member's academic freedom. But if the disputed institutional requirements are necessary to the smooth operation and administrative functioning of the college or university, institutional imperatives may trump individual faculty interests. To make this point more clearly, it is helpful to examine first some relatively noncontroversial administrative requirements imposed on faculty.

### Requiring Faculty to Distribute Course Evaluations

Under the foregoing analysis, this is properly viewed as a legitimate bureaucratic requirement to collect data for evaluating faculty performance and monitoring student satisfaction. It does not touch on intellectual concerns about the information available to students and therefore does not impinge on faculty academic freedom. The case law supports this interpretation. A professor of education at the University of Colorado at Denver was denied a merit salary increase because of her refusal to hand out a new standardized student evaluation form. Such forms were contrary to her theory of education, and in her classes she taught that student learning could not be gauged by any standardized approach. She sued the university, arguing that forcing her to distribute the form interfered with her classroom method and violated her right to academic freedom. She lost. The court held that the plaintiff was expected to discharge all "duties reasonable and regularly required to be performed by [her] as part of the responsibilities of a faculty member." She did not have to endorse the evaluation form; indeed, she could even savagely criticize its content in her class (assuming that such critique was relevant to the course's subject matter).

But she could not refuse to distribute it.[23] Claims by a former faculty member that Northern Arizona University's reliance on student evaluations to assess teaching effectiveness was a violation of his academic freedom also fell (correctly) on deaf judicial ears.[24]

## Classroom Behavior and Treatment of Students

Colleges and universities have a legitimate and legally defensible ability to insist that faculty show a basic level of civility and consideration in teaching students. While they need not strive to become modern-day versions of Mr. Chips, faculty must observe such fundamental courtesies as showing up to teach their assigned classes. No violation of faculty rights will be found if an institution disciplines (or even discharges) a faculty member for dereliction of teaching duties. "Academic freedom is not a license for activity at variance with job related procedures and requirements, nor does it encompass activities which are internally destructive to the proper function of the university or disruptive to the education process."[25] Similarly, once in class, faculty may not treat students in an abusive manner. This would include, of course, sexual harassment,[26] but also the use of obscenities or threatening language or behavior.

J. D. Martin, an economics instructor at Midland College in Texas, was terminated in 1984 for his regular and gratuitous use of profanity in class. Having been warned previously to clean up his language, he persisted in using words such as *bullshit* and *hell* and in making remarks such as "If you don't like the way I teach this God damn course there is the door." Student complaints led to his dismissal and a subsequent lawsuit over whether the use of such language was encompassed within Martin's "academic freedom." The Fifth Circuit upheld the dismissal, declaring that "repeated failure by [the plaintiff] to exhibit professionalism degrades his important mission and detracts from the subjects he is trying to teach."[27] I would argue that since the language in question is not that shocking to most people (especially to most students), the *Martin* court was really making a statement about the level of respect that faculty owe students and their institutional employers. Indeed, the court characterizes Martin's final outburst as a "castigation of the class . . . [that] implied that the students were inferior."[28]

In *Keen v. Penson*,[29] a federal appeals court upheld the demotion of a professor whose unprofessional conduct towards a former student included sending her a series of demeaning, abusive, insulting, and wildly inappropriate letters demanding an apology for her behavior in his class. As in

*Martin,* such behavior by faculty was found to be unconscionable. Again, when institutions enforce appropriate standards of classroom conduct, they are not making genuinely academic or pedagogical decisions.

Of course, courtesy in the classroom must be a two-way street. Faculty are also entitled to respect from students if they are to perform their jobs. In *McConnell v. Howard Univ.*, a federal appellate court blocked the termination of a mathematics professor who had refused to resume teaching his class until the university allowed him to "reestablish an appropriate teaching atmosphere" through the removal or other discipline of a student who had repeatedly disrupted his class.[30] The court opined that "one who is assigned to teach must have some semblance of control over the classroom. If control is lost, learning invariably will be obstructed and the teacher will be unable to fulfill a professional responsibility."[31]

## Teaching Methods

The largely routine and bureaucratic limits on faculty behavior in the classroom that we have examined in the preceding pages cross into more contested turf when they involve efforts to monitor or improve the quality of faculty teaching (and ultimately student learning). Should faculty be able to select and use whatever pedagogical methods they are comfortable with and believe will be effective? Decisions about how best to engage students' minds and present information to them are deeply intellectual and draw upon scholarly expertise. Made well, they require an understanding of what students already know, how they process new material, the meaning and significance of that new material, and how such material fits in with information and ideas yet to be presented. Faculty are uniquely well positioned to make such determinations, which lie at the core of the academic enterprise. But at the same time, institutions and students have a vital interest in making sure that the classroom instruction is lucid, engrossing, and worth the price of tuition. In circumstances in which faculty elect to use unorthodox or even intentionally disturbing methods of instruction, or in which students or administrators have rigid or unrealistic views about how best to transmit knowledge, consensus may be elusive.

Nonetheless, faculty retain enormous discretion—and primary responsibility—for selecting the teaching methods they use in their classes. While there has been some nibbling at the edges of this authority,[32] faculty are still pretty much free to teach in whatever style, relying on whatever techniques, and using whatever tools they deem appropriate. It would be a rare faculty member indeed who has experienced a direct institutional attempt to control his or her pedagogical style. This legal and practical result makes intellectual sense for the reasons noted above. Faculty have most of the knowledge upon which decisions about the promotion of student learning should be based. Making such decisions is an important responsibility— even a kind of trust. As we shall see, abdication of that responsibility (or, more generously, the failure or inability to explain how it is being thoughtfully exercised) can embroil professors in controversy.

Drawing on our earlier discussion of basic First Amendment principles,[33] since teaching methods may blend seamlessly into course content, rules or policies at state-actor institutions that extend beyond classroom decorum to reach pedagogical techniques and styles are best viewed analytically as content-based (rather than content-neutral) restrictions on speech. As such rules or policies become more detailed, they may also constitute impermissible viewpoint-based restrictions.

A recent and compelling example of case law upholding the faculty's right to select teaching methods is *Silva v. University of New Hampshire*.[34] Mr. Silva, a tenured instructor of communications at UNH, was suspended from his job for violating the university's sexual harassment policy. Among other infractions,[35] in lectures for his technical writing course he had used several sexual metaphors that made students very uncomfortable and (in their and the university's view) impeded learning. In describing the need for focus in the writing process, he told his class: "I will put focus in terms of sex, so you can better understand it. Focus is like sex. You seek a target. You zero in on your subject. You move from side to side. . . . You bracket the subject and center on it. Focus connects experience and language. You and the subject become one."[36] On another occasion, in what he described as an attempt to illustrate how a good definition combines a general classification with concrete specifics, Silva told his class that "belly dancing is like jello on a plate with a vibrator under the plate."[37]

Silva obtained an injunction blocking his suspension, successfully arguing that these classroom metaphors (which he had used with students for many years) "advanced his valid educational objective of conveying certain principles related to the subject matter of his course" and "were made in a professionally appropriate manner as part of a college class lecture."[38] His right to employ the teaching methods of his own selection, even though they upset many students, was upheld. The university was not allowed to sanction him for what it regarded as unwise and inappropriate instructional practices. The court's opinion strongly endorsed the view that "academic freedom permits faculty members freedom to choose specific pedagogic techniques or examples to convey the lesson they are trying to impart to their students."[39]

Part of the power of the *Silva* opinion stems from its unequivocal support of faculty autonomy in teaching style despite a rather unsympathetic plaintiff (an instructor who apparently liked shocking or titillating students, often made odd and inappropriate remarks to them, and had previously been warned about the use of sexually explicit stories in class). This is a strong precedent for faculty. Further support for the proposition that professors may use whatever teaching methods they think best can be found in *Blum v. Schlegel,* wherein a law professor's politically charged hypothetical questions (e.g., involving caustic criticism of national drug control policy) in a class on the First Amendment were deemed protected speech implicating academic freedom.[40] While the court wondered whether students might find such questions confusing, the professor was entitled to teach his class as he saw fit. So too in *Mahoney v. Hankin,* which expresses support for a college professor's "right to develop and use his or her own pedagogical method."[41]

Irrespective of this very positive (from a faculty perspective) line of cases however, faculty who employ unusual or likely-to-be-controversial teaching methods would be well advised to discuss those techniques with their department chair and colleagues. Input or feedback from peers about what has (or has not) worked for them in other classes, as well as suggestions on how best to carry out the unorthodox teaching plan, are very likely to improve the execution and results of innovative teaching. Beyond this, explaining one's didactic goals to colleagues can provide insulation from future attack. (There may even be circumstances in which it makes sense to lay out some of these goals to one's students.) As with any kind of peer review, if colleagues are deeply skeptical of or able to punch intellectual holes in the justification for a particular teaching method, the proponent should take such criticisms seriously. The inability to make a convincing case for such method may reveal deeper flaws.

The real flash point in disputes over teaching methods is reached when *institutions* try to make judgments about how or under what conditions students can best learn in a faculty member's class. As we have seen, colleges and universities can surely insist upon a learning environment that is inclusive (if not always comfortable). But administrative determinations of

what would work best for students are legally—and perhaps intellectually—risky. A prime example of this is the history of *Cohen v. San Bernardino Valley College.*[42] Dean Cohen was a tenured professor of English and
film studies at SBVC. He had for many years consciously employed what
he termed a "confrontational" teaching style designed to shock his students and make them think and write about controversial topics. In his
classes he discussed subjects such as cannibalism and consensual sex with
children, and he used vulgar terms and profanity. In spring 1992, while
teaching a remedial English course that was a prerequisite for other college-
level English classes at SBVC, Cohen led a discussion about pornography
(during which he argued as "devil's advocate" in favor of such works) and
then required students to write an essay defining pornography. When a
woman student requested an alternative assignment, Cohen refused. The
student filed a complaint against Cohen, and college authorities eventually
found that he had violated SBVC's sexual harassment policy through these
in-class actions. He was ordered to "provide a syllabus concerning his teaching style, purpose, content, and method to his students at the beginning of
class and to the department chair," as well as to "become sensitive to the
particular needs and backgrounds of his students, and to modify his teaching strategy when it becomes apparent that his techniques create a climate
which impedes the students' ability to learn."[43]

Viewing such restrictions as an infringement of the First Amendment
and his academic freedom, Cohen sued. The federal trial court squarely
confronted and analyzed the extent of a professor's control over teaching
methods. It recognized that "there [was] evidence in the record that Cohen's
teaching style is effective for at least some students. Cohen's colleagues
have stated that he is a gifted and enthusiastic teacher. Furthermore, according to the chair of the English Department, . . . Cohen's teaching style
[was] within the range of acceptable academic practice."[44] Nevertheless,
the court was ultimately swayed by the college's conviction that it better
understood and had a responsibility to meet the entire student body's needs.
The court upheld the strictures imposed on Cohen, declaring that "colleges and universities must have the power to require professors to effectively educate all segments of the student population, including those students unused to the rough and tumble of intellectual discussion. If colleges
and universities lack this power, each classroom becomes a separate fiefdom
in which the educational process is subject to professorial whim. . . . The

university's mission is to effectively educate students, keeping in mind students' varying backgrounds and sensitivities."[45]

This initial *Cohen* opinion was very disturbing. From a faculty perspective, its most frightening and intrusive aspect was the court's refusal to defer to a professor's knowledge of how students should best master the subject matter, despite agreement that the unorthodox teaching style in question was within the pedagogical pale. Modifying one's teaching strategy as necessary to meet varied (and perhaps shifting) student needs also seems highly impractical. In its paternalistic eagerness to ensure that all SBVC students had an opportunity to learn, the trial court lost sight of the fact that a college education should entail some level of intellectual "rough and tumble." Fortunately, the Court of Appeals reversed the lower *Cohen* court, holding that San Bernardino's sexual harassment policy was unconstitutionally vague.[46] In its much briefer opinion, the appellate court focused on the language of the contested harassment policy, declining (regrettably, in my view) to shed further light on the extent of a faculty member's authority to select his or her own teaching style.

The first *Cohen* opinion, however, points out an area in which college and university claims of autonomy periodically trump faculty responsibility for teaching methods. There is a separate line of cases—cutting in the opposite direction from *Silva* and the ultimate result in *Cohen*—that is much more supportive of institutional control over faculty teaching style. While it is possible to draw fine distinctions between the facts of various cases in an attempt to reconcile holdings, I think it wiser to recognize (and try to explain) this inconsistency.

As I read the case law, courts are sometimes willing to let colleges and universities establish and enforce *general* academic standards for the institution's student body. The argument goes as follows: beginning with student admissions, institutions gear themselves to serve or meet the needs of particular kinds of students. Thus, San Bernardino Valley College aims at and focuses on a different kind of student than does Stanford. This is reflected in everything from campus life, course scheduling, progress-to-degree requirements, program offerings, and (most immediately relevant) faculty hiring and job expectations. While faculty views may directly or indirectly shape the institution's approach to these matters, from an operational standpoint, meeting student needs and expectations is the responsibility of campus administrators. From the institution's perspective, efforts to gear the college or university at a given level and towards a certain kind of student will be brought to naught if each teacher can set his or her own standard for what students are expected to learn and in what way. Faculty must therefore accommodate some limits on teaching style in order to meet student needs and expectations and preserve institutional integrity.

Courts that uphold restrictions on faculty teaching methods tend to do so when those limits are explicitly justified as necessary to permit student learning (as opposed to avoidance of controversy or administrative convenience) and when faculty still retain considerable leeway in running their classes. (As one might expect, institutions also tend to prevail when faculty litigants have behaved outrageously and are contemptuous of student opinion.) The most important such proinstitution case is *Hetrick v. Martin*.[47] In 1970, Phyllis Hetrick's contract as an assistant professor at Eastern Kentucky University was not renewed. While there had been complaints about her teaching,[48] concerns about how slowly she was covering material, and questions about her lack of progress towards a Ph.D., the court found that the real reasons behind the nonrenewal were profound differences about pedagogical style and philosophy: "The [Eastern Kentucky] administration considered the students as generally unsophisticated and as having 'somewhat restrictive backgrounds,' and for this reason apparently expected the teachers to teach on a basic level, to stress fundamentals and to follow conventional teaching patterns—in a word, to 'go by the book.' [Ms. Hetrick's] evidence, on the other hand, tended to show that her teaching emphasized student responsibility and freedom to organize class time and out-of-class assignments in terms of student interest."[49] According to the federal appeals court, in a conflict such as this the university's assessment of what students expected and needed should prevail. Eastern Kentucky had the right "to require some conformity with whatever teaching methods are acceptable to it."[50] It mattered not whether Hetrick's teaching methods were regarded as acceptable by the profession, well within the teaching mainstream, or even educationally desirable. The university could let her go without violating the First Amendment once it concluded that her teaching philosophy was incompatible with its institutional pedagogical aims.[51]

With its sweeping language, *Hetrick* provides a juridical basis for other decisions upholding general institutional requirements on teaching methods. Thus, in *Carley v. Ariz. Bd. of Regents,* a state university assistant professor was not rehired because of an ineffective teaching methodology that involved "frequently leaving his classes unattended during appointed meeting times in order to teach students to be more self-reliant" and "emphasizing independent student work in order to reflect the expectations which students will encounter in the business world."[52] Carley argued that this classroom conduct was protected speech, but the court, which analyzed the case under First Amendment standards applicable to the public employer institution, refused to equate teaching methods with speech *content*. The university could evaluate (and ultimately discipline) him on the basis of his unsuccessful teaching. Any sanctions imposed on the professor because of his teaching methods were independent of teaching content (i.e., in First Amendment parlance, they were content-neutral).

The philosophy underlying *Hetrick*—that institutions can set broad academic policies designed to serve students—may also be extended to other topics beyond a professor's teaching style, or even past the confines of the classroom. In *Lovelace v. Southeastern Mass. Univ.*, a federal appeals court upheld the nonrenewal of the contract of a faculty member who had taken issue with the institution's academic profile. Even if (as he alleged) the professor had been let go because of his refusal to "lower standards," the university was entitled to set some common standards: "Whether a school sets itself up to attract and serve only the best and the brightest students or whether it instead gears its standard to a broader, more average population is a policy decision which, we think, universities must be allowed to set. And matters such as course content, homework load, and grading policy are core university concerns, integral to the implementation of this policy decision. . . . The first amendment does not require that each . . . professor be made a sovereign unto himself."[53]

Admittedly, the establishment of institutional academic aspirations and standards on acceptable teaching methods may be of real value if they reflect faculty consensus on these essentially academic matters (perhaps as the product of a smoothly functioning system of faculty governance). But in isolation, the language and holdings of *Hetrick*, *Lovelace* and their progeny open the door to institutionally convenient decisions divorced from relevant intellectual considerations.[54] I do not agree that institutional interpretations of student needs should automatically control faculty teaching styles. As previously noted, this view often rests on a rather paternalistic (and pessimistic) view of students' intellectual capacity. Carried to an extreme, it might compel faculty to acquiesce in the "dumbing down" of an institution—surely not a result that legal authorities should want to facilitate.

Colleges and universities are quite properly concerned with the quality of instruction, and the law clearly allows them to evaluate the faculty's teaching performance (both peer and student evaluations can be vital here). But the most thoughtful authorities in higher education law and wise academic policy continue to leave individual instructors with the ability and the obligation to make finely tailored judgments about the teaching methods and pedagogical tools needed to reach a given class of students.

## Course Content and Theoretical Emphasis

If a professor is hired to teach a course on the writings of Swift and Pope, does he have academic freedom to teach about quantum mechanics instead? If he does teach a class on eighteenth-century English literature, does he have the right to teach it from an astrological perspective? How about from a feminist perspective?

The answers to these questions (no, no, and probably yes) help flesh out what is probably the most tangled area in all of higher education law: the cases and authorities relating to the ability of faculty to select the materials to be covered in their courses and the theoretical approach taken to their subject. Because teaching style cannot always be divorced from teaching substance, there is some overlap in analysis and relevant case law between the preceding discussion of teaching methods and this discussion of intellectual coverage and slant. When controversies erupt over faculty classroom conduct, delicate distinctions between *what* is being taught and *how* it is being taught quickly blur.

We have already seen how determinations of "what shall be taught" are integral to the purposes of the academy while at the same time unlikely to command college-wide or university-wide consensus.[55] As noted earlier in this chapter, under such circumstances legal authorities are reluctant to endorse sweeping claims of faculty (or institutional) academic freedom, preferring instead to deal with disputes on an ad hoc basis. However, when we examine the applicable decisions, we again find that on the issues of deepest intellectual importance—where the faculty have the most knowledge and experience that can be drawn upon to advance student learning, where the faculty truly "live," and where they have the most to lose if their arguments for deference to scholarly judgments are rejected—on these issues, faculty continue to fare very well. Individual course instructors retain fundamental control over the selection of the ideas and information that must be presented to students; the relative importance attached to such concepts, including what to emphasize on examinations; how to synthesize key ideas (or whether they can be reconciled at all); and the broader historical, cultural, and theoretical context in which they should be viewed (including links to or comparisons with concepts from other disciplines). In short, faculty academic freedom in assembling courses is alive and flourishing where it is most needed.

Many of the justifications for institutional influence over teaching methods (most prominently, meeting students' educational expectations) would also lead colleges and universities to seek some control over the content of instruction. However, the need for institutional control is reduced in no small part by the operation of meaningful course approval processes. While regular peer review of faculty teaching is not commonplace, at most colleges and universities before new courses can be offered they must be reviewed and approved by department and institution curricular committees and often by department chairs.[56] Such scrutiny (when taken seriously) is the best safeguard against flimsy or outrageous courses and the ideal means of turning a well-intentioned but poorly conceived proposal into a solid class.

Neither law nor wise institutional policy, though, give faculty a completely free hand in this domain. Returning to the first question posed at the start of this section, faculty cannot offer courses that are completely unrelated to the officially approved and publicized subject matter, nor can they inject so much extraneous material into a course that it fundamentally subverts its character. Students who register for a course in chemistry should not receive lectures on Ottoman art. *Riggin v. Bd. of Trustees of Ball St. Univ.* upheld the termination of a business school professor for, among other grounds, failing to cover basic course material (as described in syllabi) when he was spending an estimated 50–75 percent of class time on "non-pertinent matters such as telling stories and talking about his dairy business, athletics, his experiences as a legislator, current events, lawsuits in which he had been involved, and the societal influence of bankers."[57] Said the court: "a teacher may not use his class, a captive audience, as a forum to disseminate his personal views on matters not connected with the course, wasting the time of the students who have come there and paid money for a different purpose."[58] While some extraneous matter will creep into almost any class, faculty should mind whether they are veering far from their course plans.

The acid test of individual academic freedom in the classroom, however, is whether faculty can teach a course from whatever intellectual perspective they believe appropriate. Selecting one's theoretical approach is the most basic instructional decision; it ultimately drives the choice of readings and other course materials, as well as the content of lectures. And in this critical area the autonomy of faculty is largely unchallenged. Interestingly, there is almost no case law dealing with this question—a circumstance that I believe supports the notion that faculty have wide latitude here. Colleges and universities have been very reluctant to challenge faculty choices about theoretical or ideological emphasis because such matters go to the very heart of the meaning of academic disciplines and particular fields of study.

A rare judicial opinion that addresses this issue in a thoughtful way is *Cooper v. Ross*, a 1979 decision of a federal district court in Arkansas.[59] The underlying facts and holdings of this case merit some attention. Grant Cooper was an untenured assistant professor of history at the University of Arkansas at Little Rock (UALR). In mid-July 1973, at the start of a summer school session, Cooper "informed his classes in World Civilization and American Civilization that he was a communist and a member of the [Progressive Labor Party], and that he taught his courses from a Marxist point of view."[60] At UALR, the History Department prescribed the general subject matter for its registered courses. For the world civilization course in question, which had multiple sections taught by different teachers, there was consensus among the instructors on the textbook and the periods of history to be covered. Otherwise, each instructor had great autonomy in organizing and presenting the material.[61]

Cooper's in-class statements and political affiliations became a cause célèbre, with state legislators filing suit to have him dismissed. That fall, in a meeting with the university's chancellor, Cooper was asked "whether, if instructed by the University, [he] would teach his courses from an objective point of view and refrain from identifying his own beliefs to his classes. Cooper responded that he felt it would be intellectually dishonest if he did not state his own beliefs, that he could not be entirely objective towards other points of view, and that if he were ordered not to teach from a Marxist point of view he would feel compelled to resist the order."[62] Shortly thereafter, Cooper was notified that he was not being recommended for promotion and that his 1974–75 appointment would be a terminal one. Having exhausted internal appeals, Cooper sued, claiming a violation of his First Amendment right to academic freedom.

The district court found as a matter of fact that Cooper had substantially covered the subject matter of his courses, there being no evidence that his theoretical approach limited such treatment.[63] It then addressed what it termed the "ultimate question" of whether Cooper had the right to teach his courses from a Marxist perspective.[64] While the court gingerly stepped back from directly answering this question (having disposed of the case in Cooper's favor on other grounds),[65] the opinion clearly implies that its answer would be yes. Noting first that "Cooper had a constitutionally protected right simply to inform his students [in class] of his personal political and philosophical views,"[66] the judge emphasized that there were no requirements at UALR that history courses be taught from an objective or any other specific point of view. Different faculty in fact did teach their courses from disparate viewpoints.[67] The court observed that

> other than his express announcement of his point of view to his classes in the summer of 1973, Cooper's approach to his courses was substantially the same as it had been during his three previous years at UALR. . . . It is clear that other members of the History Department were aware from the time he joined the department that Cooper personally shared the Marxist interpretation of history and economics. The Court thus concludes as a matter of fact that had Cooper not become a member of the PLP and announced his personal beliefs to his classes, *he would have been rehired, notwithstanding his Marxist viewpoint toward the teaching of history.*"[68]

The court concluded by citing with approval a series of cases upholding faculty choice of teaching methodology—a term that I believe it meant to include theoretical approach—declaring that "if Cooper's nonrenewal had in fact been motivated by his teaching methods, the Court would be inclined to invoke [the] doctrine [that academic freedom protects such choice]."[69]

*Cooper* is consistent with federal courts' antipathy towards viewpoint-based restrictions on speech and provides powerful support for the argument that faculty may determine their theoretical approach to a course's subject matter, notwithstanding the opinion's absence of a definitive ruling on that point. Such an outcome is justified on intellectual grounds if we expect (as I think we do) that faculty will not merely convey information and ideas but also help interpret what they mean.

As a practical matter, faculty are also largely free from administrative oversight or control in assembling course materials and delivering lectures. Once a course has been approved, instructors regularly add or delete readings (or retool entire units) without departmental or school review. This actual state of affairs—and the relatively scant case law about academic freedom in the determination of course content (analogous to the small number of legal disputes over a teacher's theoretical approach)—reinforce faculty claims for judicial deference in this area.

Several of the reported cases, moreover, are quite supportive of faculty autonomy. The *Sweezy* line of judicial opinions, safeguarding classroom treatment of controversial topics from external attack,[70] certainly fits this bill, as does *DiBona v. Matthews*, which upheld the right of a community college theater instructor to have his class produce a play that was likely to embroil the institution in controversy.[71] The play in question, *Split Second*, portrayed a black police officer killing a white suspect who taunted him with racial epithets. After the professor rejected suggestions that he select another play, community college district administrators canceled the drama class because of its "inappropriate" language, opposition from the local religious community, and concern that the production would inflame racial tensions in the San Diego area (which had only recently been roiled by the trial and acquittal of a young black man charged with shooting two police officers who had stopped him for a traffic violation and then allegedly assaulted him because of his race; in several respects, the facts of this case and the play were eerily similar). The court found that, "as in virtually all college-level settings," the administration had delegated to the course instructor the authority to select curricular materials, which in this case included evaluating the literary quality of and selecting a play for performance.[72] The professor was legitimately exercising his academic judgment, and his pedagogical decisions should not be second-guessed. District officials had "cited no authority—and we are aware of none—which would allow a college or university to censor instructor-selected curriculum materials because they contain 'indecent' language or deal with 'offensive' topics."[73] Administrative desire to steer clear of politically sensitive topics and avoid angering religious leaders were constitutionally impermissible justifications for in-class censorship, which ultimately might even be harmful to the local community.[74]

At the end of its opinion, though, having found for the faculty member, the *DiBona* court felt obliged to observe: "Our conclusions do not leave college administrators powerless to control college curriculum. . . . Certainly college officials may limit the drama curriculum to works of an acceptable literary quality and they undoubtedly are entitled to broad deference where such determinations are made in advance rather than, as here, some time after the class had already begun to meet."[75] This was a telling remark because, regardless of faculty professionalism in assembling courses, of peer review of new courses, of the practical hurdles in attempting to exert institutional control over curriculum, and of the legal difficulties likely to be encountered in such an effort, institutional concerns about the quality and content of courses must be taken into account. Along with cases like *Sweezy* and *DiBona* are other cogent opinions that support institutional selection and enforcement of course content. The very inconsistent holdings reflect the legitimacy of both sides' positions and the difficulty (if not impossibility) of satisfying all parties.

Having promised students instruction on a particular subject, and having hired faculty to offer such instruction, colleges and universities not unreasonably expect that teachers will teach the designated subjects through discussion and analysis of relevant and highly effective materials. Institutions properly seek to meet student desires (and those of tuition-paying parents). Hence, a faculty member who teaches a course on macroeconomics that largely neglects explanations of supply and demand and curves in order to construct arguments that only support Marx's labor theory of value has failed to perform adequately his teaching duties. But meaningful higher education must also go beyond simple customer satisfaction to include equipping students with the intellectual tools necessary to truly understand and critique subject matter. This means teaching them what they actually *need* to know about an area, as opposed to what they *want* to know (or think they want to know). Institutions pay faculty to make—and then deliver instruction based upon—this critical distinction.

Returning to the same example, if in the faculty member's professional judgment, examination of the Marxist critique of market theory is essential to fully appreciate the operation (and flaws) of supply-demand models, the macroeconomics course will be weakened—and the institution will not have done right by its students—if the students just receive an uncritical summary of standard theory. Administrators and faculty agree that determining students' intellectual needs requires giving scholar-teachers considerable discretion and independence. Input and criticism from peers should also be key ingredients in this process. So too should guidance from institutional representatives (especially chairs and deans) who are charged with evaluating student needs and welfare on a regular basis in ways that are impractical for individual faculty. While there is much common ground, inevitably different perceptions give rise to conflict. The flash point here comes when the faculty's *professional opinion on the subject matter of their courses* is questioned or somehow restricted. From the instructor's perspective, expressing those very opinions was what he was hired to do. Yet universities and colleges have frequently convinced courts to defer to their institutional judgments about course content because only they have a wide perspective that adequately takes student needs into account.

An oft-cited case for the proposition that institutions retain ultimate control over course content is *Clark v. Holmes.* Mr. Clark was hired in August 1962 as a temporary substitute teacher for the about-to-begin fall semester at Northern Illinois University (NIU), covering a required introductory health survey course. He was later asked to serve as a substitute for the following semester as well. In the spring of 1963, Clark was offered another temporary position for the upcoming academic year. But at that time Clark was also told that the university expected him to correct certain problems with his teaching, in particular, his overemphasis on sex in the health survey course. Clark took issue with this criticism, arguing that he had "surveyed his students' interests, had found that they wanted sex education and mental health emphasized and so had agreed to do so and only 'touch on' the other topics covered by the assigned text and the course syllabus" (both of which he had apparently inherited).[76] He did not modify the content of his courses, and the university chose not to rehire him. Clark sued, claiming that NIU had violated his First Amendment right to teach and say anything he wished in his classes. In holding for the university, the federal appeals court decreed, "We do not conceive academic freedom to be a license for uncontrolled expression at variance with established curricular contents and internally destructive of the proper functioning of the institution."[77] Clark was not permitted to override the judgment of his department chair, dean, and fellow faculty about the appropriate content of the health course.

Surely the result in *Clark* was influenced by the plaintiff's status as a temporary substitute and the fact that he had not been involved in putting together the disputed course. Faculty presumably have more freedom in the selection of materials for classes they have developed themselves (and which have been vetted through the regular course-approval process) than if, like Clark, they are hired right before the semester begins to substitute teach a well-established course (in which other faculty and administrators feel ownership), with a predetermined and long-standing text, syllabus, and course requirements. Still, it would be wrong to dismiss *Clark* as relevant only to faculty who are asked to teach extant courses. Other courts, building off *Clark*, have held that the "administration may at least establish the parameters of focus and general subject matter of curriculum"[78] and that "governing boards of colleges, universities, and other schools acting through their deans, department heads, and duly constituted faculty committees, have a right to develop curriculum, determine course content and impose methods of instruction. A teacher is obligated to comply with their directions in this regard."[79] Judicial deference to institutional judgments about course content is at least as common as deference to faculty academic freedom on such matters.

A more recent and influential case about the control over course materials examined the constitutionality of restrictions placed on the in-class remarks of an assistant professor of exercise physiology at the University of Alabama. Phillip Bishop "occasionally referred to his religious beliefs during instructional time, remarks which he prefaced as personal 'bias.' Some of his references concerned his understanding of the [divine] creative force behind human physiology." One spring, shortly before the final exam in his course, Bishop organized an after-class session for students and other interested parties "wherein he lectured on and discussed 'Evidence of God in Human Physiology.'"[80] Attendance at this class was purely voluntary and did not affect grades. In response to student complaints, Bishop's department head instructed him to stop interjecting his religious views into class discussions and offering optional classes on "Christian Perspectives" on academic topics. The university was concerned that this was an unwarranted departure from the typical content of an exercise physiology class, that students would feel subtle pressure to adopt Bishop's views, and that the public might regard his remarks as bearing an institutional endorsement. Bishop, predictably upset, claimed that his First Amendment rights of academic speech and free exercise of religion were being infringed.

While the trial court held for Dr. Bishop, the appellate court reversed, declaring that "educators do not offend the First Amendment by exercising editorial control over the style and content of [professorial] speech in school-sponsored expressive activities as long as their actions are related to legitimate pedagogical concerns."[81] According to the court, "Dr. Bishop and the University disagree about a matter of content in the courses he teaches. The University must have the final say in such a dispute. Though Dr. Bishop's sincerity cannot be doubted, his educational judgment can be questioned and redirected by the University when he is acting under its auspices as a course instructor.... The University's conclusions about course content must be allowed to hold sway over an individual professor's judgments."[82]

The First Circuit also stressed the narrowness of the restrictions imposed upon Bishop's speech. Alabama had "simply said that he may not discuss his religious beliefs or opinions under the guise of University courses." He remained free to adhere to whatever religious views—including religious views about his work—that he wished, to share those views in other (nonclassroom) forums, and to build them into his scholarly research.[83] He could even answer student questions *about* his religion. Likewise, he could still develop, publicize, and participate in extracurricular meetings about God's influence on human physiology. He just could not bill or hold such sessions as "voluntary" classes related to the courses he was teaching.[84]

Obviously, this detailed and carefully reasoned holding is directly at odds with the results in *DiBona* and other profaculty cases. And the court reached this outcome notwithstanding some facts and considerations that might have made Bishop's position more defensible. First, Alabama did not prohibit faculty from expressing personal views in class on other, nonreligious topics. It had not disciplined other faculty for this kind of self-revealing speech. Indeed, there was evidence that "such discussions [were] the norm used to establish rapport between faculty and students."[85] If other faculty could discuss their views on extraneous subjects, but Bishop (who never proselytized and was always careful to note when he was expressing a personal viewpoint) was prevented from doing likewise solely because the subject he chose to speak about had religious overtones, the university would seem to be making an impermissible distinction based solely on the *content* of speech.[86]

Second, the risk of student intimidation or coercion in this case seems overstated. Would college-level students, who are being taught to think independently, really conclude that Bishop's actions constituted the University of Alabama's institutional endorsement of religion?[87] Indeed, Bishop used blind grading, and therefore could not identify the exams of students who had attended the extra session. While students (even those who did not attend that session) might seek to parrot the professor's remarks on their final exam in the hopes of receiving a more sympathetic hearing and a higher grade, this danger exists in any course where faculty views on a subject can be gleaned (or even surmised).

Third—and most alarming to faculty—the court rejected the possibility that Bishop's statements about evidence of God in human physiology merited protection as his *considered professional judgment.* The university was allowed to "prevent [Bishop] from presenting his religious viewpoint during instructional time, *even to the extent that it represents his professional opinion about his subject matter."*[88] This viewpoint-based restriction on speech strikes at the heart of faculty teaching responsibilities and once again raises fears of institutional pandering to student wishes.

In *Edwards v. California Univ. of Pa.,*[89] another federal Circuit Court of Appeals endorsed institutional control over course materials. Colleagues in Edwards's department became concerned that he was teaching from a nonapproved syllabus that emphasized issues of "bias, censorship, religion and humanism" in a course entitled "Introduction to Educational Media" that had initially been designed to focus on how teachers can use classroom tools such as projection equipment and photographs. The department voted to mandate use of an earlier version of the syllabus, and the chair revoked book orders reflecting Edwards's desired curriculum.[90] The court was very direct in holding "that a public university professor does not have a First Amendment right to decide what will be taught in the classroom."[91] To the contrary, in setting the curriculum, the university was acting within its institutional right to speak, making and effecting legitimate choices about "the content of the education it provides."[92] It is important to note that in *Edwards* the court faced a situation in which an entire department had come together to reinstate the old syllabus. Thus, at some level the decision reflects deference to (collective) academic judgment. Still, a consensus is always easier to obtain in opposition to unpopular or unconventional ideas.

In our discussion in chapter 2 of freedom in the selection of research topics, I posed the case of a creationist biologist who presumably had the right to test his theories via research.[93] This hypothetical has actually materialized in the classroom setting, with mixed results (reflecting the messier status of the law concerning faculty autonomy here). At San Francisco State, a professor in an introductory biology course informed students that an "intelligent agent" may have been responsible for creating life. Since he was "troubled by gaps in the fossil record that prevented him from showing students a progression from one type of organism to another," he sought to poke holes in Darwinian theory. The biology department, convinced that he was disseminating religious views masquerading as scientific principles, barred him from teaching the course again. The local faculty senate found for the professor, however, and he was authorized to return to the classroom, notwithstanding the ire (and enmity) of his colleagues.[94] Around the same time, an adjunct professor of biology at Wright State University was dismissed after he told students enrolled in his course on evolution that he was a creationist and assigned them to write a paper on the conflict between evolution and creationism. In the university's view, he had crossed the line between permissible discussion of creationist theory and impermissible espousal of religious beliefs.[95] Unfortunately, neither of these disputes over the selection of course materials resulted in legal opinions that could shed further light in this area.

A final proinstitution case about curricular content that merits our consideration is *Scallet v. Rosenblum,* in which a former business school faculty member at the University of Virginia claimed that the First Amendment protected his use, in his section of a required first-year writing and speech course, of class materials he had selected addressing issues of diversity and business ethics.[96] The university countered that the plaintiff was not rehired because he could not work with other faculty and because his actions frustrated the purposes of this particular class and interfered with the operation of the Business School. Even though the faculty member's in-class speech may have been on matters of public concern,[97] the university could restrict such speech in order to prevent disruption of its pedagogical mission. The court found that "tight control over the ["Analysis & Communication" course] curriculum was necessary to ensure uniformity across class sections. . . . Scallet's in-class speech, in the form of the materials he used and the discussions those materials fostered, created disruption with the . . . department, hampering the School's ability effectively to deliver the A&C course to its students."[98]

The plaintiff's independent and wide-ranging course materials also created problems across the rest of the Business School, with teachers of operations, ethics, and marketing who were concerned that Scallet was poaching on the subject of their classes. Here, too, the court supported institutional authority to make judgments about curricular content: "It is proper for [the School], as an institution, to cabin the teaching of certain material within certain fora if it believes that any other pedagogical regime would compromise the delivery of the material. Thus, if school administrators believe, as they apparently do, that a required first-year class on business ethics is the most appropriate forum in which to teach issues of diversity, they are entitled to make that judgment and to bring it to fruition."[99]

Whether one agrees with them or not, precedents such as *Bishop, Edwards,* and *Scallet* dramatically enhance the legitimacy and legality of deferring to institutional views of appropriate course content.[100] Note also that each of these precedents involved public, state-actor institutions at which faculty could invoke First Amendment rights to protect their classroom expression. A non-state-actor college or university could be even more aggressive in insisting upon detailed oversight of course materials. (However, as a practical matter, the power of the constitutional law example and private institutional traditions of academic freedom and intellectual openness and tolerance substantially reduce the likelihood of such occurrence.)

The law in this area, as murky and sometimes contradictory as it is, should give neither faculty nor administrative partisans cavalier confidence simply to do as they please. I would maintain that with trust and open communication, faculty and administrators should be able to fashion a modus vivendi that leaves scholars with primary influence over classroom intellectual content while sensitizing them to legitimate administrative concerns.[101] This is the outcome towards which all parties, institutions, and courts should strive. But in the event that such accommodation and agreement prove impossible—this being a clear indicator of institutional sickness—and it becomes necessary for external legal authorities to enshrine either faculty or administrative dominion over what is taught, my (reluctant) choice would be for faculty to control course content. Faculty will always have the best understanding of what is essential in a field and how it is evolving. Since they spend more time in direct contact with students, faculty should also have a more accurate perception of current and prospective pupils' abilities and interests. With the protection of tenure, faculty are free (at least in comparison to administrators) to make honest judgments about instructional needs, irrespective of popular demand or what would be expedient. (All of the foregoing, of course, rests on the hope that faculty will rise above their narrow self-interest and convenience—which does not always occur). Buttressing my conclusion is the very practical and important fact that an institution where presidents, provosts, deans, and chairs sought to specify the substance of the courses faculty teach and the ideological perspective those courses reflect would attract neither the best students nor the best scholars.[102] It would be a far cry from our notion of a true university.

## Grading Policies and Awarding Grades

At first blush, this might seem an obvious area in which courts would defer to faculty judgments. After all, the course instructor is the only party with expertise in a given field and knowledge of what was actually discussed in class and asked for in student papers and examinations.[103] Faculty are uniquely qualified to make individual grading decisions, and the evaluation of how well students have mastered materials is certainly a core academic function. However, consensus is not always obtainable here because colleges and universities also need institution-wide grading policies (e.g., use of grading curves, time limits on grades of *Incomplete*, whether failing grades can be changed to *Withdrawal*) for reasons that are similarly close to the academic core: fairness and equity to students by assuring comparability across sections and classes; preserving quality by resisting grade inflation; and ultimately giving meaning and content to the institution's degree. Often these institutional policies are the product of lengthy faculty debate and represent the collective wisdom of the scholarly community, thereby buttressing their claims to legitimacy and enforcement.[104] Several institutions have successfully defended college-wide grading policies from faculty attack. *Lovelace v. Southeastern Mass. Univ.*, for example, approved the nonrehiring of an instructor whose personal grading practices conflicted with the university's grading standards. While the faculty member may have been frustrated by (what he perceived as) Southeastern's low academic expectations and easy grading, grading policy was a "core university concern" properly within the purview of institutional leaders.[105] In *Jawa v. Fayetteville State Univ.*, lawful reasons for firing a faculty member included lowering student grades for cutting classes when this was contrary to university grading policy.[106] General institutional guidelines on grading, then, especially if they have been adopted by faculty governance bodies, will probably be upheld as an appropriate administrative exercise of academic freedom.

There is not a large body of case law involving controversies over particular course grades. Most likely this is a consequence of both student and institutional respect for the specialized knowledge of faculty and their traditional authority within the classroom. (Consider, too, how impractical it would be for department chairs or other administrators to carry out more than a cursory statistical review of the grades assigned in a given class or by a given professor over time.) It surely reflects the effective operation of campus grade-appeal procedures that obviate the need for judicial recourse—and probably also prospective plaintiffs' calculation of the time, expense, and likely success of litigating over a grade. When a legal challenge to an individual grade occurs, though, a critical factor in the outcome is often the identity of the party disputing the grade. Faculty (and institutions) do exceptionally well in defending against *student* grade challenges.[107] Recalling our prior discussion of extra-university attacks on classroom content, it is as if student complainants are cast as external opponents of academic norms, with faculty and administrators closing ranks under the banner of academic freedom. Courts recognize that they are ill equipped to second-guess academic evaluations of student work. As long as the institution stands behind its faculty, courts are generally willing to let colleges and universities be the final arbiter of how well students are learning what is being taught.[108]

A different pattern emerges when institutional administrators initiate or support challenges to faculty grading. Notwithstanding some flowery judicial rhetoric supporting deference to instructors' judgments—and even some Pyrrhic victories—faculty are frequently unable to make their grading decisions stand. In *Parate v. Isibor*,[109] an associate professor of engineering at Tennessee State was instructed by his dean to change a student's grade in a course from a *B* to an *A*. The professor's repeated refusal to do so (though he was eventually bludgeoned into complying with the dean's orders) escalated into a deeply antagonistic relationship with the dean, whose outrageous behavior eventually included disrupting the faculty member's class and publicly humiliating him. When the professor's contract was not renewed, he sought legal redress for violation of his academic freedom. Agreeing with the plaintiff that letter grades are a form of symbolic communication to students about the quality of their work (and thus entitled to First Amendment protection), the Sixth Circuit declared that a "university professor must remain free to exercise his independent professional judgment in the assignment of grades and the evaluation of his students' academic progress."[110] The dean had therefore infringed Parate's First Amendment academic freedom when he insisted that the grade be changed. Thus far, an excellent holding from a faculty perspective. But then the court proceeded to undercut this fine language by stating that all the dean (or university) needed to do to safeguard their legitimate interest in "supervising and reviewing the grading policies" of faculty was to *administratively* change the questioned grade.[111] The deference to the faculty member's grading decision was therefore transitory, if not a sham.

The Fifth Circuit, in *Hillis v. Stephen F. Austin State Univ.*, did not even bother to acknowledge the communicative aspect of assigning grades. In upholding the nonrenewal of the contract of a faculty member who had defied his chair's order to change a student's grade (here the grade was subsequently altered by administrative fiat), the court opined that such an order did not violate the instructor's First Amendment academic freedom because it did not involve "any censorship of the content or method of his teaching."[112] And in *Keen v. Penson,* yet another federal appellate court observed that even if the First Amendment applied to faculty grading decisions, faculty rights would still have to be weighed (and might be found wanting) against the "university's interests in ensuring that its students receive a fair grade."[113] There is a clear trend here: in those relatively rare instances of full-fledged faculty-administrative legal conflict over grading, the institution tends to prevail in the end, whatever the judicial reasoning.[114]

One must conclude that institutional considerations and needs fare very well in the area of general grading policies and particular grading decisions. From a quantitative standpoint, of course, only the tiniest percentage of grades awarded by faculty are ever questioned, much less overturned. However, legally enforceable institutional policies on grading open the door to meaningful administrative oversight and a check on irresponsible faculty decisions.

## Copyright and Teaching Materials

Before making some final observations about faculty autonomy in the classroom, we must take another quick detour into the realm of copyright law to examine several important questions about the actual teaching materials—lecture notes, textbooks, class handouts, and the like—used by faculty.

We spoke earlier about faculty ownership of the fruits of scholarship and some of the questions raised by the work-made-for-hire doctrine.[115] Similar ambiguity surrounds the ownership of course outlines or teaching notes prepared by faculty in the discharge of their instructional duties. Faculty are of course hired to teach, often to teach specified courses with predetermined curricula. In some cases substitute faculty are even hired to teach from extant materials prepared by colleagues. In a variety of circumstances, then, the employer college or university can make a compelling argument that it owns these teaching materials. Thus, in the recent case of *Vanderhurst v. Colorado Mountain College District*, a federal court held that a faculty member did not hold the copyright in a course outline he had prepared on his own time and with his own materials, since its creation was "connected directly with the work [he] was employed to do and was fairly and reasonably incidental to his employment."[116]

As with faculty scholarship, however, litigation over the ownership of teaching materials is rare. Many institutional copyright policies do not even address teaching materials, simply assuming that they belong to their authors. Certainly most faculty act as if they own such items. The notion that an instructor who leaves Michigan State for Purdue must leave his lecture notes behind in East Lansing (or could only use them with the permission of his former employer) strikes us as preposterous.[117] But we may now be seeing more aggressive institutional assertions of ownership, partly in response to the rise of new markets for intellectual "product."[118] Several companies currently sell to the public audio and videotape lectures by "great teachers." Others hope to use the Internet to reach a global audience. But if these lectures are based on—or identical in content to—classroom instruction, who is entitled to license them? If the financial stakes become significant enough, faculty and institutional interests will collide, with the likely outcome a royalty split and more precise copyright policies.

In their teaching, many faculty also utilize course materials they did not write and to which they unquestionably do not hold the copyright. Accordingly, regardless of the extent of their freedom to select whatever materials they deem relevant for their classes, faculty (and their employer institutions) must avoid any legal pitfalls incident to such use. As we shall see, the law, driven by a desire to promote broad access to knowledge, is quite accommodating to faculty and student interests. But the explosive growth in the amount of information available for instruction, and especially the ease with which it can be shared with students through modern technology (photocopying machines, computer file downloads, etc.), has aroused concern and even ire on the part of publishers and "content providers" who seek to realize the full value of their copyrights. One thus sees increased legal posturing, more litigation, and even possible legislation, all in a rapidly shifting environment where waves of technological change can upend well-staked-out positions.[119]

Consider the burgeoning use of "course packs" of articles, reviews, book excerpts, and other materials for individual classes. Many faculty now rely on such tools as a regular supplement to—or even in lieu of—traditional textbooks. They do this primarily for compelling didactic reasons. Compared with having to choose between extant texts, none of which directly meet the instructor's needs, or waiting impatiently for a new edition of an old text, photocopying makes it possible, even relatively easy, for professors to tailor a set of readings to the precise subject matter of a course, drawing on the most current literature and events to present a fresh, highly relevant course. When textbook prices are high and only selected portions of existing volumes are on point, faculty and students may also favor course packs as an economical alternative to purchasing (or putting on reserve) large numbers of required texts. Recognizing these virtues, many colleges and universities use their in-house photocopying shops to produce course packs. Local and national copying businesses also fill this market niche. Such a significant change in how courses are put together and what students are expected to read may drive down textbook sales and damage the larger academic publishing market—unless publishers can efficiently capture the value of the portions of works and the more topical pieces that comprise those packs. Publishers have therefore become more aggressive in defending their property rights within the academy and in seeking to clarify the bounds of faculty use of copyrighted materials in teaching.

Delineation of those bounds necessarily begins with the recognition that many items in course packs are in the public domain, not covered by any copyright at all. This includes, for example, works of literature on which the copyright has expired (Washington Irving's *The Legend of Sleepy Hollow*) and government documents (such as the judicial opinions cited throughout this book) that were never copyrighted in the first place. Next, faculty can generally avoid any problems by obtaining the permission of the copyright holder to use all or part of a given work—a privilege for which the copyright holder may demand a license fee, charging whatever the (perhaps increasingly mercenary) market will bear. Faculty can also rely upon the legal protection offered by the doctrine of "fair use," which endorses some socially valuable uses of copyrighted works even in the absence of the holder's permission.[120] You will recall that under federal copyright law "the fair use of a copyrighted work, including such use by reproduction in copies . . . for purposes such as criticism, comment . . . *teaching (including multiple copies for classroom use)* scholarship, or research, is not an infringement of copyright."[121] Again, factual determinations of whether a given use is fair will turn on:

1. the purpose and character of the use, including whether such use is of a noncommercial nature or is for nonprofit educational purposes;
2. the nature of the copyrighted work;
3. the amount and substantiality of the portion used in relation to the copyrighted work as a whole; and
4. the effect of the use upon the potential market for or value of the copyrighted work.[122]

As I argue below, faculty who are careful in assembling course packs will be able to fit much of their designated material under the fair use rubric. Classroom teaching materials (even copies for each student distributed in packs) would seem to be the prototypical—and most easily defended— example of fair use.

For more cautious individuals and institutions, there is another alternative. In conjunction with congressional deliberations over the 1976 Copyright Act (the statute that codified the common law doctrine of fair use for the first time), representatives of educational associations and commercial publishers developed a set of guidelines on photocopying for educational uses that establish a minimum level of copying qualifying as "fair use." Anything within this "safe harbor" was clearly "fair"—though I must note that much photocopying for classroom purposes *beyond* the guidelines would also qualify as fair. At any rate, these guidelines were endorsed by House and Senate conferees "as part of their understanding of fair use."[123] The guidelines authorize fairly generous (single) copying of articles and book chapters for a professor's own use and more limited distribution of multiple copies to students in the classroom. Such classroom copies must meet rather stringent tests for brevity (e.g., complete articles of only less than 2,500 words; excerpts from longer prose pieces of 1,000 words or 10% of the complete work, whichever is less; no more than 250 words of a poem); spontaneity (e.g., there must be no time to obtain the owner's permission for such use); and cumulative effect (e.g., no more than nine instances of copying for any course; no more than one complete poem or story, or two excerpts, from the same author).[124] I find these guidelines draconian and unworkable. While courts have used them as a reference point,[125] they clearly do not have the force of law[126] and do not come close to the limits of fair use. They do, however, give some flavor of how zealously publishers wish to limit fair use.

Further evidence of publishers' antipathy to unauthorized (i.e., uncompensated) copying of proprietary materials may be found in their escalating—and very public—pattern of copyright infringement suits brought against the creators and purveyors of course packs. The first such lawsuit was brought in 1982 by a group of publishers (coordinated on their behalf by the Association of American Publishers, a prominent trade organization) against New York University, nine NYU faculty, and a copy shop near the campus. The plaintiffs sought an injunction barring unlawful copying in course anthologies.[127] Having sent a clear warning to faculty and institutions across the nation, the publishers quickly reached an out-of-court settlement with NYU that required the university to adopt, publicize, and enforce a stricter copyright policy premised on the classroom guidelines discussed above.

A few years later, building on the *in terrorem* effect of the NYU suit, publishers took aim at large copy shop chains with franchises near universities that had built up a substantial business producing course packs. In *Basic Books, Inc. v. Kinko's Graphics Corp.*, a federal trial court soundly rejected Kinko's claim that selling the packs could qualify as fair use because the purchasers employed them for educational purposes. This laughable argument ignored the profit Kinko's earned on such sales. Under the four-factor fair use test, Kinko's course packs appropriated a substantial portion of protected works and reduced both possible textbook sales and license fees.[128] A verdict for $500,000 in damages remade much of the market for course packs, forcing highly visible national copy shop chains to seek copyright holders' permission before including works in packs (with attendant time delays and price increases) or—as Kinko's did—to get out of the anthology business altogether.[129] But that still left less cautious— and less prominent—local copy shop owners. So, fresh on the heels of the *Kinko's* decision, another collection of publishers sued a small, independent operator in Ann Arbor, Michigan, who had ostentatiously refused to seek prior authorization in preparing course packs. Once again, judicial authorities (this time a federal court of appeals) found infringement, with particular reference to an increasingly well established market to license portions of works for inclusion in such packs.[130]

Publishers have chosen their targets well, building a series of precedents that strengthen their hand in each round of litigation. They focused first on the most egregious (and least sympathetic) makers of unauthorized copies: for-profit businesses. Having extracted royalties from this group, publishers may be expected to turn their fire next on nonprofit college and university-owned copy shops that produce the same kinds of course packs or other in-class handouts that allegedly infringe copyright. Such operations should therefore be careful in assessing whether requests for copies are lawful. Office staff, for example, should have a basic understanding of fair use and, if the proposed use cannot be construed as fair, should secure appropriate permissions before copying. A further caveat: if academic *institutions* accept tighter definitions of fair use, publishers may then begin to pressure individual scholars.[131] So, while faculty still retain much latitude in distributing course materials, current copyright law cautions against the blithe production of course packs.

Indeed, publishers' efforts to promote a narrow interpretation of fair use and to enforce copyright rigorously have grown in intensity and urgency with the advent of a digital environment where home computers can download entire libraries or reproduce photographic images and sounds with no discernible loss of quality—and, perhaps most disconcerting, where Internet-based and other forms of distance learning can almost instantly distribute copyrighted works much more broadly than ever before. The conflict is both simple and profound. One the one hand, academic users (faculty, students, librarians) want to employ the new technology to enhance access to the raw materials of scholarship and teaching. On the other hand, copyright owners, who have invested considerable resources in developing their "products," fear losing control over such works by placing them in computer networks or other domains where they can easily be reproduced and shared without payment. Underlying this debate is deep uncertainty about the value of "intellectual content" in the digital age: are there vast new markets that can be tapped (e.g., individual licenses to read articles or view pictures), or will vast amounts of information inevitably become digitized public goods? Little wonder that many copyright holders have taken a very conservative position, insisting that no electronic copying should occur without prior authorization.[132]

In the hopes of reaching voluntary agreement on the scope of fair use in on-line copying (and at the very least, demarcation of digital "safe harbors" analogous to that for classroom photocopying), in 1994 the U.S. Commerce Department convened publishers, software developers, music and video producers, and academic users of copyrighted materials in an inclusive

Conference on Fair Use. Topics under discussion included distance learning, educational multimedia products, interlibrary loans, and the practice of putting readings on electronic reserve. Copyright holders, led by publishers' associations and media conglomerates such as Viacom, took a tough negotiating stance, believing that colleges and universities were hotbeds of copyright infringement. University representatives ultimately concluded that the sorts of guidelines acceptable to publishers were too restrictive and that academics would have to press their arguments in other venues. After three years of negotiations, the Conference on Fair Use broke down, with educational groups formally disavowing the small number of draft proposals that had been developed and calling for colleges and universities to "reject any licensing agreement 'that implicitly or explicitly limits or abrogates fair use.'"[133] This failure to reach a negotiated solution has left the door open for congressional action, and legislators are currently considering a variety of changes to the Copyright Act, from quick patches to overhauling the entire statute to reflect new technology.[134] Given the large gulf between publishers' and academics' views of appropriate copyright flexibility and the relative pressure that each side is able to bear on lawmakers, faculty should probably not be encouraged by the prospect of new legislation.

In the meantime, where does this leave faculty who need to use published materials for teaching purposes? Still with a lot of latitude to use the desired materials, as it turns out. First, not everything is copyrighted. Second, faculty can always request and usually get permission to use copyrighted works. In many cases there may be no fee or only a minimal fee for nonprofit academic use, and the publishing industry has been working hard to make it quick and easy to obtain authorizations. An especially promising development in this regard is the creation of blanket licenses, under which a college or university can acquire the right for its faculty to use entire catalogs of participating publishers' works in course packs or other handouts in exchange for a single license payment based on the number of students enrolled at the institution.[135]

Third, faculty (hopefully assisted by counsel for their institution) may conclude that the desired use is in fact fair use under federal copyright law.[136] Returning once more to the four-factor analysis, we find that factor 1, the purpose and character of the use, need not be a problem, since course packs that are distributed free (or sold by the institution at cost) are clearly educational.[137] Factor 2, the nature of the copyrighted work, will also frequently disappear as an issue, especially if the work in question is largely factual (remember, facts are not copyrightable, though their expression is) and if it is published largely for an academic audience with little expectation of pecuniary gain (as in the case of some scholarly monographs that are printed merely because they are intellectually important, perhaps by a university press that itself does not expect to turn a profit). While the last two factors, the amount and substantiality of the portion used and the effect of such use on the potential market for the work, are clearly the most problematic, any difficulties here may also be surmounted if faculty carefully circumscribe the length of selections culled and are mindful of and seek to minimize possible adverse effects on sales of the larger copyrighted work. Certainly a decision to include a copyrighted piece in a course pack is more defensible if made solely on pedagogical grounds rather than for purposes of saving students or the university library the expense of having to buy copies of a particular book.[138] In some cases faculty can legitimately argue that including part of a copyrighted work in a course pack may actually help create demand for the larger work. Thus, a student who reads and loves a poem by William Carlos Williams might choose to purchase a volume of his poetry. As a prophylactic measure, faculty might even encourage students to buy any of the larger works that interest them, perhaps having several copies placed on order at the campus bookstore.

Although federal copyright law allows for substantial damages (including the recovery of lost profits or statutory damages of up to $100,000 for each work willfully infringed), it also contains exculpatory provisions that cushion unintentional infringers from severe penalties, and it even eliminates statutory damages altogether for faculty (or institutions) who reasonably believed their actions were covered by fair use.[139] So taking a calculated risk that one's use of copyrighted materials, if challenged (which is still not all that likely), will eventually be held to qualify as fair use may often be a rational course of action, particularly if tracking down the copyright owner would be an onerous task. Most academic uses are, after all, entirely consistent with the animating spirit of the fair use doctrine, which seeks to promote intellectual discourse.[140]

## Concluding Thoughts

When all is said and done, we return to the fundamental question of how much autonomy faculty actually have in their capacity as teachers. I would argue that despite some softening at the edges (*Bishop* and *Edwards* being prime examples), from a practical standpoint faculty at most colleges and universities remain very free to teach what they want and how they want. As long as faculty do not act abusively towards students, ignore established course content (though they can probably put their own slant even on this), use the classroom for blatant proselytizing (especially in circumstances where it looks like compulsion) or repeated discussion of extraneous matter, or aim their teaching at a different audience from their students (including pegging the course at a wildly inappropriate intellectual level), the classroom largely remains their domain. This is especially true when external challenges are made to faculty independence, but similar results obtain when institutional authorities seek to micromanage student instruction.

Perhaps the most frequently upheld basis for regulating faculty classroom conduct is that such conduct has violated institutional policies on teaching. But I would also assert that courts' willingness to defer to such policies is in large part a consequence of their having been established or reviewed by duly constituted faculty bodies (e.g., course content is the province of curriculum committees; the overall level of academic rigor is ultimately traceable to decisions of faculty admissions committees). In a very real sense, then, the *institutional* academic freedom recognized in many judicial opinions may be viewed as the sum of acts of *individual* faculty academic freedom. Conflict between these two notions may thus become illusory.

Finally, given the sometimes overshadowing influence of constitutional law in American jurisprudence, it bears repeating here (and in all other settings of our faculty typology) that even if the First Amendment does not provide the kind of ironclad protection to academic freedom at public institutions as faculty might like, *contractually based* academic freedom also operates at both public and private colleges and universities to protect faculty expectations of autonomy. Contractual promises of faculty independence may in fact be more reliable and more easily enforceable.

As we have seen, disputes about faculty teaching arise with some regularity. This will continue to be the case, given the high visibility of classroom instruction and the intense interest taken in the content and quality of teaching by current and prospective students, parents (who share a strong consumer orientation with their offspring), university administrators, outside audiences, and of course the instructors themselves. Faculty are extremely sensitive to, and will zealously guard against, any perceived or actual incursions on their independence in the classroom. Indeed, they may resist having departmental colleagues or chairs observe their classes (even with prior notice), while at the same time insisting upon peer review of scholarship. In the coming years, as all colleges and universities are increasingly held accountable to internal and external constituencies—and as both institutions and their component academic programs devote more attention to the assessment of learning outcomes—legal disputes will arise over administrative efforts to gauge what and how well students have learned and the effectiveness of faculty teaching. Institutions will seek to establish more clearly (in employment contracts, through formal policies, or by custom) their ability to monitor students' intellectual growth. But faculty will fight any measures or means that smack of censorship or stifling oversight.

Our examination of classroom case law reveals inherent tension between individual instructors and institutional leaders (department chairs as well as the more remote provosts or presidents) over the content of individual courses and the theoretical approach taken to a given subject. The respective rights and obligations of the parties, all of whom share a legitimate interest in providing students with appropriate instruction, require further legal clarification. The precedents in this area are frankly inconsistent, thereby layering confusion on a natural difference of perspectives. I described how a modicum of trust, mutually sensitive conduct by faculty and administrators, and candid communication can resolve most disputes. However, the hardest cases will still end up in court.

The now-ubiquitous Internet, together with other new technologies facilitating the exchange of information, are also certain to generate legal controversies. Commercial copyright holders will not sit idly by as university faculty and students instantly duplicate and distribute their intellectual property across the campus and around the globe. We should therefore anticipate litigation over the boundaries of fair use for academic purposes and over what constitutes a workable license in the digital age. As the concepts of copyright and of intellectual property more generally evolve—having already adapted to printing presses, photography, and television—methods of instruction and student learning styles will also change, with practical and legal effects that can only be dimly perceived.

# 4 Faculty as Institutional Citizens

The work of faculty, of course, extends well beyond classroom teaching and scholarship to an active role in shaping the character and culture of their home institutions. Both by tradition (it was thus in the proto-universities of medieval Europe) and by virtue of their expertise, faculty take the lead in establishing the curriculum and in setting standards for admission, grading, graduation, and the conduct of research. At almost all colleges and universities, faculty help select senior administrators and regularly consult with those leaders (through both formal governance structures and informal channels) about how the institution is being run and its long-range plans. Faculty also determine the future of their college or university by their control of the appointments and promotion process and the organization of academic departments and other units.

Deep faculty involvement in institutional direction-setting and governance makes sense because, especially when a tenure system is in place, faculty are the longest-term stakeholders in the life of an academic institution. Students eventually graduate, and administrators tend to come and go (even if "going" means returning to a full-time faculty position), but faculty, in their capacity as institutional citizens and repositories of the university's history and mores, serve as the collective embodiment of the institution. In the words of a former president of Stanford:

> Since everything that happens in the university is fundamentally academic, that is, involves teaching and research directly or involves activities that support teaching and research, it follows that faculty . . . are the ones most deeply affected by [and the ones who should exercise considerable influence over] policy decisions. . . . Faculty members have another, stronger case for their involvement in institutional governance. It is that the university's practicing academic members are in the best position to evaluate academic merit, and thus can best judge the consequences of the university's decisions.[1]

Faculty engagement in the life of the institution therefore ultimately makes for a stronger college or university. And faculty need sufficient autonomy and discretion to play such a role.

But at the same time, the necessities of running a large modern educational (some would say quasi-business) enterprise—meeting payrolls, maintaining an extensive physical plant, complying with lab safety ordinances and nondiscrimination statutes, and the like—require a corps of professional administrators to provide some measure of operational order and expertise.[2] Colleges and universities have a legitimate interest in internal harmony and smooth functioning. Consequently, faculty may be disciplined for violating institutional policies or rules. However, as we shall see, the border between disputes over policies that affect teaching and disputes over faculty speech (in particular on-campus speech) about intra-university affairs can be rather blurry. Many cases involve both kinds of controversy.

## Faculty Involvement in Institutional Governance and Operations

In demarcating faculty control over such intra-university matters, the law strikes a careful balance that can be illuminated by returning to my set of fundamental questions about any claim of academic freedom:

1. Is the activity in question central to the mission of a college or university?
2. Is there consensus across the university community that academic freedom is implicated and deserves protection?
3. Who stands to benefit from the purported freedom?

I would submit that a faculty member's conduct as an institutional citizen, while of genuine importance and value to a college or university, is not as essential to the work of the institution as his or her teaching and scholarship. Faculty do not come to a college or university so that they can play an active role in intramural affairs. The lack of such engagement will hurt an institution, but it will not immediately cripple it.[3] Nor is there obvious consensus on the need for academic freedom in intra-institutional governance as there is about faculty autonomy in research and teaching. Faculty will surely push for such freedom, but other constituencies will not automatically agree that individual faculty members, or even faculty as a group, should set and carry out institutional policy. In upholding a faculty union's statutory right to consult with administrators on matters of college governance (and conversely denying parallel rights to individual faculty outside the union), the Supreme Court noted that it had "never recognized a constitutional right of faculty to participate in policymaking in academic institutions."[4] Indeed, both line academic administrators (chairs, deans, provosts, and presidents) and nonacademic officials (vice presidents for human resources, student affairs professionals) will rightly assert that they are the ones charged with responsibility for managing the affairs of the institution and that—both by knowledge and by breadth of perspective—they are much better suited to do so than faculty (who, perhaps out of self-interest, often resist change and efforts at increased accountability).

In light of such tension, the answer to the question of who benefits from academic freedom in intra-university affairs depends almost entirely on whose claim of autonomy prevails. Faculty gain stature and influence over college and university operations if their bid for independent speech and action is upheld; administrators will be the direct beneficiaries if claims of *institutional* autonomy are honored. The foregoing analysis would lead us to conclude that courts will not be particularly deferential to faculty claims of academic freedom in their capacity as institutional citizens—and that is in fact the case.

Our examination of this area should begin with the recognition that, once again, different legal rules apply in the public and private sectors, and within each of these sectors there are wide local variations in faculty governance. At private institutions where the First Amendment is not in effect, faculty involvement in intra-university affairs is basically a matter of contract law. If an institution's employment agreements, faculty handbooks or policy statements, or even tradition or custom within that particular academic community allow for faculty input on operational matters such as budgets and appointments, faculty will want to participate in the decision-making processes. At other private colleges and universities, where faculty have no contractual or historical role in shaping policy, administrators will have a relatively free hand in governance. Faculty at such institutions question or interfere with administrative decisions at their own risk. Witness the dean of the graduate school and the department chair at Baylor University who were stripped of their administrative duties in 1996 for, respectively, telling a reporter that the university might be vulnerable to religious discrimination suits and criticizing the firing of the campus chaplain. Baylor's president took umbrage at these "'public and intemperate' comments indicat[ing] a 'lack of respect' for the administration," declaring that "'academic freedom had never been the right to say anything at any time.'"[5] Baylor's leadership was probably acting within its legal authority. But even administrators at private colleges with no established channels for faculty participation should appreciate how cavalier disregard of faculty opinions on matters with academic ramifications can damage morale and the healthy functioning of the institution.

Most of the legal authority about the role of faculty in intramural affairs comes from the public sector, where the overlay of First Amendment jurisprudence on contract law (itself superimposed on academic custom) makes for fascinating disputes. Over the last thirty years, federal courts have developed a relatively standard approach for reviewing faculty claims of free speech in intra-university matters. (A typical fact pattern here would be a former public university faculty member alleging that adverse employment action such as nonreappointment or denial of tenure was taken against him or her because of controversial speech about campus issues.)[6] Courts analyze such claims in four steps. First, they determine whether the faculty member's speech was "on a matter of public concern."[7] If so, as a second step the court will proceed to "balance . . . the interests of the teacher, as a citizen, in commenting upon matters of public concern and the interest of the State, as an employer, in promoting the efficiency of the public service it performs through its employees."[8] If this balance tips in favor of the faculty member, the plaintiff must then prove that his or her protected speech was a substantial or motivating factor in the employment decision being challenged.[9] Should the faculty plaintiff meet this burden of demonstrating causation, as a fourth and final analytical step the burden "shifts to the [college or university] employer to show 'by a preponderance of evidence that it would have reached the same decision . . . even in the absence of the protected conduct.'"[10] If the faculty member would have been treated in the same manner regardless of the legitimate exercise of free speech, the adverse employment decision will stand.

Resolving disputes about faculty intramural speech under this four-step framework is a fact-specific endeavor, especially the first two steps' determination of whether certain expression merits constitutional protection. Over time it has also become clear that the shoal upon which faculty claims are most likely to founder is the threshold inquiry—that is, whether the speech in question was on a matter of public concern. In making such a decision, the court will consider the "content, form, and context of a given statement."[11] The time and place of the speech thus become important but are not determinative. Speech on university-related matters can be made on campus (e.g., at a faculty meeting) or off campus (on the village green, in a letter to the editor, or even at a dinner party). While at first blush *off-campus* speech on almost any topic might seem more obviously "public" in orientation, plenty of on-campus speech has also been found to be on a matter of public concern.[12] The fundamental issue is whether the faculty member is analogous to a public-spirited citizen speaking out on a topic of political or social import to a wide range of fellow voters or is more like an employee voicing opinions about intracompany personnel decisions and working conditions. The distinction is important and deserves careful attention.

The rich case law in this area reveals that much faculty speech on intrauniversity affairs is regularly held to be on matters of public concern.[13] Prominent examples include

— oral or written commentary, in a host of venues and to a variety of audiences, about academic standards and the intellectual integrity of the institution (including admissions and grading policies, graduation requirements, and curricular weaknesses);[14]

— discussions about intellectual currents in society, or participation in campus debates on political issues;[15]

— exposing administrative waste, ineptitude, potential risks or dangers to the public fisc, or, more generally, breaches of trust on the part of college or university officials (all such speech might colloquially be characterized as "whistle-blowing");[16]

— criticism of college or university spending priorities;[17]

— faculty participation in electoral issues, including the public election of university trustees or regents;[18]

— speech in connection with faculty union (organization and collective bargaining) activity;[19] and

— some faculty intramural speech on the broadest level of institutional governance, but not speech about day-to-day operations. This might include, for example, debates over defining institutional characteristics (size, number of schools, admissions policies, and other features that verge on public concern over academic standards), as well as faculty votes of "no confidence" in the institution's president.[20] As we shall see, though, most speech on administrative matters—especially on matters that do not rise to the presidential or chancellorial level—would not be regarded as addressing matters of public concern.

These broad categories of publicly oriented speech provide faculty considerable latitude to express views on campus issues and to affect institutional policy without reprisal—assuming, of course, that the subsequent requirements of the four-step analysis are satisfied as well. But there are other types of faculty speech that smack of personal (not public) concern and which courts will not defend from institutional sanction. Chief among these are individual personnel grievances about items ranging from salary to perquisites, teaching assignments, departmental affiliation, and one's prospects for promotion.[21] As an extension of the same notion, faculty speech about a college or university's appointment and promotion policy, including commentary about decisions reached under such policy, will not be regarded as addressing a matter of public concern.[22] Likewise for criticism of a faculty colleague's scholarship or professional behavior.[23] Comments or questions about the content of university budgets or the faculty's role in the budget process that seem motivated primarily by personal interest (e.g., seeking additional funding for one's own school or department) will properly fail the first step of the legal analysis.[24] So too, I think, would abusive or vitriolic attacks on college or university administrators, even if in making such attack the faculty member is agitated over (and actually meant to discuss) issues of broad interest to the university community.[25] Finally, much speech on the "internal administration" of educational institutions will not be constitutionally protected, including complaints about the organization of faculty governance bodies and the performance of department chairs or deans.[26] On occasion, even denouncing presidential leadership will not be of public concern,[27] but the visibility of presidents makes such comments more likely to be deemed of broad community interest. For First Amendment purposes, then, much of the daily business of a college or university is not of public import.

To make this point more clearly, it is helpful to see how several courts have wrestled with the thorny first-level question of whether faculty speech on intra-university affairs is of public concern. *Johnson v. Lincoln Univ.* addressed the latest episodes of a long-standing struggle between faculty and administrators over the future direction of this historically black institution. Professor Johnson, a leader among the dissident faculty, engaged in acrimonious fights with the chair of his department and the university's president, during which he articulated his positions (even on narrow operational issues) in terms of broad views about Lincoln's academic rigor and the quality of the education it was providing students. For example, he distributed memoranda criticizing grade inflation on the campus, contacted the regional accrediting body about what he deemed unconscionably lax admissions standards to Lincoln's Master of Human Services program, published (presumably satirical) newspaper articles proposing that the university eliminate the grade of *F*, and attempted to censure faculty for allowing students to enroll in advanced courses without passing prerequisites. The federal appellate court hearing this case had no difficulty concluding that Johnson's statements on educational standards and academic policy at Lincoln went well beyond personal grievances to address matters of public concern.[28]

A similar result obtained in *Maples v. Martin*, which explored the legal consequences of a schism in the Mechanical Engineering Department at Auburn University. Here, one faction prepared a report that was highly critical of the department head's leadership and of morale within the program. This hostile document was distributed widely to faculty, students, alumni, and—most controversially—a specialized accrediting agency conducting an on-campus review of the department. After the accreditors advised the dean of engineering that the ME department had become dysfunctional, several of the report's authors were transferred to other academic units, with no change in faculty rank or salary. The transferees sued, alleging that they were being unfairly punished for exercising their right as institutional citizens to participate in and comment on university affairs.[29] The court found that the report spoke to "substantive issues that could influence the public's perception of the quality of education provided by the Department. Specifically, the Review points to weaknesses in the curriculum, inadequate facilities, a low faculty-to-school ratio and the poor performance of Auburn graduates on the professional licensing exams for engineers, all of which endanger the ability of the Department to prepare students for professional engineering careers."[30] Prospects for the program's continued accreditation (a basic institutional academic standard) therefore satisfied the "public concern" criterion.

Equally public in orientation was criticism by a nontenured professor of architecture at Iowa State of what he viewed as an overly cozy and unethical relationship between his department and the local architectural business community. This critique of the intellectual independence and integrity of the architecture curriculum (again, a matter of fundamental academic standards) was found to have been made in the faculty plaintiff's capacity as a concerned citizen and not as a self-interested employee.[31]

*Hall v. Kutztown University* is an excellent example of cases analyzing speech on broad intellectual and cultural issues. The plaintiff held a short-term appointment in Kutztown's Philosophy Department. During a discussion at a faculty meeting about a new general education model, he embroiled himself in controversy and offended many colleagues by speaking at length, in a very forceful manner, about "why multicultural education is not a good thing, in the process describing 'barbaric' practices condoned by some other cultures, such as female circumcision in the Sudan, slavery in other African countries, bride-burning in India, and discrimination against women in Islamic countries. The Plaintiff remember[ed] espousing a philosophy of moral absolutism and asserting that Westerners have a moral duty to stand up against such evils."[32] When Hall was subsequently not hired for a tenure-track position, he claimed that the university was retaliating against him for his lawful speech as an institutional and public citizen. In the court's view, Hall's remarks at the faculty meeting—while clearly sparked by opposition to any curriculum that might teach students "to accept other cultures and other cultures' practices as morally correct, rather than to apply a critical lens to such studies"—also extended considerably beyond the academic topic then before the faculty (the merits of multicultural curricula) to reach policy debates on matters of political and social concern to the entire nation.[33] He had a legal right to make such statements.

The case of *Hickingbottom v. Easley* nicely illustrates the treatment of faculty speech about careless or illegal behavior in institutional affairs. Here, a professor at an Arkansas community college alerted the state Motor Vehicle Division that the college and its president were avoiding paying taxes owed on presidential cars. Following an official investigation (during which the faculty member's whistle-blowing became known), the instructor's teaching contract was not renewed. In his subsequent lawsuit, the federal trial court decreed that "potential violation of the law should always be a matter of public concern."[34]

But contrast *Johnson, Hall, Hickingbottom,* and their progeny with cases at whose core lay the personal grievances of faculty members. In *Colburn v. Trustees of Indiana University,* two assistant professors from the minority faction of a badly divided sociology department at Indiana University–Purdue University at Indianapolis (IUPUI) were about to be reviewed for tenure. Fearful that their allegiance to the "out" group would doom their prospects, they asked senior IUPUI administrators to conduct an external review of the operations of the sociology department's appointments and promotions committee. Despite decanal intervention, the quarrels continued and the plaintiffs were eventually denied tenure. In voting against one aspirant, the promotions committee (allegedly stacked with members of the opposing dominant faction) explained that his "comments to people outside the department have hurt the image of the Sociology faculty and undermined the integrity of the peer review process."[35] The professors sued IUPUI, claiming that they had been punished for lawful intramural speech requesting a review of the committee. They lost. A federal appellate court held that "the point of their speech, given the context in which the letters [requesting the review] were written, was to highlight how the department's infighting had affected them and would affect their futures at the University."[36] The plaintiffs "were not speaking primarily as citizens, but as faculty members concerned about the private matter of the processes by which they were evaluated."[37] While such speech might be interesting to some people—and even though it was wrong for the department to allow tenure decisions to be tainted by personal bias—this speech did not directly affect the larger community and should not be classified as a matter of public concern.[38]

Similarly, in *Bunger v. University of Oklahoma Board of Regents,* the Tenth Circuit determined that faculty criticism of the procedures for selecting a committee with oversight of a business school's graduate program did not merit constitutional protection: "The organization of such internal governing bodies is not an issue of social importance or heightened public interest. Although many an academic donnybrook has been fought over such administrative rules, the issues at stake rarely transcend the internal workings of the university to affect the social or political life of the community."[39]

As a last example of cases holding that faculty speech on intra-university matters is of private—and not public—concern, consider *Kurtz v. Vickrey,* which explored the legal ramifications of a feud between an associate professor at the University of Montevallo and that institution's president. Over the course of several years, the faculty member directed a stream of disputatious, pointed, and sometimes sarcastic comments to the president, usually questioning the management of the institution. For instance, he objected when the president characterized a 5 percent salary increase as "good," publicly bickered with him about the meaning of the term *average*, chided him about misstating the precise location of the campus, and expressed embarrassment when the president announced that he was not seeking the presidency of another institution. Unwisely, the president eventually began to respond in kind.[40] When the instructor was denied promotion to full professor (allegedly in retaliation for his protected speech on institutional affairs), the court had to examine the content and context of each of his various statements. Most of his remarks, it found, "derived from [an] apparent personality conflict, a matter not of public concern."[41] These included complaints about his salary as well as half-hearted expressions of interest in the university's budget that really stemmed from his salary grievance. But others of his comments, most notably criticism of the university's spending priorities (e.g., buying a fire truck for the local community), *did* relate to matters of public import and therefore proceeded to the next stage of legal analysis, the balancing test.[42] *Kurtz* demonstrates the finely grained inquiry that must frequently be conducted to answer the "public concern" question.

Given this complexity, one is tempted to question the validity of the judicial distinction between speech on matters of public and of private concern. After all, some level of private *self*-interest is what leads us to care about even the most *public* of issues in the first place. The law is quite clear, however, that a faculty member cannot "bootstrap his individual grievance into a matter of public concern either by bruiting his complaint to the world or by invoking a supposed popular interest in all aspects of the way public institutions are run."[43] The fact that a newspaper publishes an article about an intra-university dispute does not necessarily elevate that dispute to a matter of public concern,[44] nor does the faculty's ability to stir up some interest on the part of colleagues. Courts see much wisdom in denying constitutional protection to speech about fundamentally private issues. To hold otherwise would be to hamstring the daily functioning of public colleges and universities. "Indeed, if a faculty member need only point to some verbal criticism or altercation concerning his college, its curriculum, or how things are run in order to convert an adverse personnel decision into a federal action, then nearly every [such] decision could be reviewed by a federal court."[45] The key question therefore remains whether the faculty member speaks as "a concerned public citizen, informing the public that the state institution is not properly discharging its duties . . . ; or merely as an employee, concerned only with internal policies or practices which are of relevance only to the employees of that institution."[46]

Recall that even if a faculty member's controversial speech addresses matters of public concern, in order to be legally protected the speaker's interest in (or need to) comment on such matters must outweigh the state's interest in the smooth and efficient administration of the university. This balancing test, first articulated in the 1968 Supreme Court case of *Pickering v. Board of Education*,[47] typically leads courts to look at a variety of (sometimes overlapping) factors, including the following:

1. *Is there a close working relationship between the faculty member and those he criticized,* in particular, the sort of relationship in which personal loyalty and confidence are necessary and expected?[48] Faculty speech having a detrimental impact on such relationships is not likely to be protected. Thus, in *Hamer v. Brown*, statements about the quality of campus leadership (a matter of public concern) that damaged the requisite close relationship between the director of a division and the university's chancellor were not shielded by the First Amendment.[49] But in *Rampey v. Allen*,[50] a federal appellate court overturned a decision not to rehire faculty at the Oklahoma College of Liberal Arts who criticized policies of the college's president. The president demanded absolute loyalty from all faculty and regarded anyone who did not demonstrate such obeisance as "divisive." According to the court, the former faculty members' refusal to toady in this manner and their statements disagreeing with presidential policies were protected under the First Amendment. There was no relationship between faculty duties and the president calling for unquestioned loyalty: "Whether they demonstrate [such] loyalty . . . , whether they relate to him personally and whether they have a similar philosophy is not, as we view it, a requisite . . . and there can be little question but that such demands infringe the rights of the faculty members to express legitimate views."[51] As institutional citizens, the faculty had a right to hold and express their opinions on college affairs.

2. *More generally, did the speech impair discipline by superiors or harmony among coworkers?*[52] The greater the need for such regularity and the greater the likelihood of disruption, the less freedom faculty will have to engage in critical speech. Although any complaints about campus leaders or colleagues will to some extent disturb the institutional peace, healthy colleges and universities are intellectually yeasty and fractious places. There

must always be some room for legitimate questioning of administrative or institutional actions.

3. *Did the speech have a detrimental impact on the administration and/or the regular operation of the college or university?*[53] If the answer to this question is yes, the speech is much less likely to be protected. This is why, in *Maples v. Martin*,[54] the distribution of a report savagely attacking the leadership and quality of Auburn's Mechanical Engineering Department—although addressing a matter of public concern—presented legitimate grounds for transferring the authors to other departments. The circulation of this document (timed to coincide with and to complicate a reaccreditation visit) "distracted both students and faculty from the primary academic tasks of education and research," "contributed to a lack of harmony among the faculty," and "severely hampered communication between members of the faculty and the Department Head."[55] The university's need to prevent such disruptive interference with the regular business of the department trumped the dissident faculty's claim to speak on institutional affairs. Likewise, in *Harris v. Arizona Bd. of Regents,* a disgruntled director of creative writing threatened to tell a faculty candidate that she would not be welcome in his program. University officials reasonably concluded that such speech was "so disruptive that it substantially and materially interfered with the effective operation of the creative writing program, if not the entire English Department."[56] The faculty plaintiff had no constitutional right to make statements that were "wholly inconsistent with the nature of the academic environment, and served to antagonize and alienate some faculty members."[57] Note also that the location of the speech may affect its disruptive potential (and thus its protected status). Off-campus statements about university affairs, even if such affairs are a matter of public concern, will typically be less disruptive of daily operations.[58]

4. *Was the faculty member's performance of his or her duties impeded because of the speech in question?*[59] Once again, if the answer is yes, the speech should not be protected. Faculty freedom to opine on institutional matters clearly does not supersede teaching or immediate scholarly obligations. But it would be a rare case indeed in which faculty speech about college or university operations interfered in a substantive, meaningful way with a professor's "regular" duties, especially since, for most faculty, involvement in institutional affairs (through service on committees and the like) is *itself* a job requirement.[60] Opinions analyzing the impact of faculty speech on the performance of faculty duties tend to find no disruption. A

typical example is *Hale v. Walsh*,[61] where the court held that the plaintiff department chair's union activities and his public criticism of university financial policies, both of which addressed matters of public concern, were not detrimental to the employer-employee relationship, noting specifically that "discipline and morale in the classroom were not affected."[62] And in *Booher v. Bd. of Regents*, an art professor's statement to news media that he took offense at the title of a campus exhibit (for which statement he was subsequently censured by departmental colleagues) was found to be protected speech under the balancing test. According to the court, "none of the plaintiff's reported remarks disrupted the university's teaching in classroom or studio."[63] Of course, insubordination (e.g., the outright refusal of a faculty member to perform his or her duties) is not protected speech and would provide legally sufficient grounds for the college or university to discharge an academic employee.[64]

Like all balancing tests, this *Pickering* analysis leaves courts with ample room to come down on either side, depending upon the facts of the case. It is thus difficult to generalize how faculty speech on matters of public concern will stack up against a university's need for administrative harmony and smooth operations, although faculty "whistle-blowing" on administrative malfeasance or violations of law tends to weigh especially heavy in the scales.[65] It is striking, however, how many cases examining faculty speech on intra-university affairs conduct only a cursory balancing of interests at this second stage of inquiry, devoting much more attention to the first-stage designation of the speech as being of public or private concern.

It would be fair to say that federal courts in particular often avoid becoming embroiled in intra-university personnel disputes masquerading as free speech claims. They will quickly defer to assertions of institutional autonomy if the faculty speech in question is, at its core, about individual salaries or working conditions. The four-step analysis of faculty intramural speech provides a series of opportunities for such judicial abstention. Courts may find that the speech in question was essentially private in character; alternatively, they may decide that the balancing test goes against the faculty plaintiff; and, failing this, they may still hold that the plaintiff has not proved causation.[66]

Despite the four-part framework's status as solid precedent, one also encounters periodic grumbling from commentators and litigants about the wisdom and consequences of this legal construct. For example, while the law is clear that speech on matters of public concern made privately to one's supervisor or to colleagues through institutional channels is entitled to as much constitutional protection as speech on public matters disseminated in a highly visible manner to a broad audience,[67] the heavy first-stage emphasis on the public nature of speech may induce faculty to shape the content, form, and context of their statements to be *more* public in order to enhance their freedom of participation in university affairs. But since the more public the remark, the greater is its potential for polarizing an academic community, the law may somewhat perversely promote disruption, thereby poorly serving academic interests and needs. Some commentators also argue that the standard legal analysis is not sufficiently sensitive to "the vital participatory role professors may play in shared-governance systems or the constructive impact that speech about 'institutional concerns' may have on institutional operations over the long haul."[68] And at least one scholar has contended that faculty speech on intra-university matters should not be subject to the "public concern/balancing test" approach at all, instead separating academic freedom in institutional affairs (which should be extremely broad, premised upon professional norms, and enforced by contract) from free speech under the First Amendment.[69] Nevertheless, one can reliably assume that courts will view faculty speech on college or university affairs at state-actor institutions through this legal prism and that they will afford only limited protection to such speech in recognition of the legitimacy and power of countervailing claims of institutional efficiency and (ultimately) autonomy. Remember that at private institutions where constitutional guarantees of free expression are not operative (and legal doctrines derived from constitutional law are not directly applicable or binding), different results may obtain in accordance with local policies and practice. But even there, First Amendment jurisprudence and precedent will exert a powerful influence.

## Conferences and Symposia

Any discussion of faculty nonclassroom activities within the college or university community should address scholars' participation in another staple of academic life, the seminar or public conference—if only to point out the almost complete absence of legal guidance or authority in this area. On-campus conferences, sponsored by departments or schools and often open to the public as well as to scholars from all institutions, are a critical source of intellectual exchange (and a common locus for career advancement) for most faculty. The papers presented and ideas tested in this venue make for better scholarship and enlighten student and faculty attendees. Conferences also have the potential to generate considerable controversy for their host faculty and institutions—witness the brouhaha occasioned by a 1997 conference on women's sexuality at the State University of New York's New Paltz campus that included sessions on sadomasochism and sex toys. These intentionally provocative panels (which overshadowed a host of thoughtful discussions on more conventional academic questions) brought forth the ire of conservative politicians and activists, who alleged that public moneys should not be used to support such speech, as well as impassioned defenses of free speech and academic freedom (as we have seen, not necessarily the same thing) from civil libertarians and the conference's organizers.[70]

In looking at academic conferences from a legal perspective—and without case law to serve as helpful precedent—one must decide whether such a setting is best analogized to classroom instruction, to independent scholarship, to discussions within the university community on matters of local import, or to faculty participation in debates in the "outside world"—or, alternatively, whether conferences are sui generis and require an entirely new set of governing principles.[71] Perhaps somewhat surprisingly, given the ubiquity of symposia, this is a largely open area of university law. I would argue that the wisest course to follow is to view conferences as an expanded (and in some ways more sustained and intense) version of classroom instruction and that the legal rules applicable to faculty as teachers offer the best guidance to participating persons and institutions. Conferences share features with a variety of faculty activities, not matching perfectly with any, but they are closest to advanced graduate seminars, where one shares ideas with—and one's work may in turn be tested by—protocolleagues (i.e., students and postdocs who will shortly assume faculty positions) and any departmental peers who attend. Conferences are too focused on arcane academic topics to be treated like free-wheeling discussions about faculty governance or public events. And frankly, I think we should resist creating new rules for every situation.

The strongest alternative to analogizing conferences and symposia to graduate teaching seminars is to regard them as a more public version of individual scholarship. Under this approach, courts (as well as institutional administrators and colleagues) should recognize that the type and level of faculty participation in such events is largely a matter of professorial choice. For example, faculty receive specific teaching assignments each semester but are not usually required to attend or present at conferences.[72] Those who decide to participate in conferences select their own topics, just as they do when writing articles or books (which of course often grow out of conference papers). In contrast to the duties owed tuition-paying students, presenters at symposia owe no obligations to attendees (other than observing basic rules of academic ethics such as behaving civilly and engaging in honest intellectual colloquy with questioners). Conferences may thus entail a less defined role for faculty than teaching and, conversely, a less directive role for employer institutions.

But there are also real problems with this research analogy. To begin with, presenters do have explicit obligations (often contractual in form) to conference organizers: for example, to attend the event (especially if the presenter has received an honorarium or the organizer is paying for travel and accommodations); to actually present a paper; and to present a paper on the general topic that is expected (here the similarity to course content becomes clear). When, as is often the case, the "organizer" of the event is the faculty member's own department, school, or institution, these obligations become especially hard to distinguish from teaching duties. And although a faculty member's preparing *for* a conference may involve independent scholarship, once he or she arrives at the opening session, the context and expectations change in important ways. As opposed to being closeted in a library or laboratory, the presenter is now a public representative of his or her institution (almost certainly listed as such in the conference program), much in the manner of a teacher who is paid by an employer college or university to deliver instruction in front of a class.[73] Like a classroom (and unlike individual research), conferences are relatively structured, with an expectation of dialogue and pointed questioning.

Taking all of the foregoing into account, faculty participation in conferences and symposia is best treated as an expanded version of teaching, wherein faculty will legitimately require (and should receive) even more intellectual latitude than they enjoy in a regular classroom.[74] From this starting point, I would conclude that as cases arise about conferences, faculty will be accorded broad leeway in selecting paper topics (provided again that the topic fits within the conference's rubric and is generally consistent with any subject that may have been agreed upon in advance). The content and style of a presentation, including the underlying theoretical approach, should also be left to the presenter. At the same time, however, presenters should be considerate of conference attendees' views and respectful of their questions—much like course instructors. In short, the law should give faculty as seminar participants all the autonomy they need to derive maximum benefit from such programs.

One might ask from whom faculty need academic freedom in a conference setting? I believe the answer includes administrators and faculty peers at one's home institution (who may take issue with the very occurrence of the conference, the faculty member's participation in it, or the content of what he or she presents); the conference organizers (who, especially if they are officials at the faculty member's own school, have an opportunity to stifle undesirable content); conference attendees (whose negative reaction to a proposed or actual presentation could chill speech); and perhaps even the general public (if the conference is sufficiently notorious to generate extra-university criticism). Of course, many of these parties will be able to assert their own claims of academic freedom to attack or defend the substance of the conference. This raises further analytical questions that are beyond the scope of this book but nevertheless deserve attention. For instance, if the conference organizers are faculty members, are they exercising individual or collective academic freedom in shaping and putting on the event? If the latter, how is this collective academic freedom conceptually different from *institutional* academic freedom, sometimes invoked to restrict the activities of individual faculty? (Not very, in my view.) Does the academic freedom of the organizers trump the academic freedom of individual participants or attendees? It will be fascinating to see how the law here develops over time.

## Academic Freedom at Religiously Affiliated Colleges and Universities

Before leaving the topic of faculty autonomy as a member of a college or university community, we should touch briefly on the extent of faculty independence at the hundreds of religiously affiliated colleges and universities in the United States. At these institutions, community membership entails distinctive opportunities, rights, and responsibilities.

A detailed examination of the legal principles operative at such schools is beyond the scope of this volume.[75] In most instances, the rules articulated and case law promulgated in the secular setting translate quite well into the denominational environment. This is fitting because in many respects religiously affiliated colleges and universities are very similar to their secular counterparts. Faculty conduct scholarship on topics of their choosing, teach, and play a vital role in institutional governance and defining campus culture. Students prepare for careers in nonreligious disciplines such as business, engineering, law, and biological science. Administrators (most of whom are laypersons) worry about tuition policy, fund-raising, and legal requirements. Alumni obsess about the institution's visibility and the success of its athletic teams. Yet from time to time on critical dimensions the institution's core religious mandate reasserts itself, cutting through secular trappings and practices to distinguish such colleges and universities from their sometime peers.

First, religiously affiliated colleges and universities are not state actors. Like private secular institutions, they are not bound by the First Amendment's guarantee of free speech. They also enjoy an additional level of protection from government interference in that same amendment's guarantee of the free exercise of religion.[76] Actions by legal authorities that impede a religious college or university's operations may well violate the sponsoring denomination's (and members') right to observe their beliefs. Hence, in the employment context, courts regularly uphold the ability of religiously controlled colleges and universities to hire only members of the relevant faith for positions involving ministerial functions or the exegesis and propagation of that faith (but not for entirely nonreligious jobs such as department secretary). The primary federal employment discrimination statute, Title VII, expressly authorizes such preferences.[77] Thus, *Maguire v. Marquette Univ.*[78] recognized the Roman Catholic university's right to deny a position in its theology department to a female scholar whose public views and teachings on abortion contradicted Church doctrine. There is also substantial authority that federal labor law for collective bargaining does not apply to religiously affiliated colleges and universities.[79]

A pastoral emphasis permeates student life at such institutions, with interesting consequences. A large percentage of the enrolled students, of course, typically observe the sponsoring faith.[80] Beyond this, though, the school's explicitly religious character furnishes a legally sound justification for student conduct regulations (e.g., no alcohol consumption; no coed dorms) and student discipline. An intention to provide for the moral instruction of students also extends to the classroom, where it may come into direct conflict with secular faculty norms and expectations. Denominational colleges and universities will successfully argue that they must be allowed to ensure that classroom teaching advances the religiously oriented educational goals of the institution. This may not have much impact on, say, a German class. But insistence on presenting dogma about moral and appropriate thought and behavior could dramatically reshape the study of philosophy or political theory.

When faculty assertions of in-class academic freedom collide with doctrinal interpretations and requirements at religiously affiliated institutions, faculty invariably lose. The need to provide instruction consistent with church teachings and the overt assumption of responsibility for the moral well-being of students dramatically strengthen the legal hand of administrators, giving them an additional series of arguments upon which to justify their actions.[81] *Curran v. Catholic University* rejected the plaintiff professor's argument that he had an academic freedom right (grounded in both contract law and scholarly custom) to teach theology at the university notwithstanding Church action rendering him ineligible to offer such instruction.[82] From Curran's perspective, the university was punishing him because of his unorthodox beliefs on an academic subject, which he would presumably share with students in class. But the court held that Curran's employment contract implicitly obligated him to comply with teaching requirements emanating from the Vatican. Similarly, in *Killinger v. Samford Univ.*,[83] a federal court refused to consider a faculty member's claim of religious discrimination. He alleged that the school had denied him the opportunity to teach certain courses because institutional authorities objected to his theological and philosophical positions. But since Samford was a religiously controlled institution that could hire faculty entirely on the basis of their doctrinal purity, the court found it had no jurisdiction. Class content, teaching method, and theoretical approach can thus all be under the scrutiny and control of university and church officials.

Beyond the classroom, in their capacity as scholars, faculty at religiously affiliated colleges and universities may learn the hard way that theological purity trumps conventional secular notions of academic freedom. Researchers at such institutions have jeopardized their positions by undertaking critical analyses of church actions or doctrines.[84] Consider, for example, the case of faculty at Brigham Young University. BYU, which is wholly owned by the Mormon Church, "defines itself as having a unique religious mission and as pursuing knowledge in a climate of belief."[85] Consciously balancing what it sees as a need for both individual and institutional academic freedom, the university reserves the right to restrict faculty behavior or expression that "seriously and adversely" affects BYU's mission or the Church, including speech that "contradicts or opposes . . . fundamental Church doctrine or policy; [or] deliberately attacks or derides the Church or its general leaders."[86] Recently the university has also begun to require that Mormon faculty be certified by church officials as eligible for temple privileges as a condition of employment.[87] School officials—and undoubtedly many faculty and students—maintain that as a consequence of its religious character, "for those who embrace the gospel, BYU offers a far richer and more complete kind of academic freedom than is possible in secular universities."[88]

Over the last few years Brigham Young has moved aggressively to ensure that faculty scholars do not impugn the teachings or reputation of the Church. Individuals studying the subject of Mormonism itself, as well as feminist and postmodern approaches to literature, have apparently received special scrutiny. In the view of the American Association of University Professors (AAUP), a prominent faculty watchdog and collective bargaining organization, BYU has been the site of a "widespread pattern of infringements on academic freedom in a climate of oppression and fear of reprisals."[89] So, for example:

— in rejecting a continuing appointment for a feminist professor of English, BYU's academic vice president questioned whether the concept of gender in her book project "contradicted 'fundamental Church doctrine that men and women have different roles'";[90]

— an assistant professor of anthropology who "espoused current phenomenological trends within the discipline" was criticized—and ultimately not reappointed—for employing "field work, participant observation, and 'individual reflexive description' rather than traditional empirical methods." According to the AAUP, the "subject matter . . . [of] his research ('Mormon sexuality,' 'a critique of problems within the Mormon cultural system,' Latin American perceptions of Mormon missionary efforts . . . as 'imperialistic') appears to have incurred the hostility of significant segments of the faculty, administration and board";[91] and

— a creative writing teacher whose dark and sometimes violent short stories (not required reading for his classes) disturbed some students was told by the university's provost that such fiction "was not appropriate for a Church University."[92]

In several of these (and in other similar) instances, Brigham Young authorities, including department chairs and faculty review panels, also expressed concern about the teaching and citizenship of the faculty members in question. This serves to reinforce the point that at many religiously affiliated colleges and universities, denominational concerns can profoundly shape the faculty experience.[93]

In its "1940 Statement of Principles on Academic Freedom and Tenure," the AAUP recommends that "limitations of academic freedom because of religious or other aims of the institution should be clearly stated in writing at the time of appointment."[94] This desire to preserve the broadest possible scope of faculty academic freedom at religiously affiliated institutions has brought the AAUP into frequent conflict with such entities; as of this writing, almost half of the colleges and universities on the AAUP's censure list are religious, including—as a recent addition—Brigham Young.[95]

Heeding the First Amendment separation of church and state, judicial authorities have been reluctant to delve into controversies about religious doctrine or church governance at denominational colleges and universities. Of course, when no religious questions are implicated, courts will become involved just as in other employment disputes. In order to encourage such judicial abstention, some commentators have suggested that religiously affiliated institutions specify through expansive provisions in their faculty contracts and other relevant policies that church law or religious doctrine will be binding on the parties.[96] Perhaps this is even the logical conclusion of the path opened by the AAUP "limitations clause" discussed above. But such a strategy, while legally acceptable, might foolishly undercut faculty recruitment. Many first-rate scholars will not want to join a university where they are told in a heavy-handed way, even before their arrival, that they will at all times be subject to the dictates and (perhaps anti-intellectual) judgments of religious leaders.

Tension between a desire to function as other universities do, with a free-wheeling and open scholarly environment, and the need to remain true to the tenets of the institution's founding faith is particularly acute at Catholic universities with national reputations such as Notre Dame or Georgetown that aspire to a place in the front rank of American higher education. At such institutions, the tradition of faculty scholarly achievement is strong (and growing stronger). Equally strong, however, is the

Church's central authority and its record of promulgating and enforcing doctrine that touches upon academic matters. This inherent conflict came to the fore during the development of episcopal guidelines for implementing a 1990 Papal decree on the relationship between the Church and its universities worldwide. In November 1999 the National Conference of Catholic Bishops overwhelmingly endorsed a set of measures to strengthen the religious character of America's 230-plus Catholic colleges and universities. Under these new guidelines, presidents of such institutions should be Catholics who publicly declare their commitment to the Church. To the extent possible, Catholics should also hold a majority of faculty positions and trustee slots. Most controversial, Catholic instructors of theology at these institutions will now be required to obtain an official approval or "mandatum" from their local bishop that they are teaching "authentic Catholic doctrine."[97] While the bishops recognized that the Church had no operational control over most Catholic colleges and even endorsed the colleges' autonomy and academic freedom, such institutions are nevertheless unlikely to flout the dictates of the Church from which they draw their strength and of which they view themselves as a part. The adoption of these guidelines leaves little doubt that Church authorities intend to have the decisive voice in ongoing debates about what it means for an American college or university to maintain a Catholic identity. Of course, a similar potential for conflict over faculty autonomy is present to some extent at all religiously controlled institutions.

## Concluding Thoughts

My goal in this chapter has been to show how the law recognizes the value and importance of, and therefore supports, productive faculty involvement in institutional governance and operations. The rules regulating faculty participation in the life of their home institutions provide one of the sharpest examples of the public-private dichotomy fundamental to higher education law: at private colleges and universities, faculty speech as an institutional citizen is governed by contract (and in theory can be tightly constrained, as at some religiously affiliated schools); but at state-actor colleges and universities, intra-institutional speech is protected by the First Amendment (as well as by local agreements and custom). The powerful example of constitutional law jurisprudence, however, should not be underestimated even in the private sector. Most private institutions in fact afford their faculty considerable freedom of speech and input on intramural affairs.

The law in this domain is relatively well settled, consisting of basic contract principles and especially a four-step First Amendment analysis (Was the challenged speech on a matter of public concern? Where does the balance fall between the professor's right to comment and the university's interest in smooth and efficient administration? If such balance favors the faculty member, was the protected speech the basis for an adverse employment decision? And finally, would the employer institution have taken the same action even in the absence of such speech?). It should be apparent to readers that legal determinations under this four-step test will be so fact-specific as to make general predictions difficult, especially when it comes to classifying the subject matter of speech as public or private and to balancing individual and corporate interests.

Lawsuits over intra-institutional speech (or, more precisely, over alleged institutional responses *to* such speech) will continue to be legion. As colleges and universities redefine themselves and their missions in a rapidly changing world, faculty will aggressively assert and defend their prerogative (they would say their *responsibility*) to set an institution's direction and shape its destiny. Emphasizing the academic aspects of planning (e.g., setting admissions standards, connections between student body size and teaching load), they will equate untrammeled participation in local affairs with the autonomy required for excellent research and teaching, hoping for judicial endorsement of such linkage. I am skeptical, however, that administrators or courts will cede faculty such control over institutional governance.

I also anticipate interesting if painful disputes as America's Catholic colleges and universities struggle to reconcile local traditions of faculty independence (reinforced by the open milieu of higher education in this nation) with the preservation of their denominational link and character. Lastly, test cases on faculty speech in an academic conference setting would be most illuminating—but legal scholars, like courts, must make do with the cases that actually come to bar.

# 5  Faculty as Public Citizens

At some point in the day, of course, faculty take off the hats they wear as scholars, as instructors, and as members (and employees) of an academic institution with a special interest in its health and governance, to take up their basic role as citizens within the broader populace. In this capacity, faculty understandably expect broad rights to voice their opinions on issues both great and small. And as I explain below, with one important twist—stemming (somewhat perversely) from the faculty's successful and historic struggle to define itself as a self-regulating profession—college and university faculty *do* have enormous freedom in their extramural speech.

## Faculty Extramural Speech

There is a long and checkered history of conflict over the external speech and actions of faculty. Such behavior has periodically run afoul of administrators'—and especially trustees' and political authorities'—views of propriety, resulting in attempts (sometimes successful) to discipline or discharge faculty. For example, before the Civil War, there were instances of faculty at southern universities being dismissed for supporting the abolition of slavery. At the turn of the twentieth century, a prominent Stanford professor was fired for his political advocacy of free silver and especially for his fierce public opposition to Asian immigration. During World War I, faculty at more than one institution were discharged for not being properly supportive of the war effort. The McCarthy era witnessed the persecution of faculty for pro-Communist (or insufficiently anti-Communist) beliefs. And in more recent times it has been asserted that "political correctness" casts a pall of orthodoxy even over faculty members' extra-university views or speech. But notwithstanding these various trials and tribulations—and even occasional backward steps—American higher education institutions and higher education law have moved in the general direction of increased protection for faculty speech beyond the academy's walls.[1]

By now a solid body of First Amendment case law affirms that faculty at public colleges and universities enjoy the same freedom of speech as both (1) other nonacademic public employees and (2) citizens in general. Even if they wanted to, public authorities (including public university administrators) cannot muzzle faculty extramural speech. While in theory a private college or university could contractually obligate faculty to limit their outside (or even intra-university) speech as a condition of employment, almost all institutions choose instead to ensure broad protection for faculty speech, typically through academic freedom policies or statements that acquire binding force through inclusion in faculty handbooks or collective bargaining agreements. Private colleges and universities understand that they cannot attract the best scholars and teachers without guaranteeing an equal measure of freedom in this way. Institutional structure and governance, then, do not typically constrain faculty extramural speech.

A few examples of highly publicized disputes over faculty speech will demonstrate the wide latitude accorded professors' external utterances and expressive conduct. Consider the case of Michael Levin, a tenured professor of philosophy at City College, who incurred the wrath and enmity of administrators, faculty, and students at his institution through a series of public writings—all basically unrelated to his scholarship and teaching on philosophical subjects—in which he opposed affirmative action policies and argued that blacks were less intelligent than whites and more frequently committed crimes. When Levin's private views on these subjects become public, he was condemned by colleagues (including the institution's president) and his classes were repeatedly disrupted by student activists. Although City College had not received any complaints from students enrolled in Levin's classes alleging unfair or unequal treatment on the basis of race or asserting that his controversial views compromised his teaching, the college dean, over the objections of Levin and his department chair, established an alternative "shadow" section of a required introductory philosophy course being taught by Levin. This unprecedented step was justified as avoiding interference with classroom learning and harm to students, many of whom would be uncomfortable being taught by a professor who held such views.[2] With such a parallel course available, enrollment in Levin's section plummeted. The college's president also appointed a special investigatory committee to "review the question of when speech both in and outside the classroom may go beyond the protection of academic freedom or become conduct unbecoming a member of the faculty, or some other form of misconduct." This committee, whose charge tracked faculty disciplinary language in the college bylaws, was specifically asked to consider Levin's speech.[3] Fearful of losing his job, Levin curtailed his extramural speeches and writings on race differences.

Although the review committee ultimately concluded that faculty should not be subject to discipline for external speech—and that no charges should be brought against Levin—it did endorse administrative intervention (such as the creation of shadow sections) in response to statements that denigrate students' intellectual capacity, make it difficult for them to participate in class, or prophesy their poor academic performance. With the backing of colleagues who shared his concern about the chilling effect of such measures, Levin sued City College—and was quite correctly vindicated. The Second Circuit upheld the trial court's ruling that Levin's extramural speech was protected by the First Amendment. The college could not counter the professor's public expression of his privately held views with alternative sections or a special investigation. Such retaliation violated the "long-standing, indeed historic 'understanding,' officially promulgated and fostered by the College . . . that all teachers . . . shall be free of thought control outside the classroom."[4] Levin had been unconstitutionally stigmatized for his external remarks, with genuine damage to his professional standing, reputation, and future prospects within the academic community.[5] No matter how noxious Levin's opinions were to other members of that community, both the First Amendment and commonly shared notions of academic freedom permitted him to make such statements in his capacity as a public citizen.

Another example of faculty freedom in extramural speech and activity comes from *Trister v. University of Mississippi*,[6] upholding the right of part-time law faculty at Ole Miss also to work part time for a local social justice organization when not performing their university duties. In the heat of the civil rights movement, such legal activism by state employees raised the hackles of local attorneys, university trustees, and legislators. However, university officials could not prohibit this particular form of external activity when other, less controversial, part-time employment arrangements were countenanced. The plaintiff faculty had the right to represent on their own time clients of their own choosing—and by extension, in the course of such representation, to opine about civil rights in Mississippi. While (with the benefit of hindsight spanning the civil rights movement) the facts of *Trister* may seem to present an easy case today, the same result should obtain if faculty were, on their own time and independent of their university duties, working on behalf of the Nazi Party or some other widely reviled organization.[7]

In examining the rationale behind—and the breadth of—faculty freedom in extramural conduct, it is helpful to utilize once again the conceptual framework we have applied to other realms of faculty activity. Is faculty involvement in extra-institutional affairs central to the mission of a college or university? Surely the answer is no. By definition, faculty engage in such expression and behavior when *not* meeting university obligations. While such activity may be a natural outgrowth of scholarly interests and in turn may even shape one's intellectual perspective, it remains tangential to the daily work of scholarship, teaching, and institutional citizenship. Next, is there consensus within the academic community that such activity involves academic freedom and merits protection? Here, the answer is almost certainly yes. There is typically little dispute within the academy about the propriety of faculty being free to speak their minds outside of the confines of their jobs. Some would argue that freedom of extramural speech is part of the faculty's freedom to select topics for exploration (the border between intra-university and extra-university articulation of ideas being very hazy, as discussed below). Others assert that freedom of extramural speech stems from the First Amendment and that faculty qua faculty are simply swept within the ambit of a constitutional guarantee to all citizens. Whatever the rationale (and I find merit in both arguments), there is broad agreement that faculty should have considerable latitude in their role as informed (and informing) citizens. Granted, in cases that result in litigation, some disciplinary action has been taken or some limit on faculty speech set by the employer institution—unanimity on the wisdom and necessity of faculty freedom being elusive, if not unattainable. But even in circumstances in which a lawsuit challenges institutional sanctions, I would venture that such sanctions would be very unpopular, even among many senior administrators.

The final portion of our framework asks, "Who stands to benefit from a particular claim of academic freedom?" In the case of external faculty speech, the obvious answer is "the faculty." While we can imagine institutions drawing some advantage from such extramural activity (e.g., publicity for the school; enhanced ability to recruit independent-minded faculty), the real beneficiaries of such freedom are the individual scholar-citizens who may boldly—even provocatively—express their opinions on vital issues and participate fully in the political and intellectual life of the wider community.

Compiling the responses to our framework questions, we correctly conclude that courts and institutions will generally be quite deferential to faculty assertions of academic freedom in their capacity as public citizens. Indeed, the most meaningful limits on faculty extramural conduct stem from the scholarly profession's own mores and expectations about proper behavior and legitimate roles.[8]

Courts will analyze extra-university speech by faculty at state-actor institutions under the same four-step *Pickering/Connick* test used to review faculty speech on intra-university matters. Repeating and summarizing our previous description of that test:

1. The court will first make an initial determination of whether the faculty member's speech was on a matter of public concern.
2. If so, the court must balance the interests of the faculty member/citizen in commenting upon matters of public concern against the state's interest as an employer in the efficient delivery of quality education and related public service.
3. If this balance favors the faculty member, the plaintiff must then prove that his or her protected speech was a substantial or motivating factor in the negative employment decision under dispute.
4. Should the faculty plaintiff demonstrate such causation, the burden of proof shifts to the university employer to show that it would have reached the same decision even in the absence of the protected conduct.[9]

Free-speech purists may argue that because the *Pickering/Connick* analysis endorses a public employer placing limits on employee speech in certain circumstances, extending the use of that analytic framework to new settings could blur the distinction between the faculty member's role as institutional employee and representative and his or her role as citizen,[10] thereby beginning to legitimate government restraints on speech in inappropriate realms (i.e., regulation of a citizen's high-value speech about democratic governance).

While I certainly agree that these two personae are conceptually different, the wide topical range of faculty discourse and the varied locations in which it occurs make the distinction hard to maintain. Thus, one very practical reason why courts have chosen to use the same test for evaluating the

First Amendment status of faculty speech as an institutional citizen and speech as a public citizen is the permeable "border" between intramural and extramural speech. For example, the Vietnam War was certainly external to the academy and was a legitimate matter of concern to the entire populace. College campuses served as convenient public forums for anti-war activists—some of whom held faculty positions. But American foreign policy and events in Southeast Asia also had a direct impact on the daily internal life of colleges and universities, as students sought or lost deferments and as campus protests over institutional ties to the military-industrial complex disrupted regular academic functions. Faculty therefore surely had the right as members of the academic community to express opinions about the war's effect on the campus.

Examining both "internal" and "external" speech through the same conceptual lenses eliminates the problem of mischaracterizing speech that happens to combine both types or that lies on the cusp. A shared *Pickering/ Connick* approach likewise recognizes that faculty frequently become public intellectuals—and begin to comment on the issues of the day—by virtue of their university affiliations.[11] I would argue further that the specific elements of the *Pickering/Connick* balance between a citizen's interest in public commentary and the state's interest in smooth public administration (i.e., the closeness of the working relationship between the faculty member and those he or she criticizes; whether the speech impaired workplace discipline or harmony; whether the speech had a detrimental impact on the operation of the institution; and whether the performance of the faculty member's duties was impeded)[12] are sufficiently nuanced to let courts identify protected discourse under the First Amendment and to give broad leeway to citizen-oriented speech. And it seems to me that, as compared to embracing the *Pickering/Connick* test to review faculty's extramural speech, a far greater danger to free expression would arise from looser interpretation *of* that test (e.g., an increased willingness to find that speech interfered with workplace discipline). In any event, the *Pickering/Connick* test is the legal rubric that courts have adopted.

A good demonstration of the treatment accorded extramural speech is found in *Aumiller v. University of Delaware,* where the plaintiff sought to differentiate his views and actions as an individual from those as an institutional representative. Aumiller, an openly gay man, was a lecturer and faculty advisor to a recognized student group known as the Gay Community. Delaware's president refused to renew his employment contract after he was quoted in several newspaper articles describing gay life at the university. In his successful suit alleging a violation of First Amendment rights, Aumiller proved that in interviews with reporters, he spoke—as was his right—as a public citizen (and in specific instances as a faculty advisor) and that he had neither disrupted university operations nor implied through false or misleading statements that Delaware encouraged homosexuality.[13] The *Pickering* balance thus favored Aumiller's expression of personal views over the state university's interest in avoiding unfavorable publicity.

A more recent case on point is *Hoover v. Morales*, which struck down as unconstitutional policies preventing Texas A&M professors from serving as expert witnesses or consultants to parties opposing the State of Texas in litigation. The Fifth Circuit had little difficulty finding that the first prong of the *Pickering/Connick* test was satisfied, since the prohibited faculty speech (including proposed expert testimony on the effects of tobacco use for defendant cigarette manufacturers in the state's suit against such companies) clearly addressed matters of public concern.[14] The professors also prevailed under the second prong's weighing of individual versus state interests, with the court "not see[ing] how the expert testimony of the faculty-member plaintiffs in this case will adversely affect the efficient delivery of educational services by the institutions in which these faculty members serve."[15] Having met their third prong burden of proving causation (under the disputed policies, offering hostile testimony would result in the suspension of salary), and with no possible argument from A&M or Texas officials that these overly broad policies did not seek to block speech contrary to state interests, the plaintiffs properly emerged victorious. Furthermore, the state policies violated the First Amendment as content-based restrictions on expression (only those witnesses who opposed the State of Texas were muzzled).

However, while *Hoover* and the other cases discussed above show the typical pattern of professors successfully asserting their right to free speech as public citizens, faculty interests are sometimes trumped by institutional needs. Take *Jeffries v. Harleston*,[16] which in many respects is an uncanny counterpoint to *Levin v. Harleston*. At the same time Michael Levin was offending the City College community with antiblack remarks, his fellow faculty member Leonard Jeffries (chair of the Black Studies Department) was making public statements—in his extramural role as a consultant to the State Education Department—vilifying whites, especially Jews. Jeffries's racist remarks made him a laughingstock in serious academic circles and unleashed a cascade of bad publicity on the college. When the City University of New York (CUNY) board voted to remove him as chair, he sued, alleging a violation of his right to free speech. A convoluted chain of litigation ensued, including trial and appellate verdicts for Jeffries that were vacated by the U.S. Supreme Court, eventually resolving in the college's favor. On remand, the Second Circuit found that a full *Pickering/Connick* analysis supported the college's actions. Although Jeffries's speech addressed matters of public concern (school curricula and the historic oppression of blacks), a majority of the CUNY board reasonably believed that his speech would disrupt the college. Most critically, the potential interference with college operations outweighed the First Amendment value of Jeffries' speech. The court agreed with CUNY's contention that he had been demoted because of the disruption his speech caused, not in retaliation for the particular content of that speech.[17]

It is undeniably difficult to square the final holding in *Jeffries* with that in *Levin*. (I would probably have struck a different *Pickering* balance in favor of Jeffries.) My read is that Professor Jeffries's notoriety, which exceeded Professor Levin's, made it easier for the court to find a unpalatable level of disruption in his case, while City College's blatant and ad hominem interference with Levin's courses (especially given the absence of prior complaints about his teaching) made the philosophy professor a more sympathetic figure. Of course, cynics will argue that judges more readily excuse white racism than black racism. In any event, both cases show that courts will employ the *Pickering/Connick* approach in evaluating faculty members' public statements.

In the application of this standard approach, the physical location of the expressive activity may be decisive. Speech about matters external to the academy can occur on campus, off campus, or blend from one into the other (the same is also true for speech about internal university affairs). Thus, in *Starsky v. Williams*,[18] the constitutionally protected extramural speech of a Arizona State faculty-member-cum-activist included both a public address at the cross-state University of Arizona protesting student arrests there and the on-campus distribution of materials describing the rationale behind student unrest at Columbia (such informational materials not calling for any action at ASU).[19] In an opinion that predates the crystallization of the *Pickering/Connick* analysis, Starsky's termination was invalidated and his freedom to speak as a concerned citizen on the issues of the day was upheld. According to the trial court, the Arizona Board of Regents had "confuse[d] constitutionally protected criticism with disrespect."[20] But while Starsky's behavior hardly roiled Arizona State, on-campus faculty statements about vital social and political issues *do* have special potential to disrupt colleges and universities. In this setting administrators and trustees can more persuasively argue that the individual citizen's right to expression must yield to the need for a smoothly functioning academic institution. Such claims typically wilt when applied to off-campus conduct by the same faculty.[21]

It is also important to appreciate that while First Amendment precedent affords faculty considerable freedom in their extra-university activities, professional norms and traditions *within* the academy set even higher standards for—or, depending on one's perspective, impose additional restrictions upon—faculty conduct. Such self-regulation is probably the most effective check on harmful or inconsiderate extramural behavior.

To understand why this is so, we must first recognize that faculty are expected, both by themselves and by their institutions, to function as public intellectuals. It is also anticipated that such activity may take them far from the confines of the academy. Especially at public colleges and universities, the institutional mission of service is fulfilled in part by having professors share the products of their scholarship and make themselves available to the broader community as an academic resource. The news media and citizenry regularly rely on faculty expertise, and scholars' opinions are invested with extra weight because of the years of difficult study and careful reflection that presumably underlie their formulation. At the same time, those views also gain credibility and heft through their association with the faculty member's home institution, which may have its own considerable stature.[22] Most people will listen respectfully to the views of any university professor (even outside his or her narrow field of interest) but will show additional deference to the remarks of a *Harvard* professor. Fully appreciative of such marquee value, faculty do not hesitate to wrap themselves in the mantle of an institution to generate a larger or better audience. And colleges and universities eagerly showcase their star scholars, both on and off campus. Individual professors and their employer colleges and universities thus mutually benefit from visible faculty involvement in wider society. Yet publicity—which burnishes reputations and creates new opportunities—is a double-edged sword that can also bring unwanted attention.

This duality sharpens the institution's interest in the content and tenor of faculty extramural speech and leads faculty to weigh the benefits and costs of institutional affiliation.

The American academic community's historic formulation of proper faculty extramural behavior (itself presaging the judicial balance between individual and institutional needs subsequently articulated in *Pickering*) is found in the AAUP's "1940 Statement of Principles on Academic Freedom and Tenure." As part of their early-twentieth-century struggle to define and protect faculty academic freedom, the AAUP's founders had to consider age-old problems presented by scholars' extramural conduct and reach accord with leading college and university administrators about what constituted appropriate faculty deportment. The eventual solution was to declare that

> the college or university teacher is a citizen, a member of a learned profession, and an officer of an educational institution. When he speaks or writes as a citizen, he should be free from institutional censorship or discipline, but his special position in the community imposes special obligations. As a man of learning and an educational officer, he should remember that the public may judge his profession and his institution by his utterances. Hence he should at all times be accurate, should exercise appropriate restraint, should show respect for the opinions of others, and should make every effort to indicate that he is not an institutional spokesman.[23]

This compromise language seeks to find equilibrium between faculty rights and faculty responsibilities.[24] It has been endorsed by scores of faculty and administrative groups and learned societies.

It has also been explicitly incorporated into collective bargaining and individual faculty employment agreements by many colleges and universities. And to the extent that these guidelines have become standard custom and practice within the academic community—something that the AAUP regularly asserts but that some institutions dispute—they *implicitly* bind all of higher education (at least in the absence of contrary local policies or disclaimers). Accordingly, in *Starsky v. Williams*, the Arizona Board of Regents professed to follow the 1940 Statement but, in the court's view, had unlawfully violated this standard when it discharged a faculty member for his off-duty speech.[25] In *Adamian v. Jacobsen*, a federal appellate court upheld the firing of an assistant professor at the University of Nevada at

Reno for leading a demonstration on nonuniversity matters (i.e., the invasion of Cambodia and the Kent State shootings) that disrupted a campus ceremony. University officials successfully argued that the faculty member's expressive conduct violated a section of the University Code mirroring the above-quoted portion of the 1940 Statement. The plaintiff questioned the constitutionality of such limits on his external speech, but the Ninth Circuit held that a breach of faculty decorum as described in the university policy constituted adequate cause for dismissal (relying in part, however, on supplemental AAUP interpretations of this language that narrowed administrative control over scholars' extramural remarks).[26] The AAUP language, then, was deemed by the court to be lawful and binding on the faculty and the institution.

Academic-freedom purists will correctly observe that the broadly accepted norms of the 1940 Statement require more circumspect behavior from faculty in their capacity as public citizens than is required of "ordinary" citizens under the First Amendment. While this may at first blush appear unfair (or suggest that faculty should eschew reliance on their internally developed rules in favor of constitutional safeguards), such rigorous expectations are consistent with the professoriate's traditional and enduring self-image as an independent guild. Like other learned professions that insist upon considerable self-governance (law and medicine come to mind), faculty are justified in setting (and adhering to) demanding standards.

To be sure, it was a far simpler matter to reach agreement on and enforce such standards when college and university faculties were more homogeneous in terms of race, gender, socioeconomic class, and political views. Even in 1940 there would have been wide agreement on what constituted "proper" or "respectful" behavior by faculty in their nonuniversity activities. It therefore comes as no surprise that, as faculties have grown more diverse and the courts have extended their reach into the academy, AAUP leadership has periodically revisited the hoary language of the 1940 Statement, offering new glosses that clarify (from the administrative perspective, that means expand!) the scope of extramural academic freedom.[27] However, these unilateral interpretations of faculty norms have not necessarily been adopted by the rest of the higher education community. Whether new language or old, though, the academy's internal controls clearly help direct and govern the external conduct of faculty.

As a final point in our discussion of extra-university faculty speech, we should note that electronic discourse over the Internet is raising fascinating new legal questions about when faculty speak as institutional representatives, when they speak as private persons, and whether there are circumstances in which an employer college or university has the right—or the responsibility—to limit a professor's speech in cyberspace. In theory, a faculty member–citizen should be just as free to speak electronically on matters of public concern as he or she would be to speak through other media. However, if the faculty member's electronic speech is made through university-owned and -operated computer facilities, if the faculty member uses a university Web address (perhaps resulting in voluminous responses *to* that address), or if the faculty member otherwise conveys the impression that he or she speaks as a university representative, institutional interests may be implicated and may have to be protected. With the worldwide distribution of information over the Web, the potential for misinformation or damage to a college or university's reputation is magnified.

For example, a Northwestern professor achieved notoriety for using the university's Internet server to maintain a home page that disseminated Holocaust denial tracts. However, because Northwestern did not prohibit its faculty, staff, or students from using campus computing facilities for personal business, since the professor in question (although identifying himself as a faculty member) had included on the controversial home page an express statement that the views expressed therein were not related to his position at Northwestern—and especially since the university was fiercely committed to open expression—the page was allowed to stand.[28]

Some other colleges and universities, in an attempt to avoid embarrassing situations, have taken a different approach and adopted policies mandating that institutional computers and dedicated Internet lines may only be used for official business.[29] At the very least, the AAUP suggests that "it may be appropriate to insist that special care be taken in posting or disseminating digital material, on a web page or site created and accessed through the campus computing system, to avoid or dispel any inference that the speaker represents the views of the institution or of faculty colleagues."[30] Any limitations on free expression imposed by state-actor colleges and universities must be carefully scrutinized. Content-neutral and broadly applicable restrictions on the personal use of institutional property (which could be justified by the need to preserve scarce resources such as computing lines) may well pass constitutional muster. Indeed, in *Urofsky v. Gilmore*,[31] a federal appellate court rejected a First Amendment challenge to a *non*-content-neutral Virginia law that barred state employees (including state university faculty) from using state-owned or state-leased computers to access sexually explicit material. The Fourth Circuit opined that Virginia had the authority to control how its employees discharged their duties (and presumably how they utilized state property), noting that the law in question provided an exception for viewing sexual material in conjunction with a bona fide and officially approved research project. Notwithstanding the result in *Urofsky*, I would maintain that content-based restrictions on electronic speech by public university faculty, or limits on faculty expression via private computers, are likely to be struck down.[32] In any event, it is certain that faculty speech in cyberspace will lead to future controversy and the development of new legal authority.

## Faculty Membership in Controversial Organizations

Closely related to the extra-university speech of faculty is the broad freedom enjoyed by individual professors, as citizens and on their own time, to join political and social organizations of their choice. These associational rights are also protected by the First Amendment (and reinforced by academic custom giving faculty wide latitude in their private affiliations). Faculty memberships in unpopular organizations implicate no core college or university activity. But as with free speech, this is an area in which the entire academic community will close ranks in support of professors' autonomy. Consensus is easily achieved here since today faculty affiliations are most likely to be attacked by parties outside the academy, such as local politicians. The net result is rock-solid precedent affirming the faculty's freedom of association, which is largely indistinguishable from that of the general citizenry. Professors at state-actor colleges and universities in particular have the same associational rights as all other public employees.

The most significant judicial buttress of scholars' freedom of association is the Supreme Court's 1967 opinion in *Keyishian v. Board of Regents*,[33] which struck down as overbroad and vague an intricate set of New York teacher loyalty laws and regulations designed to root out Communists in public education. Declaring in ringing tones that academic freedom had "transcendent value to all of us and not merely to the teachers" and that it was "a special concern of the First Amendment, which does not tolerate laws that cast a pall of orthodoxy over the classroom,"[34] the Court invalidated the dismissal of State University of New York faculty who had refused to sign certificates averring that they were not Communists. "Mere knowing membership without a specific intent to further the unlawful aims of an organization," said the Court, "is not a constitutionally adequate basis for exclusion from such [faculty] positions."[35]

Following the Supreme Court's lead in *Keyishian*, other tribunals have repeatedly upheld the faculty's freedom of association. In *Cooper v. Ross*, a history professor's membership in the Progressive Labor Party was deemed constitutionally protected, as was his right to inform students in class of his political affiliation and personal philosophical beliefs.[36] In *Ollman v. Toll*, litigation arose when the president of the University of Maryland rejected the proposed appointment of a Marxist to a department chairmanship. The federal trial court made it clear that "Marxist or Communist beliefs, like other political beliefs, are protected under the First and Fourteenth Amendments, and such beliefs or one's association with others holding them is protected activity for which a state may not impose civil disabilities such as exclusion from employment by a state university."[37] However, the faculty plaintiff had not shown (in line with the *Pickering/Connick* analysis used in external speech and association cases) that his extra-university political views and associations were a substantial or motivating factor in Maryland's negative hiring decision. Indeed, the university proved to the court's satisfaction that given the plaintiff's weak credentials for the chairmanship (e.g., he was only an associate professor with limited administrative and grant-writing experience), it would have reached the same decision even in the absence of his protected activity.[38]

The bottom line—consistent with the leeway they enjoy in extramural speech—is that faculty may feel very secure in their expansive associational rights. Like all other public citizens, professors may belong to and freely participate in the lawful activities of controversial political and social groups.

## Concluding Thoughts

We have examined the educational and public policy bases for, and the legal safeguards pertaining to, the extensive speech and associational rights faculty enjoy outside the confines of their regular university employment. Once again, the public-private distinction is key, with non-state-actor colleges and universities technically free to limit faculty expression in ways that would not be countenanced at public schools (although, as a practical matter, private institutions usually refrain from asserting such authority). Professors at state-actor universities, in contrast, enjoy free speech rights under the Constitution equivalent to all other citizens. Overlaying these basic principles of contract and First Amendment law are historic notions—often elevated to the status of professional norms—about the dignity of the professoriate and the responsibilities that follow from affiliation with a college or university (whose own reputation and health may be damaged by faculty speech). These norms about extramural expression lead faculty to behave in certain ways and give colleagues and employer institutions a lever to enforce "appropriate conduct."

This blend of constitutional precedent and local custom raises intriguing questions about the relationship between legal doctrine and traditional (nonlegal) conceptions of academic freedom. For instance, are the justifications for faculty autonomy in research and teaching equally relevant to extramural speech? My own view is that they probably are not. Do faculty occupy a special position in our society imposing upon them less—or, conversely, entitling them to more—freedom of expression than non-professors? Again, I would think not, arguing instead that all citizens should enjoy like freedom. But do faculty and institutional efforts to self-police external speech—using standards or assumptions that may reflect an earlier and very different professoriate—adequately protect faculty expression? There are indeed potentially serious flaws with homegrown (institution-specific or national) standards. Yet if scholars and universities rely just on First Amendment law to govern extramural faculty speech, the academy will have unwisely surrendered an important measure of its independence and distinctiveness. A better course would be to regularly question old assumptions about faculty responsibilities in order to develop (and then reinforce) a shared, university-wide commitment to updated norms.

Future litigation over faculty extramural speech (itself a category that can blur into speech about intra-university affairs) will surely present many of these policy and legal debates. An equally large area of controversy will be the attempted imposition of limits on faculty (and student) electronic speech, which frequently addresses extra-university affairs. The development of written or informal institutional policies on the "acceptable use" of university-owned or -supported computing facilities (addressing items such as control over the content of Web sites run on university servers; the acquisition and sharing of confidential personal information; the sending or receipt of threatening—or network-clogging—email; limits on access to sexually explicit or other objectionable material; and efforts to shield universities from liability for network users' violations of copyright laws, to name just a few)[39] will generate much angst and confusion, not to mention massive attorneys' fees.

# 6 Faculty as Employees

Up to this point in our analysis of the legal principles affecting faculty, we have focused on the changing roles that professors play as they move between the library or laboratory, the classroom, the faculty lounge, the campus green, and the local community. Through all of these peregrinations, though, faculty never cease to play another defining role: that of college or university employee. Faculty devotion to scholarship and teaching is both genuine and noble, but professors also draw paychecks for the provision of services. In this chapter I explore how employer-employee relationships between institutions and faculty shape the work of the professoriate.

There are, of course, innumerable ways to structure the responsibilities and privileges incident to a faculty appointment and to enforce the obligations that flow in both directions between professors and schools. Within the broad confines of applicable law (such as the constitutional protections we have discussed above and the nondiscrimination statutes reviewed below), the parties are primarily limited by their own imagination and flexibility. Contract law principles, and the actual content of the written and implied agreements that govern faculty employment, therefore assume critical importance. And although generalizations about how faculty are hired, evaluated, promoted, treated, disciplined, and discharged are inherently risky, the presence of (1) widely shared expectations about the terms and conditions of faculty jobs and (2) established custom within academe make it possible to describe and critique conventional aspects of the faculty employment relationship. Bearing all this in mind, let us examine some key legal questions facing faculty in their capacity as university employees, beginning with the appointment and promotion process.

## Hiring, Promotion, and Job Security

Litigation over faculty personnel decisions leads courts to consider the deference due to institutional judgments about a candidate's qualifications.

The need for such deference is not obvious. The activity at stake is undeniably central to the life and character of the university: in Justice Frankfurter's words from *Sweezy*, "determin[ing] on academic grounds who may teach."[1] Yet by definition there will be no consensus about adverse employment decisions. Scholars alleging impropriety in the rejection of a job application or the denial of tenure understandably take offense at the prospect that "institutional academic freedom" could shield such actions from attack, particularly since the content of the candidate's scholarship is itself meant to be protected by academic freedom. To the extent that academic freedom is recognized here, at first blush it appears to favor institutions to the detriment of individual faculty. But a more nuanced view of how academic personnel decisions are made supports the wisdom of deferring in most instances—as courts indeed do—to institutional judgments about faculty hiring and promotions.

Deference is warranted because the dominant actors by far in these personnel decisions are the current faculty of the relevant department or school. While chairs, deans, provosts, and presidents (themselves typically holders of faculty rank) must approve such actions, most of the critical steps in these processes—deciding whom to interview, whom to invite back for further consideration, whom to offer a position to, whom to reappoint, and whom to recommend for tenure—are largely controlled by the faculty of the affected unit. As the Third Circuit observed in *Kunda v. Muhlenberg*, "Although there may be tension between the faculty and the administration on their relative roles and responsibilities, it is generally acknowledged that the faculty has at least the initial, if not the primary, responsibility for judging candidates."[2]

Faculty therefore must and do have broad latitude to draw conclusions about the quality of another scholar's research and teaching and to express those views, even vehemently, in the context of a job search or promotion or tenure review. This properly reflects the fact that only faculty have the requisite specialized knowledge to evaluate a candidate's work—although the use of external reviews by noted scholars in the same field can provide a critical measure of quality and a safeguard against self-interested or short-sighted decisions. Such freedom is also tightly bound up with a faculty member's right to critique the work of *any* scholar in his or her field, regardless of whether such criticism is formally solicited as input for a personnel action. Finally, faculty dominance in this realm is consistent with the historic, guildlike nature of the faculty. By tradition the faculty is an independent, corporate body, which like other professions has the right to self-regulate.[3] Indeed, faculty will zealously defend their right to make independent assessments of peers' work. In one celebrated instance, a professor at the University of Georgia went to jail rather than revealing how he had voted in a tenure case![4]

Of course, in speaking of "faculty" decisions about appointments and promotions, it is sometimes necessary to distinguish between opinions expressed by individual scholars and the collective view of faculty peers in a department or school (typically expressed through a unitwide vote or through delegation to a committee). All faculty enjoy considerable freedom in articulating their personal opinions of another scholar's research or teaching. These individual faculty evaluations are then weighed against each other at each step in the hiring or promotion process, with no assurance that a particular scholar's view will prevail over those of colleagues within the same field. However, the collective judgment of the faculty, if driven by legitimate academic concerns, will receive much deference from local administrators in the first instance and ultimately from the courts.

## Tenure Systems: Structure, Purposes, and Consequences

With due appreciation for the centrality of the current faculty's scholarly judgments in determining the future composition and intellectual thrust of an institution's faculty, we may now examine how the unique legal and cultural concept of tenure commonly shapes a faculty member's relationship with his or her employer institution, colleagues, and students. Not all American colleges and universities have tenure systems, and of course many faculty at institutions with such systems do not enjoy tenure—but tenure's influence is so profound that no administrator or faculty member should fail to understand what tenure (or its absence) means in terms of the faculty's daily work and longer-term career expectations. Recognizing that tenure systems may vary widely, from a legal and policy perspective what are the constructs of tenure, what purposes does it serve, and what are its consequences?

Let us start with what tenure is. The best and most widely accepted definition of tenure remains the AAUP's 1940 Statement, which describes tenure as a formal employment relationship whereby, after the expiration of a limited probationary period, faculty have a right to permanent or continuous employment that can only be terminated for adequate (i.e., good) cause or under extraordinary circumstances because of financial exigencies.[5] For those not intimately familiar with the mechanics of tenure (and again, one must be cautious about generalizations that mask institutional differences), under a typical tenure system, at an appointed time in a faculty member's career, he or she will be asked to submit a dossier of materials (a curriculum vitae, copies of publications and works in progress, accounts of service to the university and the broader community, plans for future work, and the like) that make a case for the award of tenure. Very frequently and significantly, external reviews of the candidate's credentials are solicited from distinguished scholars in relevant disciplines at other institutions. The employer institution will add to this file the results of standardized teaching evaluations and materials from any annual or periodic reviews of the candidate conducted at earlier points in his or her probationary period (e.g., evaluations for reappointment). The employer may also seek additional information about a candidate's teaching from individual students or in-class observations. All of these items are carefully examined by faculty peers in the relevant department(s) or school. (Reviews may be conducted by one or more subgroups before presentation to a larger body; at some institutions a colleague is assigned the role of advocate.) Based on their assessment of the candidate's past record of research, teaching, and service and his or her future prospects, faculty peers vote either for or against tenure. Note, however, that even in the face of favorable external evaluations of a candidate's scholarship, faculty at the home institution still make the critical call on whether to award tenure. Thus, Wesleyan University prevailed in a recent lawsuit by a former assistant professor of government alleging that he had been unfairly denied tenure when his department rejected recommendations from specialists in his subfields (Western European politics and employment relations) that his work deserved tenure.[6] After this initial peer vote, further approvals are sought from a lengthy chain of academic and administrative actors attuned to school-wide or institution-wide needs and concerns: the department chair, the dean, the provost, and the institution's president. Somewhere along this line it is also common (and I believe wise) for a cross-disciplinary faculty group to add its recommendations. At the end of the process, continuous appointment is formally awarded, typically by the college or university's board of trustees.

Each college or university will establish distinct criteria for awarding tenure. Obviously, more significant scholarship will be expected for a permanent appointment at a research university than at a community college that emphasizes teaching. Private institutions may discount applied research (e.g., solving problems for business or government) in ways that would not be countenanced at a land-grant institution with a tradition of service to its state. Even within a particular college or university, there may be differences in tenure requirements and processes between individual schools and departments. Thus, teacher education and social work may focus on practice-oriented inquiry and activity rather than theoretical research;[7] and the law school may grant tenure on the basis of one or two journal articles, while humanities departments insist upon one or two completed books. Though these discipline-driven, intra-institutional variations may be understandable, they nevertheless introduce a potential legal vulnerability. It could be very difficult for a college or university to convince a court why one unit is so much more rigorous than others in awarding tenure. Deans and provosts therefore seek to raise tenure standards to the highest common denominator.

Furthermore, tenure criteria may change over time—for example, becoming more rigorous or placing more weight on a candidate's scholarship as a particular institution seeks to bolster its reputation for research or a department emphasizes a new intellectual thrust. Thus, in *Banerjee v. Bd. of Trustees*, Smith College's implementation of higher tenure standards that reflected both local aspirations and changes in the market for hiring faculty was deemed entirely legitimate.[8] College and university tenure decisions will also be driven in part by local finances (i.e., whether the institution can currently afford to make such a long-term commitment).

The AAUP quite consciously views tenure as "a means to certain ends—specifically, (1) freedom of teaching and research and of extramural activities and (2) a sufficient degree of economic security to make the profession attractive to men and women of ability."[9] Considerable numbers of higher education organizations[10] and individual colleges and universities have formally endorsed the AAUP's 1940 Statement (often along with its subsequent interpretations), incorporating it in faculty handbooks or policy statements that give it the force of law as part of an institution's employment contract with individual faculty. Furthermore, as we have seen, even institutions that have not adopted (or have not expressly disclaimed) this Statement could become bound by it should courts accept AAUP's contention that it represents standard custom and practice within academe.[11]

The 1940 Statement declares that the pretenure probationary period should not exceed seven years and that a college or university should give a faculty member at least one year's prior notice if he or she is not going to be retained after the end of that period.[12] This is why faculty at many institutions come up for tenure in their sixth year, leaving room for a terminal one-year appointment if necessary. As discussed at length later in this chapter, the 1940 Statement also mandates that a faculty member being stripped of tenure for cause is entitled to detailed notice of the charges against him or her and a rather formal hearing before a faculty committee, and that terminations for financial exigency must not be a subterfuge for other, illegitimate, reasons. Of course, since AAUP policies are not automatically binding, there are wide procedural variations across the higher education landscape. For example, at some elite private research universities (a group that has often demurred at adopting AAUP guidelines), tenure is not awarded until eight or ten years of service, and it is linked to promotion to full professor rather than associate professor. Whatever the local requirements for assembling and reviewing a tenure dossier, the faculty, chairs, deans, and other administrators involved in the effort should carefully follow each procedural link in the chain, no matter how minor, because a failure to do so will be an invitation to litigation.

Our discussion of the legal structure of tenure systems must be premised upon an understanding of why tenure exists and how well it serves its intended purposes. Proponents of tenure systems argue that

— Tenure is the linchpin of academic freedom and, through such freedom, essential advances in scholarship and human knowledge. The guarantee of tenure allows faculty to explore confidently topics of their choosing, to pursue inquiries wherever they may lead, and to share their conclusions in writing or in the classroom, all without fear of employment recrimination. Tenured professors, by their example of independence and their willingness to defend the autonomy of junior faculty, also help safeguard the academic freedom of non-tenured colleagues.

— In a related vein, the presence of tenure assures a public interested in the fruits of scholarship that faculty are honestly voicing their opinions and not trying to curry favor with vested interests in society, on the college or university's board, or within their discipline.

— As the AAUP freely admits, tenure is a tool to attract talented people to the professoriate. In the current economy, tenure represents an extraordinarily high level of job security, to which many persons attach substantial value, and thus it compensates in part for the disparities between academic salaries and the remuneration available in other fields. From a selfish institutional perspective, tenure therefore helps to keep down salary costs and to check destructive financial competition for faculty. (Of course, it can also be criticized for these very reasons.)

— Somewhat more altruistically, tenure permits faculty to concentrate their energies on research and teaching, rather than on base economic incentives. One wonders, however, whether this is really true, given the energy and burgeoning skill many faculty demonstrate in marketing their research and the encouragement—or pressure—they encounter from employer institutions to do so.

— A substantial cadre of tenured faculty promotes institutional stability, enhances shared governance, and builds collegiality and esprit de corps.

— The permanence (and thus importance) of tenure also forces colleges and universities to make hard but necessary choices about the quality of faculty performance, intellectual areas that require investment, and who they can truly afford to keep. While other mechanisms might serve these same purposes, the need to make "up or out" tenure decisions instills a vital element of rigor into institutional academic planning.

In contrast, critics of tenure identify a host of undesirable consequences that may flow from tenure systems and deep-seated flaws in the tenure process itself:

— Tenure imposes an inflexible financial burden on the employer college or university, which unfairly limits its ability to meet changing pedagogical and intellectual needs. For example, by calcifying the faculty ranks, tenure decreases colleges' and universities' ability to recruit and develop younger faculty, especially women and minority scholars, who are underrepresented in the academy. This cost is felt most keenly in parlous financial times, when new faculty slots are at a premium.

Likewise, some have argued that tenure is intellectually hidebound. It perpetuates traditional departments and disciplinary paradigms while devaluing (if not excluding outright) new or unorthodox fields and scholarship. To protect against this very real danger, members of appointments and promotions committees must always be prepared to question the theoretical foundations of their own work.

— Tenure's "guarantee" of lifetime employment can encourage—and certainly protects—mediocre or half-hearted performance. Tenure causes acute frustration when it blocks institutions from easily removing incompetent, destructive, or "deadwood" faculty unless there has been strict compliance with expensive, time-consuming, and cumbersome discharge requirements.[13]

— Because tenure systems tend disproportionately to recognize and reward excellence in research (which is often more easily appraised than pedagogical skill), they may erode the importance and quality of teaching, especially undergraduate teaching, which is less likely to be related to a faculty member's scholarship.

— Another flaw of tenure systems is that they force colleges and universities to make too-quick (and essentially permanent) judgments on the quality of a junior colleague's work and his or her intellectual promise. This places new faculty under too much pressure, too soon.[14] Institutions might respond by extending the probationary period, but that would run afoul of AAUP norms and open the door to exploitatively long "apprenticeships."

— Opponents of tenure allege that tenure systems generate large numbers of grievances and lawsuits—though it seems debatable whether other employment structures would work more smoothly in this litigious age.

— Critics of an egalitarian stripe complain that tenure is undemocratic because it concentrates power in the hands of senior faculty with permanent appointments. In order to win tenure, some junior faculty may feel pressured to tailor their intellectual views to match (or at least not to offend) those of senior colleagues, thereby defeating the whole point of academic freedom. A closely aligned (and also antielitist) argument holds that since all faculty require academic freedom in their work, tenure is not a precondition of such freedom and should be uncoupled from it. With academic freedom ensured by contract or First Amendment law, tenure should be recognized as simply a valuable privilege granted to certain employees.

— At a more practical level, tenure may be attacked for creating a "one-way street" whereby college and university employers make a commitment to the faculty member for the duration of his or her career but the faculty member is not necessarily committed to the institution, remaining free to go elsewhere. Even if entirely lawful and thoroughly negotiated by the parties, this imbalance still nags at some administrators, especially when faculty who have been courted with rich packages of salary, benefits, and research support may blithely depart at any time, often taking with them large grants, whole laboratories, and teams of junior investigators and graduate students.

As the foregoing discussion indicates, the genesis, nature, value, and cost of tenure are topics of almost endless fascination among current and prospective tenured faculty and university officials bound by tenure systems.[15] Arguments both for and against tenure have also become a staple of public debates about the work of faculty and the future of higher education. While each side obviously speaks from self-interest, I believe that the "con" position places its ultimate value on institutional planning and flexibility, with insufficient weight given to the intellectual goals at the heart of colleges and universities.

In their actual operation, the faculty appointment and promotion process and tenure systems continue to have a somewhat guildlike flavor. The critical department-level evaluation of an assistant professor's tenure case is made (predominantly if not exclusively) by the set of already-tenured faculty in the unit.[16] Promotions from associate professor are approved by the even narrower circle of full professors. Like medieval tradesmen, the advance of junior scholars through the academic hierarchy is largely controlled by the master scholars who preceded them.[17] The necessarily broad criteria governing the award of tenure (e.g., "a high degree of excellence is expected in both research and teaching;"[18] "Mastery of subject matter . . . Effectiveness in teaching . . . Scholarly ability . . . Effectiveness of University service . . . [and] Continuing growth")[19] then magnify potential "clubiness" on the part of tenured faculty and potential anxiety among nontenured colleagues about how such standards are applied.

Decisions whether to grant tenure are often wrenching for departments or schools and are certainly of career-shaping (or -breaking) importance to the candidate. Tenure denials are among the administrative actions most likely to precipitate a lawsuit between a faculty member and his or her (soon-to-be former) institution. Throughout the body of higher education law, one encounters this litigation theme under various legal guises: for example, complaints that faculty at state-actor schools were denied tenure because of their exercise of protected speech;[20] allegations that tenure was denied on grounds that violate applicable nondiscrimination laws;[21] and claims that a denial of tenure constituted a breach of the employment contract between a college or university and a professor.[22] The faculty plaintiffs' arguments in such suits often draw upon the tenure-system flaws identified above.

## Confidentiality of the Tenure Process

Given the substantial stakes involved ("lifetime" job security, additional compensation, and dramatically enhanced standing in the profession), it is essential for an assistant professor to understand the grounds on which his or her tenure case will be decided. Unsuccessful candidates, of course, have an even more acute desire for information about why they were denied tenure. The resultant conflict between trying to preserve the guildlike and confidential character of tenure decisions (and the underlying ability of faculty making such decisions to critique candidates' work freely) and trying to ensure that those decisions are wise and fair was strenuously litigated for many years and has only recently been resolved in favor of more openness in the tenure process.

In the 1990 case of *University of Pennsylvania v. Equal Employment Opportunity Commission*,[23] a unanimous Supreme Court declared that the EEOC (the agency charged with investigating claims of employment discrimination under applicable federal law) could freely examine the complete tenure files of an unsuccessful woman candidate who had filed a complaint with the commission *and* the files of several male faculty at Penn selected for purposes of comparison. These files included reviews of the faculty members' work solicited from scholars at other universities under strict assurances of confidentiality, as well as private intra-university documents about the merits of each tenure case (e.g., department chair recommendations; materials reflecting the deliberations of faculty panels).

EEOC staff had routinely demanded to examine large numbers of tenure files at a preliminary stage in their investigations.[24] Penn objected to this practice, believing instead that the commission should show a particularized need for the (usually small) portions of the files consisting of confidential peer review materials before these items were handed over.

In other words, the fact that such documents were somehow relevant to an investigation should not by itself warrant disclosure. The Supreme Court, however, unequivocally rejected Penn's argument that peer review materials were protected under a common law privilege. The justices did not wish to recognize a new exception (as any such privilege would be) to the fundamental legal rule that parties involved in litigation must share all relevant evidence in their possession so that the court can reach the correct result. The Court was also heavily influenced by Congress's express intent (when it amended the pertinent antidiscrimination law [Title VII] in 1972 to apply to higher education institutions) to ferret out and redress discrimination in faculty hiring and promotion. As the Court noted, many of the same claims of imminent harm to faculty and academic quality that Penn was now voicing were first articulated at the time of this amendment—and subsequently proved unfounded.[25]

The Court was equally disdainful of Penn's assertion that a First Amendment right of academic freedom blocked the involuntary disclosure of these materials. The university argued that the confidentiality of these items was central to faculty peer review, which lay at the heart of the tenure process, which in turn was the key to determining "who may teach" in the academy (selection of instructors being one of the essential academic freedoms articulated by Justice Frankfurter in *Sweezy*).[26] The Court, however, labeled such infringement as "extremely attenuated,"[27] noting that sharing tenure files with EEOC investigators was a far cry from questioning the *content* of speech (the behavior at issue in *Sweezy*) or mandating through the use of loyalty oaths which persons an institution can hire as instructors.[28] While the justices did leave open the possibility that universities might delete some personally identifiable information from tenure files before disclosure,[29] they found no First Amendment violation here, and they certainly did not stake out broad constitutional protection for academic freedom.

Even more ominous for future claims of institutional and individual academic freedom (recognizing that Penn's assertion of institutional autonomy also sought to protect the individual academic freedom of faculty involved in its tenure process), the overall tone of the Supreme Court's opinion in *University of Pennsylvania* is rather hostile to higher education. Rejecting notions of education as a unique enterprise, colleges and universities are analogized to writers, publishers, musicians, and other disseminators of information (a bizarre parallel is even drawn between the award of tenure and the election of partners at law firms).[30] The Court also held that disclosure of tenure files was no more destructive of the academy than subject-ing colleges and universities to taxation. "We doubt," said the justices, "that the peer review process is any more essential in effectuating the right to determine 'who may teach' than is the availability of money."[31] Such senti-ments are disturbing to faculty and institutions that must try to persuade courts of the special characteristics of higher education and the wisdom of deferring to academic decisions.[32]

In the wake of the *University of Pennsylvania* decision, faculty and ad-ministrators alike have wondered how diminished confidentiality would affect the rigor of peer review in tenure systems and thus the quality of faculty appointments. Given the likelihood that a critical evaluation will be seen and challenged by a rejected candidate, might external reviewers be reluctant to spend substantial time appraising a colleague's work? Would they begin to offer bland or meaningless reviews? Or might they simply shy away from putting anything in writing, opting instead for informal, oral reviews (which perversely could make it easier to conceal discrimination)? In my view, such gloomy predictions do a disservice to faculty, who fully appreciate the importance of the task at hand and are more likely to re-spond by being quite precise in their assessment of a candidate's scholar-ship. Now after several years' experience under a "regime of openness," the potential disclosure of peer review materials has neither severely dam-aged collegiality nor diminished the caliber of tenured faculty.[33] I would assert that the absence of confidentiality presents no significant problems to colleges and universities that make tenure decisions on legitimate aca-demic grounds. Top-flight scholars and institutions should be comfortable making and expressing hard-headed judgments about quality. With noth-ing to hide, there is nothing to fear. And any disruptions in the tenure process are clearly outweighed by increased fairness.

## The Future of—and Alternatives to—Tenure

Today's heightened scrutiny of the operation and consequences of tenure systems naturally gives rise to speculation about the future of tenure. While alternatives to tenure are frequently bandied about, and trustees and ad-ministrators occasionally bemoan its presence, to paraphrase Mark Twain, "reports of tenure's death are an exaggeration."[34] As we have seen, power-ful arguments can be mustered that tenure continues to serve essential functions in the academy. Moreover, tenure is too much a part of the culture and fabric of American higher education to be easily or blithely abandoned.

To be sure, one occasionally reads about a college or university that has officially abolished tenure, either for all new faculty hired after a certain date (for example, the College of the Ozarks and Westmark Community College)[35] or, more rarely—and more controversially—for currently tenured faculty. In 1994, as part of a comprehensive academic, administrative, and financial restructuring, Bennington College discarded its version of a tenure system and dismissed about one-third of its faculty. After six years of service, Bennington faculty had been eligible for "presumptive tenure" (for all practical purposes, this constituted permanent employment unless the faculty member was found severely deficient in a five-year review). Predictably, a multimillion-dollar lawsuit for breaching faculty employment contracts and AAUP censure for gutting tenure followed.[36] More recently, the governor of Massachusetts proposed eliminating tenure, faculty collective bargaining, and compliance with various state regulations at a small number of public "charter colleges" to be designated by the commonwealth.[37] Such dramatic breaks with tenure, however, are so infrequent and so idiosyncratically linked to the prevailing circumstances at and culture of the affected institution (e.g., at Bennington, an attempt to return to the college's historical and experimental roots with literature and the arts taught only by practicing writers, poets, dancers, and musicians) that they cannot be regarded as constituting a trend. Efforts to abolish tenure will encounter massive legal difficulties and are not likely to be worth the fight (or the inevitable AAUP condemnation). It is reasonable to conclude, therefore, that traditional tenure systems will not collapse or be savagely overhauled.

Instead, what we shall witness in the coming years are heightened administrative and trustee efforts to make "end runs" around tenure—not direct attacks, but imaginative ways of supplementing and refining existing tenure systems, expanding universities' and colleges' financial and programmatic flexibility whenever possible, and turning tenure into a more manageable institutional commitment. The most prominent of such efforts will be the increasingly widespread use of post-tenure reviews to improve faculty performance and, when necessary, to discipline faculty.[38] I would also expect many institutions to try to amend their tenure policies to enhance administrators' ability to deploy faculty resources where needed by eliminating or restructuring programs[39] or by making it easier to discharge unproductive or otherwise problematic employees.[40]

We should anticipate more part-time faculty. According to recent studies by the National Center for Education Statistics, from 1970 to 1997 the percentage of faculty working part time rose from approximately 22 percent to 43 percent.[41] The plight of part-time instructors, many of whom cobble together a living by teaching a series of courses each semester at several different institutions (or, more fortunately, landing repeat short-term assignments at the same college or university), has attracted much attention among scholarly associations and higher education commentators and many suggestions (including unionization) for improving their lot.[42] From an institutional perspective, however, hiring part-timers can not only save money but also facilitate the delivery of courses in rapidly changing fields (e.g., Web-based technology) and enhance student training in professional disciplines in which exposure to active practitioners is invaluable (e.g., architecture, health care law). Whether viewed as judicious or indiscriminate, the use of part-time faculty will continue to grow.

Even more disturbing to faculty traditionalists, the next several decades are almost certain to bring substantial increases in full-time but *fixed-term* academic appointments.[43] Such non-tenure-track jobs may or may not allow for the possibility of reappointment. AAUP data show that over a twenty-year period starting in 1975, the number of full-time non-tenure-track faculty nearly doubled, while the number of full-time faculty on the tenure track dropped by 12 percent.[44] The *Chronicle of Higher Education* reported in 1998 that at least forty institutions (Bennington among them) had adopted such arrangements in lieu of tenure, with many others using them to supplement traditional tenure systems.[45] Term contracts with faculty offer colleges and universities many of the cost savings and much of the programmatic flexibility obtained through part-time instructors. In today's market, with an oversupply of Ph.D.'s in many arts and science disciplines, colleges and universities are able to hire extremely well qualified faculty under such arrangements, who are often assigned to teach introductory courses to undergraduate students (thereby freeing up tenure-track faculty for research and upper-level instruction).

To date, efforts to allow individual faculty the choice to structure the employment relationship through voluntary term contracts have met with modest success. Boston University's Management School gives newly hired faculty a choice of going on a conventional tenure track or signing a renewable ten-year contract at an 8–10 percent salary premium (junior faculty must first undergo a six-year probationary period before they can enter into a ten-year arrangement). During the first two years of this system, half of the new hires opted for a renewable contract.[46] At the Philadelphia College of Textiles and Science, nontenure "alternative contracts" of one to four years' duration have been entered into with at least sixteen faculty who carry a full teaching load but also maintain active professional practices in architecture, design, and health care fields. Textile's deals coexist with "regular" faculty employment arrangements.[47]

However, an ongoing study of junior scholars' perceptions of tenure indicates that non-tenure-track positions still have considerably less cachet and remain much less desirable than tenure-track jobs.[48] Furthermore, even if long-term, renewable employment contracts are an attractive alternative to tenure for some institutions and scholars, such arrangements present their own problems. They can never protect faculty academic freedom quite as thoroughly as tenure, because the specter of having to come up for reappointment is always present. This produces anxiety that can interfere with the quality and independence of research and teaching, especially as the end of one's term approaches. A system of periodic reappointments is more vulnerable to faculty logrolling (or to destructive factionalism) than one-time, up-or-down tenure votes. And certainly fixed-term contracts increase the power of the administration relative to that of faculty.[49] On the other end of the bargain, term appointees (disproportionately women, many of whom were offered fixed-term contracts when a spouse was recruited for a tenure-track post) often face the same problems of lower pay, fewer benefits, and reduced stature as do colleagues with part-time jobs who were also shunted off the tenure track.[50] Notwithstanding all of these difficulties, though, the flexibility and market responsiveness of full-time, fixed-term faculty contracts are likely to make them a fixture at many institutions.

As we look to the future, at the broadest level we shall see a host of measures and new employment structures that put different faculty on distinct employment tracks and thus create a more hierarchical professoriate. At the top rung will be faculty with traditional versions of tenure; beneath them, various categories of full-time, "regular" faculty who are contractually guaranteed academic freedom and may enjoy considerable job security through multiyear, renewable (and sometimes even financially generous) contracts but who are not eligible for tenure; and at the lower rungs, an underclass of nonregular, poorly paid faculty with very little job security and few of the other emoluments (voting rights in faculty governance bodies, sabbaticals, health and other employee benefits) that are provided to more highly regarded colleagues. Different institutions may well establish their own criteria for these various ranks. For example, major research universities might explicitly downplay teaching in awarding tenure, while colleges that place a greater emphasis on instruction might move in the opposite direction (as the North Dakota University System did in 1996 by adopting a tenure code allowing faculty at certain institutions to choose to have extra weight put on teaching and service in their annual performance evaluations).[51] The overall effect will be the same: the classic tenure track will become both narrower and less crowded. The track on which a particular faculty member is placed will depend on his or her market power, as modified by individual preferences. Presumably (again depending on one's marketability) it would be possible to switch tracks—but always easier to move down than up.

With more tracking of this sort, colleges of arts and sciences will begin to resemble university medical centers with their various classifications of regular and clinical faculty and their limitations on the financial guarantees that flow from tenure.[52] More and more persons will spend large parts of an academic career holding nontraditional titles such as lecturer, research scientist, senior fellow, instructor, and clinical professor. However, the transition to this model is likely to be rocky. With traditional tenure harder to obtain than ever, we are likely to see even more litigation over tenure denials. And efforts by individual faculty, existing and nascent faculty unions, and faculty advocacy organizations like the AAUP to resist the development of alternatives to conventional tenure promise to give rise to some of the liveliest legal and policy battles in higher education during the coming years.

## The Overlay of Nondiscrimination Law

We have seen how traditional faculty prerogatives with regard to peer review, and the continued vitality of the distinctive employment relationship that is tenure, give an institution's current faculty the critical voice in shaping its *future* faculty. This guildlike control over hiring and promotion serves valuable purposes (such as ensuring that decisions about the quality of scholarship are made by experts). Courts give it legal approbation when they defer to college and university personnel decisions, which again are usually faculty-driven. But faculty and institutions do not exercise such control over academic employment in a vacuum. Layered on top of the historical autonomy of scholars and academic institutions is a latticework of nondiscrimination laws designed to ensure that individuals of widely different backgrounds and characteristics can fully participate in the life of society. These laws and their enforcement have had a powerful influence on the nature of faculty employment.

I start by repeating a point made in chapter 1 of this volume about the overlapping jurisdictions of legal authorities. Federal, state, county, and municipal governments alike have an interest in preventing discrimination in the economic, political, and social spheres. Across the nation, different governmental units have enacted widely variant antidiscrimination laws, protecting different classes of individuals for various purposes and affording the aggrieved parties a range of remedies. For example, New York City ordinances prohibit discrimination on the basis of a person's sexual orientation,[53] while New York State and federal law do not. In the following analysis, I focus on federal nondiscrimination law because of its broad applicability and high visibility. But it is essential to bear in mind that, depending on one's location, analogous—or more sweeping—requirements may be imposed on institutions and individuals by state or local law.

A few other introductory remarks are warranted before turning to an overview of the content, impact, and operation of the major federal statutes and regulations prohibiting discrimination on campuses. First, these statutes and regulations do not just apply to colleges and universities, but rather extend to much broader groups. Second, although we begin our examination of these laws through the prism of faculty employment (which is appropriate, since this is the context in which such laws most intimately affect the academy), several of the statutes and regulations discussed below do not just apply to employment arrangements (or may not be formally linked to employment at all). Third, the laws in question, even if linked to employment, do not just apply to faculty, but to *all* employees at the relevant college or university, including student employees. (Be mindful as well that several of these laws apply to student employees in their purely student capacity.) Fourth and finally, bans on employment discrimination do not just apply to the hiring, promotion, and job security decisions that we have been discussing in the preceding pages. Other terms and conditions of employment, such as salaries and benefits, working environment, and employee discipline, are covered too. I have chosen to address these laws at this point in the book because tenure and promotion decisions are the likely flash point for other, perhaps long-simmering, personnel dis-

putes. The statutes and regulations that follow provide a frequently utilized legal framework for faculty seeking redress from their employers.

## Title VII

Title VII of the Civil Rights Act of 1964 outlaws discrimination in *employment* (including hiring, firing, promotion, compensation, and other terms,
conditions, and privileges of employment) on the basis of race, color, religion, sex, or national origin.[54] (Note that it does not ban discrimination on
the basis of sexual orientation). Its neutral language encompasses not only
discrimination against minorities and women but also what is commonly
called "reverse discrimination" against nonminorities and men.[55] It applies
to all employers, public or private, who have more than a minimal number
of employees, and thus it is probably the most sweeping and significant
federal nondiscrimination statute. Interestingly enough, when Title VII
was originally enacted, it contained an exception for college and university
faculty. But in 1972 the law was explicitly amended to remove this language. The legislative record supporting this amendment reflected the sense
of Congress that a considerable amount of discrimination was occurring in
higher education and that the previously sanctioned practice of deferring
to purportedly "academic decisions" about faculty employment was not
serving the public interest. Just as Congress envisioned, since this change
in the statute, suits over faculty nonrenewals and tenure denials are often
cast in Title VII terms.

The various kinds of employment discrimination prohibited by Title VII
fall into two generic categories, labeled by courts respectively as disparate
treatment and disparate impact. Let us examine each of these templates,
which also reappear in litigation under other nondiscrimination laws. A
*disparate treatment* case (the most commonly litigated scenario) arises when
someone who was denied a job, promotion, raise, or other benefit of employment (including perhaps keeping a current position) claims that he or
she was treated less favorably than other applicants or employees because
of race, color, religion, sex, or national origin. To help sort through the facts
of a disparate treatment case, courts follow a well-established procedure
traceable to the Supreme Court's 1973 opinion in *McDonnell Douglas Corp.
v. Green*,[56] which procedure to my mind resembles a badminton volley.
The plaintiff—who at all times bears the ultimate legal burden of persuad-
ing the court that unlawful discrimination occurred—begins by trying to
make a prima facie case of discrimination. For example, to do this in a case

alleging discrimination in hiring, the plaintiff would show that (1) he or she is covered by Title VII (a cut-and-dried task, since the law protects persons of *any* race, color, religion, sex, or national origin);[57] (2) he or she applied and was qualified for a job for which the defendant employer sought applicants; (3) despite these qualifications, the plaintiff was rejected; and (4) after the plaintiff's rejection, the job stayed open and the employer continued to look for candidates with the same qualifications. The elements of a prima facie case under Title VII are basically constant but are tailored on the margins to reflect the specifics of particular employment decisions. Thus, in a suit by a woman faculty member alleging discrimination in the award of tenure, the plaintiff would need to show that although she was qualified for tenure, she was turned down while tenure was granted to male colleagues with similar or inferior qualifications. Under *McDonnell Douglas* and its progeny, if the plaintiff makes the requisite prima facie case, the defendant employer must then assume the burden of articulating a "legitimate, nondiscriminatory reason" for the action taken against the plaintiff. Once the employer does this, any presumption of wrongdoing raised by the plaintiff's prima facie case is rebutted.[58] It then falls (once again) to the plaintiff to prove that the employer's proffered reason was simply a pretext for discrimination, by showing "both that the reason was false, and that discrimination was the real reason" for what happened.[59] In other words, in a Title VII disparate treatment case, the plaintiff must prove that the employer actually intended to discriminate against him or her.

A *disparate impact* case, in contrast, arises when an ostensibly neutral employment policy or job requirement turns out to have a discriminatory effect on the plaintiff (or a group of persons similar to the plaintiff).[60] Disparate impact cases stand for the proposition that employment practices must be fair both in their form and in their operation. In such a case, it is the *consequences* of the employer's rules (rather than the intent behind its actions) that are determinative. Even an innocently created policy may violate the law.[61] Under disparate impact precedent, a requirement that excludes persons of one race, color, religion, sex, or national origin from employment or otherwise impedes their career is illegal unless the employer demonstrates that such requirement is job-related and consistent with business necessity. Thus, *Scott v. Univ. of Delaware* upheld a policy that newly appointed or promoted faculty ordinarily hold a Ph.D. or other terminal degree—even if this disqualified many black candidates—as a way of meeting the university's legitimate needs "in hiring and advancing persons who are likely to be successful in adding to the fund of knowledge in their chosen disciplines and effective in the teaching of graduate students."[62] However, even if the employer makes the requisite showing of business necessity, a disparate impact plaintiff can still prevail by demonstrating that an equally effective—but less discriminatory—alternative was available but that the defendant refused to adopt such technique. A claim of disparate impact potentially involves many more persons than an individual allegation of disparate treatment. Such claims are thus often cast as class action suits and (if they reach the litigation stage) call for complex statistical analyses of differences among sets of potential and actual employees.

Notwithstanding its sweeping antidiscrimination language and its broad applicability, Title VII still leaves academic and other employers with considerable flexibility in managing their workforce. They may make distinctions in salary and other terms of employment through seniority or merit systems (this latter option is especially important and useful to colleges and universities that, at tenure and promotion time in particular, must evaluate the quality of individual faculty).[63] Furthermore, the statute expressly allows hiring and other employment decisions based on the religion, sex, or national origin of an individual (but still not race or color) in order to satisfy a "bona fide occupational qualification reasonably necessary to the normal operation of that particular business or enterprise."[64] This relatively narrow bona fide occupational qualification exception would include gender-based requirements for positions such as locker room attendant and probably also certain campus health care or counseling jobs that involve physical contact or the disclosure of intimate information,[65] but it would not typically extend to faculty posts. For example, I think courts would reject the argument that only women can teach in a women's studies program. Religiously controlled colleges and universities enjoy another exception under Title VII that allows them to hire only employees of the relevant faith to do work connected with religious activities.[66] Considered as a whole, then, Title VII still permits colleges and universities to hire, promote, reward, penalize, or fire faculty and other employees on the basis of their job-related qualifications and performance. They just cannot make invidious distinctions on the basis of the protected classifications.

Title VII is administered and enforced by the EEOC. Complaints must be filed with the commission before bringing a private lawsuit and within

180 days after the alleged discrimination occurred (unless it was a repeated or continuing violation).[67] This six-month statute of limitations is shorter than that of several other nondiscrimination statutes—a definite downside for plaintiffs. However, as we saw in our discussion of the diminished confidentiality of tenure files, EEOC staff are often zealous in their investigation, providing complainants with thorough, government-subsidized discovery.[68] If, following the commission's own investigation, unlawful discrimination is ultimately found by the courts, successful Title VII plaintiffs are afforded a wide range of remedies, including reinstatement to their former job, back pay, attorneys' fees, and—in disparate treatment cases—compensatory and punitive damages (the latter subject to monetary caps). In disparate impact cases, courts may order employers who have discriminated to adopt and carry out affirmative action programs.

There are also rare but significant instances of courts awarding tenure or promotion to full professor as damages under Title VII. Thirty years ago, such a notion would have been unthinkable. But after the statute was amended to cover higher education faculty (and as courts became more familiar with—and less cowed by—the ways in which colleges and universities operate), judicial authorities inevitably began to look deeply into, and even became willing to reverse, decisions about academic qualifications made by faculty peers and employer institutions. The initial breach in the academy's dam of self-determination was the Third Circuit's 1980 opinion in *Kunda v. Muhlenberg*. That case considered the plight of a woman physical education instructor who was recommended for promotion to assistant professor and tenure by her department and all appropriate faculty committees but turned down by her dean and the college administration because she did not possess a master's degree. None of the plaintiff's superiors at Muhlenberg had ever told her, though, that she needed to earn her master's to acquire tenure—while Kunda's male colleagues had been so advised and several men in her and other departments had even been promoted *without* this degree. Faced with such egregious discrimination, the Appeals Court ordered, among other damages, that Kunda be promoted (back-dated to when her application was denied) and that she receive a *conditional* award of tenure: to wit, she would have two years to complete her master's degree, on the understanding that once she did so, she would automatically become tenured. In the court's view, this unusual remedy was required in order to restore the plaintiff to the position she would have occupied had no discrimination occurred (including protecting her during the next two years against changes in the college's financial position).[69] While at first blush this seems intrusive, when the *Kunda* opinion is considered carefully, it may be seen as fairly respectful of academic decision making. Rather than second-guessing the college's evaluation of the plaintiff's qualifications, the court simply took Muhlenberg officials at their word that the only reason Kunda had not received tenure was her lack of a degree and held that she should receive it once she satisfied this requirement.

A far more profound incursion on institutional autonomy followed in 1989, when the court in *Brown v. Boston University* made an outright award of tenure to an unsuccessful candidate in order to remedy sex discrimination.[70] In her sixth year as an assistant professor of English literature at BU, Judy Brown came up for tenure. In addition to her home department, the tenure committee of the College of Liberal Arts, the relevant dean, and the university-wide Appointments, Promotions, and Tenure Committee all voted in favor of tenure, in most cases by overwhelming margins. So did a 2-1 majority of a special ad hoc committee of external authorities in Brown's field that was empaneled by the university administration pursuant to its collective bargaining agreement with the faculty. However, BU's provost's office recommended against awarding tenure, and the president and the trustees sided with the chief academic officer. Brown sued, alleging discrimination in violation of Title VII. Both the trial and the appellate courts chose to conduct extremely detailed analyses of the contents of Brown's tenure file and how it compared to those of male candidates awarded tenure around the same time. For example, the courts questioned why no one in the English Department other than Brown had been pushed to finish a second book (not based on a dissertation) to get tenure, compared whose work had received reviews, considered where candidates' scholarship had been published, and even scrutinized the margin of the positive intra- and extradepartment tenure votes.[71] The First Circuit upheld the trial court's finding of unlawful discrimination and reinstatement with tenure to make Brown whole. Reading the *Brown* opinion, one cannot help but wonder whether this case might have come out differently if the university's central administration had not so blithely ignored an emerging consensus in favor of tenure. Perhaps the trial court jury was also influenced by a set of highly impolitic, if not blatantly sexist, remarks by BU's president that were admitted as evidence.[72] Still, although the courts were aware of the "risk of improperly substituting a judicial tenure decision for a university one,"[73] they plunged ahead anyway. This is hardly reassuring to defenders of academic independence.

While scattered decisions (even by distinguished appellate courts) do not make an inexorable trend, grants of tenure or promotion as a remedy for discrimination—directly shaping a college or university's faculty—raise intriguing questions about whether courts and civil rights agencies are intruding too deeply into academic appointments, especially (but not exclusively) in a Title VII context. First, judges may be beyond their depth in trying to assess the integrity of evaluations of scholarly credentials. For example, the *Brown* court reviewed BU's tenure files in a very mechanistic way, counting the number of books and articles written, the number of reviews, and the number of votes each candidate received for tenure. This is a far cry from nuanced calls made by knowledgeable faculty peers about the likely intellectual impact of ideas. Likewise, in *Bennun v. Rutgers* (a Third Circuit opinion upholding the award of a promotion from associate to full professor as damages for discrimination under Title VII),[74] the court plowed deeply through the tenure files of the plaintiff (who had been repeatedly denied promotion) and a female departmental colleague who was promoted, and then it rather simplistically matched up their ratings on Rutgers' performance criteria, paying particular attention to their respective numbers of publications over various periods, such as the three years prior to promotion review. It concluded that since the plaintiff far surpassed the comparator's totals but still scored lower on research criteria, he had been treated disparately. The court was unswayed by Rutgers' argument that it was comparing apples and oranges, as the plaintiff was a research-oriented professor and the comparator teaching-oriented.[75]

As frustrating as these two decisions are, matters can be much worse when, instead of highly trained jurists, EEOC or state human rights commission staff—who do not focus on higher education and frequently do not even grasp the difference between earning tenure through world-class research and promoting an employee with several years' experience to foreman—are expected to make determinations about the rigor and fundamental fairness of college or university employment decisions. While the foregoing arguments may strike courts (which regularly delve into the details of other complex enterprises such as the financial, health care, and computing industries) and plaintiffs' attorneys as extraordinarily arrogant, it is undeniable that judgments about academic quality often turn on theoretical constructs and terminology that are largely inaccessible to those untrained in a given field.[76]

I would also posit that courts and investigators are more easily "drawn into" disputes in the humanities and nonquantitative social science disciplines. Had Ms. Brown been a mathematician rather than a Jane Austen scholar, I doubt that the First Circuit would have so confidently expressed opinions on how her research compared to that of her colleagues. And criticism of the content of scholarship touching upon issues of race, color, religion, sex, or national origin must be carefully distinguished from discriminatory animus against members of protected classifications—in many instances including the authors of such scholarship. In *Lynn v. Regents of Univ. of California,* a woman rejected for tenure made a prima facie case of discrimination under Title VII when colleagues and superiors at UC-Irvine dismissed as insubstantial her scholarship on women in French literature. The court held that "a disdain for women's issues, and a diminished opinion of those who concentrate on those issues, is evidence of a discriminatory attitude towards women."[77] This is troubling language for scholars who take issue with the findings or even the intellectual premises of identity-based scholarship. I think a more subtle and correct reading of Title VII was reached by the court in *Jalal v. Columbia University* when it declared that

> discussion of how the work of a scholar or artist is influenced by his or her background is not only permitted by Title VII, it is an important part of the academic freedom protected by the First Amendment. . . . [Indeed,] much modern cultural and literary criticism is devoted largely to just such discussions. Those aspects of a person's background that implicate Title VII, of course, cannot be used as a basis for employment decisions. However, absent some indication that they were so used, courts must be careful to avoid chilling inquiry into this legitimate area of scholarship.[78]

The point to be stressed is that while nondiscrimination lawsuits should only be concerned with the fairness of a given employment decision, the line between such a process and the underlying academic substance can be blurry or tempting to cross. Governmental decision makers should tread warily.

Our assessment of whether courts are unwisely or unnecessarily inserting themselves into academic personnel matters by, for example, granting tenure to victims of discrimination must also take into account the practical consequences of such actions. While awarding tenure to someone who was unfairly denied it responds directly to the wrong committed, it may not actually serve the best interests of the successful plaintiff or the defendant employer. Much depends on whether opposition to the plaintiff was centered at the department level. If so, the smaller and more close-knit the department, the greater the awkwardness and unhappiness on both sides and the potential dysfunctionality. The presence of the newly tenured professor will be a daily reminder of past turmoil and—especially if the plaintiff followed the now-standard litigation practice of buttressing his or her case by attacking the credentials of tenured peers—of newer wounds that will heal slowly, if ever.[79] Nor is the battle-scarred "victor" likely to attract many offers to go elsewhere. In short, forcing the department to live with a clearly unwanted colleague "forever" (recall that mandatory retirement has been abolished) is quite different from restoring an unjustly discharged employee to a factory job.

Finally, at the most fundamental level, what many plaintiffs seek in a Title VII or other employment discrimination case is *intellectual* vindication (i.e., validation that their scholarship, teaching, and other credentials meet the standards of their discipline and that they should not be viewed as second-rate academics). No stirring language in a court opinion, award of money, title, or enhanced level of job security can completely fill this need, which raises yet another doubt about the value and efficacy of judicially imposed remedies. Still, one should never underestimate the cleansing effect of correcting injustice (in the form of employment discrimination) with justice, and the powerful warning thus provided to potential wrongdoers.

## Title VI

Title VI of the Civil Rights Act of 1964 (part of the same overarching legislation that contains Title VII) prohibits discrimination against any person on the grounds of race, color, or national origin "under any program or activity receiving Federal financial assistance."[80] It can therefore apply to both public and private colleges and universities. Here, as in many other instances, the funding acts as a legal hook—if an institution does not receive federal dollars, it will not be bound by the statute.[81] It is important to understand, however, that Title VI's definition of the aided program or activity is expansive: if a college or university accepts federal support, the law will extend to *all* of its operations, not just the particular part using government moneys (e.g., the financial aid office).[82]

Title VI is less significant than Title VII in the employment context because by its express terms it only reaches discrimination against employees when a "primary objective" of the federal aid was to provide jobs,[83] but it is a crucial piece of antidiscrimination legislation in a host of other settings such as admissions, financial aid, and racial harassment on campuses. It is frequently the basis for lawsuits seeking the desegregation of higher education systems.[84] Title VI is administered by the agency that disburses the relevant federal funds; this is why the Department of Education's Office for Civil Rights (OCR) is frequently the enforcement arm in Title VI higher education disputes. As with all of the funding-linked nondiscrimination laws discussed in this section, in the case of noncompliance the applicable agency can move to cut off support or even refer the matter to the Department of Justice for prosecution.[85] Individual victims of discrimination can also sue to enforce Title VI and may be awarded compensatory damages.

## Title IX

In language closely tracking that of Title VI, Title IX of the Education Amendments of 1972 outlaws discrimination on the basis of *sex* in any education program or activity receiving federal funds.[86] Once again, the receipt of federal dollars is the hook that makes this statute applicable to public and private institutions alike, and once again, the entire college or university must comply with Title IX even if only a small number of its units or programs directly acquire such funds. Title IX is best known as the law giving rise to controversy and enhanced gender equity in intercollegiate athletics.[87] But its scope is actually much broader, covering, for example, employment discrimination, sexual harassment, and admissions disputes (overlapping somewhat with Title VII). Note also that in distinction to Title VI, Title IX is only concerned with discrimination in federal *education* programs, and consequently OCR is responsible for its enforcement.

Statutory exceptions under Title IX authorize the continued existence of several long-standing categories of gender-based practices in higher education: for example, the ability of institutions controlled by religious organizations to observe the tenets of their faith;[88] undergraduate admissions to single-sex private colleges;[89] and the membership rules of fraternities and sororities.[90] Title IX's implementing regulations also permit drawing distinctions on the basis of sex among prospective or actual employees

to fill a job's "bona fide occupational qualifications" (paralleling Title VII).[91]
The Supreme Court's decision in *Franklin v. Gwinnett County Public
Schools*[92] established that successful individual Title IX plaintiffs (who
should expect to go through the same "badminton volley" of charges and
countercharges as a Title VII plaintiff, at all times having to prove that
intentional discrimination occurred) can receive monetary damages as compensation.[93] Title IX covers students, employees, and student employees,
and the overlap between Titles VII and IX has created some legal complications. Since Title IX suits are not subject to the damage limits governing
Title VII cases, and because Title IX may offer longer statutes of limitations for making a claim, from a plaintiff's perspective Title IX may be the
more attractive basis for litigation, even if separate counts are filed under
each law. But in *Lakoski v. Univ. of Texas Medical Branch*, the Fifth Circuit dismissed the claim of a former faculty member who, having been
denied tenure, sought money damages only under Title IX. The court declared that "Title VII provides the exclusive remedy for individuals alleging employment discrimination on the basis of sex in federally funded educational institutions."[94] Even if other courts follow *Lakoski's* rejection of
alternative Title VII and IX claims, students can still sue under Title IX, as
can employees seeking declaratory or injunctive relief rather than financial
recompense.

## Age Discrimination in Employment Act (ADEA)

As might be expected from its title, the ADEA bans discrimination in employment on the basis of age—against anyone 40 or older (with no upper
limit).[95] Persons under 40 are not covered and cannot seek protection under the law. The operative statutory language is almost identical to that of
Title VII, which serves as its model for everything from legislative scope
(both private and public employers fall within the ADEA's ambit), to types
of possible claims (both disparate treatment and disparate impact cases
are envisioned, brought by an individual or a class of plaintiffs), to the
enforcement agency (EEOC). Once an ADEA dispute proceeds past the
commission to the courts, the production of evidence and the burden of
proof also track Title VII jurisprudence. The plaintiff first makes a prima
facie case of discrimination—for example, in a disparate treatment case,
that he or she is at least 40 and was qualified for but did not receive a job or
benefit that instead went to someone younger. The defendant employer
must then show either (1) that any differentiation among employees was

not made on the basis of age but rather on other reasonable (and nondiscriminatory) factors or (2) that distinctions that *were* drawn on the basis of age stemmed from a "bona fide occupational qualification reasonably necessary to the normal operation of the particular business" (recall that there is a corresponding exception under Title VII).[96] In our hypothetical disparate treatment case, the plaintiff would then have to respond by showing that the employer's articulated reasons are pretextual and that in fact it intended to and did discriminate. If unlawful age discrimination has occurred, as in Title VII litigation, various remedies can make the plaintiff "whole," and compensatory damages are also available.[97]

The "bona fide occupational qualification" exception to the ADEA is not particularly relevant to faculty, since a scholar's age should not per se limit performance. It will have much greater impact on other employees, whose duties require skills or attributes more obviously linked to age. Thus, in *E.E.O.C. v. Univ. of Texas Health Science Center,*[98] the Fifth Circuit upheld a maximum hiring age for certain members of the center's security force that reflected the physical demands of these jobs. Interestingly, the ADEA also explicitly states that it is lawful to discharge or otherwise discipline an employee for good cause.[99] This rather self-evident proposition is not similarly highlighted in Title VII or other employment discrimination laws.

In 1986 the ADEA was amended to eliminate mandatory retirement in almost all settings. The notion behind this legislation was that an individual's desire to keep working and his or her job performance—not the attainment of some arbitrary age—should determine whether employment continued. Because mandatory retirement had been the primary means of replenishing and rejuvenating faculty ranks (and also because the higher education community aggressively lobbied for special treatment), Congress gave colleges and universities an extra seven years to adjust to the "uncapping" of tenured faculty positions (other employees were covered by the new law at its effective date).[100] Despite the hopes of some commentators and administrators that Congress would extend or institutionalize this exception, since 1994 under the ADEA faculty need not retire at 70.[101]

As described in chapter 1, pursuant to the Supreme Court's holding in *Kimel v. Florida Board of Regents,* Eleventh Amendment sovereign immunity shields state-actor colleges and universities from employees' ADEA damage suits in federal court.[102] While private institutions remain subject to such litigation—and the federal government can also enforce the act's provisions against public entities—*Kimel* certainly appears to have diminished the ADEA's reach and influence.

## Section 504

Section 504 of the Rehabilitation Act of 1973 decrees that "no otherwise qualified individual with a *disability* . . . shall, solely by reason of his or her disability, be excluded from participation in, be denied the benefits of, or be subjected to discrimination under any program or activity receiving Federal financial assistance.[103] As with Titles VI and IX, the act of taking federal money for covered programs subjects the entire institution to this nondiscrimination law. And like Title VI, Section 504 is administered by the relevant funding agency (typically OCR on behalf of the Department of Education). Given that Section 504 is an ancestor of the more comprehensive Americans with Disabilities Act (ADA) (see below), it is not surprising that there is a fair amount of overlap between these two statutes as they are applied to higher education.[104] In this and the following section, I note several instances of dual coverage and some key distinctions.

Section 504 is central to the resolution of questions about the admission of and legally required accommodations for students with disabilities.[105] But like Title IX, it is also very much concerned with fairness in employment. Under the Department of Education's implementing regulations, in making employment decisions an institution subject to Section 504 may not discriminate against a "qualified individual with a disability"— which in turn is defined as someone "who, with reasonable accommodation, can perform the essential functions of the job in question."[106] The regulations likewise mandate that covered employers must go the extra step to *make* "reasonable accommodation to the known physical or mental limitations of an otherwise qualified [disabled] applicant or employee unless the recipient can demonstrate that the accommodation would impose an undue hardship on the operation of its program."[107] Making such accommodations for faculty and nonfaculty employees may well require meaningful adjustments in college and university personnel practices.[108] However, limiting language in the regulations—the disabled person must be able to perform a job's *essential functions;* no *undue hardship* to be imposed upon the employer— in effect constitute a tempering "bona fide occupational qualification" exception similar to those found under Titles VII and IX and the ADEA.

Both Section 504 and the ADA have very inclusive definitions of *disability*, including not just classic physical and mental difficulties such as blindness or schizophrenia but also learning disabilities, contagious diseases like tuberculosis or AIDS,[109] and chronic conditions such as alcoholism[110]—in short, all kinds of impairments that limit major life activities. (The laws even protect persons who are merely *regarded* as having such disabilities.) Temporary conditions such as a broken leg, though, should not qualify. Much of the still-developing case law on disability discrimination has centered on what constitutes a disability. This is necessarily a fact-specific determination, turning on the effects of an individual's impairment in particular settings. But guidelines are emerging. For instance, the Supreme Court has held that persons who experience no substantial limitation in major life activities when using "mitigating measures" (such as medication, a prosthesis, or a hearing aid) are not disabled under the ADA. In *Sutton v. United Air Lines,* plaintiffs who could correct their myopia with eyeglasses or contact lenses were not covered by that statute.[111] Likewise, it is now clear that a "substantial limitation" of the ability to work under the ADA entails preclusion from an entire class or broad range of jobs, not just from one desired position.[112] Thus, while the nearsighted plaintiffs in *Sutton* could not qualify as global pilots, they could have worked as regional pilots or flight instructors.

As with each of the nondiscrimination statutes we have previously examined, individual victims of disability discrimination may sue and be awarded compensatory damages (and other appropriate relief) under Section 504.

### Americans with Disabilities Act (ADA)

The ADA[113] was enacted in 1990 with the goal of bringing persons with disabilities into society's mainstream. Because it is not moored to federal funding like Section 504, the ADA reaches a much broader range of entities and activities. It prohibits disability discrimination by state and local governments in their provision of public services and programs and by private entities that operate or function as places of public accommodation.[114] It requires enhanced accessibility of public transportation and telecommunications services. And large sections of the ADA prohibit discrimination in employment, which is our immediate concern.

The ADA makes it unlawful for an employer with more than fifteen employees to discriminate in its hiring, compensation, discharge, or other personnel decisions against a "qualified individual with a disability," defined, in language almost identical to that of Section 504, as someone who "with or without reasonable accommodation, can perform the essential functions of the employment position that such individual holds or desires."[115] In an extension of that precursor statute, though, the ADA outlaws discrimination not just against individuals who *themselves* have (or are regarded as having) a disability, but also against individuals who have a "relationship or association" with someone known to have a disability. Actual or prospective employees with a disabled spouse or child are therefore protected, and a whole new class of potential plaintiffs opens up.[116] Again matching up nicely with Section 504, the ADA imposes an affirmative obligation upon employers to make "reasonable accommodations" (e.g., making facilities accessible, job restructuring, modified work schedules, etc.) in response to the limitations of otherwise qualified individuals with disabilities—unless such accommodations would impose an "undue hardship" on the operation of the business.[117] I expect that litigation in the coming years will help define the scope of requisite accommodations. Similar to individualized evaluations of possible disability, the specific duties and context of a given job will determine what changes, if any, must be made. Certainly there are disabilities that cannot be accommodated in some employment settings (e.g., a school need not hire a blind bus driver). But as technology evolves, employers' ability to weave disabled persons into the workforce should grow at the same time as the cost of making meaningful accommodations decreases.

Like Title VII, the ADA is administered and enforced by the EEOC. Indeed, notwithstanding the shared language and coverage of the ADA and Section 504, it is helpful to envision the ADA (in its employment discrimination sections) as analogous to Title VII and Section 504 (with its programmatic emphasis and funding link) as analogous to Title VI. Carrying this ADA–Title VII parallel a bit further, one finds that both disparate treatment and disparate impact cases are brought under the ADA, that various ADA provisions replicate Title VII's "bona fide occupational qualification" exception, and that individual plaintiffs under the ADA must jump through the same procedural hoops as Title VII complainants (file with EEOC within 180 days, complete commission investigation before suing in court) in pursuit of the same remedies, including compensatory damages. It is also worth noting that the Supreme Court's decision in *Bd. of Trustees of Univ. of Ala. v. Garrett,* which blocked employee suits under Title I of the ADA against public universities on sovereign immunity grounds, may severely limit the import of this statute.[118]

## Executive Order 11246

The last antidiscrimination law I want to explore in detail does not carry the legislative force or endurance of a statute, but it is nonetheless significant as the locus of most federally mandated affirmative action programs. Executive Order 11246,[119] issued by President Lyndon Johnson in 1965, applies to federal contractors and subcontractors—a category that includes just about every college or university that accepts federal funding, for such dollars are frequently distributed by contract (e.g., research grants from the National Institutes of Health, many forms of student financial aid). Like Title VII, Executive Order 11246 prohibits covered entities from discriminating on the basis of race, color, religion, sex, or national origin (and requires them to put nondiscrimination language in any contracts they sign with third parties). But then it goes a step further by requiring these contractors and subcontractors to develop affirmative action plans, which are to include specific goals for developing a more diverse workforce.

Executive Order 11246 is administered by the Office of Federal Contract Compliance Programs (OFCCP), housed in the Department of Labor. Principal sanctions under the order (levied only after the contractor has been through a withering OFCCP review) are the termination of funding or debarment from entering into new contracts with the government, or both. Unlike the statutes discussed above, aggrieved individuals do not have a private right of action under this executive order.

## Consequences of Discrimination Litigation

In the preceding pages I have waded quite deeply into the alphabet and numeric soup of federal antidiscrimination law in order to equip readers with a basic understanding of key statutes and regulations. In the interests of clarity and conciseness, I have refrained from examining other federal nondiscrimination statutes that I believe faculty and administrators are less likely to encounter in their daily lives, such as the Equal Pay Act,[120] the Age Discrimination Act of 1975,[121] the Vietnam Era Veterans' Readjustment Assistance Act of 1974,[122] Section 1981,[123] and Section 1983.[124] Institutional counsel will be familiar with the details and impact of these and other relevant laws. For ease of reference, table 1 summarizes some of the salient points of the statutes and regulations that have commanded our primary attention. The foregoing discussion should also help readers appreciate that federal antidiscrimination law is a legislative patchwork rather than a well-planned or neatly coordinated system. What—or perhaps more important, who—is protected under the various statutes reflects political influence and effective advocacy at least as much as logic. Thus, the powerful American Association of Retired Persons successfully pushed for expansion of the ADEA, while the less prominent Lambda Legal Defense and Education Fund has not yet secured passage of a federal civil rights bill protecting gay men and lesbians.[125]

Note that victims of discrimination can also make claims under the Equal Protection Clause of the Fourteenth Amendment (assuming that they can show state action).[126] But as several commentators have observed, in some important respects the Constitution is a less attractive platform for challenging employment discrimination than the afore-mentioned statutes. For example, constitutionally based suits must meet more rigorous standards of proof (e.g., unintentional disparate impact discrimination under Title VII would not violate the Equal Protection Clause), and plaintiffs do not have EEOC or other agency investigatory and enforcement mechanisms at their disposal.[127] Still, for individuals or groups not covered by federal antidiscrimination laws (such persons under 40 or gays and lesbians), claims under the Constitution may provide the only avenue into federal court.

TABLE 1. SUMMARY OF ANTI-DISCRIMINATION LAWS

| Statute | Covered Groups | Linked to Federal $ ? | Enforced by | BFOQ Exception |
|---------|----------------|-----------------------|-------------|----------------|
| Title VI | Race, color, national origin | Yes | Funding agency (typically OCR/ED) | No |
| Title VII | Race, color, religion, sex, national origin | No | EEOC | Yes |
| Title IX | Sex | Yes | OCR/ED | Yes |
| ADEA | Age (40 and over) | No | EEOC | Yes |
| Section 504 | Disability | Yes | Funding agency (typically OCR/ED) | ° |
| ADA | Disability | No | EEOC | ° |

° Tied in with whether someone is "qualified."
Key: ADA, Americans with Disabilities Act; ADEA, Age Discrimination in Employment Act; EEOC, Equal Employment Opportunity Commission; OCR/ED, Office of Civil Rights (of the Department of Education)

Earlier in this section we considered the intrusiveness of some of the remedies fashioned by courts in response to illegal discrimination. Our discussion of the content and significance of antidiscrimination laws should now conclude by looking at the likely outcomes of litigation under such statutes. According to a study of faculty discrimination lawsuits from 1971 to 1984, plaintiffs only prevailed in about 20 percent of cases.[128] But overall plaintiffs do much better than these statistics suggest, since employers will settle out of court for many reasons, especially when their liability is clear. Claims of sex discrimination by women faculty are most common,[129] with age discrimination suits occurring relatively infrequently.[130] Perhaps somewhat counterintuitively (especially given the discrimination laws' animating impulse), white plaintiffs suing historically black institutions were more often successful than black plaintiffs suing historically white institutions.[131]

Discrimination litigation is very costly to individuals and institutions. Unless wrongdoing is obvious, colleges and universities are inclined to fight such cases tooth and nail to preserve the integrity of their faculty hiring and peer review processes. Beyond the substantial sums spent on attorneys' fees[132] (and potentially in damages), the time and energy expended on such disputes are incalculable. Departments can be ripped apart, scholars and institutions diverted from their real mission of research and teaching, and the campus culture transformed by the adoption of legalistic (and perhaps overly defensive) ways of doing business. For example, in settling a sex discrimination suit, the University of Minnesota had to agree to a ten-year period of federal oversight of its employment practices, including the creation of goals and timetables for hiring women in each department, dramatically expanded record keeping, and the use of court-appointed special masters to resolve complaints.[133] Plaintiffs are likewise forever changed by the litigation experience. The same 1987 study found that more than half of them switched jobs, if not careers, within a short period of time after their lawsuits, many expressing great frustration with the legal process.[134]

So is discrimination litigation necessary and worthwhile? The answer is clearly yes. Antidiscrimination laws and the suits brought under them are an avenue to justice and a strong and visible deterrent against future misconduct. Certainly colleges and universities should take preventive measures to avoid liability (e.g., giving feedback on employees' performance so that adverse actions are less of a surprise; affording broad access to tenure files; providing internal grievance mechanisms to appeal negative reappointment, tenure, or promotion decisions). I would also hope that government agencies and courts would focus on procedural aspects of employment decisions and defer whenever possible to institutional judgments about intellectual substance. But given that we live in a litigious society, and that egos and careers are on the line, plaintiffs and institutions must be able to count on judicial redress in extreme circumstances, though recognizing that courts are not the ideal venue to resolve fundamentally academic disputes.

## Affirmative Action in Faculty Hiring

Most colleges and universities seek greater representation of minorities and women[135] in their workforce and especially on their faculties. A diverse faculty, they believe, will promote more lively and varied intellectual discourse, which will lead to more thoughtful scholarship. It can also enhance the quality of instruction by exposing students to new ideas and perspectives. Many educators further contend that it is vital for minority students to work with and be mentored by academic role models with similar backgrounds. Such noble aspirations—and less selfless considerations such as compliance with federal law—have led institutions to craft affirmative action programs for the recruitment and hiring of minority faculty and other employees.

Colleges and universities employ a variety of techniques to achieve their affirmative action goals, ranging from literally reserving faculty slots for minorities,[136] to "two for one" deals (where a department that hires a minority scholar is rewarded with another faculty line or the minority hire is not regarded as filling an available slot), to setting aside pots of money to use in wooing minority faculty (and then cutting whatever deals are necessary to retain such individuals), to less controversial—indeed, now almost conventional—search techniques such as advertising jobs in publications with a large minority readership or having chairs and deans insist that lists of job finalists include one or more minority candidates. Many institutions establish precise and aggressive goals for minority representation among faculty and staff (such goals constitute a key part of the required affirmative action plan for federal contractors under Executive Order 11246). And almost every school includes lofty rhetoric about the value of diversity in its official policy statements and publications. In some instances, universities have launched and run their affirmative action programs with great

fanfare in pursuit of goodwill and publicity;[137] others (especially those using discretionary funds to pay for minority hires) have labored more quietly.

There is considerable tension between the objective of building a more
diverse workforce through affirmative action and the strong prohibitions
under Title VII and other statutes (and, for state actors, the Constitution)
against drawing distinctions among current or prospective employees on
the basis of their race or sex. This conflict, of course, has implications well
beyond the hiring practices of colleges and universities. (For example, the
white-hot legal and policy debate over affirmative action in student admissions is currently the most controversial and fluid area in all of higher education law.) But affirmative action in employment is also being challenged,
and the legality of such efforts is at present very unsettled.

Significant legal differences exist between mandatory and voluntary
affirmative action programs. Affirmative action will be upheld when required as a remedy under Title VII or other nondiscrimination statutes
pursuant to a formal finding (by the cognizant administrative agency or the
courts) of past discrimination by a college or university. The far more common *voluntary* affirmative action programs, though, are legally vulnerable.
Such programs will probably fare better in the private sector, where they
do not have to meet the requirements of the Fourteenth Amendment's
Equal Protection Clause and its deep skepticism of government policies
that classify individuals by personal characteristics, especially race. But for
public colleges and universities—and all other entities regarded as state
actors under the Constitution—the law seems to be evolving in ways that
make voluntary affirmative action in employment almost impossible to
sustain.[138]

The Supreme Court's 1995 decision in *Adarand Constructors, Inc. v.
Pena*[139] made it clear that race-based preferences will be subjected to "strict
scrutiny"—the most difficult level of Equal Protection review to satisfy—
and will only be upheld if they serve a compelling institutional interest and
are narrowly tailored to further that interest. It is increasingly difficult to
meet these standards. Indeed, the only interests that the Supreme Court
has regarded as "compelling" in the affirmative action context are (1) remedying the present effects of past discrimination by the relevant institutional actor (a good example here would be court-ordered affirmative action in a Title VII disparate impact case) and (2) arguably—at least for the
moment—promoting diversity in education.[140] Other justifications offered
for affirmative action in faculty hiring (remedying the effects of discrimi-

nation in society at large; increasing the representation of minorities in particular fields; providing role models) have not passed constitutional muster.[141] And even the two established compelling interests are open to attack and limitation. For example, in *Hopwood v. State of Texas*,[142] the Fifth Circuit rejected the concept that seeking diversity in education was constitutionally "compelling" and held instead that race could not be used as a factor in a university's admissions decisions. This same reasoning could of course be extended to faculty hiring. Equally disturbing to proponents of affirmative action, many courts seem to be raising the level and specificity of past discrimination whose remediation merits race-based distinctions.

The uncertainty surrounding a public college or university's affirmative action program will not dissipate if courts agree that it serves a compelling interest. Faculty hiring preferences must also be "narrowly tailored." In conducting this portion of their "strict scrutiny," courts will carefully examine the operational details of the program in question. For example, lawful affirmative action plans seek to "eliminate conspicuous racial imbalance in traditionally segregated job categories."[143] To gauge whether a particular program does this would typically involve statistical analysis of whether the need for such program has been established and its goals set with reference to appropriate pools of actual and prospective job candidates. Now at most institutions, women and minority scholars have never constituted a large proportion of the faculty (significant exceptions being women's colleges and historically black colleges and universities). This certainly supports the legitimacy of narrowly tailored affirmative action plans. However, the combination of the unfortunate facts that (1) there are not many senior-level minority faculty and (2) in many fields only small numbers of doctorates are awarded each year to minority candidates may make it hard for institutions—especially those where a Ph.D. is required of all new hires—to demonstrate that a gap exists between the number of qualified minorities in a given field and their representation on campus that would justify the imposition of hiring preferences.[144] Filling this "pipeline" is the long-term solution to achieving faculty diversity. Until significant numbers of highly qualified minority scholars are in the job market, institutions will fight savagely over available minorities and cries will continue for race- or gender-based hiring preferences to address short-term needs. This last point leads us back to other important determinants of whether an affirmative action program is "narrowly tailored." When scrutinizing a challenged program, courts want to ensure that it is limited in duration (i.e., it seeks to eliminate disparities rather than to prescribe a new balance). They must also make certain that the affirmative action plan does not "unnecessarily trammel" the rights of third parties by, for example, precluding them from consideration for employment opportunities.[145]

The overarching issue in this latter prong of a court's Equal Protection analysis is whether an alternative, narrower program could have accomplished the same purposes as the disputed affirmative action plan. If so, the program at issue will be struck down. In *Bakke v. Regents of Univ. of California*—the Supreme Court's only opinion to date on affirmative action in higher education—the outcome of this "narrow tailoring" inquiry was to prohibit the use of explicit racial quotas in a medical school's admissions process and to confirm that race may used as *a* factor (but not the dispositive factor) in college and university admission decisions.[146] The question that now confronts colleges and universities is whether the long-presumed parallel to *Bakke* in the workforce setting—that an institution can use race or gender as a positive factor in making employment decisions in order to achieve a more diverse faculty and staff—is valid.

There is scant case law offering guidance. Presumably, minority candidates, even if unsuccessful, are unlikely to contest the legality of affirmative action programs of which they are potential beneficiaries. It also seems that many current faculty feel they have little to gain and perhaps much to lose by challenging employers' programs (being labeled racist and sexist, limiting their marketability, even possible reprisals).[147] Rejected nonminority applicants—the obvious aggrieved parties—frequently sue, but their claims and the resultant judicial opinions tend to focus more on the details of particular hires (disparate treatment cases are more common than disparate impact suits) without reaching the constitutionality of affirmative action policies. And most colleges and universities that consider race and gender in faculty hiring are of course content to keep this issue low-profile.[148] At least until now, the net result has been a silence that is almost deafening when compared with the volume of litigation over affirmative action in admissions.

A recent opinion from the Supreme Court of Nevada strongly supports the legality of affirmative action in faculty employment. *Univ. and Comm. College System of Nevada v. Farmer* approved a "two for one" minority hiring incentive plan. In a ringing affirmation of *Bakke* and a rejection of *Hopwood*, the court concluded that "the University demonstrated that it has a compelling interest in fostering a culturally and ethnically diverse faculty. A failure to attract minority faculty perpetuates the University's white enclave and further limits student exposure to multicultural diversity. Moreover, the minority bonus policy is narrowly tailored to accelerate racial and gender diversity."[149] The university prevailed because "in addition to considerations of race, [it] based its employment decision on such criteria as educational background, publishing, teaching experience, and areas of specialization. This satisfies *Bakke's* commands that race must be only one of several factors used in evaluating applicants."[150] Also heartening to affirmative action proponents was a 1998 California decision upholding a state law authorizing community colleges to employ hiring preferences to correct for the effects of discriminatory employment practices.[151] (This result ran counter to the spirit of a 1996 referendum amendment to the California constitution banning preferential treatment on the basis of race, sex, color, ethnicity, or national origin in public employment, education, and contracting.)[152]

However, on the opposite side of the ledger, a couple of 1999 precedents support the proposition that race- and gender-based hiring preferences at public universities are constitutionally infirm and may soon be a relic of the past. In two separate instances, affirmative action hiring decisions in the University of Wisconsin System were struck down. A federal trial court held that the La Crosse campus had violated Title VII when, contrary to *Bakke* and the provisions of its own affirmative action plan, it used race as the determining or governing factor in hiring an Asian man over a white man.[153] And the Seventh Circuit held that the Whitewater campus violated Title VII when a dean who wanted the Psychology Department to hire a woman to meet its affirmative action goals refused to let that department offer an open job to a man. Again contrary to *Bakke,* the university had made gender the dispositive (if not the sole) factor in a faculty search. Furthermore, the court observed, Whitewater's affirmative action plan did not require such conduct.[154] Interestingly, the Seventh Circuit's opinion includes statistical analysis showing that "a plan to have every department duplicate the pool from which it was drawn cannot be sustained. . . . Such a plan neither rests on a powerful justification nor uses sex in a way that is narrowly tailored to the justification."[155] This analysis and reasoning may be a precursor of decisions to come.

Beyond what may be growing judicial hostility, affirmative action in employment also faces legislative and state constitutional complications. In 1998 Washington State voters followed Californians in passing a ballot measure barring racial preferences in state hiring. Similar referenda and statutes have already been and will certainly be proposed in other jurisdictions. With tension high, some colleges and universities are ending their minority faculty recruitment plans.[156] Others are proceeding with "business as usual" but trying to avoid drawing attention to their affirmative action efforts. And the entire higher education community anxiously awaits further legal guidance arising from litigation about affirmative action in undergraduate and professional school admissions, which many observers expect to reach the Supreme Court.

## Terms of Employment

Even after their basic job security has been established, faculty remain vitally concerned with the terms and conditions of their employment. This is a realm in which contract law is king. One must always remember that faculty are employees bound to their employer colleges or universities by written or unwritten contract and that the rights and obligations flowing between the parties are determined by those contracts. In theory, and increasingly in practice, just about any conceivable term of employment is a potential subject for contract negotiation, especially at private institutions, which may be more accustomed to entering into side deals or ad hoc arrangements with professors. Topics of negotiation often include teaching loads; endowed chairs; start-up packages (for research equipment and setting up a lab, computers, and enhancements to library collections in a scholar's field); new research centers; eligibility for leaves and sabbaticals; housing allowances; travel funds; tuition remission and other benefits; the employer's contribution to retirement plans; office space and secretarial support; the allocation of graduate assistants; and (especially for incoming chairs) the number and level of new hires in a department.

Of course, salary always moves to the forefront. Today's faculty are quite sophisticated in demanding and receiving full market value for their services, with such value frequently established (and a professor's negotiating leverage substantially enhanced) by soliciting offers from other employers. Likewise, colleges and universities are increasingly willing to pay considerable differentials based on a scholar's stature and his or her academic discipline.[157] Computer scientists, who are avidly pursued by industry, thus command a premium over classicists. Institutions have also become rather creative in structuring faculty compensation, moving well beyond merit pay to propose (and sometimes even implement) salary arrangements linked to student enrollment or faculty receipt of research grants.[158] In a 1998 state court decision, the payment of a salary was even uncoupled from tenure in a medical school setting. An Illinois judge upheld Northwestern's "zero-based salary" plan pursuant to which a tenured faculty member literally received a university salary of zero dollars (the underlying notion being that the plaintiff's tenure was basically honorific and that he would earn his living through his separate clinical practice).[159]

In the current highly competitive faculty market, colleges and universities set salaries with careful attention to what peer institutions are paying. There are a variety of means of obtaining such information, ranging from monitoring individual offers received by professors, to focused exchanges of data among selected schools, to national salary surveys that may be either discipline-specific or institution-wide.[160] However, in compiling and using such materials, colleges and universities must avoid the pitfall of antitrust violations. The Sherman Antitrust Act, which applies to the nonprofit business of higher education as well as other sectors of the national economy, bars contracts, combinations, and conspiracies "in restraint of trade or commerce."[161] Among the activities outlawed are horizontal price-fixing among competitors, either directly by outright agreement or indirectly through means such as pooling information that ineluctably leads to common prices. The price paid for the services of faculty (their salaries) is usually one of the largest and most visible costs of operating a college or university and therefore will be scrutinized by faculty, rival institutions, and federal regulators for antitrust compliance.

Indeed, as part of the Department of Justice's 1991 investigation of undergraduate financial aid awards at the Ivy League schools and MIT, the government alleged that these colleges and universities had violated the Sherman Act by circulating data about faculty salaries to artificially depress such costs. Eight of the nine institutions ultimately signed a consent decree limiting their ability to exchange "information concerning [their] plans or projections, including budget assumptions, regarding . . . general Faculty Salary levels."[162] I would argue that these charges reflected an extremely aggressive approach to antitrust enforcement (driven in no small part by the Justice Department's desire to make a political splash) and that it is still perfectly legal for colleges and universities to share salary information—like that found in most national surveys—that is available to the general public, and even for them to participate in multiparty data exchanges not clearly linked to price-fixing. Still, these events provide unmistakable evidence that the market for faculty is and will be treated by the federal government as essentially commercial in character.

A critical threshold question in understanding the nature and terms of a faculty member's employment is whether the relevant contract is between an individual professor and his or her home institution or whether the professor is covered by a collective bargaining (i.e., union) agreement. In a nonunion environment, each scholar is free to cut the best possible deal with his or her employer, to disregard (or negotiate away) issues and potential contract terms of perceived low value, and to seek to renegotiate an old contract in his or her favor any time that circumstances so warrant (e.g., receipt of another job offer, publication of an important new book). Conversely, in a unionized setting, faculty negotiate as a bloc through their elected representatives, and personalized salary or other employment arrangements are typically not made or welcomed. Unionized faculty also enjoy the protections that can be gleaned—and the enhanced bargaining clout that may result—from membership in a larger group. (Needless to say, such protections will have more significance to "ordinary" faculty than to a superstar who can basically write his or her own ticket.)

## The Nonunion Setting

In a nonunion setting, formal written contracts with faculty are unusual. What typically exists in their stead is a collection of correspondence directed to individual faculty, including offer and appointment letters spelling out key initial terms of employment, a reappointment letter at the conclusion of each fixed term, letters formally advising the faculty member that he or she has been awarded tenure and promoted to associate (and then full) professor, and annual salary notifications. However, all of these letters—if carefully drafted—will contain blanket references to "applicable" institutional policies, which will constitute the bulk of the faculty member's employment contract. These would include, for example, procedures and criteria for tenure and promotion decisions, faculty discipline codes, sexual harassment policies, institutional statements on academic freedom, copyright and patent policies, consulting guidelines, and rules establishing eligibility for health and other benefits. Recall also that in addition to written documents, unwritten institutional customs and practices can form part of the contract, especially when professors have clearly relied on their continued relevance. This rather informal and loosely structured employment

relationship reflects professors' and institutions' desire for collegial relations and promotes the contracting parties' flexibility, but often it lacks
clarity about what is expected on each side of the bargain. The nascent
confusion can lead to disputes and litigation (e.g., breach-of-contract suits
arising from the denial of tenure). Understandably, one of the big attrac-
tions of collective bargaining (which is briefly discussed in the following
pages) is the level of certainty it provides about the respective rights and
duties of the college or university and its faculty (and other) employees.

## Unionization

The laws governing collective bargaining at colleges and universities; the
strategies followed by unions to organize a campus and by institutions to
defeat such efforts; the scope, interpretation, and enforcement of collective bargaining agreements; and the practical consequences to both employers and employees of operating in a unionized environment comprise
a vast and specialized area of higher education law. Institutions with faculty or graduate student unions and the employees represented by those
unions typically require the assistance of sophisticated labor counsel to
navigate these shoals. Thus, most university administrators and faculty are
not (and need not be) familiar with the arcana of labor law. Accordingly, in
this section I have sought to lay out only the basic legal concepts and principles necessary for readers to understand how their institutions are (or
might be) bound by collective bargaining agreements, how such agreements are likely to affect their daily work, and (as promised at the start of
this volume) when to ask their attorneys for more particularized advice.

   In 1996 academic unions represented 250,716 professors on 1,097 campuses.[163] As I explain below, though, for much of the last two decades faculty unionization has not been a particularly prominent issue in higher
education law. Efforts at unionization (especially at private colleges and
universities) were dealt a major setback by the Supreme Court's 1980 holding that faculty at Yeshiva University—and by implication at many other
universities—were ineligible to form unions because they helped manage
their institutions.[164] A separate line of precedent dating from the mid-1970s
held that graduate teaching instructors and research assistants were students, as opposed to employees entitled to bargain collectively. However,
unionization efforts appear to be gathering steam once more in a faculty
job market and academic climate characterized by (1) unabated financial
pressure on employer institutions; (2) the resultant bleak employment pros-

pects for newly minted Ph.D.'s and junior faculty (e.g., continued growth in part-time and non-tenure-track positions; reluctance to award tenure); (3) faculty discomfort and anger over what is seen as the encroachment of "corporate values and practices" into the academy (e.g., administrative use of "Total Quality Management" principles and efforts to "right-size" an institution); and (4) conscious efforts by unions to expand their membership and influence in nonindustrial settings like college and university campuses.[165] Under these conditions, established arguments and precedents against unionization, especially collective bargaining by graduate students, are being challenged anew.

Here I want to make a critical point bearing on any analysis of the merits or effects of collective bargaining in higher education. Given the basic philosophical and legal structure of American labor law, unionizing academic employees often resembles jamming a square peg into a round hole. Federal and state labor laws are premised on a classic industrial model of unionization with a sharp division between management and labor. Put simply, management determines the business that will be engaged in, the current product lines, the methods of production, and the sales price. Labor just makes the product. This model works reasonably well on the assembly line, but the distinction between management and labor is much less obvious with scholarly employees like faculty who actually control the content and mode of delivery of the university's research and teaching "product"—or who perhaps should even be viewed *as* that product. Suddenly the question of who exercises power in the workplace, and thus who should be bargaining with whom about what, becomes rather complex.

In addition to the complications posed by an ill-fitting industrial model, labor law is one of the many realms where public and private institutions are subject to different legal authorities. Unionization at private colleges and universities (and for all other private employers) is governed by *federal* labor law, most significantly the National Labor Relations Act (NLRA).[166] This statute is interpreted and enforced primarily by the quasi-judicial National Labor Relations Board (NLRB) in Washington and its staff in regional offices across the country. However, appellate courts have carved out a major exception under the NLRA for religiously controlled and operated colleges and universities, which can refuse to bargain collectively with their faculty. In *Universidad Central de Bayamon v. N.L.R.B.*,[167] a split First Circuit did not enforce an order requiring a Catholic university to negotiate with a faculty union, citing the Supreme Court's opinion in

*N.L.R.B. v. Catholic Bishop of Chicago* that rejected board jurisdiction over parochial school faculty as an unconstitutional entanglement of church and state.[168] Half of the *Bayamon* judges feared that mandatory negotiations over "the college curriculum (including religious requirements), the manner of teaching (according to Christian principles), [and] the teachers' obligations to counsel the students (and the moral or religious principles that underlie the counseling)" would inevitably and impermissibly mix terms of employment with religious doctrine.[169]

Unionization at public colleges and universities, in contrast, is governed by *state* law. As of 1997, thirty-three states and the District of Columbia had authorized faculty collective bargaining by express statute or policy of the relevant state labor board (such boards usually parallel the NLRB in structure and authority).[170] In the remaining states, collective bargaining is still illegal for public employees. Further, where the law allows unionization, the relevant statutes are not always respectful of educational values and goals and the university environment. California's Higher Education Employer-Employee Relations Act takes a relatively sophisticated approach, wisely removing from the scope of union representation a series of traditionally "academic" subjects such as admission requirements; conditions for the award of certificates and degrees; the content of courses, curricula, and research programs; and policies for appointment, promotion, and tenure.[171] But other state laws are much less sensitive and fail to draw helpful distinctions between faculty and other state workers. In contrast to private employer unions under the NLRA, public college and university unions typically cannot strike. Indeed, in some jurisdictions (New York being a prime example), statutes expressly bar the use of this "ultimate" labor weapon.[172] In lieu of strikes, state laws frequently mandate fact-finding or arbitration to resolve labor disputes. The use of such terminal mechanisms is not required under the NLRA and is much less common in the private sector.

Where collective bargaining is allowed at either public or private institutions, faculty may create their own independent unions or choose to affiliate with a national labor organization such as the American Federation of Teachers, the National Education Association, or even traditional "blue collar" unions like the United Autoworkers (these larger groups may in turn be affiliated with umbrella labor organizations like the AFL-CIO). Affiliation with statewide or national unions may enhance a local unit's bargaining clout and allow it to tap additional resources (such as strike funds) and to draw on the parent union's expertise in contract negotiations or settling grievances. In this regard, it is essential to note that the AAUP—which we have encountered elsewhere in this volume in its self-appointed role as codifier, interpreter, and guardian of academic mores—often moves beyond its historic status as a faculty advocacy group to become the legally recognized collective bargaining agent for professors on a particular campus. According to the most recent *Directory of Faculty Contracts and Bargaining Agents,* the AAUP and its affiliates represented over 28,000 faculty in sixty-one bargaining units.[173] It is therefore critical for administrators to understand the legal status of the local AAUP chapter (i.e., whether or not it is a formal bargaining agent) before giving credence to, much less accepting, the chapter's positions.

## FACULTY ELIGIBILITY TO UNIONIZE

Notwithstanding the public-private divide, the NLRA (as seminal collective bargaining legislation) and the case law arising under it also frequently serve as a model for the crafting, interpretation, and enforcement of state labor laws.[174] Consider, for example, the vital threshold question of which employees are eligible to form unions. The NLRA explicitly declares that *professional employees* (the definition of that term clearly seems to envision college and university professors)[175] can organize to bargain collectively with management. However, reflecting an industrial model, the act excludes from its coverage "supervisors" who have "authority, in the interest of the employer, to hire, transfer, suspend, lay off, recall, promote, discharge, assign, reward, or discipline other employees, or responsibly to direct them, or to adjust their grievances, or effectively to recommend such action."[176] Under that same model (though not pursuant to express statutory provision), courts have consistently held that "managers" may not unionize either. The fear is that union membership and participation in contract negotiations would create a risk of divided loyalty for these employees who "formulate and effectuate management policies by expressing and making operative the decisions of their employer."[177] Predictable complications arise when ostensibly "professional" faculty members assume roles and responsibilities that could be characterized as "supervisory" or "managerial" under the NLRA. This happens with some frequency because, in the words of one prominent commentator, "faculty have much more influence in the organizations in which they work than any other professionals previously included under the [act]. But faculty are also much less accountable to higher authority than many of the people the NLRB had excluded as managers."[178] The classification of an institution's faculty is thus both delicate and entirely determinative of their right to unionize.

Large-scale faculty unionization first occurred in the 1960s, and litigation over its propriety promptly followed. From 1971 to 1980, the NLRB routinely held that faculty were "professional employees" eligible to bargain collectively. Then, in *N.L.R.B. v. Yeshiva Univ.*, the Supreme Court ruled in a controversial 5-4 decision that Yeshiva's full-time faculty—and, by extension, faculty at other similar "mature private universities"—were managerial employees excluded under the NLRA because they formulated and implemented the academic policies that essentially drove the "educational business" of the institution and because their professional interests were closely aligned with (indeed, could not be separated from) those of the employer university.[179] According to the majority opinion, Yeshiva's faculty

> decide what courses will be offered, when they will be scheduled, and to whom they will be taught. They debate and determine teaching methods, grading policies, and matriculation standards. They effectively decide which students will be admitted, retained, and graduated. On occasion their views have determined the size of the student body, the tuition to be charged, and the location of a school. When one considers the function of a university, it is difficult to imagine decisions more managerial than these. To the extent the industrial analogy applies, the faculty determines within each school the product to be produced, the terms upon which it will be offered, and the customers who will be served.[180]

In *Yeshiva* the Supreme Court did not resolve the question of whether professors were also barred from unionizing as *supervisory* employees— though it implied that faculty dominance over hiring, tenure, promotions, and sabbaticals might well lead to exclusion under the NLRA.[181] Note also that in addition to overseeing the work of junior colleagues, faculty regularly supervise the activities of graduate student and postdoctoral-level research and teaching assistants.

As one might expect, the *Yeshiva* decision checked the national trend towards unionization. Colleges and university administrations quickly embraced this powerful legal precedent against union certification. At some institutions, organizing efforts faltered and prospective bargaining agents withdrew; at others, agents were actually decertified when faculty were held to be managerial employees. For example, the AAUP union chapter at Boston University lost its bid to represent faculty when the NLRB and a federal appellate court determined that at BU "as in Yeshiva, in the promulgation of the University's principal business, which is education and research, the faculty's role is predominant, and 'in any other context unquestionably would be considered managerial.'"[182] Since the *Yeshiva* decision, the NLRB has only granted bargaining rights to private-college faculty on a handful of occasions.[183] And although *Yeshiva* is a private-sector case, much of the Supreme Court's reasoning would also appear to block the formation of faculty unions at public colleges and universities in states with similar limits on the union eligibility of managers and supervisors. Nevertheless, as unionization efforts again gather momentum for the reasons noted above, union advocates will certainly try—and may be able—to distinguish the *Yeshiva* opinion and thus limit its reach. By the Court's own characterization, Yeshiva was a "mature" institution with well-established and substantive faculty governance. Considerable numbers of colleges and universities will not fit this pattern or exhibit the same traditions. Furthermore, the *Yeshiva* holding does not address the status of part-time faculty. It arguably does not cover faculty off the tenure track or scholars on soft-money research appointments. And it certainly does not extend to graduate students serving as teaching or research assistants. *Yeshiva* was and remains a critical legal turning point, but it was not the final word in this area.

Several additional points must be made about faculty eligibility to unionize and the consequences of defining an appropriate bargaining unit. Under *Yeshiva* and its progeny, senior-level academic administrators such as deans and provosts would clearly be excluded under the NLRA (and analogous state acts) because of their managerial-supervisory duties, even if they hold faculty appointments. Legal authority on the status of department chairs, however, is very muddled, with conflicting precedents that reflect the institution-specific nature of the chair's role (and probably also some sloppiness or confusion on the part of the NLRB).[184] Administrators and union supporters alike should also know that colleges and universities are not obliged to negotiate automatically with nascent faculty unions. In most circumstances, the employer should first insist upon holding a formal certification election under the NLRA. To do otherwise might subject the employer to liability for recognizing a minority union (in egregious cases, minority unions might be controlled by management) or for recognizing any particular union when a rival labor organization still claims to enjoy substantial support. Once a union wins a certification election, though, it will represent all eligible faculty, even those who elect not to become dues-paying members. The union can charge these nonmembers a fee to help cover the cost of the services it provides related to collective bargaining (but not for other activities such as political advocacy).[185]

## BARGAINING SUBJECTS

The NLRA requires employers to bargain with employee unions over the "mandatory subjects" of "wages, hours, and other terms or conditions of employment."[186] If the employer refuses to bargain in good faith about a mandatory subject of negotiation (or subsequently violates the terms of the signed contract), it can be charged with having committed an unfair labor practice under the act. According to this taxonomy, any subject that is not mandatory is a "permissive" subject for bargaining—meaning that even if one party wishes to negotiate about it, the other side may elect otherwise. State labor laws, which as we have seen are frequently modeled after the NLRA, also typically subscribe to this mandatory/permissive dichotomy.

Obviously, if both employers and unions (or adjudicating labor boards or courts) take an inclusive view of what constitutes mandatory subjects, the parties will have a broad array of potential topics for negotiation. Alternatively, if mandatory subjects are circumscribed to exclude issues of importance to most professors—such as matters implicating academic freedom—faculty unionization may lose much of its appeal. Given the diversity of jurisdictions, institutions, and points of contention, it is hardly surprising that there are no settled definitions of what is mandatory. But typically the formal procedures or criteria that fix a faculty member's status would be mandatory, while institutional policy directions or strategies would be permissive (and therefore could be withdrawn from the bargaining table).[187] The AAUP's former staff counsel has argued that courts treat "many issues of substantial professional interest as outside the scope of mandatory bargaining, including curriculum, student-faculty ratio, policies on academic freedom and professional ethics, and decisions to hire, promote, award tenure, and retrench."[188] Of course, a college or university administration that elects not to bargain over a permissive subject can still choose to consult with its faculty formally or informally about that same matter, and perhaps administrators would be well-advised to do so. But this does not address the underlying problem that a narrow interpretation of mandatory subjects is not easily reconciled with faculty notions of responsibility for institutional mores and academic governance. In short, while they draw paychecks on the same account, in fundamental ways faculty are not employees in the same way that janitors are, much less the graduate teaching assistants, to whom we next turn. What this again points out is the inadequacy of applying industrial models of labor relations to the business of higher education. As the NLRB itself has recognized, "from the standpoint of educational policy, the nature of collective bargaining is such that it is not particularly well suited to academic decisionmaking."[189]

## GRADUATE STUDENT UNIONIZATION

The ability of teaching and research assistants to form unions is a hotly contested and fluid area of college and university law at public and private institutions alike. The legal debate centers on whether graduate students are fundamentally *employees* (and thus entitled to organize) or *students*. However, recent events indicate that graduate student unionization may be emerging as a national trend. Recognized unions now exist at at least twenty-seven public colleges and universities in ten states and, over the last decade, membership in such unions has reached almost 40,000. In 1999 the movement won a huge victory when the University of California ended fifteen years of acrimony (including threatened and actual strikes) by recognizing teaching assistant unions on eight UC campuses.[190] And in late 2000, the NLRB held for the first time that graduate students at a private higher education institution—in this case, NYU—were eligible to bargain collectively with their university employer.[191] As I explain below, the legal and policy battles in this realm are intense and far from over.

Graduate student unionization at public colleges and universities is regulated (if it is permitted at all) by state collective bargaining statutes. At private institutions (as with faculty unionization) the NLRA is controlling. And historically, private universities have refused to negotiate contracts with unions representing their graduate teaching and research assistants, relying on a series of NLRB decisions from the 1970s that held that graduate students who provided services to universities that were directly related to or an integral part of their educational programs were primarily students and not covered employees under the NLRA. For example, in 1974 the board declared that graduate research assistants in Stanford's physics department were not employees because the payments they received from the university were stipends or grants permitting them to engage in advanced research that was required as "part of the course of instruction, a part of the learning process."[192] It thus seemed relatively settled that private colleges and universities need not bargain collectively with graduate-level workers because the "mutual interests of the students and the educational institution in the services being rendered are predominantly academic rather than economic in nature."[193]

However, we may now be witnessing a seismic shift in this legal ground. The first indication of such change came in 1996, when NLRB attorneys embraced the position that graduate teaching assistants *were* employees entitled to unionize;[194] the government attorneys even filed a complaint against Yale for retaliating against teaching assistants (TAs) who refused to turn in grades as a protest against the university's refusal to recognize their union. Then in 1999 (in a case involving Boston University's medical center), the NLRB reversed more than twenty years of precedent by holding that interns, residents, and clinical fellows were employees covered by the NLRA.[195] These physicians-in-training were deemed employees because they "work for an employer . . . are compensated for their services . . . receive fringe benefits and other emoluments . . . and provide patient care."[196] That they also obtained educational benefits from their employment did not alter this fundamental status. Substituting the phrase "undergraduate teaching" for "patient care," much of the NLRB's reasoning in *Boston Medical Center* could easily be extended to reach Ph.D. students. And the board did exactly that in its October 2000 *New York University* decision, declaring that "graduate assistants plainly and literally fall within the meaning of 'employee'" under the NLRA.[197] According to the NLRB, "workers who are compensated by, and under the control of, a statutory employer . . . [may not be deprived] of their fundamental statutory rights to organize and bargain with their employer, simply because they also are students."[198] As one might expect, the combination of graduate student activism and these regulatory-adjudicatory about-faces has created legal turmoil.

Understandably, determination of the "employee status" of graduate students blends into the debate about whether unionization is in the best interests of such students and the academy. Each side has powerful arguments at its disposal.[199] Advocates of unionization begin with the economic proposition that (educational rhetoric to the contrary) graduate students are a source of cheap and abundant labor that colleges and universities increasingly rely upon to meet their teaching needs. At many institutions TAs earn fifteen thousand dollars or less, with meager benefits, for what amounts to a half-time faculty job. They are frequently called upon (and to eke out a living are often willing) to teach subjects far removed from their field of graduate study, with minimal supervision, undercutting claims that their instructional duties are connected to their education.[200] Unionization can therefore be seen as a response to current workplace exploitation and bleak job prospects, particularly for students in overcrowded humanities and social science disciplines.[201] According to union activists, organizing graduate students (and other faculty) will help block colleges and universities from replacing tenured and tenure-track positions with cheaper and lower-quality adjuncts. To forestall concerns that collective bargaining will pervert academic decisions, perhaps the parties might even agree to negotiate only about monetary issues.

Organizers also identify educational benefits that may flow from unionization. For example, with better wages and benefits, graduate students would not need to find extra jobs that pull them away from dissertation writing and extend their time-to-degree. More generous stipends would permit students from a broader range of socioeconomic backgrounds (and perhaps better students as well) to pursue graduate study. A unionized environment offers graduate students clear, formal channels to contribute ideas to enhance undergraduate teaching and to fight for improvements such as smaller classes and better training for TAs.[202]

Finally, considerations of equity drive the graduate student union movement. Beyond the tangible rewards sought through enhanced bargaining power, unionization in this context is very much about earning respect and recognition for the critical role graduate teaching and research assistants play in providing baccalaureate instruction and conducting scholarship. Collective bargaining also promotes fairness by ensuring consistent treatment of union members' concerns and grievances and by giving graduate students a greater measure of control over their lives.

The case *against* graduate student unionization is a potpourri—the predictable consequence of institutions using any and all available arguments to ward off the union threat—but nonetheless very cogent. Interestingly, it employs many of the same conceptual lenses used by union proponents (e.g., the effect of unionization on graduate students themselves and on undergraduate education) to reach diametrically different conclusions. At the heart of the antiunion position is the conviction that the "defining relationship between faculty members and graduate students is the educational one that brought them together, not the relationship of employer and employee."[203] Graduate students are apprentice scholar-teachers preparing for a career that they have not yet entered; the pedagogical training acquired as a TA is an integral part of their education.

Painted most starkly, collective bargaining with graduate students will "reshape academic life . . . dramatically and destructively."[204] First, there are several ways in which unionization may hurt the quality of graduate education. In a union setting, Ph.D. training could easily become homogenized. Graduate students might lose the flexibility to determine the content and timing of their own educational programs in areas covered by the bargaining agreement (for instance, if the contract called for them to acquire teaching experience by certain dates). Conversely, union contracts may reduce departments' and senior instructors' ability to use teaching fellows as educationally appropriate. Once the extent and timing of graduate student teaching responsibilities become negotiable (recalling here that mandatory subjects of bargaining under the NLRA include the hours of employment), the TA union may press for additional teaching duties or even guaranteed slots for its most senior or experienced members, even if faculty supervisors feel that novice teachers would benefit more from such opportunities. Or the union might demand more teaching experience for all its members than they actually need. The mechanics of negotiating and administering labor contracts can also deleteriously affect graduate education. Blocks of time devoted by students to such endeavors may come at the expense of more swiftly achieving primary intellectual and career goals.[205] Moreover, from the perspective of graduate student autonomy, individual TAs will not have much control over the bargaining positions taken by the union on their behalf. Indeed, local chapters may rely heavily on national affiliates for advice and expertise, in which case nonacademic "outsiders" will shape both the local's stance and the final contract.

The second charge against graduate student unions is that they will impede, if not prevent, the development of desired collegial, nurturing bonds between doctoral students and faculty, resulting instead in relationships that are bureaucratized and even polarized. For example, reflecting their industrial genesis, collective bargaining agreements would typically move past the (sometimes informal) procedures in place to resolve graduate student complaints to establish official mechanisms for filing grievances with the full political backing and the financial and legal support of the union.

Formal and more adversarial union charges, which might wend their way to the NLRB, could then be brought against faculty supervisors on issues such as stipend levels, grades, the ability to continue in the program, approval of dissertation topics, receipt of departmental honors, and the content of references. Meritless complaints would be more difficult to dispose of.[206] At the same time, graduate student unions may "curtail and supplant existing forms of [graduate] student government and participation in faculty committees."[207] Graduate student–adviser relationships are symbiotic (and ideally mutually beneficial), intense, and even in a nonunion environment occasionally flare into controversy over students' need for independence, the attribution of ideas and labor, and faculty exercise of intellectual or career power.[208] Creating a graduate student union, however, raises the stakes by giving structure and permanence to these inherent tensions and feeding the perception (cynics might say recognizing the reality) that graduate-level education is fundamentally an arms-length, quasi-commercial transaction between equally wary students and faculty.[209]

Opponents of unionization also envision how collective bargaining with graduate teaching or research assistants could infringe upon academic freedom. According to this line of thought, recognizing a union (in particular under the NLRA) will make bargainable subjects of matters with regard to which the faculty (sometimes in conjunction with the university as an institution) has enjoyed tremendous historical and legal autonomy, including program (and curricular) content, standards for student advancement and graduation, evaluations of student work, and instructors' teaching methods. Any incursion into these realms, from whatever source (governmental, trustee, or—as in this case—student), will encounter fierce faculty resistance. From both a faculty and an institutional academic freedom perspective, a related risk is that collective bargaining dispute resolution procedures may invest arbitrators or mediators (who have a very limited understanding of the academy) with the power to make decisions about educational matters.[210] Furthermore, the concern has been raised that in a union environment faculty will be reluctant to express their views on the propriety of the union's positions for fear of opening themselves to claims of retaliation in their capacity as supervisors of graduate student employees or (unless a shop steward participates in such discussions) unlawful interference with the union's role as sole bargaining agent. Extreme pessimists worry that faculty will temper their scholarly criticism of graduate students' work, especially if a particular instructor has been the target of a prior union grievance. I disagree with this last point, believing that faculty have considerable integrity and will not be so easily cowed. But as Yale's provost has correctly observed, "restrictions on what could be legally discussed with an 'employee' would strike at the freedom of expression central to the whole conception of the university as an intellectual community."[211]

Last but not least, union foes assert that recognizing TA unions will harm the quality of *undergraduate* education. Contractually imposed limits on how faculty may utilize graduate assistants in structuring and teaching baccalaureate courses may make no pedagogical sense. One can easily conceive of union leadership demanding the creation of more (and more highly compensated) TA positions notwithstanding undergraduate students' need and desire to receive a greater proportion of their instruction from regular faculty. Most obviously, undergraduates will be the immediate and direct victims of any strikes or "job actions" engaged in by the union as part of its recognition and negotiation strategy.

Underlying and reinforcing all of these qualms about graduate student unions are legitimate fears about the incremental cost of collective bargaining agreements. Even without unions, most institutions provide substantial financial support to their Ph.D. students. For example, a typical Yale doctoral student would receive a multiyear commitment of tuition waivers, stipends, and a dissertation fellowship totaling more than $135,000.[212] In an era of constrained resources and growing needs, universities understandably balk at the prospect of further subventions of graduate education or otherwise making this notoriously costly and inefficient activity even more uneconomical. But as I have shown in the preceding paragraphs, partisan claims that skinflinted selfishness is the only reason universities and faculty resist unionization are overly simplistic, if not just plain wrong. Note also that many institutions would dispute union figures about the extent of their reliance on TAs in staffing courses.

One prominent dispute over graduate student union organization came to a head when a budding union of Yale teaching assistants (with the legal backing of NLRB regional staff) filed an unfair labor practice charge against the university for retaliating against member TAs who participated in a 1995 "grade strike" that was part of a recognition drive. In November 1999 the NLRB ruled in Yale's favor on what might be deemed technicalities (i.e., withholding fall semester grades while still meeting with students, grading course materials, writing recommendations, and planning to teach in the spring constituted an unlawful "partial strike" under the NLRA; the student papers and test materials that were withheld were Yale's property).[213] Although the board remanded the case to an administrative law judge for a determination of whether the graduate students were employees under the act, Yale and the NLRB entered into a settlement agreement without further findings on or resolution of this critical issue.[214]

In the meantime, however, the parallel NYU case wound its way through several administrative layers of the legal system. In finding that the bulk of the university's graduate assistants were statutory employees under the NLRA, local NLRB staff observed:

> The Employer has specific expectations of graduate assistants that are often spelled out in departmental or program handbooks, by job descriptions, or by NYU representatives. NYU representatives supervise the work of the graduate assistants. The Employer provides the supplies and the place of work for the graduate assistants. In the case of TAs, NYU provides extensive training as to the nature of the services to be provided, including training on the application of NYU policies to the undergraduates. As for their compensation, graduate assistants' stipends are treated like any other personnel salary [and unlike fellowship or scholarship awards] in that they are processed through the payroll department and distributed in bi-weekly checks. The IRS treats the stipends as taxable income. . . . Finally, graduate assistants are subject to removal or transfer.[215]

The national board was unequivocal—even blunt—in agreeing with this determination. Said the NLRB: "graduate assistants perform services under the control and direction of the Employer, and they are compensated for these services by the Employer. . . . The graduate assistants' relationship with the Employer is thus indistinguishable from a traditional master-servant relationship."[216]

NYU's arguments that, unlike the house staff physicians in *Boston Medical Center*, these Ph.D. candidates had not yet earned their graduate degrees, spent a much smaller portion of their time performing required duties, and were not directly paid "for" their teaching and research all fell on deaf ears. Although formally enrolled at NYU, the graduate assistants did not pay tuition or complete coursework like "traditional" students. They may have worked fewer hours than hospital house staff, but they were still engaged in work. And much of that work did not appear to be educationally driven. The NLRB noted "that this is work in exchange for pay, and not solely the pursuit of education, is highlighted by the absence of any aca-demic credit for virtually all graduate assistant work. . . . working as a gradu-ate assistant is not a requirement for obtaining a graduate degree in most departments. Nor is it a part of the graduate student curriculum in most departments."[217] In short, the NYU graduate students were NLRA-covered employees notwithstanding the fact that they acquired some educational benefit from their employment.

The NLRB also rejected NYU's contention that graduate student unions were highly undesirable on educational and public policy grounds. The board discounted claims that unionization would imperil academic free-dom by, for example, requiring negotiations over course content and deliv-ery. Observing that the Supreme Court had been undeterred by "attenu-ated and speculative claims of injury to academic freedom" when it upheld EEOC access to tenure files,[218] the board declared, "We are confident that in bargaining concerning units of graduate assistants, the parties can 'con-front any issues of academic freedom as they would any other issue.'"[219] Previously, the NLRB regional director had concluded that collective bar-gaining "can be limited to only those matters affecting wages, hours, and other terms and conditions of employment."[220] If (as NYU warned) the allegedly clear boundaries between academic and employment matters turned out to be blurry, the local NLRB chief had retorted that "the obli-gation to bargain does not involve the obligation to *concede* significant interests."[221] Now, in affirming that director's decision, the NLRB expressly held, "We cannot say as a matter of law or policy that permitting graduate assistants to be considered employees entitled to the benefits of the [NLRA] will result in improper interference with the academic freedom of the in-stitution they serve."[222]

The board's *NYU* opinion clearly endorses the NLRA's view of collective bargaining as a path towards economic fairness. Under that statute, a uni-versity cannot preserve its market power (and keep its costs down) by dic-tating terms of employment to graduate assistants in individual negotia-tions, rather than dealing with the united voice of all similarly situated employees.

NYU eventually threw in the towel, agreeing to bargain collectively with its TAs and declining any judicial challenge to the NLRB's decisions. But some other private research university that is faced with graduate student unionization will undoubtedly take up this gauntlet in the federal appellate courts (with the full support and legal backing of peer institutions across the country). Whichever one turns out to be the test case, its final outcome is likely to have *Yeshiva*-like repercussions. Recognizing the hazards of prediction, how will things shake out? In my view, contrary to the NLRB's latest position, graduate assistants are fundamentally students and not employees. However, in order to stretch limited resources as far as possible and to placate senior faculty who do not wish to teach low-level undergraduate courses, many universities have strayed too far from this largely unassailable legal ideal. If they hope to avoid graduate student unions, institutions must at the very least relink students' teaching duties to their educational programs, perhaps requiring such service as an integral (even credit-bearing) part of Ph.D. training, and ensure meaningful faculty oversight of such activity. But even this may not stem a growing unionization tide.

## Faculty Discipline

Inevitably, some faculty at some colleges and universities—like employees everywhere—will fail to meet their responsibilities with regard to the quality of work or the level of professionalism that is fairly expected of them. They fall short in their performance, harm or take unfair advantage of other members of the college or university community, hurt their employer institution or block the attainment of its goals, or even injure broader society. When such unfortunate events occur, faculty—again like all other employees at educational and commercial businesses—are subject to discipline by their employers (and may also incur civil or criminal liability).

Institutions therefore need well-understood and well-accepted means of monitoring the effectiveness of faculty employees and, if necessary, enforcing standards of performance. Faculty have, of course, always been held accountable in various ways, ranging from high barriers to entering the professoriate, to the widespread use of teaching evaluations, to periodic reviews of probationary appointees, to rigorous reappointment and tenure processes, to having their scholarship subject to formal peer review and their ideas (and behavior) subject to the constant scrutiny of colleagues at their institutions and within their disciplines. However, higher education today faces unprecedented demands to demonstrate productivity and efficiency to all its stakeholders: legislators, donors, granting agencies, and tuition check-writers, who fund the enterprise; students, who increasingly view themselves as educational consumers; employers, who seek assurances of the value of an institution's degree; and a general public that is often ignorant of or skeptical about what colleges and universities actually do. In this environment, institutions—and occasionally professors themselves—have placed new emphasis on faculty accountability. Further, since colleges and universities must meet the needs of an ever-more-rapidly changing world, they have to be nimble and flexible enough to accommodate shifting intellectual currents and financial circumstances notwithstanding faculty tenure (and the compelling justifications on which it rests). Here, too, institutions require administrative tools to ensure that faculty will respond appropriately to changing conditions—and if the faculty fail to do so, institutions require the ability to change *faculty* as part of *their* response to those new conditions.

In this final section of our examination of faculty in their role as employees, I review the legal structures and rules that have evolved allowing colleges and universities to be confident that they have the faculty in place to do the work at hand and that such work is in fact being done. Because employers' insistence about such matters often leads to controversy, I also explore the legal (in some circumstances constitutional) safeguards that protect faculty from unfair or wrongheaded actions by their institutions. All of this falls under a rubric that I term *faculty discipline*.

Obviously, faculty conduct that warrants institutional discipline may take an infinite variety of forms. And expectations about proper faculty conduct, and the consequences for violating them, will likewise differ from one college or university to another. The terms of applicable faculty employment contracts, whether collective bargaining agreements with a union or agreements (written or unwritten) with individual professors, are the primary source of such rules and of the procedures for their enforcement. But local history and culture also exert a powerful influence on faculty discipline (for instance, insubordinate faculty remarks to a dean or president may be regarded much more seriously at a small denominational college than at a large public research university).

Predictably, the more grave the misconduct (or the more frequently or repeatedly it occurs), the more serious the sanctions that are likely to ensue. However, at almost every institution there will be many checkpoints along the path of graduated employee discipline. Typical steps before dismissal would include, in increasing severity: (1) an informal conversation between the faculty member and the chair or dean; (2) a lower-than-normal (or even zero) salary increase; (3) loss of perquisites or privileges (i.e., premium office space, discretionary funds, research assistantships); (4) a formal warning or reprimand, which might be placed in the faculty member's personnel file; (5) being put on probation; and (6) being put on involuntary leave. In the following pages, I focus primarily on types of faculty misconduct that may result in the loss of one's job. This approach helps demarcate the outer limits of acceptable faculty behavior. But readers should always bear in mind that before such limits are reached, more modest or isolated faculty transgressions will result in lesser (though potentially escalating) penalties. Indeed, even behavior that may warrant dismissal is often met with a less severe punishment. In all of these respects, general legal rules authorizing employee discipline once again translate neatly into the faculty context.

## Post-Tenure Review

Prior to earning tenure, junior faculty are of course probationary employees, whose term appointments (for periods as short as a semester or as long as several years) will not necessarily be renewed.[223] At many colleges and universities, these nontenured faculty undergo annual or periodic performance reviews, which are critical inputs in chairs' or deans' decisions about retention. Depending on the institution and the provisions of any applicable employment agreement, such reviews will vary in formality and frequency. But in almost all cases they can be a structured and highly effective means of identifying—and hopefully eliminating—employee problems (if not problem employees). Even if a professor on the tenure track is reappointed for another term, a pretenure review can provide critical feedback about areas requiring improvement and the individual's current prospects for tenure. In the alternative, advising an instructor or assistant professor that he or she is not performing as anticipated may lead that junior faculty member to seek employment elsewhere, thus avoiding the loss of face and potential damage to reputation associated with a nonrenewal or the denial of tenure. Entirely apart from the issue of reappointment, pretenure reviews may also lead to sanctions for undesirable or improper faculty conduct.

Moreover, an increasingly common and accepted method for colleges and universities to oversee the quality of faculty work is to require periodic reviews of professors' teaching, scholarship, and service even after the award of tenure. Scores of institutions across the country have already adopted some version of formal post-tenure review, with many more sure to follow. According to a 1996 survey of 680 colleges and universities, 61 percent had post-tenure review policies in place and another 9 percent were considering imposing such a requirement.[224] As explained below, post-tenure review has been especially popular among public institutions in response to legislators' and citizens' demands for faculty and institutional accountability.[225]

Post-tenure reviews have as many variations as tenure and promotion policies. For example, a key distinction is between across-the-board reviews mandated for all faculty at certain times and individual reviews triggered by events such as poor teaching evaluations or below-average merit raises. Post-tenure reviews also vary by their periodicity, their use of internal or external evaluators, the types of feedback given to reviewees, the kinds and levels of resources associated with the review program (in particular, whether post-tenure reviews generate funds and other assistance to improve faculty performance), and, significantly, the consequences or sanctions that may follow from an adverse assessment.

Debates over the wisdom and effectiveness of post-tenure reviews are quite heated—though at present the proponents of such reviews are clearly ascendant. Supporters claim that post-tenure review is critical to increased public confidence in and willingness to support higher education, especially at state-operated colleges and universities, and especially during times when resources are tightly constrained (as is all too often the case). Such reviews seek to ensure that faculty continue to take their responsibilities seriously and to perform their jobs well. They may be all the more necessary and valuable now that mandatory faculty retirement has been eliminated. Some advocates go a step further to assert that post-tenure reviews by faculty peers promote collegial responsibility for assessment and thus actually strengthen faculty governance and the tenure system. "By assuring the public that the faculty is accountable for its own performance, post-tenure review not only enhances the reputation of the institution but also protects academic freedom by diminishing the likelihood of public intervention."[226] Even the AAUP concedes that if post-tenure reviews must occur, the faculty should take the lead in crafting and administering them.

But opponents of post-tenure review claim (frequently in rhetoric tinged with hysteria) that it changes—indeed, cheapens—tenure to a series of multiyear contracts because faculty must essentially be recertified every "x" years and that it is ultimately an assault on the very foundations of academic freedom. According to this view, post-tenure review's focus on managerial accountability can redirect faculty priorities. The prospect of an impending review puts faculty under time pressure to produce "results" demonstrating their fitness and worth. This can undercut the quality, creativity, and boldness of scholarship. "More frequent and formal reviews may lead faculty members to pick safe and quick, but less potentially valuable, research projects to minimize the risk of failure or delayed achievement."[227] One wonders, however, whether the anxiety generated by such reviews would actually reach the extreme level needed to alter a tenured professor's research agenda. Persons so easily swayed lack the temperament necessary for successful scholarship. It is certainly true, though, that heavy reliance on periodic post-tenure reviews is at odds with the fact that careers in research are often characterized by lengthy periods of quietude and reflection punctuated by bursts of creativity. Thoughtful post-tenure reviews must recognize that scholarship is neither regular nor terribly efficient.

Post-tenure review, say its proponents, provides a necessary mechanism to address the rare but inevitable situations in which faculty members are not doing their jobs. It can help these underperforming faculty to improve (e.g., in response to a critical review, a professor might be required to craft and adhere to a professional development plan).[228] Post-tenure reviews can also help faculty who are performing adequately to do even better. Reviews can be constructive rather than negatively judgmental, enhancing faculty motivation and spurring renewal and growth. Recognizing these purposes (but still deeply skeptical about possible adverse uses and consequences of post-tenure reviews), the AAUP takes the position that in order for such assessments to have utility they must be "supported by institutional resources for professional development or a change of professional direction."[229]

An obvious counterargument to claims that post-tenure reviews promote faculty improvement is that such reviews offer a solution considerably worse than the problem they were meant to address. Periodic across-the-board post-tenure reviews, done well, are extraordinarily time-consuming, costly, and cumbersome. Consider, for example, how the effort required to review annually one-fifth of an entire tenured faculty as part of a five-year cycle would dwarf the effort expended in reviewing the cohort of assistant professors coming up for tenure that same year. Practical-minded skeptics would assert that instead of conducting mandatory reviews of all tenured faculty—with their risk of logrolling among faculty reviewers via "routinized and mutualized plaudits"[230]—colleges and universities would be far wiser to concentrate their energies on the handful of genuine "problem" professors who in most cases are already well known to campus administrators. "The at-best marginally useful reassessment of the overwhelming proportion of the faculty who are discharging their responsibilities conscientiously and competently is too blunt an instrument and too wasteful an enterprise if the purpose is to identify, even for developmental purposes let alone for discipline, the extremely small number who are seriously underperforming."[231] From this perspective, periodic reviews are tantamount to using a howitzer when a rifle shot would suffice.

The alternative to across-the-board post-tenure reviews—reviews triggered by subpar faculty performance—have the advantage of focusing on problem faculty but give rise to different complications. Not the least of these is the stigma associated with such individually targeted evaluations, which makes it very difficult for these reviews to be seen as (or to be) truly diagnostic or helpful. Triggered reviews also have heightened potential for damaging relationships among colleagues. Still, focused reviews are much more efficient and quite possibly more effective than their "blanket" counterparts.[232] To fully achieve its objectives, of course, a system of post-tenure reviews will require some level of monitoring and follow-up by the relevant department or school.

Opponents of post-tenure review are quick to argue that such reviews are redundant because tenured faculty at most institutions are continuously being evaluated in one form or another. According to the AAUP, faculty are subject to

> annual reports for purposes of determining salary and promotion, reviews for the awarding of grants and sabbaticals, reviews for appointment to school and university committees, to graduate faculties and interdisciplinary programs, and to professorial chairs and professional societies. More narrowly focused reviews include course-by-course student teaching evaluations, peer review and wider public scrutiny of scholarly presentations and publications, and both administrative and collegial observation of service activities. Faculty members are also reviewed in the course of the program reviews required for regional or specialized accreditation and certification of undergraduate and graduate programs.[233]

However, those faculty who *are* coasting through their careers may not put themselves in positions where their work will be scrutinized by, for example, publishing or seeking grants. Annual salary reviews are too often perfunctory, especially when the raises at stake are relatively insubstantial. Student teaching evaluations can be easily dismissed as popularity contests (and at some institutions these data are not publicized in any way or even shared with department chairs). And many of the other myriad opportunities for review do not typically involve in-depth examination of the work of individual professors.

At least in theory, post-tenure reviews could be an addition to or conducted on a completely separate track from long-standing faculty disciplinary proceedings. Indeed, a 1998 AAUP policy statement on post-tenure review calls for just such uncoupling. No matter how benignly post-tenure review is envisioned and structured, though, it is of course still premised on the notion that consequences of some kind will follow from a poor rating. From this starting point, it is but a short intellectual and administrative step to the realization of the faculty's basic fear about post-tenure reviews: that their inclusion in the standard set of institutional responses to (or sanctions for) weak performance can short-circuit the regular discipline process by transforming the institution's traditional burden of demonstrating a professor's unacceptable performance into an obligation on the part of that same faculty member to demonstrate good performance. Such a shift would make it easier for colleges and universities to dismiss faculty.[234]

Cynics dismiss post-tenure review as public relations fluff, but other commentators regard it as a deft political counterstroke that silences higher education critics while advancing important institutional interests. Post-tenure review

> creates a beneficial impression of responsiveness to public concerns and a recognition that faculty are not beyond the reach of performance evaluations. (Legislating post-tenure review is equally astute for elected officials, because they thereby demonstrate sensitivity to constituents' discontent while averting a showdown with higher education.) From the faculty's viewpoint, post-tenure review is a fire wall to protect institutions from even greater damage, such as board resolutions, legislative proposals, or public referenda to abolish tenure altogether.[235]

Notwithstanding these manifold benefits, the impact of individual post-tenure reviews will be blunted if they are not linked to funds for faculty development or if colleges and universities prove reluctant (or find it exceedingly difficult) to use them to address directly the problem of carrying "deadwood" faculty. This has led Richard Chait to suggest that "post-tenure" reviews address the performance of entire academic *departments* (as opposed to examining the work of individual professors). Conventional academic program reviews focus on intellectual strengths and future directions; under Chait's recommended approach, internal or external reviewers would "delve more deeply into the policies and practices the department employs to gauge and regulate faculty quality."[236] These would include the "standards, criteria and procedures used for routine or annual faculty evaluations; the documentation of faculty-development activities; the degree to which the department rewards excellence (e.g., the distribution of merit pay); and the process invoked to reinvigorate or prune subpar performers."[237] Such departmental reviews would reinforce the faculty's collective responsibility for quality and might facilitate strategic consideration of each unit's long-term value to the institution.[238] The introduction of wide-ranging departmental reviews might be easier than mandating individual faculty evaluations, particularly at colleges and universities accustomed to periodic program reviews. Moreover, the two could even be combined, with a poor departmental review resulting in individual reviews of all department members.

From a technical legal perspective, adopting and managing a system of post-tenure review raises no serious problems. In a unionized setting, requiring such reviews and specifying how they will be conducted and used are entirely appropriate topics for collective bargaining and eventual inclusion in a labor contract. In a nonunion environment, institutions can easily supplement their personnel policies to include post-tenure review— though, as with any change in the terms and conditions of employment for extant faculty, the employer college or university would be well advised to have the faculty who will henceforth be subject to post-tenure review formally acknowledge the applicability of new or amended policies by means such as countersigning reappointment or salary increase letters. Furthermore, I am aware of no significant judicial opinions or other precedent centered on post-tenure review. Once in place, such reviews merely become part of the employment agreement and are interpreted and governed by established principles of contract law.

Foes of post-tenure review will surely claim that there are less onerous ways of reinvigorating or redirecting faculty or, if need be, inducing them to resign. Peer pressure can be extraordinarily effective; if this fails, it is incumbent upon the department chair or dean to confront the recalcitrant

scholar. But sometimes nothing short of a hammer will do. In such circumstances, post-tenure reviews—particularly if they are in fact preliminary or
otherwise linked to formal disciplinary procedures—can be a necessary
arrow in an employer institution's administrative quiver. Colleges and universities must not be paralyzed into fearful inaction when faculty do not
perform the jobs they were hired to do. This last observation leads us neatly
into a discussion of more serious faculty discipline and possible termination "for cause."

## Loss of Tenure

Contrary to popular misperceptions, tenure does not amount to a lifetime
guarantee of employment. A tenured professor can still lose his or her job.
Even so staunch a defender of faculty prerogatives and tenure as the AAUP
acknowledges in its fundamental 1940 Statement that tenured faculty may
be terminated "for adequate cause, . . . [for] retirement [for] age, or under
extraordinary circumstances because of financial exigencies."[239] With the
application of federal age discrimination laws to colleges and universities
(and the concomitant uncapping of mandatory retirement), the elimination of tenure for retirement is now obsolete.[240] But in the following pages
I discuss in turn the continuing legal and operational validity of the two
remaining grounds for breaking tenure that have historically been recognized by the AAUP, as well as other justifications that have evolved in recent years.

### TERMINATING TENURE "FOR CAUSE"

It is beyond cavil that faculty—even tenured faculty—may be discharged
for cause. But invoking this principle hardly ends our inquiry. What constitutes legitimate or adequate cause for termination? The AAUP admits that
the definition of "adequate cause" has been a "persistent source of
difficulty,"[241] in effect recognizing that it is impossible and unwise to specify
every type of faculty misbehavior justifying dismissal. Most colleges and
universities have adopted termination policies, which are contractually binding on faculty. For example, the University of North Dakota defined adequate cause in its faculty handbook as "(a) demonstrated incompetence
or dishonesty in teaching or research, (b) substantial and manifest neglect
of duty, (c) personal conduct, including but not limited to moral turpitude
or criminal conduct which substantially impairs the individual's fulfillment
of institutional responsibilities, or (d) a physical or mental inability to per-

form assigned duties."[242] A Ball State handbook required each teacher to "devote his energy to developing his motivation and improving his scholarly competence, [to] exercise self-discipline and good judgment and practice intellectual honesty; and . . . [to] accept his share of faculty responsibilities for the governing of the institution."[243] Faculty at public universities may also be subject to state education or administrative procedure laws governing the grant and withdrawal of tenure.[244] And entirely apart from any institution or system-specific rules, the AAUP has promulgated its own policies on termination (with special attention to the procedures it believes should be followed in such proceedings). Not surprisingly, this faculty interest group says that to justify such action there must be a direct and substantial relationship between the conduct in question and a faculty member's professional fitness in the capacity of a teacher or researcher.[245] The AAUP also takes comfort in the Ninth Circuit's holding in *Adamian v. Jacobsen* that "'adequate cause' must be interpreted in the context of traditional standards of faculty behavior."[246]

This multiplicity of policies and guidelines, however, actually reveals considerable agreement about types of behavior that could lead to a termination "for cause." I would identify four such broad categories: *incompetence* (inability to perform), *insubordination* (unwillingness to perform), *breaches of academic integrity*, and *moral turpitude* (which would encompass all kinds of reprehensible personal conduct, including sexual harassment).

**Incompetence.** A faculty member who simply cannot perform the basic elements of the job can and will be fired. An solid example is *Riggin v. Bd. of Trustees of Ball St. Univ.*, in which a tenured professor was discharged for, inter alia, being unprepared and disorganized for class, using wildly outdated course materials, his students' failure to learn the subject area, conducting no research or scholarly activities, and not engaging in departmental or university service.[247] Poor teaching,[248] not preparing for class,[249] difficulty interacting with or maintaining poor relations with students,[250] glaring inefficiency, and sloppy or undocumented research[251] all fit under this rubric. So too would a medical disability that renders a faculty member incapable of fulfilling the essential functions of his or her job (though of course campuses may not unlawfully discriminate against employees on the basis of disabilities that do not affect the quality of job performance).[252]

**Insubordination.** Insubordination encompasses all varieties of unwillingness or conscious failure to perform one's job, ranging from dereliction of duty to defiance to disruptive behavior. It extends beyond teaching and research tasks to cover faculty obligations for institutional service.[253] Thus, tenured faculty members have been lawfully terminated for refusing to teach courses to which they were assigned;[254] refusing to develop new courses as instructed by the dean;[255] boycotting a mandatory faculty workshop and refusing to participate in commencement exercises as required;[256] refusing to follow university grading policies;[257] refusing to submit required reports for contract research projects or a requested list of publications;[258] unexcused absences from class;[259] failing to cover basic course material (as described in syllabi) and spending the majority of class time on nonpertinent matters;[260] failing to keep office hours for advising students;[261] and refusing to participate in departmental affairs or to serve on committees.[262]

Noncompliance with any of the terms and conditions of a faculty employment contract can result in discharge, including the failure to generate research grants to cover one's salary (or run one's lab) when the procurement of such grants is required by the contract. For instance, the case of *Texas v. Walker* concerned a tenured surgeon who was fired for violating his practice plan agreement by not remitting the fees he earned as an expert witness.[263] Abusive, disruptive, or otherwise insubordinate relationships with colleagues can also cost professors their jobs. In *Fong v. Purdue University*, a federal court refused to enjoin Purdue from dismissing a tenured chemist who had engaged in a multiyear pattern of threatening and harassing faculty peers, administrators, and staff and who had made improper public accusations of criminal misconduct/fraud against university and public officials.[264] Finally, even rather trivial transgressions, such as not attending faculty meetings or not opening mail from one's supervisor, may lead to termination if numerous enough or combined with more serious insubordination.[265] Simply put, the employer college or university "has a right to expect a teacher to follow instructions and to work cooperatively and harmoniously with the head of the department."[266]

Efforts to discipline tenured professors for insubordination, however, are particularly likely to give rise to claims of First Amendment violations (at public universities) or the stifling of academic freedom (at both public and private institutions). Insubordination cases "often involve the collision of important values—on the one hand, academic freedom and free speech, and on the other, the right of colleges and universities to expect cooperation and loyalty from their faculty."[267] Certainly, faculty have the right—perhaps even the duty—under the constitution to make known their views on issues of public concern and higher education governance. But, as our previous discussion of faculty intra-institutional speech made clear, under the controlling *Pickering/Connick* line of precedent, the First Amendment does not protect faculty speech that disrupts close working relationships or the basic functioning of a college or university.[268] Likewise, at non-state-actor institutions, local academic freedom or free speech policies will be written and interpreted so as to limit—even to the point of authorizing punishment for—unnecessarily provocative or disruptive speech. In short, a faculty member "does not immunize himself against loss of his position simply because his non-cooperation and aggressive conduct are *verbalized*."[269]

Note also that firings for classroom-based insubordination—including improper practices such as abusing or proselytizing one's students or devoting large amounts of time to extraneous or outdated material—pull us back into the vital issue (discussed at length in chapter 3) of the scope of academic freedom in teaching.[270] Recalling that discussion, administrators and professors alike must understand that in proper (albeit limited) circumstances faculty can indeed be disciplined or terminated for classroom misconduct.

**Breaches of academic integrity.** A third set of faculty behaviors likely to result in a termination "for cause" embraces all manner of scholarly transgressions, including the failure to meet expected standards of veracity and honor in one's academic work. The AAUP accurately reflects the views of both the national professoriate and the general public when it calls upon faculty to "practice intellectual honesty."[271] Courts will therefore not hesitate to uphold dismissals for plagiarism (or for the similar wrong of misallocating credit for authorship). For example, in *Yu v. Peterson*, the University of Utah lawfully fired a professor of engineering for representing as his own work a research report that had involved a coauthor and two publications that were essentially the work of his students.[272] In *Agarwal v. University of Minnesota*, the legitimate grounds for discharging a tenured faculty member included plagiarism in the preparation of physics lab manuals.[273] Faculty have also been terminated for falsifying or otherwise misrepresenting their own academic credentials (e.g., degrees awarded).[274]

Colleges and universities can surely fire either tenured or nontenured faculty for research fraud or other scientific misconduct. Indeed, federal regulations and policies on the integrity of government-sponsored research, as well as the specific terms of research contract or grant documents themselves, seek to hold researchers to impeccable scientific standards. Notably, in late 2000 the federal Office of Science and Technology Policy adopted a new government-wide policy that would more sharply define research misconduct ("fabrication, falsification, or plagiarism in proposing, performing or reviewing research, or in reporting research results") and establish basic guidelines for responding to allegations of such misconduct, including procedural safeguards.[275] When a professor tailors or buries his findings to reach a financially advantageous result, the preservation of scholarly integrity is mixed with an institution's need and legal right to enforce its conflict-of-interest policy and protect its own good name, even breaking tenure as necessary.

Regrettably, the foregoing breaches of faculty integrity in scholarship are paralleled by breaches of integrity in teaching that likewise justify dismissal. Such dishonest or noxious instructional practices include awarding students better (or worse) grades than they have fairly earned,[276] leaving students to flounder through a lack of vital course information or woefully inadequate advising, and making a mockery of the ideal student-teacher relationship (and perverting the learning process) by taking advantage of students or treating them in an abusive or demeaning manner. Rutgers, for example, fired a tenured professor of chemistry for exploiting visiting Chinese scholars (e.g., making them perform domestic work for him), engaging in research grant and other kinds of fraud, and securing an appointment as a postdoctoral fellow for an unqualified individual.[277] This behavior unequivocally violated the professional norm that faculty members "adhere to their proper roles as intellectual guides and counselors."[278]

***Moral turpitude or reprehensible personal conduct.*** In this last category of faculty behavior that constitutes adequate cause for termination, we move beyond violations of purely academic norms to offenses against broader society. This would certainly include criminal acts by faculty members. Breaking the law—even in ways that are unconnected to one's academic duties—can cost a scholar his or her job. For example, *Samaan v. Trustees* vindicated Cal State–Sacramento's actions in firing a tenured professor for committing health insurance fraud in his private counseling practice.[279] Among the overlapping factors that institutions will legitimately weigh in deciding whether to sanction faculty for criminal conduct (and that will also be central to any judicial examination of such sanctions) are the type and seriousness of the crime in question, how recently the crime occurred, the proximity of the crime to the campus, the publicity associated with the crime, whether the crime is connected to academic pursuits, and whether the crime involved students or otherwise harmed the academic community. It is worth noting that there is no legal requirement that colleges or universities wait until a faculty member has actually been convicted of a crime before meting out its own discipline. Colleges and universities have genuine reputational interests and operational concerns (e.g., a faculty member's involvement in a scandal may irreparably damage his or her effectiveness as a teacher; the need to avoid disruption within a department) that may best be protected by punishing faculty for behavior that ultimately falls short of conviction. Still, institutions should be wary lest a precipitous rush to judgment place the accused professor in a legally untenable position without adequate procedural safeguards or simply strike a peer review panel or court as unfair.[280]

Tenured faculty have also been dismissed for *immoral* (but still noncriminal) behavior—for example, private acts that offend widely shared concepts of propriety. In *Corstvet v. Boger*, a tenured professor of veterinary medicine at Oklahoma State was lawfully fired for moral turpitude after he was caught soliciting sex in the student union building, even though all parties agreed that he was "a very good teacher with excellent research capabilities."[281] Similarly, in *Board v. Stubblefield*, a permanent faculty member was discharged when he assaulted a police officer who discovered him having sex in a car with a student and tried to evade arrest.[282] Sexual or racial harassment of students or faculty colleagues would qualify as moral turpitude. So would having *consensual* sex with one's student (even if otherwise legal). Entirely apart from (perhaps disputed) notions of proper sexual behavior, such harassment or such intimate relationships constitute profound breaches of trust with students and, I would argue, pervert the ideal of faculty member as mentor.[283] At private, especially religiously controlled, colleges and universities, faculty morality may even be regulated by employment contract. Professors at such religiously affiliated schools have a straightforward choice: accept and abide by the institutionally mandated moral strictures or leave (either voluntarily or involuntarily). A perfect example of a private institution's ability to enforce its own standards of personal behavior arose several years ago when the Catholic University of Puerto Rico fired a female faculty member who (like all of her fellow faculty) was bound by an institutional policy to "conduct [herself] in accordance with the ethical principles of the Catholic Church (both within and without the University)" because she had remarried outside the Church.

An outraged AAUP censured the university,[284] but there was no legal basis to void such action.

All kinds of dishonesty or fraud (e.g., embezzling institutional funds, falsifying payroll records or travel reimbursement forms) fit under the "moral turpitude" rubric. Thus, in *Zahavy v. Univ. of Minnesota*, the court upheld the firing of a professor who was "double-dipping" by simultaneously holding tenured positions at two universities without the permission of either school.[285] Professor Zahavy's conduct "was a misuse of the University's resources and time that interfered with [his] usefulness to the University"[286] and "undermine[d] a basic, necessary trust" that must exist between the institution and its faculty.[287] And in *Ivey v. Univ. of Alaska*, a director of vocational education was lawfully discharged for pretending to teach (and being paid for teaching) phony classes and giving students credit for such fake courses.[288] I would also categorize violations of institutional conflict-of-interest or conflict-of-commitment policies—which are contractually binding on faculty[289]—as additional examples of morally reprehensible behavior justifying termination (alternatively, these might be viewed as forms of insubordination). Faculty may not flagrantly ignore the primary allegiance owed to their employer.[290] Likewise, a researcher who makes unauthorized profits off his university scholarship is certainly as much of a scoundrel as one who misstates his findings for nonpecuniary gain.

Many of the foregoing scenarios involving faculty discharge for moral turpitude stand for the proposition that "a tenured professor's 'fitness in a professional capacity' need not necessarily be tied to [his or her] teaching, scholarship, and service."[291] And although "reported judicial decisions of the dismissal of faculty members for off-campus bad acts are fairly rare, probably reflecting that such problems . . . are most often resolved without litigation,"[292] it is clear that courts and public opinion alike will support the breaking of tenure for egregious extra-university conduct. To be sure, efforts to discipline faculty for moral turpitude—particularly private misbehavior—may generate freedom-of-expression or (at public institutions) First Amendment challenges analogous to those in insubordination cases.[293] Such claims, however, are not likely to prevail.

Admittedly, my "for cause" categories of incompetence, insubordination, breaches of academic integrity, and moral turpitude sometimes blur. University administrators or courts may encounter faculty misdeeds that defy easy classification (e.g., failing to supervise the work and review the findings of graduate lab assistants may demonstrate both incompetence and a lack of academic integrity) as well as problem faculty who meet the criteria for several categories of misconduct.[294] There are alternative ways of conceptualizing standards of faculty behavior.[295] Nevertheless, these broad headings accurately reflect how institutions and judges have analyzed and resolved questions of serious faculty wrongdoing.

Some prominent commentators have argued that colleges and universities should craft very precise policies governing terminations "for cause," with sharp definitions of proscribed conduct and specific criteria for applying those definitions to individual cases.[296] This approach is unrealistic and misguided. Employer institutions must have standards that are flexible enough to be effective in an unpredictable world. They simply cannot anticipate and enumerate all possible kinds of faculty malfeasance. As the Sixth Circuit observed in a faculty discipline case, "it is not feasible or necessary . . . to spell out in detail all that conduct which will result in retaliation. The most conscientious of codes that define prohibited conduct of employees include 'catchall' clauses prohibiting employee 'misconduct,' 'immorality,' or 'conduct unbecoming.'"[297] Nor need commonsense notions of faculty conduct be reduced to writing to be enforceable. In *San Filippo v. Bongiovanni,* the court held that as a matter of course "a tenured professor [may] be expected to behave decently towards students and coworkers, to comply with a superior's directive, and to be truthful and forthcoming in dealing with payroll, federal research funds or applications for academic positions."[298] That case rejected a "void for vagueness" attack on a Rutgers policy that defined "adequate cause" for firing tenured faculty only in general terms: to wit, "failure to maintain standards of sound scholarship and competent teaching, or gross neglect of established University obligations appropriate to the appointment, or incompetence, or incapacitation, or conviction of a crime involving moral turpitude."[299]

Notwithstanding the resolution of any questions about the requisite level of specificity in an institution's termination policy, it is also necessary to recognize the massive practical and political hurdles that must be overcome when a college or university moves to discharge a tenured faculty member "for cause." It is no easy matter to fire a tenured faculty member, nor should it be. From a purely operational standpoint, dismissal proceedings are often protracted (typically involving several levels of rigorous review) and always complicated. For example, the termination hearing before a panel of Rutgers faculty in *San Filippo* lasted 250 hours over forty-six days.[300] A recent case at the University of Kansas required thirty-three days of hearings (with testimony from 49 witnesses) and generated a transcript of more than eight thousand pages! Faculty who are asked to serve on peer discipline panels may therefore have to disrupt substantially their schedules and careers.[301]

Moreover, colleges and universities endeavoring to fire tenured faculty "for cause" pursuant to local policies must strictly comply with the express terms of those policies—especially any procedural safeguards set forth therein—lest they open themselves to claims of breach of employment contract. These procedural hoops offer innumerable opportunities for institutional mistakes that can impugn if not void the termination proceedings. Such errors are especially likely because terminations "for cause" are rare and administrators may be unfamiliar with the operative rules. So, in *McConnell v. Howard Univ.*, a federal appeals court held that Howard's failure to follow precisely its dismissal procedures (e.g., giving the board of trustees just a summary of a grievance committee's findings rather then its full report) would, if proven, constitute a breach of the plaintiff faculty member's contract.[302] Likewise, in *Klinge v. Ithaca College,* the demotion of a tenured professor for plagiarism was invalidated because the college had departed from the terms of its handbook by imposing a new (albeit more modest) punishment not contemplated by that manual.[303] While adherence to institutional policies is of course a concern for both public and private entities, the stakes are higher for state actors whose failure to observe procedural requirements can assume constitutional dimensions. Note further that even if an employer college or university is unencumbered by a written termination policy, it should still try to conduct any faculty discharge proceedings in ways that would strike disinterested observers as fundamentally fair.[304]

Under any circumstances, faculty termination proceedings are extraordinarily painful for everyone involved. Such public washings of personal and institutional "dirty laundry" get quite ugly, with considerable potential for embarrassment. Moreover, once the damning charges have been circulated and supported by evidence—and in spite of the principle underlying peer review that "faculty must be willing to recommend the dismissal of a colleague when necessary"[305]—faculty are often singularly lenient towards their colleagues and balk at actual firings.[306] If we add to this natural reluctance to fire one's peers the AAUP's admonition that "presidents and governing boards must be willing to give full weight to a faculty judgment favorable to a colleague,"[307] senior administrators or boards that overturn (or decline to follow) faculty panel determinations in discipline cases must appreciate that they are practically inviting litigation. Of course, this should still not deter them from doing what is right for their institution. It has been estimated that nationwide there are still about fifty official terminations "for cause" of tenured faculty each year.[308] However, when colleges and universities fully take into account the risks and costs of trying to fire a tenured faculty member "for cause," they usually choose to dispense with formal charges and settle on the side, perhaps by buying out the remainder of the faculty member's contract at a discount (the acquiescence of the accused faculty member is typically gained by intense pressure to resign from school or departmental colleagues). Such a course of action may be eminently wise and is perfectly legal.

This last observation helps reinforce the important point that frequently the best means of changing a wayward professor's behavior—and the most effective sanction that can be imposed upon him or her—is not a formal institutional response (no matter how onerous or fear-inducing that may be) but rather is peer pressure from faculty colleagues. Knowledge that misconduct will cause one to fall sharply in departmental peers' estimation, or may even lead to professional disgrace or being shunned, is, in my view, the very strongest incentive for rectitude.

**Sexual harassment.** A particularly significant subcategory of faculty misbehavior constituting moral turpitude and justifying dismissal "for cause" (and drawing increased legal and media attention in recent years) is sexual harassment. Sexual harassment of students by professors deeply offends our sensibilities because it is a betrayal of time-honored norms and expectations that faculty be committed to advancing their pupils' academic growth. Serving as an "intellectual guide" of necessity includes showing "respect for students as individuals" and avoiding their "exploitation, harassment, or discriminatory treatment."[309]

As a matter of black letter law, sexual harassment is a subset of discrimination on the basis of sex. Drawing upon our earlier survey of nondiscrimination law, the relevant statutes are therefore Title VII (discrimination in employment) and Title IX (discrimination in education and employment in covered programs). Recall as well that from a plaintiff's perspective, bringing suit under Title IX has the advantage of uncapped monetary damages.[310] While the standards of proof and institutional liability are still very much evolving in this "new and difficult area of federal law,"[311] some of the operative legal principles are becoming clear. For example, although the vast majority of incidents of sexual harassment involve men harassing women, the applicable statutes also cover women harassing men and same-sex harassment.[312] There can be illegal sexual harassment by a supervisor against an employee, by one co-worker against another, by customers of a business against its employees, by a teacher or administrator against a student, and even—pursuant to the Supreme Court's 1999 decision in *Davis v. Monroe County Bd. of Ed.*[313]—between fellow students.

Two prototypes of sexual harassment are commonly recognized by federal regulatory agencies and courts: *quid pro quo* harassment and *hostile environment* harassment.[314] Quid pro quo sexual harassment occurs when (1) submission to unwelcome sexual advances is made a term or condition of an individual's employment (or, under Title IX, an individual's status as a student) or when (2) submission to or rejection of such advances is used as the basis for employment or educational decisions affecting such individual. Note that unlawful harassment may be found even if the employee or student victim gives in to the harasser's sexual advances or threats (though such submission would raise questions about the "unwelcomeness" of such attention).[315] Put bluntly, "if the plaintiff is threatened, and if the plaintiff is rewarded or punished, then there is quid pro quo harassment."[316] In order to explain this concept, consider the following examples of quid pro quo sexual harassment:

— In *Korf v. Ball State Univ.*, a tenured professor was fired for offering students good grades contingent on sexual involvement with him. He also gave students gifts and money in return for sexual favors. Such conduct was found to be a clear violation of university policy (which incorporated the AAUP Ethics Statement).[317]

— In *Lipsett v. Univ. of Puerto Rico*, quid pro quo sexual harassment infected a surgery residency program in contravention of Title IX when senior residents and medical supervisors made sexual advances to the plaintiff and, after she rebuffed those overtures, became hostile and highly negative in their professional dealings with her.[318]

— In *McDaniels v. Flick*, the court rejected a procedural attack on the discharge of a tenured professor who offered a student the chance to improve his course grade if he assented to what the professor termed (in language heavy with sexual innuendo) "tough love" counseling and then threatened the student that he would "get him" if he told anyone about this offer.[319]

— Finally, in *Kadiki v. Virginia Commonwealth Univ.*, the trial court called for further fact-finding to determine whether a professor (who had previously spanked a female student for poor performance on an exam) conditioned her retaking the test upon her consent to another spanking if she did not achieve a certain score. If proven, such conduct would constitute quid pro quo harassment.[320]

Hostile environment sexual harassment, in contrast, occurs when unwelcome sexual attention is sufficiently severe or pervasive to interfere with an employee's work (or a student's ability to participate in or benefit from an educational program) or when such attention creates an intimidating, hostile, abusive, or offensive working (or educational) environment.[321] While supervisors or teachers can commit either quid pro quo or hostile environment harassment, harassment by co-workers or fellow students will always be of the latter variety, lacking the threat of adverse employment or educational consequences that would furnish added "bite." Prime examples of hostile environment sexual harassment include

— *Lipsett v. Univ. of Puerto Rico,* in which a female surgery resident was subjected, inter alia, to comments by senior residents that women should not be surgeons and that they would drive her out of the program; to repeated crude and sexual remarks in front of or about her; and the open display (in a room where all residents ate and worked) of *Playboy* centerfolds, a sexually explicit drawing of the plaintiff, and a list of sexually charged nicknames of female residents, including her.[322]

— *Maas v. Cornell Univ.,* in which a tenured professor was lawfully disciplined for harassing female student assistants by inappropriate kissing, hugging, and touching (one student claimed he grabbed her breast) and for making sexually oriented suggestive comments to these young women and buying them presents.[323]

— *Jew v. Univ. of Iowa,* in which a hostile environment was created when co-workers spread false rumors that the plaintiff faculty member had gained favor with her department head by engaging in a sexual relationship with him. The illegal harassment also included a series of sexually and racially derogatory comments made about the plaintiff.[324]

— *Lehman v. Bd. of Trustees of Whitman College,* upholding the discharge of a tenured professor for making sexual advances to female students, staff, fellow faculty, and wives of faculty and staff.[325]

A significant development since 1998 has been the Supreme Court's clarification of the circumstances under which employer colleges and universities will be liable for sexual harassment pursuant to Titles VII and IX. In particular, we are seeing growing differences between the legal standards used to enforce each of these statutes. Under Title VII, vicarious liability attaches to employers whose supervisors engage in sexual harassment (whether labeled quid pro quo or hostile environment) of their supervisees that culminates in a tangible employment action such as a hiring, firing, demotion, reassignment, or significant change in benefits. However, when no such tangible employment action has been taken, the employer may avoid liability for its supervisor's misbehavior if (1) it exercised reasonable care to prevent and correct promptly any sexual harassment by the supervisor and (2) the plaintiff employee unreasonably failed to take advantage of any preventive or corrective opportunities.[326] Beyond this vicarious liability for the harassing conduct of its supervisors, an academic (or any other) employer will also be liable under Title VII for a sexually hostile environment created by *co-workers* if it knew or should have known of the problem but nevertheless failed to take appropriate remedial action.[327] This "negligence" standard of conduct is considerably more tolerant than the essentially "automatic" liability that may flow from the acts of an employer's supervisors.

In contrast, a college or university will only be liable for sexual harassment damages under Title IX if an institutional official with authority to correct the problem had *actual knowledge* of the wrongdoing and, with deliberate indifference, failed to respond adequately.[328] Knowledge of the harassment will not be imputed to create vicarious liability. This standard now governs both teacher-on-student and student-on-student sexual harassment in federally funded education programs (the latter misconduct, again, always stemming from a "hostile environment"). Predictably, the Supreme Court's adoption of a higher threshold for liability in Title IX suits than in Title VII cases upset advocates who regard students as more vulnerable to sexual harassment (especially by authority figures such as faculty) than employees in the workplace.[329]

One dilemma often encountered by colleges and universities—which the recent Supreme Court holdings help resolve—is how to respond when an employee or a student makes allegations of sexual harassment but requests that they be kept confidential. In light of these newly articulated standards, administrators should not make such a guarantee. In addition to the institution's legal duties to the complainant, possession of such information could lead to liability if the harasser, left unchecked, subsequently preys on others. Bear in mind also that sexual discrimination suits may be brought by third-party employees or students when peers who submit to a harassing supervisor or instructor are singled out for special favors (e.g., better grades, raises). So, confronted with direct knowledge of harassment, institutions must take action—at the very least, make further inquiries and perhaps even pursue charges that will inevitably lead to disclosure of the accuser's identity.

Many significant legal and policy questions involving sexual harassment remain unresolved. For instance, what conduct rises to the level of a "hostile environment"? And in whose eyes? Determinations of what is "sufficiently severe or pervasive" to constitute harassment will necessarily be driven by the facts and context of each particular case. However, lest academic institutions and supervisors be too confident in the protection furnished by their current antiharassment policies and procedures, there is extant legal authority that even one isolated incident, if severe enough—such as a professor slapping his departmental secretary on the buttocks[330]—may create an unlawful hostile environment. In evaluating whether conduct is offensive, courts will consider how a reasonable person would react or feel in the plaintiff's situation. The Ninth Circuit, in *Ellison v. Brady,* endorsed a "reasonable woman" standard for female complainants in hostile environment cases.[331] By this same logic, would it be necessary to use a "reasonable man" standard for male plaintiffs (for example, the young man at Cal. State–Sacramento who claimed—unsuccessfully—that his female professor created a hostile environment by discussing female genitalia and masturbation in a psychology course)?[332] Rather than plaintiff-specific, gender-based standards, the far better course of wisdom is for university officials and courts adjudicating harassment complaints to keep "both the man's and the woman's perspective in mind,"[333] thereby reflecting more fully the changing mores between (and within) the sexes. The essential point here is that sexually oriented discourse or behavior that would have been tolerated twenty years ago is not acceptable today. Thus, it is no longer regarded as humorous to use pinups as teaching aids in an anatomy class, to ridicule homosexuals, or to assume that women want men to be sexual aggressors. Faculty must understand and adapt to such societal changes in their relationships with colleagues and students, and even in their teaching.

In chapter 3 I examined controversies involving the unorthodox or otherwise offensive teaching styles of faculty members, especially their use of sexually oriented material in class, that led to charges of sexual harassment. As we have seen, given the confluence of strong personal, institutional, and societal interests in faculty having broad academic freedom in the classroom, professors are likely to prevail in such disputes. Faculty should and do serve as the primary arbiters of what pedagogical techniques and teaching materials should be used to impart certain knowledge and to facilitate the intellectual growth of their students.[334] But in this era of jangled sensitivities and still-evolving social standards, further controversies are inevitable. For instance, a former sociology professor at Colby College recently claimed that he was denied tenure when students complained about (and cast as sexual harassment) being assigned to write papers about their families and personal lives. According to the instructor, such papers made theoretical material more relevant by helping students "realize how their lives had been shaped by social forces."[335] If accurate—and if this were the only questionable act by the professor—such assignments would fall well within the pale of legitimate teaching style and would not amount to a hostile environment violative of either Title VII or Title IX. But these disputes are never so clear-cut or so easily solved.[336]

At the most basic level, if there is a nationwide trend of sexual harassment litigation, and if courts have shown themselves willing to impose vicarious (as well as negligence) liability on college or university employers, how are academic institutions to protect themselves against the misbehavior of "lecherous professors"?[337] Among the obvious keys to avoiding liability are written—and widely disseminated—policies prohibiting sexual harassment;[338] regular peer and supervisor training on how to prevent and handle claims of harassment; and fostering a campus culture in which harassment is reviled and will be met with zero tolerance. Some institutions have sought to shift the ultimate liability back onto the transgressor faculty. Two public universities that were sued under Title IX responded by filing complaints against the professors whose actions spawned the original litigation. However, the contention that these universities could not exercise appropriate control over their faculty fell on deaf judicial ears.[339] In theory, a university could contractually require faculty harassers to hold it harmless for any damages assessed because of their wrongdoing. But such agreements will be pointless if the faculty member has no money to satisfy the judgment.

Beyond these ideas for limiting legal exposure, should colleges and universities adopt policies prohibiting *consensual* sexual relations between faculty or staff and students, or even between senior and junior faculty? Many institutions have taken steps in this direction. An early and prominent example is the University of Iowa, which requires that "no faculty member shall have an amorous relationship (consensual or otherwise) with a student who is enrolled in a course being taught by the faculty member or whose academic work (including work as a teaching assistant) is being supervised by the faculty member."[340] In effect, Iowa faculty are forced to choose between the continuance of any such relationship and the performance of their professional responsibilities. A parallel policy at the University of Pennsylvania prohibits as well sexual relations between graduate or professional students and an undergraduate (or between advisors, program directors, or other administrators and students) when the former has supervisory academic responsibility for the latter, between department chairs and students in the department, and between graduate group chairs and students in the group. Indeed, Penn goes so far as to explicitly discourage *any* sexual relations between members of the faculty (or administration) and undergraduates.[341]

Proponents of consensual-relationship policies argue that the inherent power imbalance between faculty and students creates massive potential for future complications, if not disaster. Perhaps this differential means that there can never been true "consent" to such a relationship.[342] The case for such policies also draws strength from visceral notions about the essence of the teacher-student bond, the proper behavior of professors, and students' innocence and defenselessness. In contrast, such policies are deemed by many to be impermissibly intrusive. "Consensual sexual relationships are not unlawful. Furthermore, those involved do not violate any specific duty owed to the public, and no harm is done to any individual."[343] From this standpoint, what transpires between two responsible adults is solely their business. No one else should care about a faculty-student relationship if the student is not in the professor's class (much less if the student is enrolled in a program in which he or she is unlikely ever to take a class from the instructor in question). Policy opponents have also claimed that it is unfair to condemn just this one type of favoritism shown by faculty towards particular students—as opposed, say, to club advisors excusing members' missed classes or assignments, or African American professors making a special effort to mentor black students. In each of these circumstances, third parties will perceive the teacher-student relationship as unfairly disadvantaging them and therefore "wrong." However, becoming romantically or sexually involved with a student goes well beyond these other connections in terms of the level of intimacy.[344] Lastly, it has been argued that consensual-relationship policies are not justified by data that show actual harm done to students but rather stem from stereotypes about female students' vulnerability and overt gender politics. According to this view, such policies are "merely a pretext for an inappropriate and misplaced political and social agenda."[345]

Regrettably, much of the angry debate about the propriety of consensual-relationship policies fails to focus on the practical effect of such rules. Opponents inaccurately assume that the policies will be zealously enforced by a squad of chaperones. But no college or university administration has the means (or the stomach) to monitor faculty behavior to ensure compliance. Policy proponents just as inaccurately overestimate the ability of a policy per se to change persons' minds or the campus culture. Attempts to legislate human love and passion will fail. And although undesirable personal behavior can be punished after the fact, this assumes that knowledge and evidence of the behavior is available (no easy task as long as the relationship remains truly consensual). I share the worry that promulgating a policy acknowledged as largely symbolic may blunt the impact of other university rules that are meant to be rigidly enforced,[346] such as conflict-of-interest and sexual harassment policies.[347] However, I ultimately support consensual-relationship policies because I believe it is fundamentally inappropriate for faculty or administrators to become romantically involved with junior colleagues or students. Such policies can help foster a strong campus ethic or taboo against this noxious behavior. The *in terrorem* effect of a policy will dissuade some individuals from entering into such liaisons. And when such relationships inevitably arise, even if (as seems likely) there is no formal prosecution, having the policy on the university's books will strengthen the hand of peers and administrators who seek to drive home the seriousness of this misconduct and prevent its recurrence. In the last analysis, though, regardless of the existence of a formal policy (or any prosecutions under it), this behavior will stop most quickly when those who engage in it are ostracized.

Colleges, universities, and their faculty will encounter other unresolved issues in this still-fluid area of law. For example, when a professor who has engaged in sexual harassment moves from one school to another, does the former employer have a moral or legal duty to advise the new institution of this prior misconduct? Does it make a difference if the faculty member has only been accused of such wrongdoing, rather than found guilty? At present there is no such legal obligation under either circumstance. The harasser's old institution will be sorely tempted to remain quiet—either in delight at the prospect of the miscreant's departure or out of caution that sharing such information could be viewed as defamation.[348] In fact, institutional reticence may be required if (as often occurs) the university and the faculty member have negotiated a "scripted" employer reference as part of the informal settlement of a complaint or as a result of a formal finding of harassment. Moreover, at some public and private institutions, state law prohibits the disclosure of information in an individual's personnel file without his or her consent.[349] Such silence, however, might put students or colleagues from the professor's new school at serious risk.[350] Plaintiffs' attorneys will surely claim that when a college helps a problem faculty member find a job elsewhere through a carefully worded reference or a diplomatic silence, it should be liable for the foreseeable harm thus done to future victims. I know of no such judicial holding, but in 1994 a young woman who alleged that she was sexually harassed by an instructor at the University of Pennsylvania sued not only Penn but also the faculty member's previous employer, Bates College, for "fobbing him off" on Penn. The lawsuit was settled out of court after the professor resigned.[351] One obvious lesson here is that a hiring institution should pose careful questions to candidates and their references to explore as delicately as possible whether a potential colleague's past is clouded by scandal.

Granted, such inquiries about previous sexual misconduct—not to mention the sort of public disclosure sought in some quarters—make it extraordinarily difficult for harassers to put the past behind them. For example, Ohio State withdrew a job offer it had made to a Yale mathematician when it learned that he had been sanctioned for sexual harassment in New Haven.[352] OSU's actions were not only lawful (new information had come to light before the appointment was approved that materially altered the university's view of the potential hire) but also probably prudent. Once a professor is publicly accused of sexual harassment, no matter what the final outcome of the case, his or her career is incalculably damaged. Cynics point out that this creates an entirely new kind of "power differential" between faculty members and disgruntled students, and they rightly caution that colleges and universities must avoid placing so much emphasis on the eradication of harassment that they neglect fair treatment of the alleged wrongdoer.[353] However, given the direction of federal sex discrimination law and the heightened sensitivity within the academy and society to the evils of sexual harassment, institutions can confidently hold faculty accountable for such misconduct, even if it means breaking tenure.

## TERMINATING TENURE FOR FINANCIAL EXIGENCY

Entirely apart from problematic job performance or personal behavior, faculty can also be discharged for "impersonal institutional reasons"[354] that are beyond an individual's control. Such terminations do not directly threaten the core academic values (such as free inquiry) that tenure is designed to safeguard. However, as I explore in the following pages, dismissals of this kind raise important questions of legal fairness and the employer institution's continued academic and fiscal strength.

The most widely recognized of these "neutral" bases for terminating faculty is financial exigency. It is now settled law that a college or university facing a fiscal crisis may let even its tenured faculty go, provided that it acts in good faith. Quite often, terminations for exigency are addressed by the formal language of the faculty member's employment contract.[355] But numerous courts have also opined that discharges for financial exigency are lawful even if they are not expressly authorized in that contract. Academic institutions have an implied right and ability to take such action.[356] This is consistent with the AAUP's stance that tenured faculty may be terminated in "extraordinary circumstances because of financial exigencies," while cautioning that the exigency must be "demonstrably *bona fide*."[357] The last big round of litigation over financial exigency firings occurred in the late 1970s and early 1980s. In these suits colleges and universities typically prevailed and terminations for exigency were upheld.

The obvious threshold questions in this area of higher education law are (1) What qualifies as a financial exigency? and (2) Who decides whether the institution is in such dire straits? The AAUP contends that an exigency is "an imminent financial crisis which threatens the survival of the institution as a whole and which cannot be alleviated by less drastic means."[358] This "survival standard" is of course very difficult to meet and would dramatically limit the number of exigencies. Courts, however, have not generally accepted this standard. Instead, there is a small but solid body of precedent holding that an institution faces an exigency if it is merely running deficits in its operating budget and that it need not invade its endowment or sell off its capital assets to be in exigent circumstances. Thus, in *Krotkoff v. Goucher College,* the fact that Goucher had accumulated deficits totaling more than $1.5 million over an extended period and suffered a steady drop in enrollment over that same time constituted an exigency. Said the court: "The existence of financial exigency should be determined by the adequacy of a college's operating funds rather than its capital assets."[359] And in *A.A.U.P. v. Bloomfield College,* New Jersey appellate judges rejected a lower court's finding that there was no exigency when a college could have sold a valuable parcel of land (on which it envisioned building a new campus) to reduce its current fiscal peril. As opposed to imminent bankruptcy, the appeals court simply equated financial exigency with a "state of urgency," which it did find to be present.[360]

There is also case law holding that, in direct contradiction of the AAUP's view, an exigency can be limited to one department or academic unit of an institution. In 1977 the Supreme Court of Nebraska upheld faculty terminations stemming from a financial exigency confined to Creighton University's School of Pharmacy. No contention was made that Creighton as a whole faced an exigency; nevertheless, the court declared that the university's administrators had to be afforded "sufficient discretion to retrench in areas faced with financial problems."[361] Judicial support exists as well for the proposition that a financial crisis short of an officially declared exigency may necessitate the closure of programs and the dismissal of faculty. In *Bd. of Trustees v. Adams,* a Maryland appeals court ratified Essex Community College's "pre-exigency" termination of tenured professors as legitimate "attempts to resolve the present and anticipated financial shortfalls in order to solve the financial problems without the necessity of taking [the] last step [of declaring an exigency]."[362] Holdings like this, though, begin to blur any distinction between discharges for exigency and discharges occasioned by the elimination of academic programs, since the latter may also have financial roots.[363]

Courts are clear that the determination of whether an exigency exists should be made by the college or university's governing board.[364] Consequently, the burden of proving an exigency is placed on the *institution.* This is both right and fair because "the numerous facts and considerations which went into the . . . decision to declare a financial exigency were specially within [its] knowledge."[365] Needless to say, the institution's case will be all the stronger if it can show that it considered a variety of less drastic responses to its financial problems before moving to dismiss faculty. Such preliminary measures might include postponing the addition of new academic programs; cuts in nonacademic services (e.g., building maintenance, extracurricular and cultural programs); slashing supply and travel budgets; shifting resources between units or between the operating and capital budgets; raising teaching loads in pursuit of enhanced productivity; offering faculty and staff early retirement incentives; hiring or salary freezes; salary reductions; making full-time appointments part time; employee furloughs; terminating nonacademic staff; and (rather than just reducing expenses) all kinds of creative efforts to generate additional revenue (e.g., bolstering enrollments or marketing new intellectual products).[366] Predictably, the AAUP mandates that colleges and universities must pursue all feasible alternatives before letting faculty go.[367]

If an exigency does exist, who determines how the institution will respond? Here, too, the law is relatively straightforward. A finding of exigency is typically but the first link in a longer chain of necessary but delicate personnel decisions: Are faculty terminations required because of the exigency? What part of the institution should incur such losses? What criteria will be used to make terminations? Which particular faculty are to be discharged? Courts will leave each of these decisions to the wisdom and discretion of the college or university's governing board. The board, in turn, may delegate decision-making responsibility to senior administrators. As the court stated in an exigency case from Nebraska's Peru State College, "where lack of funds necessitated releasing a sizeable number of the faculty, certainly it was peculiarly within the province of the school administration to determine which teachers should be released, and which retained."[368] However and whatever the institution decides, it should apply the same criteria to all faculty being considered for termination, and it must not act in an arbitrary or capricious manner.[369] These, however, are rather modest limitations on institutional autonomy.

*Johnson v. Bd. of Regents* reviewed the constitutionality of the University of Wisconsin's layoffs of tenured faculty in response to hefty budget cuts. In examining the procedural protections owed the terminated scholars, the federal trial court affirmed the limited role carved out for faculty in the chain of exigency decisions. The affected professors need not be given the chance to argue or otherwise persuade administrators that "departments within their respective colleges, other than theirs, should have borne a heavier fiscal sacrifice; that non-credit-producing, non-academic areas within their respective campus structures should have borne a heavier fiscal sacrifice; that campuses, other than their respective campuses, should have borne a heavier fiscal sacrifice; or that more funds should have been appropriated to the university system."[370] The faculty did, however, have the right to challenge the legitimacy of what the court termed the "ultimate" decision selecting them for discharge.[371]

Nonetheless, while they may not be required to do so, colleges and universities facing financial exigencies should still give the faculty a prominent role in termination decisions because the professoriate is particularly well equipped to judge how proposed retrenchments will affect the quality of academic programs.[372] The AAUP, of course, would heartily endorse such sentiments. Under its model regulations, faculty should participate in any decision that an exigency exists or is imminent (and presumably also in any decision that the exigency calls for reductions in academic staff). The AAUP says that faculty, not administrators, should have primary responsibility for determining where within the overall academic program any terminations for exigency should occur and for determining criteria for identifying persons whose appointments are to end. Finally, the faculty should take some part in the actual identification of those unfortunate individuals, at the very least designating or approving the party or parties making such decisions.[373] But despite the very real value of faculty input in framing a response to financial exigencies, college and university administrators must recognize that professors are often extraordinarily reluctant to take adverse action against their colleagues. In the words of one of the drafters of the AAUP's exigency regulations, faculty tend to shrink "at the sight of blood."[374] For example, in *Krotkoff* a faculty committee that should have offered guidance on which of two German faculty ought to be terminated recommended instead that *both* teachers be retained and an assistant dean be dismissed![375] Administrators should therefore avoid being locked into following the faculty's recommendations. By refusing to cede such final control, the institution may in fact be preserving its ability to take hard but necessary personnel actions to secure its future.

While due process requirements in faculty discipline are treated at length later in this chapter,[376] some brief mention is appropriate here of the safeguards afforded faculty before, and perhaps even after, they are terminated for financial exigency. Most significantly, because these faculty are being discharged through no fault of their own, they neither need nor are entitled to the level of procedural protection mandated when a termination is "for cause" (e.g., a more comprehensive hearing to learn what actually transpired). Faculty dismissed as a result of financial exigency receive a scaled-down process that the *Johnson* court held must include "[1] furnishing [the faculty member] with a reasonably adequate written statement of the basis for the initial decision to lay off; [2] furnishing [the faculty member] with a reasonably adequate description of the manner in which the initial decision had been arrived at; [3] making a reasonably adequate disclosure to [the faculty member] of the information and data upon which the decision-makers had relied; and [4] providing [the faculty member] the opportunity to respond."[377]

Beyond what the Constitution requires in the way of process, the AAUP has tried to institutionalize a set of substantive rights and benefits for faculty terminated as a result of financial exigency. In considering these guidelines, however, recall that colleges and universities are not automatically bound to observe AAUP policies. Indeed, the hortative nature of such pronouncements and the association's unabashedly partisan outlook should be borne in mind during all discussions of faculty terminations, regardless of their cause.[378] The AAUP states, for instance, that in an exigency tenured faculty should be retained over nontenured colleagues except "in extraordinary circumstances where a serious distortion of the academic program would otherwise result."[379] Yet institutions are not regularly required to extend such preference. In *Brenna v. Southern Col. State College*, a tenured professor was let go in favor of a nontenured colleague in order to give his department more versatility and flexibility in its intellectual coverage. Without convincing proof that the college had endorsed the AAUP's view on preserving tenured lines, the Tenth Circuit refused to read this term into the plaintiff's employment contract.[380]

Next, the AAUP urges that faculty discharged for financial exigency receive at least a year's prior notice (or severance pay in lieu thereof).[381] But courts have upheld terminations with far quicker triggers, even as brief as thirty days.[382] As a third safeguard, the association would require colleges and universities to make every effort to find new positions for discharged faculty somewhere else in the institution.[383] In *Krotkoff*, however, the court declared that while Goucher was obliged (if not by explicit contract language, then in accordance with academic custom) to make a reasonable effort to find alternative employment for the plaintiff, this duty did not include retraining her to teach in a completely new discipline.[384]

Lastly, to ensure that exigency terminations are truly driven by financial need, the association would restrict colleges and universities that declare exigency from hiring new faculty at the time of the dismissals[385] and from filling each vacated position for three years thereafter (unless the discharged employee has declined reinstatement).[386] To be sure, making new hires when exigency has just been invoked or faculty recently laid off may raise serious doubts about the severity and genuineness of the institution's financial difficulties.[387] Faculty will take particular offense if full-time professors are replaced with part-time employees who offer the same courses. Still, as a Washington State appellate court observed, "the hiring of faculty is not necessarily inconsistent with a bona fide financial exigency necessitating the layoff of tenured faculty in other departments."[388] Notwithstanding the AAUP's very aggressive advocacy on behalf of faculty interests, its model institutional responses to financial exigency provide some useful guidance. In general, judges and juries will look favorably on—and accord more leeway to—colleges and universities that act fairly and show sensitivity towards any employees they discharge.

Given the unremitting fiscal pressure on most institutions of higher education, I would expect that the coming years will bring further litigation (and the development of additional case law) on schools' ability to terminate tenured faculty for financial exigency. The AAUP has not abandoned its "survival standard," and faculty will reliably assert that the purported financial constraints do not rise to the level of exigency or are a sham.[389] We can also anticipate the adoption of detailed institutional rules (or the refinement of existing rules) in faculty handbooks or collective bargaining agreements defining what constitutes an exigency and how it can be met (e.g., will employees' length of service be factored into retrenchments).[390] Having such guidelines in place before an exigency occurs is good planning and will accrue to all parties' advantage. Finally, we shall see more litigation over the procedural protections afforded dismissed scholars. Tenured faculty who lose their jobs are not likely to be satisfied with the minimal procedures courts have imposed to date; they will demand additional checks against unfair termination decisions.

## TERMINATING TENURE BECAUSE OF PROGRAM ELIMINATION

Termination for program discontinuance or elimination, the second of the two impersonal or neutral justifications for lawfully discharging faculty, is a relatively recent focus of higher education law. The key case, *Jimenez v. Almodovar,* dates from 1981. In that case the University of Puerto Rico dismissed three (of five) tenured faculty in its Physical Education Department when it inactivated a pilot associate degree program in physical education and recreation. The decision to end this course of study was not made on financial grounds (no exigency was claimed), but rather because of weak enrollment and the results of an academic evaluation of the program. The First Circuit held that the university had an "implied right of *bona fide* unavoidable termination on the ground of change of academic program."[391] Program eliminations on academic grounds may have a variety of causes, among them lack of faculty expertise in requisite areas; recognition (or at least belief) that a particular discipline has become stagnant or even obsolete; the need to adapt to new intellectual currents or priorities; inadequate library collections to support proper research and instruction in a field; and changes in student—or broader societal—interests, often evidenced by permanent reductions in enrollment. Program closures may be driven by academic leaders within the institution[392] or carried out in response to external stimuli such as commands from state coordinating boards or legislatures to avoid program duplication and achieve greater efficiency.[393] Periodic program eliminations are, in fact, a sign of the intellectual health and vibrancy of a college or university.[394] Even the AAUP acknowledges the legitimacy of faculty terminations stemming from program closures. Although such dismissals are not addressed in the 1940 Statement, the association's subsequent "Recommended Institutional Regulations on Academic Freedom and Tenure" declares that discharges "may occur as a result of *bona fide* formal discontinuance of a program or department of instruction,"[395] provided that they are "based essentially upon educational considerations" and primarily determined by faculty.[396]

"A decision to discontinue a program is viewed by the courts as an exercise of academic discretion that is not subject to strict judicial review."[397] But such deference, while entirely proper, begs the question of who within the institution exercises the authority to make program elimination decisions. The college or university's charter and bylaws (for private institutions) or the applicable state constitutional provisions and statutes (for public institutions) provide a first-level answer: namely, that the governing board is usually vested with broad policymaking authority over all aspects of the institution, including curricular offerings.[398] Thus, in *Ahmadieh v. St. Bd. of Agriculture*, significant changes in the University of Southern Colorado's mission led the board to overhaul USC's courses of study (in particular adding baccalaureate and graduate-level degrees and phasing out two-year programs), thereby eliminating many tenured faculty lines. The resulting lawsuit by terminated faculty (alleging breaches of employment contracts and violations of constitutional rights) failed because the board had not delegated control over program and curriculum development to the formal faculty governance bodies. This case stands for the proposition that assertive boards will have wide latitude in closing programs.[399]

However, by virtue of expertise and academic custom, if not by more formal delegations of authority, an institution's faculty typically take the lead in crafting—and directing on a daily basis—the program mix and content delivered to students.[400] From both an intellectual and a practical standpoint, it is a foolish board or administration that arrogates program discontinuance decisions to itself. Faculty are simply more knowledgeable about the college or university's current and potential academic strengths and more attuned to student needs. Without faculty support, any programmatic or curricular changes can also be subverted. While administrators and boards must ensure that societal and institutional requirements are addressed and must guard against faculty recommendations that reflect narrow self-interest (including logrolling to protect jobs), I would assert that it is even more essential to involve faculty in program eliminations than in framing a response to a financial exigency.

Of course, substantive faculty involvement does not equate to dictation of process or outcomes. When the University of Iowa terminated its dental hygiene program, a federal appeals court found no legal right of program faculty to be appointed to the committees reviewing the closure recommendation or to participate in the planning for the phaseout (the plaintiffs had, however, testified before at least one review committees).[401] Nor will faculty involvement necessarily insulate a program discontinuance from further challenge. In *Apte v. Regents of the Univ. of California*,[402] a clinical (i.e., nontenured) associate professor in UC-Berkeley's School of Public Health was discharged when the two federally funded training programs he directed (Community Mental Health and the Native American Program in Mental Health Planning and Administration) were terminated pursuant to a vote of the school's faculty. The school's leadership wanted to eliminate these sorts of "soft money" programs and direct the priorities of the school elsewhere. Despite a unanimous vote in favor of closure, the court found that Berkeley's termination decision was arbitrary and capricious—in part because, subsequent to that vote, funding prospects for the primary program brightened considerably, yet the issue of closure was not resubmitted to the faculty.

This is a very troubling decision, as it flies in the face of a clear faculty vote—based on then-accurate information—to terminate the programs (indeed, the tenured faculty member who served as the principal investigator on the program grants sponsored the closure resolution). A close reading of the opinion reveals that the court was influenced by compassion for the plaintiff, who had been at Berkeley for thirteen years and who had argued (correctly, as it turned out) that the federal government would continue the program funding. The fact that a faculty appeals panel had sided with the plaintiff also helped his case. Still, I think *Apte* was wrongly decided; as Berkeley's chancellor argued in rejecting the findings of the appeals panel, reinstating the plaintiff would "hamper the University in ending 'programs that are evidencing difficulty, unduly straining resources, such as space and time, better used otherwise, and shaping curricula unwisely.'"[403] Courts should rely whenever possible on the academic judgment of the duly assembled faculty. Here there was even a formal vote in favor of closure, which—as any dean who has sought to effect a program closure can attest—is no small feat.

Given the horrible adverse publicity associated with a declaration of financial exigency, as well as the likely effect of such a declaration on enrollments, alumni donations, and faculty morale and recruitment, many institutions that encounter financial crises will view program eliminations as a far more palatable option. The resulting litigation should help clarify several of the currently unresolved issues in this area of college and university law. For example, there is no common understanding of what constitutes an academic "program." If a program's boundaries are drawn narrowly enough, it could include only one or two faculty, and thereby raise doubts about the true motivation for the closure. Nevertheless, in a world of increased intellectual specialization and the proliferation of options for focused training, there *are* many small and narrow academic programs. Some colleges and universities have tried to end such debates by establishing their own definitions of *program* for use in a discontinuance scenario. The University of Washington, for instance, defines a program as "1) A department or other degree-granting unit (other than a school or college) ... [or] 2) Either a sub-unit within a department, or a group of faculty from one or more departments, which offers a distinct degree, or a track within a degree that is described as a distinct option [in the relevant catalog] . . . or is customarily noted as such on student transcripts."[404] Such guidelines are a helpful, albeit institution-specific, start in shedding necessary legal light on the problem of program scope.

If a college or university terminates a degree program, questions may also arise about potential liability to enrolled students. As a general proposition, students expect that if they pay their tuition bills, obey the school's disciplinary rules, and perform the academic work required of them, they will in fact receive their desired degrees.[405] "Once a student is admitted to a degree program, he/she has an enforceable expectation that the institution will continue that program for the length of time normally necessary for the student to graduate."[406] An institution that deprives students of the opportunity to earn their degrees because of a program closure may therefore have to pay damages for breach of contract.[407] *Behrend v. Ohio* concerned Ohio University's decision to close its School of Architecture. The impending closure blocked the school's accreditation and therefore breached an implied term of the student-university contract that the program the architecture students had enrolled in would be accredited. Even though the university was willing to let the students complete their course of study, they could incur compensable damages (e.g., difficulty in transferring to other schools, having to repeat courses, not being eligible to take the state licensure exam).[408]

In a tightly constrained financial environment, pure academically driven program closures may be rare events. After all, "it is entirely natural that the educational value of fields of instruction or research should be viewed with a colder eye in bad times than in good."[409] Administrators and faculty alike may therefore wonder whether it makes any legal difference if a program is being eliminated, and tenured faculty discharged, on a mixture of financial and academic grounds. Should an institution be required to declare an exigency if it elects to discontinue academic programs in part (or primarily) because of its finances? Indeed, should program eliminations that are conceived and carried out *solely* in response to an exigency be treated like academic decisions at all?[410] The answers to these questions become particularly important if the procedural protections or substantive rights available to terminated faculty (e.g., severance pay or reinstatement options) are greater in an exigency situation. Although there have been several judicial opinions involving (and authorizing) program closings necessitated in whole or in part by financial reasons, the courts have not really focused on the "mixed motives" in these cases or on the possibility that program eliminations might be used to make "end runs" around stricter exigency requirements.

A Washington State appellate court upheld a community college's layoff of a tenured agriculture instructor for both insufficient funds and a change in academic program. The college's declaration of a financial emergency demanded faculty retrenchments and lent urgency to an ongoing review of its academic programs and priorities. When a report from an advisory committee concluded that the present agricultural offerings were not meeting student or community needs and should be replaced with a tree fruit production program, the college's course of action became clear. The agriculture program (and with it, the plaintiff's job) were eliminated. Financial exigency may have been the catalyst, but this lawful program closure was also justified by powerful academic arguments.[411] And, as discussed earlier in this chapter, in *Bd. of Trustees v. Adams,* a community college legally closed its office technology program because of financial pressure that had not yet blossomed into an exigency. The *Adams* court identified three possible bases for discharging tenured faculty (beyond firings "for cause"): "1) the necessary or preferred discontinuance of courses or programs; 2) declining enrollment that alleviates the need for programs; or 3) when financial problems result in the necessity for termination of programs, positions, or courses."[412] The case at bar supposedly fell into this third category. However, office technology had been selected for elimination on the basis of enrollment, section size, and other (presumably academic) considerations.[413] In my view, the faculty dismissals in *Adams* were neither a classic exigency situation nor a pure program elimination. A third case demonstrating the complexities of dismissals for mixed financial and programmatic reasons is *Rymer v. Kendall College.* Here, a tenured faculty member was lawfully placed on involuntary leave when declining enrollments led Kendall to stop offering his physics course. In interpreting the language of the employment contract, an Illinois appeals court refused to draw distinctions between possible underlying causes for the course cancellation (i.e., it made no difference whether it stemmed from a drop in enrollment or flowed entirely from intellectual concerns).[414]

In the near future, courts will be called upon to define the boundaries, if any, between faculty terminations for financial exigency and terminations for program elimination/discontinuance. I would predict that, because of the frequency of financially driven program closures and the near impossibility (for both institutional decision makers and reviewing judges) of clearly separating and weighing scholarly versus fiscal goals, that any legal differences between such employment actions will blur over time to the point of nothingness.

Another open question is whether colleges and universities have the ability to *reduce* programs rather than to eliminate them entirely. There is some case law support for faculty dismissals linked to program reductions. For example, *Rose v. Elmhurst College* upheld the discharge of a tenured religion professor when his department was curtailed (but apparently not shut down completely) because of lackluster enrollment.[415] Likewise, in *Hooper v. Jensen,* a school of osteopathic medicine could lawfully decide not to renew a nontenured professor's contract when it scaled back its pathology program. The employer in *Hooper* acted under the rubric of a state Board of Regents policy that authorized program reductions as well as discontinuances.[416] Such policies, though, may not exist in other states or at other institutions. Note also that the closure of a highly circumscribed program, such as the soil mechanics and hydrology instruction eliminated in *Browzin v. Catholic Univ.*, is really equivalent to a reduction in a larger and more comprehensive academic unit (in this same example, Catholic's School of Engineering and Architecture).[417]

Consideration of program reductions leads to the even more interesting (and equally contestable) domain of program *restructuring*. While there is clearly some overlap between these two, I believe a restructuring is more likely to reflect nonfinancial imperatives such as covering critical new developments in a discipline or shifts in academic priorities. Restructuring could also involve adding faculty lines. At present, some colleges and universities have already adopted policies permitting staff changes driven by the redesigning of programs. University of Wisconsin System rules, for instance, give the chancellor of each campus the right to lay off even tenured faculty as part of the "modification" or "redirection" of an academic program.[418] At other schools, however, even abstract discussions of program restructuring have generated intense and painful debate. Several years ago, the regents of the University of Minnesota, seeking flexibility for that institution, proposed that faculty salaries might be cut for reasons other than financial exigency and that tenured professors could be terminated if their programs were closed or restructured. When such proposals were aired, Minnesota's faculty reacted negatively and vehemently. A unionization effort gathered enough steam to block implementation of the regents' plan. Eventually, a compromise solution was reached with the adoption of a new tenure code authorizing college-specific or university-wide salary cuts in circumstances of financial "stringency" (as opposed to a more dire "exigency") and permitting faculty reassignments—but not dismissals—if departments or programs were eliminated. The singularly fractious concept of terminations for "restructuring" was abandoned—at this particular university, and at this particular time.[419]

Nevertheless, the related reduction and restructuring "flavors" of program elimination will be a flash point of future litigation. From an institutional, an administrative, and even an intellectual perspective, program restructuring makes perfect sense. A restructuring is much more finely attuned to the preservation of academic quality than the blunderbuss approach of a wholesale program closure. It allows a college or university to focus on the most significant areas within a particular field (while keeping a scholarly flag securely planted in the wider discipline), to nimbly accommodate changing student interests, and to permit enrolled students to graduate from their programs.[420] One could argue (and undoubtedly some plaintiffs will) that while program eliminations are impersonal, entirely academic, decisions, the potential for targeting unpopular or troublesome faculty members (and hence the risk of a violation of academic freedom) is much greater in the context of a program reduction or restructuring. Under this line of reasoning, tenured faculty who are discharged pursuant to a reduction or restructuring deserve more procedural protection than professors whose programs are simply shut down. In the eyes of the AAUP, program reduction terminations would in fact be equivalent to terminations "for cause," since in both scenarios individual faculty have been singled out for dismissal.[421]

Indeed, a last area where the legal standards applicable to program eliminations are still fluid is the safeguards extended to faculty who are let go. For reasons discussed above, it will be particularly interesting to see how these still-evolving protections compare with those required for financial exigency discharges. Drawing quite intentionally upon its guidelines for exigencies, the AAUP asserts that a college or university that terminates faculty pursuant to a program elimination must make every effort to place those individuals elsewhere in the institution (this would include financial and other support for retraining) and, if no suitable positions are found, to make equitable severance payments reflecting the duration of the professors' past and potential service.[422] The potential intrusiveness of such regulations explains why colleges and universities should only agree to comply with AAUP policies after careful deliberation.[423]

A Fifth Circuit opinion, *Texas Faculty Ass'n. v. University of Texas at Dallas*,[424] spelled out the constitutional due process afforded faculty in the event of a program elimination. There, the university decided to close its Special Education and Environmental Sciences Programs in response to declining enrollments and falling research support. Environmental Sciences in particular was viewed as peripheral to UTD's mission and as a "worthwhile experiment that failed."[425] The court drew a distinction between the requisite process for (1) a decision to eliminate a given program and (2) a decision to terminate a specific professor. For the former, "only the barest procedural protections of notice and an opportunity to be heard need be afforded the individual faculty member."[426] This meant giving faculty a chance to contribute to the debate over the program closure, but not any authority to make such a call. In contrast, when the institution faced an individual termination decision, the affected faculty member was "entitled to a meaningful opportunity to demonstrate that, even if his or her program was to be discontinued . . . he or she should nevertheless be retained to teach in a field in which he or she [was] qualified."[427] The intricacies of such tenure termination decisions lead us into a more comprehensive discussion of the protections enjoyed by faculty against all manner of adverse employment actions.

## Procedural Protections for Faculty in Personnel Decisions

The first legal principle in this area is that both public and private colleges and universities must carefully abide by the terms of their employment contracts with faculty. Those contracts, as interpreted under applicable state contract law, will frequently establish the kinds and levels of procedural safeguards afforded faculty in various personnel matters.[428] Usually this is accomplished through institutional policy statements that are explicitly or implicitly incorporated in the employment contract. As usual, the AAUP has its own rules on the proper procedures in disciplining faculty— which are only binding on colleges and universities that choose to follow them.[429] Institutions must also comply with relevant state legislation granting such procedural protections, such as state administrative procedure acts that cover public higher education entities. And, of course, colleges and universities that are state actors are also subject to federal constitutional requirements when making personnel decisions and changes. Most significantly, the Fourteenth Amendment guarantees that states will not deprive any person of liberty or property "without due process of law."[430] In the following pages I consider what Fourteenth Amendment due process safeguards are provided to faculty at such institutions.

The legal rules for evaluating due process at state-actor colleges and universities are by now well settled. Quite simply, the constitutionality of faculty personnel decisions depends on the answers to two questions. First, "Is the faculty member being deprived of a liberty or property interest?" If the answer to this question is no, there is no Fourteenth Amendment problem with the institution's process (or lack thereof). But if the answer to this first question is yes, then the faculty member is entitled to due process, and courts will turn to the second question, "*What* process is 'due' under these circumstances?" Reviewing courts will—and administrators at state-actor institutions always should—run through this two-step Fourteenth Amendment analysis whenever adverse personnel decisions are being made against faculty in order to ensure that they are acting in accordance with constitutional dictates.

## WHAT LIBERTY OR PROPERTY INTERESTS DO FACULTY HAVE?

A faculty member is deprived of a constitutionally protected *liberty interest* when (1) a state actor (this could include a public university acting through its official leadership) makes a public charge against the professor that might seriously damage his or her standing and associations in the community or (2) a government-imposed stigma or other disability forecloses that person's freedom to take advantage of other employment opportunities.[431] The obvious fact that individuals will be less marketable as a result of adverse employment action does not necessarily mean that liberty interests have been implicated. "Although any dismissal or denial of reappointment, for whatever reason, may reflect negatively upon a professor, this stigma alone is not of a constitutional magnitude."[432] Thus, to trammel a faculty member's liberty interest via employee discipline, the reasons for the disciplinary action must be published or otherwise made widely known.[433]

A faculty member's *property interests* are involved whenever a professor has a "legitimate claim of entitlement" to a given term or condition of employment or to a particular benefit—claims that must be independently grounded in law (typically state law).[434] The seminal cases defining faculty property rights in employment are *Board of Regents v. Roth* and *Perry v. Sindermann.*[435] The underlying facts of these 1972 companion Supreme Court decisions are similar, both concerning the nonrenewal of a college teacher's term contract. In *Roth,* the Court found that neither a liberty nor a property interest was implicated when, at the conclusion of his initial one-year appointment, the plaintiff assistant professor at Wisconsin State University–Oshkosh was simply not rehired.[436] But in *Perry,* while the justices again found no liberty interest at stake, they held that a professor who had been reappointed for four successive years under one-year contracts might be able to demonstrate that he had acquired de facto tenure that would constitute a protected property right. In reaching this result, and in distinguishing *Perry* from *Roth,* the Court pointed to Texas state education board guidelines vesting teachers with seven or more years' service in the state college system with "some form of job tenure"[437] and to an unusual provision on "Teacher Tenure" in the faculty guide at Mr. Perry's home institution stating that "Odessa College has no tenure system. The Administration of the College wishes the faculty member to feel that he has permanent tenure as long as his teaching services are satisfactory and as long as he displays a cooperative attitude toward his co-workers and his superiors, and as long as he is happy in his work."[438] The combination of these policies and the plaintiff's heretofore regular annual reappointment may have resulted in a legitimate expectation of continued employment.[439] I think that considerations of equity (i.e., the unfairness of seeing a longtime professor summarily turned out) must also have influenced the *Perry* outcome.

Under *Roth, Perry,* and their progeny, when are constitutionally protected property or liberty interests being taken from faculty?

— *Breaking tenure* certainly entails a deprivation of property. Continuous and contractually enforceable employment lies at the very heart of tenure; faculty who have earned this designation expect to remain in their positions.[440]

— *Ending a term appointment before the end of the term* also clearly implicates a faculty member's property interest.[441] Probationary faculty lawfully anticipate that they will be allowed to complete their current contracts, even if they have received no assurances about renewal.

— *Nonrenewal of a term appointment at the end of the term* would *not* generally be a limitation or taking of property,[442] although one could construct scenarios to the contrary (e.g., if institutional rules or practices, or clear understandings with the faculty member, create renewal rights or implied tenure as in *Perry*). Ordinarily, though, a term appointee has no right to be reappointed.

— *Denying tenure* would not infringe the unsuccessful applicant's property (except in the most extraordinary circumstances). No nontenured faculty member is *entitled* to tenure. Tenure is "a privilege, an honor, a distinctive honor, which is not to be accorded to all assistant professors."[443] Nontenured faculty are probationary employees whose performance and credentials for tenure are judged by subjective and discretionary standards. Eligibility for tenure is thus very far from a job guarantee. As the court opined in *Johnson v. Univ. of Pittsburgh,* "a mere expectancy that plaintiff might be retained if she did certain things [i.e., academic achievements of a level meriting tenure] is clearly not enough to invest her with a property right in her employment at the University."[444]

— *Denying a promotion in faculty rank* (e.g., from associate to full professor) would be viewed as equivalent to a denial of tenure, with no property interest involved. Faculty must earn such promotions, which do not occur as a matter of course.[445]

— *Transfers of faculty between academic departments* do not implicate property interests either. For example, in *Maples v. Martin* the Eleventh Circuit found no deprivation of property when disruptive Mechanical Engineering faculty were reassigned to other engineering departments at Auburn, all without any loss of tenure, rank, or salary. The plaintiffs had no "entitlement to continued assignment in the ME Department."[446] Nor could they show that the transfer stigmatized them or damaged their job prospects in ways that amounted to a constitutionally protected liberty interest.[447]

— *Removal as chair of a department* also should not constitute a loss of property or liberty, at least as long as the nonrenewed (or even deposed) chair remains a fully tenured member of the faculty.[448] However, while no "tenure" in a chairmanship is consistent with faculty culture in the arts and sciences, one wonders whether a similar result would obtain in an academic medical center, where department chairs typically have more seniority and security in their posts.

— *Loss of perquisites or special privileges* does not entitle a professor to due process. In *Mahaffey v. Kansas Bd. of Regents,* constitutionally protected property was not at stake when the plaintiff was given no (or small) merit raises, stripped of specific committee assignments, reduced from a twelve-month to a nine-month appointment (presumably with no loss of salary), moved to a smaller office, and ceased to have control over certain audiovisual equipment.[449] And in *Samad v. Jenkins,*[450] the court found no property right in being granted (or even being considered for) "Professor Emeritus" status. Although such emoluments might technically be characterized as "conditions" of employment, trivial or contingent items like these do not ordinarily merit constitutional safeguards.

Note as well that statements in faculty handbooks or appointment letters that individuals will be evaluated for reappointment or tenure pursuant to specific criteria and processes do not create property interests for Fourteenth Amendment purposes. "A contractual right to have certain procedures followed does not create a property interest in the procedures themselves."[451] "Property" instead requires a more substantive entitlement. But although promises to observe enumerated procedures do not rise to the level of constitutionally protected property, faculty may still have a contract claim (typically under state law) if those procedures are ignored. Put differently, a college or university's failure to adhere strictly to its own rules would not violate the Constitution—but it may be a breach of contract or a violation of state administrative procedure law.[452]

Readers should recall that in any of the situations described above, an institution's actions could implicate *liberty* interests even if no property interests are involved (e.g., public disclosure of charges or sanctions that damage a faculty member's reputation; barring future employment at the college or university). But in an academic environment where both custom and comity frown on public disparagement of disciplined or departing colleagues, losses of property will be much more common than infringements of liberty. Finally, remember that the only legal consequence of having a property or liberty interest implicated is that the affected individual must *receive* due process before a deprivation of such interests occurs—not that he or she will be able to preserve them.

## ASSUMING ONE IS ENTITLED TO DUE PROCESS, WHAT PROCESS QUALIFIES AS "DUE"?

In answering this second question in the due process analytical framework, judges will apply the legal test enunciated by the Supreme Court in *Matthews v. Eldridge,*[453] balancing (1) the private interest at stake or being affected; (2) the risk of an erroneous deprivation of liberty or property through the procedures currently being used, and the probable value (if any) of additional or other safeguards; and (3) the state actor's interest, including both the nature of the governmental function involved (in this case, education) and the fiscal and administrative burden that additional or other procedural protections would entail. By such balancing, over an almost-thirty-year (and ongoing) series of cases, courts have provided detailed guidance on the constitutionally mandated procedures to effect various faculty personnel actions.

Significantly, there is no standard checklist of due process requirements for particular actions, places, or times. The boundless variety of underlying fact patterns, together with the necessity for courts to spell out with some precision the procedural flaws or needs in each case, precludes rigidity or uniformity. As the First Circuit observed in *Newman v. Burgin,* "The Due Process Clause . . . does not require [a] University to follow any specific set of detailed procedures as long as the procedures the University actually follows are basically fair ones."[454] The crux of Fourteenth Amendment due process, however, is usually some form of *notice* of the action being taken against the faculty member and the reasons for it, and some kind of opportunity for a *hearing* at which the faculty member can make a case against the proposed action. As long as these baseline elements are present, college and university employers will have considerable discretion in crafting procedures that reflect their culture and meet their operational goals. With these principles in mind, let us now explore how courts have viewed constitutional due process for some common forms of faculty discipline.

*Breaking tenure "for cause."* A faculty member facing this most severe penalty should receive the following:

— a written statement of the reasons justifying his or her termination (this document should also alert the professor to the evidence allegedly supporting the charges);
— adequate notice of a hearing about the proposed discharge;
— an actual hearing before an impartial body, held within a reasonable

period of time, where the affected faculty member can challenge
the grounds for dismissal; and
— a final written statement of the bases for dismissal if it does occur.
(This last document should set forth the facts adduced at the hearing and the evidentiary basis for them.)[455]

While there are variations in the case law, there is strong legal authority for
the proposition that the due process hearing required before a college or
university can terminate a tenured faculty appointment need not be a comprehensive judicial proceeding. The official(s) considering the dispute do
not have to follow the Federal Rules of Evidence or Civil Procedure.[456]
The faculty member probably does not have the right to be fully represented by counsel as if this were an adversarial trial (though many institutions permit attorneys to attend and quietly advise their clients),[457] nor
would the professor be entitled to cross-examine witnesses or to obtain an
official transcript of the deliberations.

Sometimes an employer college or university may need (or at least believe that it needs) to move swiftly to discharge a problem tenured faculty
member. In such a scenario, the institution may seek to dismiss the professor immediately while offering him or her a post-termination hearing.
However, employers' freedom and flexibility to rely upon post-termination
procedural safeguards has been limited by a line of judicial precedent originating with the Supreme Court's 1985 decision in *Cleveland Bd. of Education v. Loudermill*. In that case the Court declared that even in circumstances in which a fired public employee with tenure would be granted a
post-termination appeal hearing, *prior* to his or her discharge the employee
was nevertheless entitled "to oral or written notice of the charges against
him, an explanation of the employer's evidence, and an opportunity to
present his side of the story."[458] More succinctly, as a preliminary check
against mistaken dismissals, faculty must get notice, an explanation of the
charges, and an opportunity to respond (irrespective of any postremoval
rights). In an important gloss on *Cleveland Bd. v. Loudermill*, lower courts
have subsequently clarified that the requisite notice must apprise faculty
both of the specific charges against them *and* of the contemplated disciplinary actions.[459]

The Third Circuit's opinion in *McDaniels v. Flick* provides a good example of how federal courts will interpret the pretermination due process
owed to faculty under the Fourteenth Amendment. In that case, constitu-

tional mandates were satisfied when a tenured community college professor had pretermination opportunities to rebut student allegations of sexual harassment (both during an investigatory meeting with college officials and for several weeks thereafter until the college trustees formally approved his discharge), as well as post-termination rights of appeal. Reflecting judicial willingness to give colleges and universities procedural leeway at the pretermination stage, the court held that the obligatory *Cleveland Bd. v. Loudermill* pretermination "hearing" could even be before an interested party (the faculty member's dean), as long as post-termination recourse could still be had to a neutral decision maker.[460]

Overall, the constitutional procedural hoops that colleges and universities must jump through to terminate tenured faculty "for cause" cannot be characterized as very demanding. This means that, from a faculty perspective, Fourteenth Amendment due process is a rather thin reed on which to hang one's job security or career.

***Ending a term appointment before the end of the term "for cause."*** The process "due" in this situation would be equivalent to that owed when an institution strips a faculty member of tenure. However, litigation on this subject would be very unusual, since colleges and universities will find it simpler just to let the problematic faculty member's contract expire. This will also be regarded as kinder to that instructor; and, more cynically, it reduces the risk of claims for deprivation of liberty or property.

***Discharges for financial exigency.*** As described earlier,[461] faculty who are dismissed because of a financial exigency are only granted an abridged set of constitutional protections. "Where termination or elimination of a position was due to fiscal exigencies, procedural due process requirements are less strict than in cases where plaintiffs have been terminated for cause or other personal reasons."[462] The operative legal and policy analysis here has been that because these kinds of discharges are not at their core decisions based on facts about individual performance (and involve no assignment of fault), less process is needed. Accordingly, in the frequently cited case of *Johnson v. Board of Regents,* the University of Wisconsin System was merely required to furnish the faculty member with a written statement explaining the rationale behind the decision to terminate and the mechanics of how that decision was made, to share key data driving the termination decision, and to afford each employee slated for termination a chance to argue against that action.[463] However, in identifying which faculty to let go out of some larger group (such as a department or a school), factual questions about each person's quality and merit will inevitably arise, thereby bolstering plaintiffs' arguments for more comprehensive Fourteenth Amendment due process.

**Discharges for program elimination.** As this subfield of higher education law evolves, it will be interesting to see whether the procedural safeguards extended to faculty when their programs are closed or retrenched vary in any meaningful way from those given to faculty who are terminated because of financial exigency. (My strong sense is that there will be no substantial distinctions). Once again, though, courts have authorized a much less elaborate process for program elimination dismissals than they demand when a dismissal is "for cause."[464]

In the *Texas Faculty Ass'n* case,[465] a federal appeals court assumed (and perhaps tacitly agreed) that faculty members' property interests were implicated both by the decisions to close their programs and by the decisions to eliminate each of their particular jobs. This reflected the conceptual and practical difficulty of cleanly breaking these decisions apart. But when the court then reached the second-level inquiry of what process was "due" to protect those property interests, it treated the two elimination decisions differently. It said that no formal or adversarial hearing was required on the decision to close an academic program. Notice of the closure decision and an opportunity to meet with the dean to discuss it sufficed. However, in the context of decisions on whom to lay off, the faculty members slated for termination had a Fourteenth Amendment right to make an argument why they should be retained elsewhere in the institution.[466] If no such showing were made, the matter would end with a brief written statement of reasons for the dismissal. But if an affected faculty member *could* make a colorable case for reassignment, he or she must then receive a very informal "hearing" to present that argument to the relevant university decision maker and to explore alternatives to termination. At this hearing, the faculty member would not be entitled to representation by counsel, to cross-examine witnesses, or to a transcript.[467] The court even held that the hearing could be before the university official(s) who made the prior decision to eliminate the particular program.[468] If the decision maker did not change his or her mind as a result of such a hearing, as a final requisite step in the process the faculty member should receive a written statement of the official's conclusions.

I want to reiterate here an earlier point that the procedural safeguards for faculty facing dismissal for exigency or program elimination are a likely source of future litigation. The constitutional protections that federal courts have typically demanded in such circumstances are rather modest, and they fall well short of what the AAUP would mandate: namely, an on-the-record adjudicative hearing before a faculty committee, with representation by counsel (and presumably the cross-examination of witnesses), and with such panel free to delve into the existence and extent of the condition of financial exigency or the educational justification for the program closure, as the case may be.[469]

Our discussion of Fourteenth Amendment due process in faculty employment actions should conclude with several important caveats. First, in addition to complying with relatively detailed requirements about the kinds and timing of notices and hearings, all of these adverse personnel decisions must be made in good faith, in reliance upon objective criteria, and not in an arbitrary or capricious manner. Such notions of fundamental fairness involve *substantive* due process under the Constitution (as opposed to *procedural* due process, which has been our focus in these last several pages). Carefully made (even if close or controversial) choices about faculty hires, reappointments, tenure, and discipline should ordinarily comport with substantive due process. The Supreme Court has noted that "when judges are asked to review the substance of a genuinely academic decision . . . they should show great respect for the faculty's professional judgment. Plainly, they may not override it unless it is such a substantial departure from accepted academic norms as to demonstrate that the person or committee responsible did not actually exercise professional judgment."[470] Well-considered personnel actions by academic administrators such as chairs, deans, provosts, and presidents will of course receive like deference.[471] Still, there are occasional examples of institutions that are found to have violated the substantive due process rights of faculty—as in *Johnson v. San Jacinto Junior College*, where a too-hasty demotion procedure unfairly denied the plaintiff an opportunity to explain his conduct.[472]

Second, all of the above-described procedural protections are merely the constitutionally required *minima* or floors. Nothing in the Fourteenth Amendment blocks a college or university from electing to furnish additional safeguards, and many do. (Institutions must, of course, rigorously comply with any procedural rules they establish. And they should be mindful that the more detailed and comprehensive the process provided, the more complicated and time-consuming faculty discipline becomes, with a greater likelihood of procedural errors.) Third, as previously noted, being entitled to constitutional due process does not mean that a faculty member will be able to achieve a desired outcome (e.g., retaining his or her position). And fourth, from a technical legal standpoint, constitutional due process is only applicable to institutions that are state actors.

However, at non-state-actor colleges and universities, written faculty contracts, local custom and practice, or state statutes or state constitutions may furnish employees with at least as much procedural protection as they would receive in the public sector. Both state and federal courts also use Fourteenth Amendment standards as a guide or benchmark in reviewing procedural fairness even when the Constitution is not formally applicable.[473] Consequently, private colleges and universities may not blithely assume that they have a free hand in disciplining their faculty.

In my view, the procedural protections that will be required in faculty employment actions should not be troubling to either public or private institutions. These are in fact the sort of commonsense safeguards that colleges and universities would adopt on their own, without any legal compulsion, for reasons of fairness, maintaining employee morale, and smart legal and public relations. As William Kaplin and Barbara Lee correctly observe, procedural checks on faculty personnel decisions can avoid or rectify improper actions, help protect the faculty's academic freedom, foster professors' confidence in the institution (this will positively affect the recruitment and retention of scholars), and encourage the internal resolution of disputes rather than immediate resort to litigation.[474] Indeed, in some instances state courts may require the exhaustion of intra-institutional or other administrative remedies before they will entertain a suit.[475] Even if no such exhaustion doctrine applies, a college or university that has—and has followed—fair internal personnel procedures will look eminently more reasonable when (inevitably) one of its actions is challenged in court.

## Concluding Thoughts

This chapter exceeds all others in scope and length for the obvious reason that, no matter what activity they are engaged in at a particular moment (conducting research, teaching, participating in committee meetings) faculty are always institutional employees who draw paychecks and are subject to some form of accountability and administrative control. Questions turning on a professor's role or status as a college or university employee thus run the gamut. Still, there are several key concepts that shape this area.

First among these is the dominance of contract law and principles of contract interpretation. At institutions both public and private, research- and teaching-oriented, and with or without collective bargaining, faculty are always bound by some form of employment contract. The terms of such contracts, whether memorialized in writing or established more informally, set the nature and conditions of a professor's work, including the salary, benefits, and other rights received in return for his or her labor; the duration of his or her appointment; opportunities for promotion; specific duties; and the consequences of failing to perform those duties. Post-tenure review, for example, can only occur when authorized by or consistent with an agreement between faculty and their employer institution. (Such agreement may result from lengthy negotiation, or, at the other extreme, local policy or custom may empower the university to impose such evaluations unilaterally.)

A second overarching concept is the impact of federal, state, and local employment discrimination law. Whether prohibiting actions based on the race, sex, religion, age, disability, or other protected characteristic of a prospective or actual employee, such rules provide a common legal framework (probably second in use only to breach-of-contract suits) for aggrieved parties to shape and pursue claims against college and university employers (e.g., Ms. X was denied tenure because she was a woman, thereby violating Titles VII and IX).

Third, the law of faculty employment at state-actor institutions is heavily influenced by the Fourteenth Amendment's mandate that individuals receive due process before the state can strip them of property or liberty. What qualifies as a constitutionally protected property or liberty interest, as well as what specific procedural safeguards are required, is by now well established and unlikely to be dramatically recast.

However, there are other zones of faculty employment law that are much more fluid, and where future statutes and litigation will establish the operative legal principles. I have identified and discussed the most important of these areas in the preceding sections. Summarizing briefly, commentators and courts should expect the following developments.

***Innovative employment arrangements aimed at reducing the cost and rigidity of traditional tenure systems.*** The variety of types of faculty lines will increasingly resemble the range of positions found at academic medical centers, with even larger numbers of part-time, fixed-term, and other non-tenure-track instructors. Consistent with growing faculty entrepreneurism (as seen in the pursuit of research sponsors and in scholars who hopscotch between schools), many institutions will offer professors additional short-term compensation in exchange for reduced long-term job security. Of course, the response from faculty unions and advocacy groups will be fiercely negative.

*Expanded protections against employment discrimination.* Examples of such new safeguards will be laws prohibiting discrimination on the basis of sexual orientation (which I expect to multiply) and more inclusive interpretations of what constitutes a disability. As our knowledge of the genetic code grows, additional physical and mental conditions beyond an individual's control may be deemed covered by the ADA, Section 504, and equivalent statutes. Within the subfield of sexual discrimination law, courts need to develop sharper definitions of sexual harassment (for example, what level and frequency of behavior creates a hostile workplace or educational environment) and hopefully will craft more sturdy legal protections for serious classroom discussion of sexually oriented topics. I also expect that courts will become even more intrusive in their examination of the bases for faculty personnel decisions, to the dismay of peer reviewers and administrators. This may encourage less candor in tenure and promotion cases—which in turn might lead to even more lawsuits. One significant development that may reduce employment discrimination litigation, though, is the Supreme Court's apparent embrace of a broad Eleventh Amendment prohibition on suits brought against a state (including a state university) by one of its citizens. This jurisprudential approach has already cast doubts on the enforceability of federal age and disability discrimination law. If this approach is extended to other antidiscrimination statutes, the law of faculty employment might begin to look very different.

*Heightened tension over the composition and diversity of faculties.* As faculties across the nation become more "gray" because of the end of mandatory retirement and a concomitant desire by some professors to work into their 70s, many schools, especially research universities, will encounter financial pressure from carrying numerous highly compensated senior scholars, human-resource pressure from clogged lines of promotion and occupied chairs, and especially intellectual pressure to rejuvenate the professoriate with fresh ideas and individuals. Colleges' and universities' responses will write new chapters in employment law. In a related vein, the diversification of faculties with women and minority scholars (in my view a wise and valuable effort) will inevitably be challenged by male and nonminority job candidates and employees alleging reverse discrimination. Bloody legal battles are coming over the constitutional validity of current affirmative action efforts in student admissions and faculty hiring and promotion. Should such programs be struck down, fights will then follow over the legal and policy impact of alternative approaches to the problem of diversity.

*New struggles over unionization.* I noted earlier how the stressful existence and uncertain job prospects of graduate (especially Ph.D.) students has given rise to a unionization movement, which may have received significant impetus from the NLRB's ground-breaking fall 2000 approval of collective bargaining by graduate students at the private New York University. While faculty unionization at private colleges and universities was set back by the Supreme Court's *Yeshiva* decision, the AAUP and other trade union advocates are becoming more aggressive in light of the financial pressures encountered by current and potential faculty and the perceived "corporatization" of higher education.

*Litigation over institutional responses to financial constraints.* We have seen that many legal problems are connected to the combination of tightly limited university resources and ever-growing costs. Genuine and unavoidable financial pressures might lead to a new round of faculty terminations for exigency (in which case courts will clarify how focused and severe fiscal problems must be to justify discharges). However, they are much more likely to result in closing specific programs for mixed financial and academic reasons (an area where the law is still murky), and especially in reducing or restructuring programs and departments to achieve strength and distinctiveness. Legal guidance will be necessary on whether and how colleges and universities can effect such focused redeployment of faculty resources.

It is evident, therefore, that faculty members' legal relationship with their employer institutions and their status as employees will continue to generate disputes requiring judicial intervention and guidance.

# Final Observations on Faculty Law

In concluding our examination of the law pertaining to faculty, we need to step back and consider from a broad higher education policy perspective how legal formulations and rules affect the daily work, lives, and status of college and university faculty and their home institutions. My key point in this regard is that—notwithstanding substantial and continuing growth in the statutory, regulatory, and case law applicable to higher education (in particular, law relevant to the professoriate)—faculty essentially remain as free as they always have been to explore new ideas, to teach, and to participate in institutional and civic affairs.

As we have seen, in their capacity as scholars, faculty enjoy wide discretion in selecting their own research topics, in pursuing external funding to support such research, and in disseminating their results in a manner and at a time of their own choosing (while exercising proper caution about the accuracy and completeness of their findings). Furthermore, the overlay of individual contracts and institution-specific patent and copyright policies on basic principles of intellectual property law gives professors considerable control over, and financial stake in, efforts to tap the commercial value of their scholarship. In their capacity as teachers, faculty are still for the most part the masters of their classrooms, able to determine what is taught, from what intellectual perspective, and in what style. Even the modest checks imposed on faculty control over curriculum and pedagogy are often derived from decisions made by the faculty as a collective (e.g., through duly constituted curriculum committees). In their capacity as institutional citizens, faculty are expected to shape (and at the very least, to carefully critique) local policies about admissions and academic standards, hiring and promotions, college or university goals and priorities, and norms of community behavior. In their capacity as public citizens, faculty of course enjoy the First Amendment rights of free speech and association granted to all citizens. However, faculty members' expertise, erudition (and sometimes their institutional affiliations) afford them special opportunities to engage in public service and to comment on current political, economic, or social issues. While professors and employer universities alike must be mindful of any perceived or actual conflicts of faculty interest or commitment (and of the necessity of distinguishing between individual and institutional statements or actions), faculty involvement in the nonacademic world is generally welcomed. Finally, in their capacity as employees, faculty have great freedom to contract with college or university employers on terms that they find personally advantageous, and they are afforded meaningful substantive and procedural safeguards against wrongful personnel decisions.

## The Risk of Personal Liability

Turning to different kind of legal question from most of those explored in this volume, faculty members and academic administrators will understandably want to know about the potential personal legal liability they face as a result of their actions. For the reasons set forth below, they are likely to find the answer to that question very reassuring. However, because an actual determination of liability is both extremely fact-specific and dependent upon the intricacies of contract, personal injury, criminal, or other law in a specific jurisdiction, this is an area where there can be no substitute for consultation with legal counsel.

Most litigation involving faculty as *defendants* will arise from students (or their parents) who feel they have received inadequate redress from institutional grievance procedures (or who, through inadvertence or a predisposition towards litigation, have not availed themselves of such procedures). Typical examples would be challenges to grades or academic discipline (e.g., expulsion for cheating). But as we saw in the grading context, suits about course work are viewed as extra-university attacks on the academy, with a united academic community and the courts quick to uphold faculty judgments.[1] Suits by a college or university against its *own* faculty, in contrast, are rare—not because of a dearth of arguments between these parties, but because by contract or custom, or both, such disputes will be handled through internal faculty disciplinary proceedings. In the event that the institution does not prevail in these forums, it would be most unlikely to pursue matters further in court.[2] Academic and other administrators, however, are frequently sued in both their individual and official capacities by a host of parties, ranging from disgruntled (or wronged) faculty, to students, to for-profit businesses, to government regulators.

Generally speaking, the keys to gauging a faculty member's or an academic administrator's legal exposure are whether the challenged action was within the scope of that individual's employment and whether it was taken in good faith. If the faculty member, chair, dean, or provost was faithfully attempting to perform assigned job duties or taking legitimate steps necessary to carry out the job (elastic concepts that include the exercise of professional discretion and even the making of honest mistakes), he or she should have little to fear. For example, faculty who make candid evaluations of a student's course work, a manuscript sent for review, a case for tenure, or (in a peer discipline panel) a colleague's personal or professional conduct, should face no genuine legal risk. Likewise, if a chair or dean makes requisite administrative decisions (hires, promotions, raises, employee discipline, the expenditure of resources, the establishment of priorities, etc.) in good faith, no liability will attach to such actions. In contrast, when faculty members or administrators act outside the scope of their employment, in bad faith, or beyond their delegated authority (e.g, committing a crime, sexually harassing a student, signing contracts without permission), liability tends to arise.[3]

Of course, since one's decisions or actions will sometimes cause disappointment or pain to others, and because we live in a litigious time, there is no way to insulate faculty or administrators from legal controversy. But colleges and universities (and higher education law) have responded to the legitimate concerns of their employees that they enjoy sufficient freedom of thought and action to do their jobs well and that they not be liable for behavior in their roles as official representatives of employer institutions. Accordingly, faculty members, academic administrators, and other staff (and even trustees) will typically be *indemnified* by their institutions from legal risk associated with the performance of their duties. In layman's terms, this means that in the (unlikely) event that a court actually levies a judgment against an individual employee, the employer college or university will assume such liability and actually pay the bill. Moreover, the employer will also typically provide, at its expense and throughout the entire course of threatened or actual litigation, appropriate representation by counsel for any employees named as defendants or otherwise involved in a legal dispute.[4]

The means for accomplishing these results will vary. Thus, many colleges and universities have explicit policy statements or rules on employee indemnification, setting forth any conditions upon and the mechanics of such protection.[5] Sophisticated institutions will also typically purchase liability insurance policies to guard against litigation risks. But even in the absence of such formal safeguards, colleges and universities customarily defend and indemnify their faculty and staff from legal entanglements that arise as they carry out their jobs.[6]

The availability and scope of indemnification must be resolved early on, for an employee who is not indemnified must engage private counsel. This is why the immediate step professors or administrators should take upon learning that they are embroiled in a legal controversy (typically through receipt of a threatening letter from an attorney, and in any event upon service with a complaint) is to contact the college or university's attorneys for an explanation of their rights and clarification of their (and the institution's) expectations.[7] Obviously, during the course of any such dispute, individuals should not make a legal move except under counsel's direction, regardless of who is responsible for the legal bills.

## Basic Sources of Legal Tension

Throughout this volume I have sought to identify areas of future controversy, to show where higher education law remains underdeveloped or unclear, and to point out some of the conceptual directions in which I think the law pertaining to faculty (and, for that matter, good administrative practice) should move. There are, obviously, a host of legal flash points (many of which are reiterated at the ends of the previous chapters). But there are also several underlying trends helping to generate and drive more specific disputes.

The first of these is the growing number of constituencies with a profound interest in the work of colleges and universities. In addition to "internal" audiences of faculty, students, and administrative staff, even an "independent" private institution must consider the views of trustees; alumni; national, state, and local political leaders; parents of students; prospective students; prospective employers of students; the media; neighbors; corporate sponsors; federal funding agencies; and (at religious institutions) denominational authorities. At public institutions, this list must be expanded to include governors, legislators, coordinating boards, university system administrations, rafts of other state agencies, and of course taxpayers, who help foot the bills. With so many cooks having an interest in the educational soup, sharp differences of opinion, escalating into legal disputes, are inevitable. All the more so when higher education is (correctly) viewed as a life-changing investment for students, and universities have assumed roles as beacons of service and engines of economic development.

Second, the core university community of faculty, staff, and students is much less homogeneous and more splintered than ever before. Departmental colleagues no longer share the same cultural background or intellectual underpinnings; faculty in different disciplines may not know each other (much less be able to understand one another's work). Student bodies are also increasingly diverse in age, race, gender, and many other dimensions. From an intellectual and educational perspective, all of this diversity can be spectacularly valuable. But it also undeniably leads to tensions, for example, with student "humor" that offends members of particular racial or ethnic groups, or heated arguments within the English department about the merits of reader response theory. Intra-university disciplinary hearings and extra-university lawsuits are extreme forms of unresolved community conflict.

A third basic source of legal tension is the burgeoning institutional and faculty pursuit of outside funding and profits. Rules and relationships that were workable twenty (or even five) years ago, when the fruits of faculty scholarship and the intellectual content shared in classes were viewed as having no real monetary value and when the costs of embarking upon a research project were relatively modest and the stakes were low, today look obsolete or unfair to faculty, administrators, or both. The combination of potential new sources of funding and long-standing financial pressure is incendiary. Resentment between faculty and institutions will simmer and erupt into disputes unless these old rules and relationships are revamped, or at the very least justified.

Finally, technological change is generating intense confusion about the respective legal rights, roles, and responsibilities of faculty and employer institutions. As scholarly research, teaching, student learning, and the very notion of intellectual discourse are transformed by digital technology, the pace and scope of the necessary adaptation by higher education will be unprecedented—and almost certainly jarring.

There are, of course, countless other causes of unrest and threatened or actual litigation involving faculty. But I am struck by how many of the legal arguments examined in this book—and the disputes that I think will fill the pages of future volumes and judicial opinions—can be traced back, at least in part, to these four factors.

## Assessing the Law's Impact

It would be fair to say that in this study I have frequently endorsed a somewhat faculty-centric view of how higher education (and colleges and universities) should operate. This reflects my belief that an institution is ultimately only as good as its faculty. As I noted at the very beginning, students and scholars are not drawn to a university or college, nor will it attract grant funding or donations, because of its superb administration (although such stewardship does directly enable great teaching and research). Of course, faculty sometimes act and speak in ways that are blatantly self-serving, greedy, obstreperous, or otherwise deeply damaging to the process of education, the discovery of truth, and the health of their institutions. This volume certainly contains many examples of such unfortunate behavior, and also identifies appropriate and lawful institutional responses and remedies. Still, college and university administrators (including counsel)—and especially external judicial and other governmental authorities—should always be sensitive to the likely effects of legal rules or decisions on the core academic business, which is largely entrusted to faculty. To the extent that laws or legal formulations choke off inquiry or chill the delicate (and sometimes necessarily painful) exchange of ideas in a classroom or around a seminar table, higher education will not be well served.

The law has had both positive and negative impacts on faculty.[8] On the plus side of the ledger, the development of college and university law has resulted in the articulation of stronger and more powerful defenses for academic freedom and autonomy—not just for individual professors, but also for colleges and universities as institutions. Faculty benefit as well from the law's push towards increased fairness in academic decisions. For instance, nondiscrimination statutes prevent the denial of tenure to minority or women faculty on the basis of race or sex. I would optimistically assert that college and university law's support for open decision making (e.g., no assured confidentiality for tenure files) has increased the recognition of merit in faculty hires and promotions. Some commentators have opined that clearer legal definitions of research fraud and faculty conflicts of interest and commitment (coupled with meaningful enforcement of such standards) have fostered higher levels of academic integrity. Certainly health and safety conditions in laboratories and offices have improved because of statutory mandates.[9] Last but not least, the explosion in higher education law has led to a clearer and sharper understanding of the role of faculty within their institutions (including how they relate to other constituencies such as colleagues, students, and administrators), the role of those institutions themselves (e.g., how they should deal with their faculty, other colleges and universities, and the wider world), and how symbiotic and fragile each of these roles are.

On the negative side, increased reliance upon legal rules and reasoning has left many faculty with a diminished sense of control over their professional lives. Even if this is just a perceived (rather than an actual) loss of control, the damage to faculty morale can be immense. Should a cautious desire to avoid any legal problems allow "hesitancy [to creep] into the process of evaluation and critical judgment, teaching and scholarship can be compromised."[10] There is also a danger that legal processes may overwhelm the substance of academic decisions. For example, in discharging a tenured faculty member for cause, more time and energy may be spent arguing over the precise procedural steps to be followed than in examining the alleged misconduct. As both faculty and employer institutions (as well as students) have proved increasingly willing to defend aggressively—if not to seek to expand—their legal rights, we have also witnessed new levels of tension and adversariness within the academy. Historically, direct conflict has been "a last resort in an educational environment. Yet conflict is natural to the legal process, and the threat of adversary procedures hovers inevitably around lawyers, and around legal formulations."[11]

These problems are genuine—and undoubtedly sometimes painful—but still fall well short of mortal blows to faculty work or culture. Confirming that the law does not seriously impede the activities of faculty, very little of the day-to-day business of most university legal offices involves faculty issues. Most faculty will go through their entire career without ever dealing directly with their institution's attorneys. It is also interesting to note that the most serious and potentially intrusive legal constraints imposed on colleges and universities stem from societal concerns extending well beyond the academy (e.g., ending workforce discrimination; preventing sexual harassment).

On balance, the law has added real value and fairness to American higher education while maintaining the ability of faculty and institutions to fulfill their academic missions. I see no real threat to the work or the integrity of faculty because of the growth in college and university law over the last several decades or because of any directions in which that law is likely to evolve. Indeed, faculty at both public and private institutions can confidently pursue their teaching, research, and service without fear of legal incursion, and academic administrators can turn to relevant legal principles in making wise personnel decisions, in structuring employment and research contracts, and in formulating effective policies.

# Notes

## Introduction

1. This discussion of the benefits and disadvantages of a more legalistic academy draws upon a fuller exposition in T. Wright, *Faculty and the Law Explosion: Assessing the Impact—A Twenty-five Year Perspective (1960–1985) for College and University Lawyers,* 12 J.C. & U.L. 363 (1985), 373–79.

2. *See* W. Kaplin & B. Lee, *The Law of Higher Education* (Jossey-Bass: 1995).

3. My highly segmented analysis of the various roles and activities of faculty derives in part from more rudimentary classifications used by R. O'Neil in *Academic Freedom and the Constitution,* 11 J.C. & U. L. 275 (1984).

4. As of this writing, there are 4,096 two- and four-year colleges and universities in the United States. *Chronicle of Higher Education, Almanac,* September 1, 2000, 7.

## 1 The Lay of the Land

1. As this volume will make clear, higher education is a heavily regulated enterprise like telecommunications (although it has not yet risen to the level of regulation governing meatpacking). Almost every aspect of the work of colleges and universities has been subjected to legal attack or scrutiny in one context or another. The following discussion of sources of law relies in part on Kaplin & Lee, cited in introduction, n. 2, at 13–16, 18–20.

2. Pp. 11–16.

3. At the same time as the First Amendment limits the ability of public institutions to discipline faculty or students for the exercise of protected speech, its guarantee of freedom of religion affords *private* sectarian institutions considerable latitude in how they conduct their affairs, even allowing them to discipline faculty or students for espousing heterodox beliefs. See *Curran v. Catholic Univ.,* No. 1562-87 (D.C. Super. Ct., Feb. 28, 1989) (private university, acting pursuant to Vatican ruling, can prohibit professor from teaching theology courses).

4. *See, e.g., United States v. Fordice,* 505 U.S. 717 (1992) (equal protection clause requires Mississippi to dismantle any remaining aspects of a dual system of higher education).

5. 20 U.S.C. §1681 (a).

6. 34 C.F.R. Part 106, with the athletics regulations found at Section 106.41.

7. Just to complicate matters further, the Title IX regulations themselves operate at a number of different levels. In addition to the regulations contained in the C.F.R., the department has issued a Policy Interpretation that explains its rules. And the department's *Investigator's Manual* sets forth the procedures to be followed in formal inquiries.

8. For example, regulations proposed in 1995 by the Office of Management and Budget would require universities to use the same Cost Accounting Standards under federal grants as are used by for-profit defense contractors. 60 Fed. Reg. 7104 (February 6, 1995). These standards would obligate universities to obtain federal approval—on a grant-by-grant basis—of any intra-institutional accounting changes. The Council on Government Relations (an umbrella group of university officials responsible for federal affairs) contended that OMB had wildly underestimated, perhaps by a factor of 10 to 15, the time required to complete the proposed rules' disclosure forms. M. Goldberg to A. Rivlin, May 11, 1995, and attachments (on file with author).

9. U.S. Const. Art. VI.

10. *See, e.g.,* Cal. Const. Art. IX, §9, which creates the University of California.

11. Cal Const. Art. I, §1.

12. K. Lively, "42.8-Billion for Public Colleges," *Chronicle of Higher Education,* October 14, 1994, A43.

13. Using Illinois law as an example, *see* 110 ILCS 205/0.01 et seq. (creating the Illinois Board of Higher Education); 805 ILCS 105/101.01 et seq. (general not-for-profit corporation law); 110 ILCS 70/0.01 et seq. (State Universities Civil Service Act); 720 ILCS 120/0.01 et seq. (hazing illegal); and 235 ILCS 5/6-20 (prohibiting consumption of alcohol by persons under 21). A recent California statute (Cal. Educ. Code §94367) gives students at private colleges and universities the same free speech rights and protections as students at public institutions. Ohio Rev. Code Ann. §3345.45 requires public universities in that state to develop standards for faculty instructional workloads "with special emphasis on the undergraduate learning experience." This bill, which was intended to effect at least a 10% increase in professors' teaching time, was upheld by the U.S. Supreme Court in *Central State Univ. v. AAUP,* 526 U.S. 124 (1999) (Equal Protection Clause not violated by exempting faculty workload policies from collective bargaining).

14. *See, e.g.,* 6 NYCRR §372 (generation and transportation of hazardous waste); 12 NYCRR §§461–64 (hearings on eligibility for unemployment benefits); and 8 NYCRR §§72.1–72.6 (licensing of psychologists).

15. The combination of innumerable jurisdictions and ordinances leaves any thorough treatment of local law beyond the scope of this volume.

16. J. Tokasz, "City Using Law to Get CU Money," *Ithaca Journal,* November 22, 1994, 1A; "Ithaca's Mayor Blocks Cornell's Construction Projects," *New*

*York Times,* May 3, 1995, B9; W. Skinner, "Mayor Yields on Frozen CU Permits," *Ithaca Journal,* June 1, 1995, 1A.

17. *See, e.g.,* Title 8, Administrative Code of the City of New York (New York City Human Rights Law), especially §8-107 (prohibiting discrimination based on, inter alia, sexual orientation). In the past, municipalities have even passed laws amounting to their own "foreign policy," for example, declaring themselves places of sanctuary for Central American refugees or prohibiting commercial ties with companies doing business in South Africa, Burma, Nigeria, Switzerland, Cuba, and Tibet. V. Merina, "Cities vs. the INS; Sanctuary: Reviving an Old Concept," *Los Angeles Times,* November 17, 1985, 1:1; R. Willing, "Some Localities Want to Decide Own Foreign Policy," *USA Today,* March 22, 2000, 4A. However, the Supreme Court's decision in *Crosby v. National Foreign Trade Council,* 530 U.S. 363 (2000), striking down a Massachusetts law barring state entities from purchasing goods or services from companies doing business with Burma, has now reasserted federal primacy in the conduct of foreign affairs.

18. Of course, the names of the various tribunals in different jurisdictions are often wildly inconsistent. Consider New York State, where the trial-level court is known as the Supreme Court and the supreme-level court is known as the Court of Appeals.

19. I.e., the U.S. Court of Appeals for the Fifth Circuit. As here, throughout this volume federal appellate courts are periodically referred to simply by their circuit numbers.

20. Readers seeking additional basic background on the structure, operation, and history of the U.S. legal system may turn, for example, to K. Hall, *The Magic Mirror* (Oxford University Press: 1989).

21. The answer appears to be that Penn is a private actor and not an instrumentality of the state. The state appropriation accounts for only a small percentage of the university's overall budget, and Penn has always exercised great autonomy in admitting students and setting academic standards. *See* judicial dicta in *Schier v. Temple Univ.,* 576 F. Supp. 1569, 1573, and 1577 (E.D. Pa. 1984), *aff'd sub nom Krynicky v. Univ. of Pittsburgh,* 742 F.2d 94 (3rd Cir. 1984), that as a "state-aided" institution, Penn was not as closely tied to the commonwealth as the "state-related" Temple University. (In contrast, Temple was found to be a state actor [p. 14].) The *Schier* dicta, however, did predate the 1994 appointment of Penn's new Commonwealth Trustees.

22. The state-action inquiry has "been characterized variously as a 'paragon of unclarity,' a 'protean concept,' and an 'impossible task.'" *Frazier v. Bd. of Trustees of Northwest Miss. Regional Med. Center,* 765 F.2d 1278, 1283 (5th Cir. 1985).

23. *Lugar v. Edmondson Oil Co.,* 457 U.S. 922, 938 (1981).

24. *Jackson v. Metropolitan Edison Co.,* 419 U.S. 345, 351 (1974) (emphasis added).

25. *See, e.g., Blum v. Yaretsky,* 457 U.S. 991, 1004 (1982); and *Imperiale v. Hahnemann Univ.,* 776 F. Supp. 189, 199 (E.D. Pa 1991).

26. *Blum,* supra, at 1004.

27. 429 F.2d 1120 (2nd Cir. 1970)

28. N.Y. Educ. Law 6450 (McKinney 1985), commonly known as the Henderson Act.

29. *Coleman,* cited in n. 27, at 1125.

30. The debate still rages as to whether the Henderson Act turns otherwise private colleges into state actors. In *Albert v. Carovano,* 851 F.2d 561 (2nd Cir. 1988) (en banc), the same court concluded that Hamilton College's suspension of protesters (once again under regulations adopted and filed with the state pursuant to the act) was not state action, largely because over time the state's role under the act had been limited to keeping file copies of various colleges' rules. A dissenting opinion argues that this student discipline is state action traceable to the coercive power of the Henderson Act. Ibid., at 574–78 (Oakes, J., dissenting).

31. *Jackson,* cited in n. 24, at 353. Courts often rely upon this "public function" test in cases where the government, perhaps in an effort to avoid constitutional strictures, has transferred a function to a private entity, and in cases concerned with powers (such as the supervision of elections) that are almost always exercised by the government. *Krynicky v. Univ. of Pittsburgh,* cited in n. 21, at 98 n. 4.

32. Many cases confirm that colleges and universities do not satisfy this "public function" test. *See, e.g., Stone v. Dartmouth College,* 682 F. Supp. 106, 108 (D.N.H. 1988) (post-secondary education not public function); *Martin v. Delaware Law School,* 625 F. Supp. 1288, 1301 n. 11 (D. Del 1985), *aff'd without opinion,* 884 F.2d 1384 (3rd Cir. 1989) (operating law school not public function); *Cohen v. Harvard College,* 568 F. Supp. 658, 661 (D. Mass 1983), *aff'd,* 729 F.2d 59 (1st Cir. 1984) (scientific research not public function); *Tynecki v. Tufts Univ. Sch. of Dental Med.,* 875 F. Supp. 26, 32 (D. Mass 1994) (graduate student discipline not public function).

33. *Burton v. Wilmington Parking Auth.,* 365 U.S. 715, 725 (1961).

34. *Martin,* cited in n. 32, at 1301.

35. Cited in n. 33.

36. *See, e.g., Cohen,* cited in n. 32, at 661 ("the symbiotic relationship category is very narrow").

37. 457 U.S. 830 (1982).

38. Ibid., at 843. It is difficult to reconcile the Court's holdings in *Burton* and *Rendell-Baker:* "both cases involved a significant degree of financial integration between the public and private actors; indeed, Massachusetts's funding in *Rendell-Baker* arguably rose to a greater level of governmental involvement than did the Wilmington Parking Authority's lease to and profit-by-association with the Eagle Coffee Shoppe." *Frazier,* cited in n. 22, at 1287. This discrepancy is perhaps best explained by a more activist *Burton* Court seeking to redress a clear social wrong.

39. Cited in n. 25.

40. Cited in n. 21.

41. Pa. Stat. Ann. Tit. 24, §2510-2(7) (Purdon Supp 1983).

42. In a companion case involving the interpretation of an almost-identical statute governing relations between the commonwealth and the University of Pittsburgh, Pitt was also found to be a state actor. *Krynicky,* cited in n. 21.

43. *Imperiale,* cited in n. 25.

44. Ibid, at 197.

45. Ibid, at 198. Pennsylvania's rather Byzantine classification of public, state-related, and state-aided (all as distinguished from private) institutions has engendered considerable litigation on the status of individual colleges and universities. In addition to *Schier, Krynicky,* and *Imperiale, see also Smith v. Duquesne University,* 612 F. Supp. 72 (W.D. Pa. 1985) (Duquesne not a state actor).

46. Cited in n. 32.

47. One also finds reference to other state-action tests: *see, e.g., Adickes v. S.H. Kress & Co.,* 398 U.S. 144, 170 (1970) (a "state compulsion" test that I would argue is incorporated in the "close nexus" test); Kaplin & Lee, cited in introduction, n. 2, at 48 (a "government contacts" test that is really the "symbiotic relationship" test). *But see Lugar,* cited in n. 23, at 938 (various "tests" are really just different ways of characterizing the same fact-based inquiry).

48. 84 N.J. 535, 423 A. 2d 615 (N.J. 1980), *appeal dismissed,* 455 U.S. 100 (1982).

49. For example, the University of Pennsylvania declares that "the freedom to experiment, to present and examine alternative data and theories; the freedom to hear, express, and debate various views; and the freedom to voice criticism of existing practices and values are fundamental rights that must be upheld and practiced by the University." §I.A., "Guidelines on Open Expression," University of Pennsylvania 1999–2000 *PennBook.*

50. Indeed, courts have on at least one occasion explicitly measured the adequacy of disciplinary procedures at a private university against the elements of constitutional due process required at public institutions. *Slaughter v. Brigham Young University,* 514 F.2d 622 (10th Cir. 1975).

51. For a much more thorough and analytical discussion of the field of constitutional law, *see, e.g.,* G. Stone, L. Seidman, C. Sunstein & M. Tushnet, *Constitutional Law* (Little, Brown: 1996); and L. Tribe, *American Constitutional Law* (Foundation Press: 1999).

52. U.S. Const. Amend. I.

53. 385 U.S. 589, 603 (1967).

54. Ibid., quoting *United States v. Associated Press,* 52 F. Supp. 362, 372 (S.D.N.Y. 1943).

55. Stone et al., cited in n. 51, at 1086–87.

56. 336 U.S. 77 (1949).

57. 408 U.S. 104 (1972).

58. 468 U.S. 288 (1983).

59. *R.A.V. v. City of St. Paul*, 505 U.S. 377, 382 (1992).

60. *See, e.g., Brandenburg v. Ohio*, 395 U.S. 444 (1969) (mere advocacy of criminal acts to achieve political ends—stopping short of incitement to imminent lawless action—was protected by the First Amendment). Readers should beware that sometimes it is far from obvious whether a particular rule is content-neutral or content-based (for example, if an ordinance is content-neutral on its face but was clearly enacted to suppress a particular message, it may have to be struck down). *See* Stone et al., cited in n. 51, at 1331–34.

61. 424 U.S. 828, 839 (1976). *See also Lehman v. City of Shaker Heights*, 418 U.S. 298 (1974) (plurality opinion upholding local policy banning political ads, but not commercial advertising, in rapid-transit cars). For a more thorough discussion of subject matter–based and viewpoint-based restrictions, see G. Stone, *Restrictions of Speech because of Its Content: The Peculiar Case of Subject-Matter Restrictions*, 46 U. Chi. L. Rev. 81 (1978).

62. *Rosenberger v. Rector and Visitors of University of Virginia*, 515 U.S. 819 (1995).

63. Ibid., at 831.

64. 500 U.S. 173 (1991).

65. *Rosenberger*, cited in n. 62, at 833.

66. Contract law is especially significant in the private college or university setting. Since these institutions are not bound to follow constitutional rules regarding individual rights and due process of law, contractual commitments ensure that these parties deal with their various constituencies in an orderly, consistent, and basically fair manner.

67. Contractual relationships may also exist between students and individual faculty; for example, when the student is hired as a research assistant. One could even argue that contractual obligations exist between a professor and each of the students enrolled in his or her class (the professor assuming a duty to offer the course described in the catalog and syllabus, to treat students courteously, and to evaluate them fairly; the student perhaps assuming a duty to put forth an honest effort)—but since the professor would actually be carrying out his or her duties as an employee, the student's real claim here in the event of breach would be with the institutional employer.

68. *Krotkoff v. Goucher College*, 585 F.2d 675 (4th Cir. 1978) (national academic community's conception of tenure). Judicial reliance upon common academic practice may present a danger for institutions that buck national trends (e.g., not following tenure review or revocation standards recommended by the American Association of University Professors).

69. 377 F. Supp. 227 (W.D. Wis. 1974), *aff'd without opinion*, 510 F.2d 975 (7th Cir. 1975). *See* pp. 228–30, 246.

70. 489 N.E. 2d 616 (Ind. Ct. App. 1986). *See* pp. 81, 209.

71. *Faro v. New York Univ.*, 502 F.2d 1229, 1231–32 (2nd Cir. 1974).

72. *See* pp. 64–69 for further discussion of academic freedom being equated with legal deference.

73. *Ross v. Consumers Power Company*, 420 Mich. 567, 597, 363 N.W. 2d 641, 650 (1985), discusses the original justifications for this rule. One such explanation was that "the sovereign (the king) was somehow 'divine' or above the law. As such, the king could commit no wrong and was, therefore, never properly sued. The second explanation was that the king was superior to the courts which he had created and vested with a portion of his power. As such, while the sovereign could do wrong, there was no entity with power to enter judgment against [him]. Only by the sovereign's consent (essentially, a self-inflicted judgment) could a party recover for an injury caused by the sovereign." In modern times, sovereign immunity is often justified as a means of protecting the public purse. *Messina v. Burden*, 228 Va. 301, 307, 321 S.E. 2d 657, 660 (1984).

74. Unless, of course, the government has waived immunity by authorizing such litigation.

75. Annot., "Modern Status of Sovereign Immunity as Applied to Public Schools and Institutions of Higher Learning," 33 A.L.R. 3rd 703 (§5a).

76. 467 N.W. 2d 431 (N.D. 1991). (However, in 1994 the Supreme Court of North Dakota abolished the state's sovereign immunity from tort liability. *Bulman v. Hulstrand Constr. Co., Inc.*, 521 N.W. 2d 632 [N.D. 1994].) For other recently successful university assertions of sovereign immunity, *see,* inter alia, *Greenhill v. Carpenter,* 718 S.W. 2d 268 (Tenn. Ct. App. 1986) (tort and contract claims against Memphis State University and individual university officials barred); and *Raymond v. Goetz,* 262 Ill. App. 3d 597, 635 N.E. 2d 114 (1994), *appeal denied,* 157 Ill. 2d 521 (1994) (Board of Trustees of the University of Illinois is an arm of the state for sovereign immunity purposes and can only be sued in the state's Court of Claims).

77. U.S. Const. Amend. XI ("The judicial power of the United States shall not be construed to extend to any suit in law or equity, commenced or prosecuted against one of the United States by citizens of another state"). This provision has also been interpreted to bar federal suits brought against a nonconsenting state by one of its *own* citizens. *Kimel v. Fla. Bd. of Regents,* 528 U.S. 62 (2000). A large number of cases hold that state universities and colleges are equivalent to the state government for purposes of Eleventh Amendment immunity. *See, e.g., Hall v. Medical College of Ohio at Toledo,* 742 F.2d 299 (6th Cir. 1984), *cert. denied,* 469 U.S. 1113 (1985), and cites therein at 300–301.

78. Recent Eleventh Amendment immunity cases include *Seminole Tribe of Fla. v. Florida,* 517 U.S. 44 (1996) (blocking suits about Indian gaming activities); *Regents of the Univ. of California v. Doe,* 519 U.S. 425 (1997) (blocking a breach-of-contract suit); *Florida Prepaid Postsecondary Ed. Expense Bd. v.*

*College Savings Bank,* 527 U.S. 627 (1999) (blocking patent infringement suits); *Alden v. Maine,* 527 U.S. 706 (1999) (blocking suits under the Fair Labor Standards Act, 29 U.S.C. §201 et seq.); and *Kimel,* cited in n. 77 (blocking suits under the Age Discrimination in Employment Act, 29 U.S.C. §621 et seq.).

79. For a fuller discussion of the ADEA, *see* pp. 169–71.

80. *Bd. of Trustees of Univ. of Ala. v. Garrett,* 531 U.S. 356 (2001) (suits under Title I of Americans with Disabilities Act barred by Eleventh Amendment.

81. Private institutions occasionally invoke an analogous doctrine of "charitable immunity" in tort actions. This theory is based on the idea that "an agency or institution devoted to the public good should not be subjected to liability for injuries suffered by individuals, or, stated otherwise, that an injured individual rather than the charitable institution should bear the burden of the injury." Annot., "Immunity of Private Schools and Institutions of Higher Learning from Liability in Tort," 38 A.L.R. 3d 480 (§2a). The viability of the doctrine of charitable immunity is very much in question these days, as courts treat nonprofit corporations more like their for-profit counterparts and seek to spread the risk of injury across the wider group represented by the charity. Ibid.

82. *Lister v. Board of Regents of the Univ. of Wisconsin Sys.,* 72 Wis. 2d 282, 299, 240 N.W. 2d 610, 621 (1976) (registrar can claim official immunity in making state residency determinations). *See also Messina,* cited in n. 73, at 308, 660–61 (immunity extends to superintendent of buildings at Tidewater Community College). Courts and commentators refer variously to "sovereign," "governmental," "constitutional," "official," and "state employee" immunity. I would argue that much of the confusion here results from a failure to distinguish between the immunity of the state qua state (which has some theoretical grounding) and the more practically oriented immunity required by state officials. One jurist asserts that these different concepts become blurred from "undue reliance upon the truism that government can act only through the acts of its employees." *Messina,* cited in n. 73, at 314, 664 (Poff, J., concurring).

83. *Board of Trustees v. City of Los Angeles,* 49 Cal. App. 3d 45, 122 Cal. Rptr. 361 (Cal. Ct. App. 1975) (sovereign immunity extends to governmental functions of a state university, not to leasing a campus facility to a circus).

84. *See, e.g., Courtney v. University of Texas Sys.,* 806 S.W. 2d 277 (Tex. Ct. App. 1991).

85. *Lister,* cited in n. 82, at 300–301, 621–22.

86. *Harlow v. Fitzgerald,* 457 U.S. 800, 818 (1982) (analyzing public officials' qualified immunity from suit under 42 U.S.C. §1983).

87. *See, e.g., Board of Trustees of Howard Community College v. John K. Ruff, Inc.,* 278 Md. 580, 588, 366 A.2d 360, 365 (Ct. App. Md. 1976) (legislation giving a community college the power to sue and be sued constitutes a waiver of sovereign immunity).

## 2    Scholarship

1. *But see* discussion of compelled disclosure of faculty research findings, pp. 48–55.

2. As I shall argue throughout this chapter, claims of "academic freedom" in any context and from any quarter are more likely to receive legal protection to the extent that they find support across the entire college or university community: faculty, students, administrators, and trustees.

3. *See, e.g.,* 1999–2003 Agreement between the State of New York and United University Professions, §9.1 (copy on file with author): "It is the policy of the University to maintain and encourage full freedom, within the law, of inquiry, teaching and research."

4. A formal policy statement endorsed by the American Association of University Professors (AAUP) and many other academic organizations declares that "the teacher is entitled to full freedom in research and in the publication of the results." AAUP, "1940 Statement of Principles on Academic Freedom and Tenure (with 1970 Interpretive Comments)," in *Policy Documents & Reports* (AAUP: 1995), at 3 ("1940 Statement").

5. "Judge Dismisses Lawsuit over Tobacco Research," *Chronicle of Higher Education,* December 12, 1997, A8.

6. R. Wilson, "Colo. Regents Reject Promotion of Erotic-Literature Scholar," *Chronicle of Higher Education,* September 28, 1994, A24.

7. Ibid.

8. "Professor of Erotic Literature Is Promoted after All," *Chronicle of Higher Education,* November 2, 1994, A19. Of course, as a simple matter of legal authority, the regents can approve or disapprove of any promotion. But overriding the faculty's academic judgment in this way is highly provocative and potentially damaging to the institution.

9. P. Healy, "Idaho Board Settles Lawsuit by Professor Who Lost Grant to Study Gay Communities," *Chronicle of Higher Education On-Line,* April 20, 1998. This article also notes that the Idaho legislature, upset over the controversy and lawsuit, had voted to discontinue the entire grant program, making this a rather Pyrrhic victory for the cause of academic freedom.

10. *See, e.g., S.E.T.A. UNC-CH, Inc. v. Huffines,* 101 N.C. App. 292, 399 S.E. 2d 340 (1991) (student activists seek access to data about faculty experiments on animals). *See* more generally, A. Schneider, "The Academic Path to Pariah Status," *Chronicle of Higher Education,* July 2, 1999, A12 (researchers advocating discredited [they say unpopular] ideas are shunned: grant applications are rejected, their work is panned, graduate students are discouraged from working with them, and they are marginalized in everything from speaking invitations to committee assignments). There is, of course, a huge gulf between lawful condemnation of a colleague's scholarship and the illegal theft of research animals,

the destruction of labs or data, and threatening or even physically harming researchers. *See* W. Weissert, "Animal-Rights Activists Are Charged in Siege on Home of Primate Researcher," *Chronicle of Higher Education On-Line,* August 25, 1999; and A. Schneider, "Animal-Rights Group Sends Booby-Trapped Letters to Dozens of Researchers," *Chronicle of Higher Education,* November 5, 1999, A20.

11. K. Magnan, "A & M's 'Alchemy Caper,'" *Chronicle of Higher Education,* January 19, 1994, A19.

12. J. Thomson, "Ideology and Faculty Selection," in W. Van Alstyne, ed., *Freedom and Tenure in the Academy* (Duke University Press: 1993). Thomson would distinguish the wrongheaded mathematician (whom she would regard as "*intellectually* less than fully competent") from a historian who claimed that the Holocaust did not occur. The latter position, she argues, is not self-contradictory and, at least in theory, might be supported by evidence. Ibid., at 170–71. I would question this distinction. The Holocaust denier's position flies just as much in the face of all accumulated knowledge. Perhaps all such knowledge is indeed flawed, but then so too might be the basic principles of arithmetic.

13. *See* pp. 208–15.

14. Institutional, school, or departmental reluctance or refusal to commit discretionary funds to support a scholar's projects—even if necessitated entirely by financial constraints or the demands of other priorities—can operate as another form of pressure on faculty selection of research topics. *See* R. Dworkin, "We Need a New Interpretation of Academic Freedom," in L. Menand, ed., *The Future of Academic Freedom* (University of Chicago: 1996), 186. Dworkin recognizes that distinctions are frequently made in hiring faculty, but he argues that our desire to "advance truth and useful discussion by not wasting scarce academic resources on plainly false opinions or trivial projects" should also logically lead us to restrict the selection of research topics by existing faculty. According to Dworkin, the fact that such restrictions are deemed violative of academic freedom means that academic freedom ultimately rests on deeper ethical grounds than a simple search for truth.

15. Thomson, cited in n. 12, at 163.

16. D. Rabban, *Does Academic Freedom Limit Faculty Autonomy?* 66 Texas L. Rev. 1405, 1411 (1988).

17. Thomson, cited in n. 12, at 163. *But see* J. P. Byrne, *Academic Freedom: A "Special Concern of the First Amendment,"* 99 Yale L.J. 251, 284 (1989), noting that scholars who challenge accepted wisdom are likely to be held to higher standards of competence.

18. *See* Byrne, supra, at 285, for the proposition that the doctrine of academic freedom was not intended to provide rules to settle arguments over disciplinary paradigms.

19. Pp. 139–40.

20. 518 F. Supp. 1196 (D. Md. 1981), *aff'd,* 704 F.2d 139 (4th Cir. 1983).

21. The legal intricacies of federal research grant and contract requirements are largely beyond the scope of this book.

22. 60 F. Supp. 2d 31 (E.D.N.Y. 1999).

23. 612 F.2d 285, 288 (7th Cir. 1979).

24. *See, e.g.,* 50 App. U.S.C. §1 et seq. (Trading with the Enemy Act), prohibiting contracts (which would include research funding agreements) with enemies of the state. Agreements *requiring* illegal activity by a faculty member or institution would of course be improper, too. Typically faculty will also have to disclose any conflicts of interest created by their sources of research funding (see pp. 55–60).

25. D. Wheeler, "Biologist with Contrarian View of AIDS Raises Private Funds to Support His Lab," *Chronicle of Higher Education On-Line,* March 5, 1999.

26. *See, e.g., University of Pennsylvania Handbook for Faculty & Academic Administrators (Penn Handbook),* §III.A, "Guidelines for the Conduct of Sponsored Research," §4 (the university "neither seeks nor accepts security clearance for itself or any administrative unit"); and *Penn Handbook,* §V.D, "Relationships between Members of the University Community and Intelligence Organizations." This policy does not prevent faculty from obtaining individual clearance.

27. Of course, institutional policies that contravene lawful statutes and ordinances are unenforceable.

28. *See* D. Bok, *Beyond the Ivory Tower* (Harvard University Press: 1982), 266–79. *See also* R. Eisenberg, *Academic Freedom and Academic Values in Sponsored Research,* 66 Texas L. Rev. 1363 (1988), 1378–84, 1390–91.

29. Faculty who engage in such research, though, will likely encounter ridicule from colleagues and considerable peer pressure to abandon such experiments.

30. Some of the merits and risks of sponsored research agreements are discussed at pp. 55–57, 61–62.

31. 17 U.S.C. §102(b).

32. 447 U.S. 303 (1980) (permitting the award of a patent to a manmade, genetically engineered bacterium).

33. Ibid., at 309, quoting *Funk Brothers Seed Co. v. Kalo Inoculant Co.,* 333 U.S. 127, 130 (1948). *See also* R. Gorman, "Copyright and the Professoriate: A Primer and Some Recent Developments," 73 *Academe* 29 (September–October 1987), at 30 ("scholars . . . cannot use copyright law to claim exclusive use of the ideas, theories, concepts or principles they formulate, and cannot bar others from using the discoveries or facts they unearth").

34. U.S. Const. Art. I, Sec. 8, clause 8 (the Congress shall have the power to "promote the Progress of Science and useful Arts, by securing for limited Times to Authors and Inventors the exclusive Right to their respective Writings and Discoveries").

35. *See, e.g.,* S. Kulkarni, *All Professors Create Equally: Why Faculty Should Have Complete Control over the Intellectual Property Rights in Their Creations,* 47 Hastings L.J. 221 (1995).

36. Trademark constitutes a third and final category of intellectual property. Trademark law establishes and protects property rights in symbols or names that are used to identify particular products, companies, or institutions, including educational institutions. Trademark issues most frequently arise in a college or university setting in connection with the use of institutional logos (for example, on sportswear or novelty items marketed to the public). *See, e.g., University of Pittsburgh v. Champion Products, Inc.,* 566 F. Supp. 711 (W.D. Pa 1983). Federal trademark law is codified at 15 U.S.C. §1051 et seq.

37. 17 U.S.C. §102(a).

38. Ibid.

39. 17 U.S.C. §101 (definition of a "fixed" work).

40. 35 U.S.C. §101. This description applies to *utility* patents (the vast majority of all patents), which cover functional or mechanical innovations. There are also *design* patents (which cover original and ornamental designs for articles, as opposed to their functionality) (*see* 35 U.S.C. §171) and *plant* patents (which cover newly developed varieties of plant not found in nature) (*see* 35 U.S.C. §161).

41. Manmade life forms that do not occur in nature are patentable. *See Diamond v. Chakrabarty,* cited in n. 32 (oil-eating bacteria); *Ex Parte Allen,* 2 U.S.P.Q. 2d (BNA) 1425 (1987) (upholding in principle the patentability of genetically altered oysters); K. Schneider, "Harvard Gets Mouse Patent, a World First," *New York Times,* April 13, 1988, A1:5 (award of first-ever animal patent, for a transgenic mouse).

42. This is reflected in the relatively greater cost and complexity of obtaining a patent.

43. P. Chew, *Faculty-Generated Inventions: Who Owns the Golden Egg,* 1992 Wis. L. Rev. 259, 276 n. 65 ("courts are divided on whether and when software is patentable, copyrightable, or both").

44. *See, e.g., Parker v. Flook,* 437 U.S. 584 (1978).

45. *Manual of Patent Examining Procedure,* §2106 (2000) (establishing procedures for reviewing patent applications on computer-related inventions).

46. 35 U.S.C. §281. In all of the following discussion, I deal exclusively with federal copyright and patent law, which preempt state law. 17 U.S.C. §301 and *Del Madera Properties v. Rhodes and Gardner, Inc.,* 820 F.2d 973 (9th Cir. 1987) (federal copyright law dominant); *Bonito Boats, Inc. v. Thunder Craft Boats, Inc.,* 489 U.S. 141 (1989) (federal patent law preempts inconsistent state statutes and regulations).

47. 17 U.S.C. §201 (a). In the case of a joint work by more than one author, all authors are deemed co-owners of the copyright. Ibid.

48. Typically, the life of the author plus seventy years. 17 U.S.C. §302(a).

49. 17 U.S.C. §106.

50. 17 U.S.C. §101 (definition of "work made for hire"); 17 U.S.C. §201(b).

51. Chew, cited in n. 43, at 275 n. 64.

52. *See Williams v. Weisser,* 273 Cal. App. 2d 726, 78 Cal. Rptr. 542 (Cal. Ct. App. 1969). The *Williams* plaintiff, a faculty member at UCLA, successfully enjoined a local firm from transcribing and publishing versions of his in-class lectures. Interpreting California copyright law, the state court rejected the publisher's argument that UCLA owned the professor's lecture notes as works made for hire. It is worth noting that the university, while not a party to this litigation, endorsed the faculty member's claim of ownership.

53. *See* T. Simon, *Faculty Writings: Are They "Works Made for Hire" under the 1976 Copyright Act,* 9 J. C. & U.L. 485 (1982–83) (institutions now have much stronger claim to ownership); L. DuBoff, *An Academic's Copyright: Publish and Perish,* 32 J. Copyright Soc'y 17 (1985) (work for hire could include scholarship). *But see* L. Lape, *Ownership of Copyrightable Works of University Professors: The Interplay between the Copyright Act and University Copyright Policies,* 37 Vill. L. Rev. 223 (1992) (1976 act does not abolish professor's exception; faculty should and do hold copyright in their scholarship); M. Nimmer & D. Nimmer, *Nimmer on Copyright,* vol. 1, §5.03[B][1][b][i], at 5-33 to 5-34 (1996) ("if a professor elects to reduce his lectures to writing, the professor, and not the institution employing him, owns the copyright"); and R. Dreyfuss, *The Creative Employee and the Copyright Act of 1976,* 54 U. Chi. L. Rev. 590, 642 (1987) (if institutions claim ownership of faculty scholarship under the work-made-for-hire doctrine, severe damage will occur to the "social fabric" of the university).

54. Simon, cited in n. 53, at 502–4. ("Few schools will consider publications totally outside a professor's field in tenure reviews"). Ibid., at 502–3. *See also* Gorman, cited in n. 33, at 31.

55. Simon, supra, at 504.

56. Pp. 25–30. *See also* Gorman, cited in n. 33, at 31; Chew, cited in n. 43, at 302 ("Faculty expectations are that their research topics and objectives may be predicated on their personal and professional interests, not dictated by university administration").

57. R. Gorman & J. Ginsburg, *Copyright for the Nineties,* 269 (Michie Company: 4th ed. 1993).

58. Gorman, cited in n. 33, at 31; Chew, cited in n. 43, at 278.

59. However, some written materials prepared by faculty in their professional capacity are and clearly should be deemed institutional property, such as committee reports on academic and nonacademic matters.

60. Gorman, cited in n. 33, at 31, noting that this probably reflects the meager royalties flowing from most academic work.

61. 811 F.2d 1091, 1094 (7th Cir. 1987) ("The statute is general enough to make every academic article a 'work for hire'"); *Hays v. Sony Corp. of Am.*, 847 F.2d 412, 416 (7th Cir. 1988) ("it is widely believed that the 1976 Act abolished the teacher exception").

62. Significantly, though, the university did not claim that *it* was the owner. *Weinstein*, cited in n. 61, at 1094 ("The University concedes that a professor of mathematics who proves a new theorem in the course of his employment will own the copyright to his article containing that proof").

63. *Hays,* cited in n. 61, at 416 (emphasis added).

64. I am aware of no comprehensive data on the incidence of such policies. Lape, cited in n. 53, at 251–53, asserts that as of the early 1990s most institutions did not have formal copyright policies. However, of the 70 major research universities she surveyed (a category of institutions rather likely to have adopted such rules), 59 had extant or draft policies. One can assume that copyright policies are becoming more common.

65. 17 U.S.C. §201(d).

66. Simon, cited in n. 53, at 506; Lape, cited in n. 53, at 246–50 (each stressing the necessity of an agreement signed by both parties to effectuate a transfer. Thus, an appointment letter referring to policies in a faculty handbook should at the very least be countersigned by the appointee in order to make such policies legally binding).

67. *See* Lape, cited in n. 53, at 256–64, for a survey of a large group of policies.

68. Ibid., at 257–58. *See also* University of Chicago Policy, "New Information Technologies and Intellectual Property at the University" (April 27, 1999) ("Chicago Intellectual Property Policy") (copy on file with author) ("the University owns the intellectual property the faculty create at the University or with substantial aid of its facilities or its financial support").

69. *Stanford University Research Policy Handbook*, Document 5.2, "Copyright Policy," §1.B, September 1, 1994 ("In accord with academic tradition . . . Stanford does not claim ownership to pedagogical, scholarly, or artistic works, regardless of their form of expression"). *See also* Lape, cited in n. 53, at 262, citing inter alia at n. 163 a University of Rochester policy "not [to] claim for itself copyrights in those books, articles, theses, papers, novels . . . and similar works which are intended to disseminate the results of the academic research, scholarship, and artistic expression of its faculty."

70. Lape, cited in n. 53, at 256.

71. S. Carr, "A For-Profit Subsidiary Will Market Cornell's Distance Programs," *Chronicle of Higher Education On-Line*, March 14, 2000; S. Carr, "Faculty Members Are Wary of Distance-Education Ventures," *Chronicle of Higher Education,* June 9, 2000, A41.

72. K. Arenson, "N.Y.U. Sees Profits in Virtual Classes," *New York Times,* October 7, 1998, B8.

73. K. Arenson, "Columbia to Put Learning Online for Profit," *New York Times,* April 3, 2000, B3. The university's partners include the New York Public Library, the British Library, the Smithsonian's Museum of Natural History, the London School of Economics and Political Science, and Cambridge University Press.

74. G. Blumenstyk, "A Company Pays Top Universities to Use Their Names and Their Professors," *Chronicle of Higher Education,* June 18, 1999, A39; S. Carr, "Closely Watched UNext Rolls Out Its First Courses," *Chronicle of Higher Education,* May 12, 2000, A50. The universities will retain ownership of the intellectual property developed pursuant to their agreements with UNext .com.

75. D. Carnevale & J. Young, "Who Owns On-Line Courses? Colleges and Professors Start to Sort It Out," *Chronicle of Higher Education,* December 17, 1999, A45.

76. Pp. 182–83.

77. J. Young, "A Debate over Ownership of On-Line Courses Surfaces at Drexel U.," *Chronicle of Higher Education,* April 9, 1999, A31; Carnevale & Young, cited in n. 75.

78. A. Marcus, "Seeing Crimson," *Wall Street Journal,* November 22, 1999, A1:6.

79. *See* pp. 58, 214.

80. J. Young, "Harvard Considers Limits on Teaching Online Courses for Other Institutions," *Chronicle of Higher Education On-Line,* April 25, 2000.

81. "Chicago Intellectual Property Policy," cited in n. 68. This parallels Chicago's treatment of royalties from printed or electronic texts, which also flow to faculty.

82. Ibid. According to Chicago's new policy, because of the pace of technological change, "the most important obligation of faculty who exploit [information] technologies is early disclosure of what they are doing to their chairs or deans. The disclosure should be less formal than that involved for discoveries and inventions, but it should also come much sooner."

83. D. Carnevale, "Duke U. Moves to Set Policies on Online Courses," *Chronicle of Higher Education,* June 9, 2000, A47.

84. 35 U.S.C. §101.

85. However, while patent law has no analogue to the work-made-for-hire doctrine, as discussed in the rest of this section, employers will frequently insist that employees sign over any patent rights arising in connection with their work.

86. *United States v. Dubilier Condenser Corp.,* 289 U.S. 178, 187, *amended,* 289 U.S. 706 (1933) (the employee retains the patent "if the employment be

general, albeit it cover a field of labor and effort in the performance of which the employee conceived the invention").

87. Chew, cited in n. 43, at 266–71 (sardonically observing at 266 n. 24 that "if faculty are 'hired to invent,' the university employer is certainly benevolent and patient since the vast majority of research does not yield any inventions"); P. Lachs, *University Patent Policy*, 10 J.C. & U.L. 263, 281 (1983–84); Kulkarni, cited in n. 35, at 232–33. *But see Speck v. North Carolina Dairy Foundation*, 311 N.C. 679, 319 S.E.2d 139 (1984), concerning ownership rights in a secret (apparently unpatentable) process, discovered by a North Carolina State University faculty member, for producing "Sweet Acidophilus" milk. The state supreme court held that the university owned this process because it had "permitted and encouraged . . . the precise research which led to the discovery and perfection of the secret process." Ibid., at 686, 144. The *Speck* plaintiffs were typical faculty: the university paid their salaries and provided research facilities but did not direct them to focus on milk production. This holding has been sharply criticized as contrary to established doctrine, including *Dubilier.* Chew, cited in n. 43, at 298–304; Note, *The Souring of Sweet Acidophilus Milk: Speck v. North Carolina Dairy Foundation and the Rights of University Faculty to Their Inventive Ideas*, 63 N.C.L. Rev. 1248 (1985).

88. 409 F. Supp. 190 (N.D. Ill. 1976), *rev'd on other grounds sub nom. Kaplan v. Corcoran*, 545 F.2d 1073 (7th Cir. 1976).

89. Ibid., at 200. Not only was the physician in *Kaplan* not hired just to invent, but he was certainly not hired to invent this particular camera system.

90. Chew, cited in n. 43, at 270, suggests that since shop rights will usually be of little value to nonprofit colleges and universities, it might be more equitable for faculty patent holders to reimburse institutions for the value of the resources used in developing the invention.

91. This latter course avoids disputes about faculty notice of the policy's content and demonstrates mutual acceptance of the terms.

92. G. Blumenstyk, "A 40% Increase in Income from Inventions," *Chronicle of Higher Education*, November 9, 1994, A37 (117 research universities received $242 million in royalties in fiscal 1993); K. Grassmuck, "Gatorade Brings U. of Florida $17 Million—and 5 Court Actions," *Chronicle of Higher Education*, June 12, 1991, A25 (university did not originally pursue a patent on the drink, but acquired royalties as a result of litigation with faculty inventors and their licensees). Never mind that most patented inventions do not even recover the costs of obtaining the patent. Chew, cited in n. 43, at 272 n. 24 ("Of 2,751 discoveries disclosed by University of Wisconsin faculty, only 73 have produced incomes greater than expenses"); Note, *Reform for Rights of Employed Inventors*, 57 S. Cal. L. Rev. 603, 604 (1984) (citing estimates that only 1 in 100 inventions conceived by corporate employees will be economically viable).

93. The Patent and Trademark Law Amendment Act of 1980, 35 U.S.C.

§§200–211 (the Bayh-Dole Act). As some commentators have pointed out, though, the Bayh-Dole Act permits but does not *require* institutional ownership. Chew, cited in n. 43, at 293–96.

94. Patent policies antedate copyright policies at many institutions. Lape, cited in n. 53, at 251.

95. As with copyright, comprehensive comparative data on institutional patent policies is not readily available. See n. 64. Chew, cited in n. 43, compiles data from one set of prominent research universities.

96. Chew labels these the resource-provider, maximalist, and supramaximalist approaches, respectively. Ibid., at 276–81.

97. Ibid., at 286–93, in part criticizing faculty members' naive acquiescence to patent policies.

98. Ibid., at 305–9. Of course, the same might be said for faculty ownership of patents.

99. Ibid., at 309–10.

100. Ibid., at 284–85, suggesting that more attractive patent policies may help institutions recruit faculty.

101. Ibid., at 310. *See also* Dreyfuss, cited in n. 53.

102. *Stanford University Research Policy Handbook,* Document 5.1, "Inventions, Patents and Licensing," §§ 1.A.1 and 3(1), February 1, 1996. The remaining two-thirds of net revenues are split between the inventor's department and school (all this after the university has taken 15% of gross revenues for overhead and deducted direct expenses such as filing fees).

103. Lape, cited in n. 53, at 265–66.

104. Pp. 36–43. This would include copyright to articles or monographs describing patentable inventions.

105. *But see* L. Guernsey, "A Provost Challenges His Faculty to Retain Copyright on Articles," *Chronicle of Higher Education,* September 18, 1998, A29, discussing a proposal that Caltech faculty and their employer institute jointly retain copyright of faculty scholarship and then license such works to journal publishers in order to counter the publishers' current market dominance.

106. 17 U.S.C. §107. This common law doctrine was codified for the first time in the 1976 Copyright Act.

107. Ibid.

108. *See* pp. 95–101.

109. 60 F.3d 913 (2nd Cir. 1994), *further amended,* July 17, 1995.

110. Ibid., at 916. The court understood that while faculty were not motivated to write articles by the prospect of royalties, a royalty stream was necessary to induce publishers to produce journals that were the vehicle for disseminating scholars' work. Ibid., at 927.

111. B. Mishkin, "Urgently Needed: Policies on Access to Data by Erstwhile Collaborators," *Science* 270: 927, 928, November 10, 1995.

112. *But see* R. Poch, *Academic Freedom in American Higher Education: Rights, Responsibilities, and Limitations,* ASHE-ERIC Higher Education Report No. 4 (George Washington University, School of Education and Human Development: 1993), 69–72 (arguing that, in addition to these factors, courts will also focus on the probative value of the research in question, the burden of compliance, the subject matter of the research, and whether confidentiality has been promised to research subjects).

113. 672 F.2d 1262 (7th Cir. 1982).

114. The scholars would also have had to update Dow on "additional useful data" they obtained. Ibid., at 1276.

115. Ibid., at 1273.

116. Ibid., at 1276. Indeed, the court expressed fear that "a large private corporation, through repeatedly securing broad-based subpoenas . . . relating to on-going studies, could make research in a particular field so undesirable as to chill or inhibit whole areas of scientific inquiry." Ibid., at 1276 n. 25.

117. Ibid., at 1274. *See also Richards of Rockford, Inc. v. Pacific Gas & Electric Co.,* 71 F.R.D. 388 (N.D. Cal. 1976), blocking a civil plaintiff's attempt to compel a faculty research assistant to testify about confidential interviews with PG&E employees about the company's decision making on environmental issues. ("Compelled disclosure of confidential information would without question severely stifle research into questions of public policy." Ibid., at 388.) The information sought by the plaintiff was largely supplemental (in other words, this was a "fishing expedition"). Indeed, the sole article published by the faculty member as a result of the research in question made no mention of the issues being litigated.

118. S. Greenhouse, "Cornell Professor Fights a Slander Suit," *New York Times,* April 1, 1998, A14:4; J. Basinger, "Judge Dismisses Suit against Scholar Accused of Libeling Nursing-Home Chain," *Chronicle of Higher Education On-Line,* May 28, 1998.

119. *In re: Cusumano,* 162 F.3d 708, 714 (1st Cir. 1998).

120. Ibid., at 714.

121. Ibid., at 717. However, the protection afforded scholars in the Microsoft case is difficult to square with the Supreme Court's holding in *Branzburg v. Hayes,* 408 U.S. 665 (1972), where newsmen, like all other citizens, were required to testify before grand juries about criminal conduct, even if this breached the confidentiality of their sources. (For another example of the Supreme Court's refusing to extend special protection to news gathering, *see Herbert v. Lando,* 441 U.S. 153 [1979] [libel plaintiffs may inquire into the state of mind of reporters and publishers].) Perhaps the *Cusumano* court would have distinguished *Branzburg* on the grounds that that precedent concerned criminal investigations in which the need for accurate and complete evidence from all sources is especially compelling. Even more likely, in stating that academic investigators

merited protection equivalent to that of reporters, the First Circuit may have been seeking to replicate the effect of the "shield laws" enacted in many states after *Branzburg* that create *statutory* privileges for newsmen (*see, e.g.,* Mich. Comp. Laws §767.5a [2000]; Minn. Stat. §§595.021–.025 [1999]).

122. *Wright v. Jeep Corp.,* 547 F. Supp. 871 (E.D. Mich. 1982).

123. Ibid., at 876.

124. 880 F.2d 1520 (2nd Cir. 1989).

125. Ibid., at 1529.

126. Ibid., at 1530.

127. 740 F.2d 556 (7th Cir. 1984).

128. Ibid., at 560.

129. Ibid., at 565 (emphasis added).

130. It is no coincidence that all of the cases cited here involve companies requesting scholars' data to block or defend product liability suits. According to some press accounts, embattled industries are aggressively seeking access to underlying research materials in order to uncover methodological flaws or expose what they regard as faculty members' ideological biases. *See, e.g.,* S. Burd, "Scientists See Big Business on the Offensive," *Chronicle of Higher Education,* December 14, 1994, A26 (companies using state open-records laws and federal and state rules on research misconduct to obtain information; detailing in particular how the R. J. Reynolds Tobacco Company obtained supporting data for published studies on the impact of its "Joe Camel" character on children).

131. 5 F.3d 397 (9th Cir. 1993), *cert. denied,* 510 U.S. 1041 (1994).

132. Ibid., at 399.

133. P. Monaghan, "Facing Jail, a Sociologist Raises Questions about a Scholar's Right to Protect Sources," *Chronicle of Higher Education,* April 7, 1993, A10.

134. P. Monaghan, "Sociologist Is Jailed," *Chronicle of Higher Education,* May 26, 1993, A10.

135. 750 F.2d 223 (2nd Cir. 1984).

136. *In re Grand Jury Subpoena,* 583 F. Supp. 991 (E.D.N.Y. 1984), *reversed,* 750 F.2d 223.

137. *In re Grand Jury,* supra, at 225.

138. Ibid.

139. Even with postpublication disclosure, such context may still be ignored by unsophisticated or biased audiences, but at least the scholar will have had an opportunity to make a complete case.

140. G. Low, "The Organization of Industrial Relationships in Universities," in T. Langfitt et. al., eds., *Partners in the Research Enterprise: University-Corporate Relations in Science and Technology* (University of Pennsylvania Press: 1983), 77.

141. Conflicts of interest can also arise in other, nonresearch settings; for example, if a faculty member or a member of her family has a financial stake in

a company supplying goods or services to the university or in an entity that directly competes with the university for external funding or business opportunities (e.g., a faculty-owned economic forecasting firm that bids against the university for government contracts). And, of course, even when there are no prospects for extra-university financial gain, nepotism (hiring one's relatives) constitutes a classic conflict of interest.

142. *See* Eisenberg, cited in n. 28, for a fuller exposition of the argument that externally funded research threatens the core values (such as free inquiry, objectivity, dissemination of results) that underlie academic freedom.

143. *See, e.g., Stanford University Research Policy Handbook,* Document 4.1, "Faculty Policy on Conflict of Commitment and Interest," ("Stanford Conflict Policy"), §3, "Free and Open Exchange of Research Results"; *University of Chicago Faculty Handbook* (1996), "Outside Professional and Commercial Interests of Faculty and Conflict of Interest" ("Chicago Conflict Policy"), p. 30, ¶¶A–B.

144. NSF regulations at 60 Fed. Reg. 35820 (July 11, 1995); PHS regulations at 60 Fed. Reg. 35810 (July 11, 1995). *See also* "Chicago Conflict Policy," supra; and University of Chicago "Revised Supplemental Guidelines: Compliance with Federal Policies" (copy on file with author) for an example of how one institution has responded to these heightened agency requirements.

145. In some circumstances, however, the favorable publicity accruing to a college or university through a professor's purely external activities (i.e., activities not even classifiable as service) may still be very desirable to the institution. See pp. 135–36.

146. Of course, conflicts of interest and commitment are not entirely severable. Paid consultancies can divert faculty energies while also establishing financial incentives that may taint research. The use of college or university equipment or facilities for private gain can also raise both kinds of conflict. It is therefore fairly common for institutions to consolidate their various conflicts policies. *See, e.g.,* "Stanford Conflict Policy," cited in n. 143; "Chicago Conflict Policy," cited in n. 143; *Penn Handbook,* cited in n. 26, §II.E.10, "Conflict of Interest Policy for Faculty Members" ("Penn Conflict Policy") (the first section of this policy is entitled "Conflict of Interest in the Allocation of Time and Effort to Extramural Activities").

147. "Professor Accused of Double Dipping Is Fired," *Chronicle of Higher Education,* April 21, 1995, A20 (University of Minnesota discharges a tenured faculty member who, unbeknownst to it, had also accepted a tenured position at UNC-Charlotte and was commuting between the two institutions).

148. 522 F. Supp. 90 (N.D.Ill. 1981).

149. Ibid., at 97.

150. 61 F. Supp. 2d 81 (S.D.N.Y. 1999).

151. 620 F.2d 109, 110 (6th Cir. 1980).

152. "Chicago Conflict Policy," cited in n. 143. Of course, disclosure does not

in itself manage or eliminate the conflict. That task follows upon recognition that a potential problem exists.

153. *See, e.g.,* "Penn Conflict Policy," cited in n. 146, §II (total extramural commitments should not exceed 1 day per 7-day week during the academic year); "Chicago Conflict Policy," cited in n. 143 (no more than 11 days each 10-week quarter of residence without specific authorization); "Stanford Conflict Policy," cited in n. 143 (no more than 13 days during a 13-week academic quarter). (*See also Stanford University Research Policy Handbook,* Document 4.3, "Outside Consulting Activities by Members of the Academic Council.") The NYU policies violated in *Marks,* cited in n. 150, at 90–91, included both a "one day per week" external employment rule and separate prohibitions against teaching at another institution without permission.

154. For example, the "Chicago Conflict Policy," cited in n. 143, declares that "there is a presumption in favor of allowing faculty members to act in dual roles once the conflict of interest has been disclosed."

155. Broad disclosure would seem especially appropriate when a scholar is reviewing a peer's work (for grant support or publication) in an area in which the reviewer has a conflict of interest.

156. *See* "Stanford Conflict Policy," cited in n. 143, §7 (automatic appointment of oversight group for conflicts involving advanced clinical trials); D. Wheeler, "Pressure to Cash In on Research Stirs Conflict-of-Interest Issues," *Chronicle of Higher Education,* April 12, 1989, A29 (group of biomedical researchers set their own conflict policy banning the ownership of stock in companies whose drugs they were testing).

157. J. Nicklin, "University Deals with Drug Companies Raise Concerns over Autonomy, Secrecy," *Chronicle of Higher Education,* March 24, 1993, A25.

158. "Chicago Conflict Policy," cited in n. 143, §XI; "Stanford Conflict Policy," cited in n. 143, §7.

159. Pp. 39–43.

160. The Morrill Federal Land Grant Act of 1862 supported colleges "where the leading object shall be, without excluding other scientific or classical studies, to teach such branches of learning as are related to agriculture and the mechanic arts." Quoted in F. Rudolph, *The American College & University* (University of Georgia Press: 1990), 252.

161. T. Veblen, *The Higher Learning in America* (Transaction Publishers: 1993), 35. This book was originally published in 1919.

# 3    In the Classroom

1. Witness the proliferation of undergraduate college rankings in annual guides and publications such as *U.S. News & World Report,* the significance attached to the National Research Council's 1993 ranking of doctoral programs, and accrediting agencies' insistence that colleges and universities assess student learning

outcomes. *See, e.g.,* Commission on Higher Education of the Middle States Association of Colleges and Schools, *Characteristics of Excellence* (1994) (requiring assessment of student learning).

2. *See Piarowski v. Illinois Community College Dist. 515,* 759 F.2d 625, 629 (7th. Cir. 1985), *cert. denied,* 474 U.S. 1007 (1985) (academic freedom "is used to denote both the freedom of the academy to pursue its end without interference from the government . . . and the freedom of the individual teacher . . . to pursue his ends without interference from the academy; and these two freedoms are in conflict"). *But cf. Urofsky v. Gilmore,* 216 F.3d 401, 410 (4th Cir. 2000), *cert. denied,* 531 U.S. 1070 (2001) ("Our review of the law, however, leads us to conclude that to the extent the Constitution recognizes any right of 'academic freedom' above and beyond the First Amendment rights to which every citizen is entitled, the right inheres in the University, not in individual professors").

3. To some extent, of course, the law does defer to several of these experts in their respective domains. Battlefield orders, and military justice more generally, are not very susceptible to conventional legal challenge. *Parker v. Levy,* 417 U.S. 733 (1974) (upholding court-martial for speech that disrupted unit order and discipline). Prison guards and wardens can mandate and enforce restrictions on inmates' conduct that would not be countenanced in regular society. *Turner v. Safley,* 482 U.S. 78 (1987) (upholding regulations prohibiting correspondence between inmates at different prisons). In both of these settings— like the university setting described in the main text—the presence of a special and spatially or temporally constrained environment (i.e., war, prison) justifies legal nonintrusiveness.

4. This of course raises a profound question whether an institution where faculty inquiry is channeled (or worse, directed) by religious or other authorities can truly be called a "college" or "university." *See* pp. 120–25.

5. A survey of the very rich literature in this area should certainly include: R. Hofstadter & W. Metzger, *The Development of Academic Freedom in the United States* (Columbia University Press: 1955) (a seminal work by affiliated authors); *Developments in the Law—Academic Freedom,* 87 Harv. L. Rev. 1034 (1968) (an early and significant law review treatment of this subject); L. Joughin, ed., *Academic Freedom and Tenure* (University of Wisconsin Press: 1967); T. Emerson, *The System of Freedom of Expression* (Random House: 1970), 593–626; E. Pincoffs, ed., *The Concept of Academic Freedom* (University of Texas Press: 1975); M. Finkin, *On "Institutional" Academic Freedom,* 61 Texas L. Rev. 817 (1983); O'Neil, cited in introduction, n. 3; M. Yudof, *Three Faces of Academic Freedom,* 32 Loyola L. Rev. 831 (1987); symposium papers compiled at 66 Texas L. Rev. 1247–1659 (1988); Byrne, cited in chap. 2, n. 17; W. Van Alstyne, "Academic Freedom and the First Amendment in the Supreme Court of the United States: An Unhurried Historical Review," in Van Alstyne, ed., cited in

chap. 2, n. 12 (this entire volume—also a collection of symposium papers—is worth examining); and L. Menand, ed., cited in chap. 2, n. 14.

6. A sense of the scope and flavor of such debates is highly instructive. For example, some commentators have argued that academic freedom in faculty scholarship and teaching falls solidly within the rights safeguarded by the federal Constitution, and that judicial recognition of this will help protect the fundamental work of the academy. *See* Van Alstyne, "Academic Freedom and the First Amendment," cited in n. 5. But J. Peter Byrne asserts that "academic freedom" (defined as the individual "liberties claimed by professors through professional channels against administrative or political interference with research, teaching and [institutional] governance") should be distinguished from the "constitutional academic freedom" that protects academic *institutions* from governmental interference. Byrne contends that faculty should not place their faith in courts and the Constitution for the enforcement of traditional norms of faculty autonomy. Byrne, cited in chap. 2, n. 17, quote at 254. The central premise of his argument—with which I concur—is that the scholarly purposes served by the concept of academic freedom (such as the right and concomitant obligation of faculty to exercise independent critical judgment in reviewing the work of their peers) are ill served and even denigrated by being squeezed into a Procrustean legal bed. Basic disagreement also exists among scholars about the existence and legitimacy of "institutional" academic freedom. Matthew Finkin argues that academic freedom, properly understood, relates only to the scholarly labors of individual instructors and students. In his view, when universities claim such freedom (as in making faculty personnel decisions), they are simply packaging their desire to avoid legal supervision in a faculty-specific concept. Finkin, cited in n. 5. But Mark Yudof argues that the benefits derived from scholars' and students' autonomy do not provide a sustainable constitutional justification for academic freedom. He notes unavoidable limits on such autonomy (e.g., the need for faculty to teach courses they are hired to teach) and sees as additional (and largely independent) bases for academic freedom the need to limit government control over expression and the importance of autonomous action by private schools. Yudof, cited in n. 5.

7. 665 F.2d 547, 552 (5th Cir. 1982), *cert. denied*, 457 U.S. 1106 (1982). *See also* Byrne, cited in chap. 2, n. 17, at 257 ("The [Supreme]Court has been far more generous in its praise of academic freedom than in providing a precise analysis of its meaning"); and *Cohen v. San Bernardino Valley College*, 883 F. Supp. 1407, 1411 (C. D. Cal. 1995), *reversed in part, affirmed in part*, 92 F.3d 968 (9th Cir. 1996) ("the cases, shorn of panegyrics, are inconclusive, the promise of their rhetoric reproached by the ambiguous realities of academic life").

8. Courts generally view with disfavor purported "constitutional rights" covering only a limited class of citizens. In *Urofsky*, cited in n. 2, the Fourth Circuit rejected the claim that state university professors had a constitutional right to

academic freedom, opining that the very notion that such faculty might have greater freedom of inquiry than a state-employed psychologist was "manifestly at odds with a constitutional system premised on equality." Ibid., at n. 13.

9. Byrne, cited in chap. 2, n. 17.

10. Pp. 25–30.

11. As we shall see throughout this volume, consensus about whether a particular action falls under the protective umbrella of academic freedom may be hard to obtain or may easily disintegrate. Controversies that proceed to litigation will, by definition, involve a lack of such agreement. My objective in posing this overview question is to show that in circumstances in which the academy *does* coalesce (or even largely rally together) in support of a given activity or local administrative decision, this shared sentiment will offer powerful protection against legal interference with such action. Obviously, in the absence of consensus, courts will become more deeply involved in evaluating the quality and fairness of institutional decisions and weighing the merits of the respective claims. But the potential impact of such consensus should in fact encourage constituencies within a college or university to reach agreement whenever possible, thereby enhancing internal control over the institution's (and local actors') own destiny.

12. While one might argue that there are also "losers" (i.e., that unhappiness will also result) when a scholar chooses to research Topic A as opposed to a dean's or trustee's or legislator's preferred Topic B, there is no third-party coercion in the research setting analogous to that which arises when students are required to study something against their (or someone else's) wishes. Nor will trustees or legislators typically have given funds to the university on the express condition that a particular topic be investigated. In contrast, tuition is paid on the assumption or promise that students will receive germane and useful instruction in the courses for which they are registered. The sense of "loss" or "betrayal" is thus likely to be more keen in classroom disputes.

13. 354 U.S. 234 (1957).

14. Ibid., at 244–45.

15. Ibid., at 262 (Frankfurter, J., concurring).

16. Ibid., at 263 (quoting statement of prominent South African scholars). This ringing language from Frankfurter's concurrence has been repeatedly cited and relied upon as evidence of judicial support for academic freedom, although it never obtained the support of a majority of the Court.

17. 13 Cal. 3d 757, 533 P. 2d 222 (1975).

18. Ibid., at 770, 231.

19. *Hammond v. Brown,* 323 F. Supp. 326 (N.D. Ohio 1971), *aff'd,* 450 F.2d 480 (6th Cir. 1971).

20. Ibid., at 349.

21. Ibid., at 350.

22. Giving rise to the court's dictum in *Lamb v. Univ. of Hawaii*, 1998 U.S. App. LEXIS 10775, 4 (9th Cir. 1998), that "neither the Supreme Court nor this Circuit has determined what scope of First Amendment protection is to be given a public college professor's classroom speech."

23. *Wirsing v. Bd. of Regents of the Univ. of Col.*, 739 F. Supp. 551, 553 (D. Col. 1990), *aff'd without opinion*, 945 F.2d 412 (10th Cir. 1991). Rather than endorsing the plaintiff's personal claim of academic freedom, the court characterized teacher evaluation as part of the university's *institutional* academic freedom. Ibid., at 554.

24. *Carley v. Arizona Bd. of Regents*, 153 Ariz. 461, 737 P. 2d 1099 (Ct. App. Ariz. 1987).

25. *Stastny v. Bd. of Trustees of Cent. Washington Univ.*, 32 Wash. App. 239, 647 P. 2d 496 (Ct. App. Wash. 1982), *cert. denied*, 460 U.S. 1071 (1983), at 249–50, 504 (faculty member lawfully discharged following intentional absence from class, having earlier received letters directing him to be present). *See also Smith v. Kent State Univ.*, 696 F.2d 476 (6th Cir. 1983) (professor terminated for repeated failure to teach assigned class); *Jawa v. Fayetteville State Univ.*, 426 F. Supp. 218 (E.D. N.Car. 1976), *aff'd without opinion*, 584 F.2d 976 (4th Cir. 1978) (tenured faculty member dismissed for, inter alia, refusal to teach assigned courses and failure to keep office hours for students); *Riggin*, cited in chap. 1, n. 70 (reasons for professor's discharge included failure to teach classes); and *Carley v. Ariz. Bd. Of Regents*, cited in n. 24 (problems with instructor's teaching methods that justified nonrenewal, including frequently leaving classes unattended). *But see Starsky v. Williams*, 353 F. Supp. 900 (D. Ariz. 1972), *affirmed in part and reversed in part on other grounds*, 512 F.2d 109 (9th Cir. 1975) (faculty member cutting one class viewed as minor incident not warranting termination, especially in light of selective enforcement of class attendance policy). The main text's treatment of lawful institutional demands on faculty is also directly applicable to discussions of faculty terminations "for cause" at pp. 208–26.

26. *See* pp. 217–26.

27. *Martin v. Parrish*, 805 F.2d 583, at 585 (5th Cir. 1986). *But see* J. Pulley, "Federal Judge Orders Reinstatement of Professor Who Was Suspended for Swearing," *Chronicle of Higher Education On-Line*, August 30, 1999.

28. *Martin*, supra, at 584.

29. 970 F.2d 252 (7th Cir. 1992).

30. 818 F.2d 58, 63 (D.C. Cir. 1987).

31. Ibid., at 66.

32. Often in the form of judicial dicta or catchphrases.

33. Pp. 16–19.

34. 888 F. Supp. 293 (D. N. H. 1994).

35. Silva's out-of-class behavior (verbal and physical encounters with students) also ran afoul of the policy.

36. *Silva,* cited in n. 34, at 299.

37. Ibid. Interestingly, the court found that this belly-dancing statement was not of a sexual nature because the word "vibrator" need not connote a sexual device. Ibid., at 312–13. While I agree with the *Silva* result, this holding strikes me as a real stretch.

38. Ibid., at 313.

39. Ibid., at 330, citing affidavit of W. Van Alstyne.

40. 18 F.3d 1005, 1011 (2nd Cir. 1994).

41. 593 F. Supp. 1171 (S.D.N.Y. 1984) (plaintiff professor may conduct in-class discussion of current college controversies, assuming they are related to the curriculum, in a political science course). The court endorsed dicta in prior cases that "freedom to teach in the manner of one's choice is a form of academic freedom that is universally recognized, if not invariably protected, at the college level." Ibid., at 1174, citing *East Hartford Educational Association v. Bd. of Ed.,* 562 F.2d 838, 843, *vacated on rehearing en banc,* 562 F.2d 838 (2nd Cir. 1977). *See also Hillis,* cited in n. 7, at 552–53 (dicta on both content *and method* of teaching being protected by academic freedom).

42. *Cohen,* cited in n. 7.

43. Ibid., at 1409–11, quote at 1411.

44. Ibid., at 1419.

45. Ibid., at 1419–20.

46. As might be expected, the *Cohen* reversal was enthusiastically greeted by higher education law experts. R. O'Neil, "Protecting Free Speech When the Issue Is Sexual Harassment," *Chronicle of Higher Education,* September 13, 1996, B3.

47. 480 F.2d 705 (6th Cir. 1973), *cert. denied,* 414 U.S. 1075 (1973).

48. For example, Ms. Hetrick apparently raised hackles when, in seeking "to illustrate the 'irony' and 'connotative qualities' of the English language, she told her freshmen students 'I am an unwed mother,'" not explaining that she was divorced. The court found, however, that her nonrenewal was not based on incidents such as this but rather on fundamental differences over teaching style. Ibid., at 706.

49. Ibid., at 707.

50. Ibid.

51. Ibid., at 709.

52. *See, e.g., Carley,* cited in n. 24, at 463, 1101. These teaching methods were criticized by students in course evaluations, which were a key element in Carley's nonrenewal.

53. 793 F.2d 419, 425–26 (1st Cir. 1986). The First Amendment was invoked

here because the employer university was a state actor. At private institutions, the terms of faculty employment contracts and local policies, rules, and custom will govern faculty speech.

54. For an extreme—and I think wrongly decided—example of administrative interference with faculty teaching methods, *see Parate v. Isibor,* 868 F.2d 821 (6th Cir. 1989). In this bizarre case, a dean made an unannounced appearance in a faculty member's class, repeatedly interrupted the teacher, ordered him to complete a problem from the text on the blackboard (and then came up to work on that same problem himself), and publicly criticized the teacher in front of his students. Later, the dean removed the professor as course instructor but directed him to attend the class as a *student!* Ibid., at 825. Amazingly, the court (while holding for the professor on other grounds) found no violation of the professor's First Amendment right to academic freedom in teaching method, citing *Hetrick* for support.

55. P. 68.

56. For example, proposed new courses in the University of Pennsylvania's School of Arts and Sciences (SAS) must ordinarily be reviewed by the school's Curriculum Committee and approved by the SAS faculty. SAS policy documents (on file with author). The utility and importance of the course-approval process is a recurrent theme in this section.

57. Cited in chap. 1, n. 70, at 626. Other lawful bases for Riggin's termination for cause included a failure to engage in research or scholarly activities, lack of adequate preparation for class, failure to meet classes, and destructive relations with colleagues. Ibid.

58. Ibid., at 630.

59. 472 F. Supp. 802 (E.D. Ark 1979). Surprisingly, this case has not received a great deal of attention from commentators.

60. Ibid., at 804.

61. Ibid., at 807. The opinion does not contain analogous detail about the structure of the American civilization course.

62. Ibid., at 805.

63. Ibid., at 808. Interestingly, the *Cooper* opinion includes several dicta affirming the university's right to determine curriculum and subject matter. See discussion at pp. 85–91.

64. Ibid., at 812.

65. Namely, a faculty member's right to join political organizations, which is discussed at p. 139–40.

66. Ibid., at 811.

67. Ibid., at 813.

68. Ibid. (emphasis added).

69. Ibid., at 814.

70. *See* pp. 69–71.

71. 220 Cal. App. 3d 1329, 269 Cal. Rptr. 882 (Cal. Ct. App. 1990), *cert. denied,* 498 U.S. 998 (1990). *See also Wirsing,* cited in n. 23, at 554 (faculty may say what they want in class; evaluation forms are unrelated to course content and thus do not impede professor's academic freedom); and *Hillis,* cited in n. 7, at 552 (academic freedom protects against infringements on classroom *content* and method). All of these cases, however, arose at public institutions, where First Amendment protections applied.

72. *DiBona,* supra, at 1341–42, 889, noting that the district had no policy requiring or even allowing for the review of materials before use in class. The clear import, however, is that the administration has initial control over curriculum, which (at least in theory) it could choose *not* to delegate. This is consistent with the court's reliance, which I think is misplaced, on high school cases affirming administrative control over curriculum.

73. Ibid., at 1346–47, 893. Interesting parallels and contrasts might be drawn here to efforts by local authorities to control the selection of books in public libraries and public schools. Courts have shown hostility to the suppression of ideas by removing volumes from library collections. *Board of Educ., Island Trees Union Free School Dist. v. Pico,* 457 U.S. 853 (1982) (unconstitutional to remove books from school library because of opposition to the concepts they express). But fundamental legal and cultural differences between higher education and public K-12 instruction (e.g., the relative sophistication of students; K-12 education having as an express goal the inculcation of particular social mores and values) make it easier for administrators to remove books deemed educationally unsuitable or otherwise to restrict expression in the elementary or secondary school setting. *See, e.g., Hazelwood School Dist. v. Kuhlmeier,* 484 U.S. 260 (1988) (upholding censorship of articles in high school newspaper).

74. *DiBona,* cited in n. 71, at 1344, 891.

75. Ibid., at 1347–48, 894.

76. 474 F.2d 928, 929 (7th Cir. 1972), *cert. denied,* 411 U.S. 972 (1973). Clark was also criticized for counseling an excessive number of students instead of referring them to NIU's professional counselors, and for belittling other staff in conversations with students. Ibid.

77. Ibid., at 930–31.

78. *Mahoney,* cited in n. 41, at 1174 (supporting both the administration's right to regulate curriculum content and a teacher's right to use his or her own pedagogical method, which could include discussion of controversial topics related to the approved curriculum). *See also Lovelace,* cited in n. 53, at 426 ("course content . . . [is a] core university concern"); and *Keen,* cited in n. 29, at 257 ("supremacy of the academic institution in matters of curriculum content").

79. *Riggin,* cited in chap. 1, n. 70, at 630.

80. *Bishop v. Aronov,* 926 F.2d 1066, 1068–69 (11th Cir. 1991), *cert. denied,* 505 U.S. 1218 (1992).

81. Ibid., at 1074 (relying in part on *Clark, Mahoney,* and other cases discussed supra).

82. Ibid., at 1076.

83. Ibid., at 1075. This is of course consistent with faculty freedom in the selection of research topics, discussed at pp. 25–30.

84. Ibid., at 1075–76.

85. Ibid., at 1069.

86. *See Rosenberger,* cited in chap. 1, n. 62 (student activity funding decisions based on religious content of speech impermissible).

87. In *Bishop* (and in *Edwards v. California Univ. of Pa.,* 156 F.3d 488 [3rd Cir. 1998], *cert. denied,* 525 U.S. 1143 [1999]), the court relied heavily on secondary school precedents in arguing for institutional control of course content. I think this is unwise given the profound differences between high school and university environments. For support of my position, *see, e.g., Scallet v. Rosenblum,* 911 F. Supp. 999, 1011 (W.D. Va. 1996), *aff'd without opinion,* 106 F.3d 391 (4th Cir. 1997), *cert. denied,* 521 U.S. 1105 (1997) ("the pedagogical interest in restricting teacher's in-class speech is not as strongly implicated in the context of higher education").

88. *Bishop,* cited in n. 80, at 1077 (emphasis added).

89. *Edwards,* cited in n. 87.

90. Ibid., at 489–90.

91. Ibid., at 491.

92. Ibid. quoting *Rosenberger,* cited in chap. 1, n. 62.

93. P. 29.

94. M. Collison, "Creationism Gets Biologist into Trouble," *Chronicle of Higher Education,* January 19, 1994, A20.

95. C. Mooney, "Devout Professors on the Offensive," *Chronicle of Higher Education,* May 14, 1994, A18.

96. Cited in n. 87.

97. The court here employed a legal test drawn from *Pickering v. Bd. of Ed.,* 391 U.S. 563 (1968), discussed at pp. 114–16, noting that it hesitated to apply this test to the *in-class* speech of university faculty. *Scallet,* cited in n. 87, at 1011. As explained later, I think such an extension of *Pickering* was an error.

98. *Scallet,* cited in n. 87, at 1016.

99. Ibid., at 1017.

100. At some level *Bishop* and *Edwards* reflect the explosive nature of debates over religion in American society. One wonders what might have transpired had the plaintiff professors opined on different topics. *See also* M. Olivas, *Reflections on Professorial Academic Freedom: Second Thoughts on the Third "Essential Freedom,"* 45 Stan. Law Rev. 1835, 1847 (1993).

101. Indeed, at some institutions the faculty's authority to select course materials is ensured through *contract* with the employer college. *See, e.g., Carr v.*

*Bd. of Trustees of the Univ. of Akron,* 465 F. Supp. 886, 891 (N.D. Ohio 1979), *aff'd without opinion,* 663 F.2d 1070 (6th Cir. 1981) (faculty manual provided that "selection of texts is the prerogative of the instructor subject to departmental policies").

102. "University officials are undoubtedly aware that quality faculty members will be hard to attract and retain if they are to be shackled in much of what they do." *Bishop,* cited in n. 80, at 1075.

103. Faculty will almost always have the ability to select exam (or required paper) topics. *Cohen,* cited in n. 7.

104. For example, the Stanford faculty's 1994 decision to reinstate a failing grade. B. Workman, "Stanford Votes to Restore Failing Grade," *San Francisco Chronicle,* June 3, 1994, A1.

105. Cited in n. 53, at 425–26.

106. Cited in n. 25, at 221, 223.

107. "Generally, in any situation in which students' rights are pitted against those of faculty, academic tradition will prevail and faculty rights will triumph." Olivas, cited in n. 100, at 1841.

108. This is why O'Neil would include the "evaluation of student performance" within his conception of First Amendment academic freedom. O'Neil, cited in introduction, n. 3, at 283. The combination of specialized faculty expertise, the relatively abstract means used to assess student achievement (e.g., papers, tests, class participation), traditional (if waning) judicial deference to academic judgments, and the unique nature of the academy will make faculty decisions about student performance much harder to overturn through litigation than, say, supervisors' evaluations of employees at for-profit businesses. With grading, there are usually no concrete or measurable work product and no third-party customers or clients from whom views on student performance are solicited.

109. Cited in n. 54.

110. *Parate,* cited in n. 54, at 827–28, quote at 828.

111. Ibid., at 830. Forcing the professor to change the grade, however, was deemed an infringement of his right to free speech.

112. *Hillis,* cited in n. 7, at 553. The court deemed both classroom content and teaching methods worthy of academic freedom (and First Amendment) protection. Such an approach recognizes that the line between content and method is often fuzzy (*see* pp. 73–74, 80–81). However, the court rejected the plaintiff's argument that refusing to change a grade constituted a "teaching method." *Hillis,* cited in n. 7, at 553.

113. *Keen,* cited in n. 29, at 257–58.

114. This should especially prove true at private colleges and universities where faculty cannot mount a First Amendment defense.

115. Pp. 34–46.

116. 16 F. Supp. 2d 1297, 1307 (D. Col. 1998), *subsequent appeal*, 208 F.3d 908 (10th Cir. 2000).

117. Gorman, cited in chap. 2, n. 33, at 31.

118. *See Stanford University Research Policy Handbook*, Document 5.2, "Copyright Policy," §1.F ("Courses taught and courseware developed at Stanford belong to Stanford"); and pp. 39–43 supra.

119. For a thoughtful discussion of the current flux, *see* C. Mann, "Who Will Own Your Next Good Idea," *Atlantic Monthly* 282, no. 3: 57–82, September 1998.

120. *See* previous discussion of fair use at pp. 47–48.

121. 17 U.S.C. §107 (emphasis added).

122. Ibid.

123. "Agreement on Guidelines for Classroom Copying in Not-for-Profit Educational Institutions with Respect to Books and Periodicals," in H.R. Rep. No. 94-1476, 94th Cong., 2d sess. 68 (1976).

124. The complete text of the photocopying guidelines, and a parallel set of equally stringent guidelines concerning "Off-Air Recording of Broadcast Programming for Educational Purposes" (e.g., recordings may only be shown once [and repeated once] and that within 10 school days of the original broadcast date), may be found at H.R. Rep 94-1476, supra, and *Congressional Record* at E4751, October 14, 1981, respectively.

125. *See, e.g., Marcus v. Rowley*, 695 F.2d 1171, 1177 (9th Cir. 1983); *Basic Books, Inc. v. Kinko's Graphics Corp.*, 758 F. Supp. 1522, 1536 (S.D.N.Y. 1991).

126. *Princeton Univ. Press et al. v. Michigan Document Services, Inc.*, 99 F.3d 1381, 1390–91 (6th Cir. 1996), *cert. denied*, 520 U.S. 1156 (1997); "Photocopying for Educational Uses," University of Pennsylvania *Almanac*, March 28, 1978, 4–5.

127. *Addison-Wesley Publishing Co. v. New York Univ.* (Civil Action No. 82 Civ. 83333, S.D.N.Y.).

128. *Basic Books*, cited in n. 125, at 1531–33. It was no coincidence that both of these suits were brought in New York City, headquarters to much of the publishing world and a sympathetic venue.

129. D. Magner, "Copy Shops, Publishers Still Seek Common Ground on Permissions Process," *Chronicle of Higher Education*, June 16, 1993, A15.

130. *Princeton Univ. Press*, cited in n. 126.

131. However, unless institutions enforce rigorous copyright policies (as in the NYU settlement), faculty may be able to shift this legal risk back to their employers under institutional policies indemnifying faculty from personal liability for actions carried out in the scope of their duties.

132. R. Jacobson, "No Copying," *Chronicle of Higher Education*, March 10, 1995, A17. Colleges, too, have been urged to be very cautious in securing all

necessary copyrights and in protecting themselves against unauthorized use in connection with distance learning. S. Steinbach & A. Lupo, "The Hidden Legal Traps in Distance-Learning Programs," *Chronicle of Higher Education*, February 6, 1998, A52.

133. R. Jacobson, "The Furor over 'Fair Use,'" *Chronicle of Higher Education*, May 10, 1996, A25; G. Blumenstyk, "After 3 Years, Academics and Publishers Reach No Clear Conclusions on 'Fair Use,'" *Chronicle of Higher Education*, May 30, 1997, A32; "On Line," *Chronicle of Higher Education*, June 13, 1997, A23 (quoting joint statement of educational groups).

134. Mann, cited in n. 119.

135. G. Blumenstyk, "A License to Copy," *Chronicle of Higher Education*, September 29, 1995, A59. Indeed, in *American Geophysical Union*, cited in chap. 2, n. 109, at 930–31, the Second Circuit regarded the availability of blanket photocopying licenses through the Copyright Clearance Center (a clearinghouse established by publishers) as evidence that a viable market had evolved for copies of scientific journal articles. This in turn led to a holding that the unauthorized copying of such articles was not fair use.

136. Again, while there are state copyright statues, federal law sets the prevailing tone in this area.

137. The situation becomes more complex when profit-making motives are involved. *See* pp. 39–43.

138. However, courts are still likely to care more about the practical effect of such action than its underlying motivation.

139. 17 U.S.C. §504 (c)(2). Of course, with the increasing visibility of copyright law and debates over fair use, it becomes harder to claim ignorance.

140. Fair use, though, can be a double-edged sword, as the University of Florida learned when it unsuccessfully sought to block a company from selling notes of faculty lectures. M. Cage, "U. of Fla. Loses Suit to Bar Company from Selling Summaries of Lectures," *Chronicle of Higher Education*, January 5, 1994, A46.

## 4   Faculty as Institutional Citizens

1. D. Kennedy, *Academic Duty* (Harvard University Press: 1997), 120.

2. *See* L. Veysey, *The Emergence of the American University* (University of Chicago Press: 1965), at 311–17, for a discussion of the birth of administrative bureaucracies at colleges and universities.

3. *But see* M. Finkin, *Intramural Speech, Academic Freedom, and the First Amendment*, 66 Texas L. Rev. 1323, 1341 (1988), for a different appraisal of the centrality of such faculty activity: "Although intramural criticism, debate and protest do not contribute to the discovery of a disciplinary truth, they conduce toward something almost as important in the life of the university. In developing

and executing its policies, institutions seek not truth but wisdom: a decision on admissions, curriculum or tenure is not true or untrue, but is wise or unwise. Thus, the professoriate, vitally affected by educational policies and charged with carrying them out, refused to concede to the administration the possession of all wisdom in such matters."

4. *Minnesota St. Bd. for Community Colleges v. Knight,* 465 U.S. 271, 287 (1983) (lawful for state to give collective bargaining agent exclusive representation in "meet and confer" sessions with the administration. The First Amendment rights of nonunion faculty did not extend to direct participation in governance. In other words, the right to speak was not equivalent to the right to be listened to).

5. "2 Staff Members at Baylor U. Demoted for Criticizing President," *Chronicle of Higher Education,* November 8, 1996, A8.

6. *See, e.g., Johnson v. Lincoln University,* 776 F.2d 443 (3rd Cir. 1985); *Coats v. Pierre,* 890 F.2d 728 (5th Cir. 1989), *cert. denied,* 498 U.S. 821 (1990); *Ghosh v. Ohio University,* 861 F.2d 720 (6th Cir. 1988), *cert. denied,* 490 U.S. 1006 (1989); *Gardetto v. Mason,* 100 F.3d 803 (10th Cir. 1996); and *Anderson-Free v. Steptoe,* 993 F. Supp. 870 (M.D. Ala. 1997), citing *Watkins v. Bowden,* 105 F.3d 1344 (11th Cir. 1997).

7. This threshold requirement can be traced to *Connick v. Myers,* 461 U.S. 138 (1983).

8. *Pickering,* cited in chap. 3, n. 97, at 568. Together with the *Connick* "public concern" inquiry, this balancing test determines whether the speech at issue was constitutionally protected.

9. *Mt. Healthy City Sch. Dist. Bd. of Educ. v. Doyle,* 429 U.S. 274 (1977).

10. *Gardetto,* cited in n. 6, at 811, quoting *Mt. Healthy,* supra, at 287. It is important to note that *Pickering, Connick,* and *Mt. Healthy* (and other seminal opinions that have shaped this area of law) are First Amendment cases and thus not controlling at private institutions where limits on faculty speech do not constitute state action. Furthermore, since these precedents do not involve disputes over speech in a university setting, they have had to be grafted (sometimes a bit awkwardly) to the higher education environment.

11. *Connick,* cited in n. 7, at 147–48.

12. *See, e.g., Mumford v. Godfried,* 52 F.3d 756 (8th Cir. 1995); *Gardetto,* cited in n. 6; and *Anderson-Free,* cited in n. 6.

13. The case law is rich in number because disgruntled faculty frequently seize upon First Amendment claims over intramural speech as a mechanism to bring employment disputes into federal court.

14. *Johnson,* cited in n. 6 (discussed infra); *Maples v. Martin,* 858 F.2d 1546 (11th Cir. 1988) (discussed infra); *Mumford,* cited in n. 12 (discussed infra); *Anderson-Free,* cited in n. 6 (grading policies; quality of graduates); *Coats,* cited in n. 6 (allegations of favoritism towards athletes and premed students and fac-

ulty exchanging sex for grades); *Sinott v. Skagit Valley College,* 49 Wash. App. 878, 746 P.2d 1213 (Ct. App. Wash. 1987) (state court case involving criticism of intellectual integrity of welding program); and *State ex rel. Richardson v. Bd. of Regents,* 70 Nev. 347, 269 P.2d 265 (S. Ct. Nev. 1954) (pre-*Connick* case involving faculty complaints about weakened admissions standards). However, there are also scattered cases holding that disputes over curricula and syllabi are not matters of public concern. *See Ballard v. Blount,* 581 F. Supp. 160 (N.D. Ga. 1983), *aff'd without opinion,* 734 F.2d 1480 (11th Cir. 1984) (challenges to new freshman English syllabus relate only to internal college affairs); and *Blum v. Schlegel,* 830 F. Supp. 712 (W.D.N.Y. 1993), *aff'd,* 18 F.3d 1005 (2nd Cir. 1994) (suggestions about school policies and curriculum not public matter). Faculty speech about grades awarded to individual students would not be protected either.

15. *Hall v. Kutztown Univ.,* 1998 U.S. Dist. LEXIS 138 (E.D. Pa. Jan. 12, 1998), *reconsideration granted in part on other grounds,* 1998 U.S. Dist. LEXIS 2418 (E.D. Pa. Feb. 23, 1998) (discussed infra); *Scallet,* cited in chap. 3, n. 87 (remarks at faculty meeting about wisdom of inserting issues of diversity and social responsibility into curriculum; posting articles about diversity on office door); *Blum,* cited in n. 14 (articles in campus publications attacking federal drug policy; advocacy of civil disobedience in public debate); *Booher v. Bd. of Regents,* 1998 U.S. Dist. LEXIS 11404 (D. Ky. July 22, 1998), *appeal dismissed,* 163 F.3d 395 (6th Cir. 1998) (newspaper interview fanning fires of campus debate about controversial art exhibit); and *Starsky v. Williams,* cited in chap. 3, n. 25 (distributing materials about student demonstrations on other campuses).

16. *Hickingbottom v. Easley,* 494 F. Supp. 980 (E.D. Ark. 1980) (discussed infra); *Powell v. Gallentine,* 992 F.2d 1088 (10th Cir. 1993) (whistle-blowing on grade fraud); and *D'Andrea v. Adams,* 626 F.2d 469 (5th Cir. 1980), *cert. denied,* 450 U.S. 919 (1981) (contacting state auditors about alleged misuse of university funds); *Gardetto,* cited in n. 6 (accusing president of misrepresenting his academic credentials); and *Hullman v. Bd. of Trustees,* 725 F. Supp. 1536 (D. Kan. 1989), *aff'd,* 950 F.2d 665 (10th Cir. 1991) (raising questions with officials about management of public money).

17. *Kurtz v. Vickrey,* 855 F.2d 723 (11th Cir. 1988) (faculty complaints about university funds not being spent for educational purposes); *Hullman,* supra (attacks on university financial practices such as how budgets were used and how scholarship programs were funded); and *Hale v. Walsh,* 113 Idaho 759, 747 P.2d 1288 (Ct. App. Id. 1987) (newspaper interview criticizing university's handling of financial crisis). *See also* "Jury Says College Fired Advocate of Pay Raises," *Chronicle of Higher Education,* October 30, 1998, A14 (pushing for across-the-board salary increase and leadership of faculty professional group).

18. *Gardetto,* cited in n. 6 (faculty member's public support for slate of nonincumbent board candidates).

19. Faculty collective bargaining rights are addressed later in this volume. *See* pp. 185–92. Union organization and periodic contract negotiations, while they do directly affect individual members, clearly address matters of public concern. *See Hale*, cited in n. 17, at 766, 1295.

20. *Honore v. Douglas*, 833 F.2d 565 (5th Cir. 1987) (running disputes with law school dean over admissions policy, size of student body, administration of school budget, and untimely certification of graduates' bar eligibility); *Gardetto*, cited in n. 6 (urging faculty vote of "no confidence"); and *Narumanchi v. Bd. of Trustees*, 1986 U.S. Dist. LEXIS 19512 (D. Conn. Oct. 6, 1986), *aff'd in part, rev'd in part on other grounds*, 850 F.2d 70 (2nd Cir. 1988) (faculty member's opposition to reorganization of school matter of public concern as it involved the allocation and use of state funds). The *Narumanchi* holding, however, begins to impede on operational matters not typically deemed of public concern.

21. *Kurtz*, cited in n. 17 (questions about salary not matter of public concern); *Ghosh*, cited in n. 6 (complaints about professor's merit rating and compensation due for an undersubscribed course); *Ballard*, cited in n. 14 (internal disputes about course assignments and a less-than-average salary increase); *Dorsett v. Bd. of Trustees*, 940 F.2d 121 (5th Cir. 1991) (concerns about teaching assignments and the work environment); *Ayoub v. Texas A&M Univ.*, 927 F.2d 834 (5th Cir. 1991), *cert. denied*, 502 U.S. 817 (1991) (long-standing salary grievance); *Mahaffey v. Kansas Bd. of Regents*, 562 F. Supp. 887 (D. Kan. 1983) (salary increases, perks, departmental "home"); and *Blum*, cited in n. 14 (letters to colleagues about plaintiff's promotion).

22. *Boyett v. Troy State Univ. at Montgomery*, 971 F. Supp. 1403 (M.D. Ala. 1997), *aff'd without opinion*, 142 F.3d 1284 (11th Cir. 1998) (comments on university's proposed tenure and promotion policy, opposition to faculty evaluation process, and unfavorable reactions to a particular tenure case not matters of public concern); *Harris v. Ariz. Bd. of Regents*, 528 F. Supp. 987 (D. Ariz. 1981) (obstructionist behavior in connection with a search, including complaints about lack of influence over the outcome, criticism of the successful candidate, and threatening to dissuade her from accepting appointment); *Ballard*, cited in n. 14 (objections to denial of tenure to colleague); and *Hamer v. Brown*, 641 F. Supp. 662 (W.D. Ark. 1986), *aff'd*, 831 F.2d 1398 (8th Cir. 1987) (statements to campus visitors about personnel actions and allocations of funds). *But see Narumanchi*, cited in n. 20 (dispute over appointment is public concern because it involves allocation and use of state funds); and *Curtis v. Univ. of Houston*, 940 F. Supp. 1070 (S.D. Tex. 1996), *aff'd without opinion*, 127 F.3d 35 (5th Cir. 1997) (questionable faculty hiring practices are public concern).

23. *Williams v. Alabama State Univ.*, 102 F.3d 1179 (11th Cir. 1997); *Simons v. West Virginia Univ.*, 1996 U.S. App. LEXIS 10425 (4th Cir. 1996) (memo attacking colleague's conduct and then questioning chair's directive that no further such memos be circulated was not speech on matter of public concern).

24. *Boyett,* cited in n. 22 (efforts to secure increased funding for plaintiff's division); *Kurtz,* cited in n. 17 (personally motivated questions about budget).

25. *Starsky,* cited in chap. 3, n. 25, at 910–11, 924–25, stands for the proposition that personal invective cannot be on a matter of public concern and will not be protected. *See also Gardetto,* cited in n. 6 (abusively warning president not to terminate one of plaintiff's supervisees under a reduction-in-force policy not a matter of public concern, even though criticism of that policy before the college's board of trustees *was* protected speech). More recently, a tenured professor at the University of Central Arkansas was censured (and then allegedly fired) for behaving rudely and sarcastically towards university officials, including snorting at them as they passed by and making an obscene gesture to the university president. Such expressive conduct is not likely to be deemed a matter of public concern. J. Reynolds, "U. of Central Arkansas Fires Tenured Professor," *Chronicle of Higher Education,* May 22, 1998, A15.

26. Quotation from *Hullman,* cited in n. 16, at 1545. *See Colburn v. Trustees of Indiana Univ.,* 973 F.2d 581 (7th Cir. 1992) (discussed infra); *Bunger v. Univ. of Okla. Bd. of Regents,* 95 F.3d 987 (discussed infra); *Boyett,* cited in n. 22 (criticism of method of election to internal governance body and questioning level of faculty input into budget process); *Garvie v. Jackson,* 845 F.2d 647 (6th Cir. 1988) (department chair's complaints to provost about supervising dean's administrative actions not shown to be matter of public concern); *Harris v. Merwin,* 901 F. Supp. 509 (N.D.N.Y. 1995) (vocal criticism of the appointment of an "unqualified" chair to head plaintiff's department); *Roseman v. Indiana Univ. of Pa.,* 520 F.2d 1364 (3rd Cir. 1975), *cert. denied,* 424 U.S. 921 (1976) (intra-university complaints about conduct of department chair); and *Pressman v. Univ. of North Carolina at Charlotte,* 78 N.C. App. 296, 337 S.E. 2d 644 (Ct. App. N.C. 1985) (comments at faculty meeting about dean's administrative incompetence stemmed from plaintiff's own grievances and were not on a matter of public concern).

27. *Kurtz,* cited in n. 17 (dispute over how the university should be managed, including criticism of president's choice of language in policy statements, not matter of public concern).

28. *Johnson,* cited in n. 6, at 452–53.

29. *Maples,* cited in n. 14, at 1548–49.

30. Ibid., at 1553.

31. *Mumford,* cited in n. 12.

32. *Hall,* cited in n. 15, at 62.

33. Ibid., at 67. This call to arms against multicultural education and specific practices in non-Western cultures was also distinguished from a faculty member's "abstract theorizing" by its clear and concrete political and moral agenda, Ibid., at 71.

34. *Hickingbottom,* cited in n. 16, at 984.

35. *Colburn,* cited in n. 26, at 584.

36. Ibid., at 587.

37. Ibid., at 588.

38. Ibid., at 586.

39. *Bunger,* cited in n. 26, at 992.

40. *Kurtz,* cited in n. 17, at 728–29.

41. Ibid., at 729.

42. Ibid., at 729–30.

43. *Mahaffey,* cited in n. 21, at 890.

44. *Harris,* cited in n. 26, at 514.

45. *Ballard,* cited in n. 14, at 163. *See also Harris,* cited in n. 26, at 514 ("every inter-departmental squabble about faculty appointments [does not] implicate the First Amendment").

46. *Mumford,* cited in n. 12, at 760.

47. *Pickering,* cited in chap. 3, n. 97. *Pickering* is not itself a higher education case.

48. *Pickering,* supra, at 569–70. *See also Gardetto,* cited in n. 6, at 815; *Maples,* cited in n. 14, at 1554; *D'Andrea,* cited in n. 16, at 474–75; and *Hamer,* cited in n. 22, at 665.

49. Hamer, supra, at 666.

50. 501 F.2d 1090 (10th Cir. 1974).

51. Ibid., at 1098.

52. *Pickering,* cited in chap. 3, n. 97, at 569–70. *See also Gardetto,* cited in n. 6, at 815; *Maples,* cited in n. 14, at 1554; *Hamer,* cited in n. 22, at 665; *Hale,* cited in n. 17, at 767; *Sinott,* cited in n. 14, at 881, 1216; and *Rampey,* cited in n. 50, at 1098.

53. *Pickering,* cited in chap. 3, n. 97, at 573. *See also Gardetto,* cited in n. 6, at 815; *Maples,* cited in n. 14, at 1554; *Hale,* cited in n. 17, at 767; and *Sinott,* cited in n. 14, at 882, 1216 (speech of faculty balanced against the "need to prevent activities disruptive of the educational process and to provide for the orderly functioning of the university").

54. *Maples,* supra, discussed at p. 110.

55. Ibid., at 1554.

56. *Harris,* cited in n. 22, at 999.

57. Ibid. *See also Scallet,* cited in chap. 3, n. 87 (faculty member's interest in expression [posting articles and cartoons about sexism and other public topics on an office door] did not disrupt university and outweighed any institutional interest in an "aesthetic" environment). *But see Burnham v. Ianni,* 119 F.3d 668 (8th Cir. 1997), for an alternative analysis of the faculty's right to post materials. In this bizarre case, run-a-muck officials at the University of Minnesota–Duluth removed photos of two history professors (who had posed with weapons related to their scholarly interests) from a public display about the department. The

pictures were apparently regarded as aggravating a climate of fear on the campus. When the faculty sued, a federal appellate court held that the display case had been opened up for precisely such expression, and that the professors' speech had been impermissibly censored because of its content. The court further declared that *Pickering* and its progeny were inapplicable since those cases involved employee discipline (and that even if they did apply, these pictures did not disrupt the campus). While this holding is undoubtedly correct, one cannot read this case without regretting the time and money wasted in trying to regulate—and then litigating over—such trifles.

58. *D'Andrea,* cited in n. 16, at 475–76 (university failed to show detrimental impact of plaintiff's off-campus communication to state officials about possible financial improprieties. These remarks were protected speech).

59. *Pickering,* cited in chap. 3, n. 97, at 572–73. *See also Gardetto,* cited in n. 6, at 815; *Maples,* cited in n. 14, at 1554; *Hamer,* cited in n. 22, at 665; *Hale,* cited in n. 17, at 767, 1296; and *Sinott,* cited in n. 14, at 881, 1216.

60. While one could conceive of a faculty member's participation in institutional affairs consuming such huge blocks of time that it genuinely interfered with the performance of more central (and conventional) obligations, I am aware of no such case.

61. Cited in n. 17. Although *Hale* is a state court opinion, the Idaho Court of Appeals employed a fairly conventional *Pickering/Connick* analysis.

62. *Hale,* cited in n. 17, at 767, 1296. While the plaintiff's speech—in particular his formal request for an interpretation of state regulations on course waivers—was likely to annoy some administrators with whom he had no close working relationship and to strain several such extant relationships, the level of disruption was not enough to tip the *Pickering* balance against him.

63. *Booher,* cited in n. 15, at 43. Furthermore, any disruption of the plaintiff's relationship with his department chair (who had refused to change the exhibit's title) was deemed relatively minor. Ibid. at 44.

64. *See* discussion of faculty terminations "for cause," pp. 209–11.

65. *Powell,* cited in n. 16, at 1091; *Hickingbottom,* cited in n. 16, at 985–86; and *Gardetto,* cited in n. 6, at 816. Note that in the nonfaculty case of *Waters v. Churchill,* 511 U.S. 661 (1994), the Supreme Court held that the government could discharge employees for speech it reasonably *believed* would disrupt the workplace, as opposed to speech actually *having* such effect.

66. *Coats,* cited in n. 6, at 732–33; and *Sinott,* cited in n. 14, at 885–86, 1218. In *Sinott,* while the faculty member's statements were a factor in his termination, the defendant college demonstrated (under the fourth and final prong of the analysis) that it would have taken the same employment action even in the absence of such speech. *See also Franklin v. Atkins,* 562 F.2d 1188 (10th Cir. 1977), *cert. denied,* 435 U.S. 994 (1978) (University of Colorado lawfully refused to hire a scholar dismissed from the Stanford faculty for disruptive speech.

The plaintiff did not show that his Stanford speech was constitutionally protected or that it was a substantial factor in Colorado's hiring decision; further, Colorado would have apparently reached the same decision even in the absence of such speech).

67. *Givhan v. Western Line Consolidated School District,* 439 U.S. 410 (1979).

68. Kaplin & Lee, cited in introduction, n. 2, at 320.

69. M. Finkin, *Intramural Speech,* cited in n. 3.

70. *See, e.g.,* R. Kimball, "A Syllabus for Sickos," *Wall Street Journal,* November 5, 1997, A22:3; K. Arenson, "At SUNY, a Conference about Sex Is Criticized," *New York Times,* November 7, 1997, B5:1; and K. Arenson, "Furor over a Sex Conference Stirs SUNY's Quiet New Paltz Campus," *New York Times,* November 8, 1997, B1:2.

71. My focus in this discussion is on faculty as conference presenters rather than as passive attendees.

72. Of course, if seminar or conference participation is an ingrained part of the departmental culture or an expectation in building a plausible case for tenure or promotion, the faculty member's "choice" may be nominal.

73. Conflicting claims of faculty autonomy and responsibility as an "institutional ambassador" are also raised by a professor's extra-academy speech as a public citizen. Pp. 127–39.

74. This logic might lead to a "sliding scale" of instructionally oriented academic freedom, with faculty autonomy being the most limited in large, introductory, lower-division courses (where content and teaching methods are most likely to be of institutional concern); growing larger in upper-division courses for departmental majors (where more intellectual intercourse with students is expected); expanding still further in graduate-level seminars (where the instructor-pupil relationship begins to evolve into an dialogue among peers); and reaching its height in full-fledged scholarly exchanges with disciplinary colleagues (tantamount to mutual instruction) in organized conference settings. Perhaps this notion should be developed further by commentators or courts.

75. For a more thorough examination of this topic, *see, e.g.,* P. Moots & E. Gaffney, *Church and Campus* (University of Notre Dame Press: 1979); M. McConnell, "Academic Freedom in Religious Colleges and Universities," in Van Alstyne, ed., cited in chap. 2, n. 12; and C. Curran, *Academic Freedom and Catholic Universities,* 66 Texas L. Rev. 1441 (1988).

76. "Congress shall make no law. . . prohibiting the free exercise [of religion]." U.S. Const. Amend. I.

77. 42 U.S.C. §§2000e-1(a) and 2000e-2(e)(2). See p. 162. While it might be argued that all teachers at a religiously affiliated institutions are asked to serve as exemplars, thereby inserting a moral element into their work, I think such colleges and universities could not legally justify faith-based requirements for many faculty positions (e.g., professor of mathematics).

78. 814 F.2d 1213 (7th Cir. 1987). *See also Pime v. Loyola Univ.*, 803 F.2d 351 (7th Cir. 1986) (university could reserve slots in its philosophy department for Jesuits).

79. *See* pp. 186–87; and *Universidad Central de Bayamon v. N.L.R.B.*, 793 F.2d 383 (1st Cir. 1986), with a divided court blocking Labor Board jurisdiction over this denominational institution.

80. Approximately 85% at Notre Dame, 70% at Catholic University, and 50% at Georgetown. K. Lively, "A Debate over Crucifixes Provokes Larger Questions at Georgetown U.," *Chronicle of Higher Education*, November 28, 1997, A45.

81. Under the Constitution, *nonsectarian* private institutions (that are not state actors) also have the freedom to control the behavior of faculty, staff, and students to preserve the local culture and promote the moral health and growth (along whatever lines desired) of community members. Thus, Harvard or Oberlin could *theoretically* impose restrictions on faculty inquiry and activity (e.g., no deconstructionist literary analysis; professors must live near campus). Such rules, if adopted, should properly take the form of explicit contract provisions or formal institutional policies. There are, however, two major differences—one legal, the other cultural—between religious and secular private institutions in this regard. Religiously controlled institutions have an extra legal plank upon which to stand in defending such restrictions in the form of the First Amendment's Free Exercise clause. That provision obviously cannot be invoked by a nonsectarian college or university. Perhaps even more important, while measures to preserve doctrinal and cultural purity may have value at denominationally run schools (at least in the eyes of religious authorities, trustees, and some administrators and faculty), the very *notion* (much less the enforcement) of such purity is antithetical to the basic purposes of most secular universities.

82. *Curran,* cited in chap. 1, n. 3.

83. 917 F. Supp. 773 (N.D. Ala. 1996), *aff'd,* 113 F.3d 196 (11th Cir. 1997).

84. Faculty at such schools may also anticipate that in their nonprofessional private lives they will also be expected to adhere to the sponsoring religion's standards of behavior in a way that extends far beyond a secular institution's ability to discharge faculty "for cause," such as moral turpitude. *See* pp. 212–14.

85. *BYU Faculty Handbook*, "Statement on Academic Freedom at Brigham Young University," April 1, 1993.

86. Ibid.

87. D. Manger, "A Test of Faith," *Chronicle of Higher Education*, February 23, 1996, A17.

88. Ibid.

89. "Academic Freedom and Tenure: Brigham Young University," 83 *Academe* 52, 68 (September–October 1997).

90. Ibid., at 58. *See also* "Brigham Young Denies Tenure to Scholar for Non-Mormon Views," *Chronicle of Higher Education*, June 21, 1996, A15.

91. "Academic Freedom and Tenure," cited in n. 89, at 61. *See also* "Professor Says Church Tries to Intimidate Him," *Chronicle of Higher Education,* October 16, 1991, A5; "Brigham Young U. Won't Extend 2 Scholars' Contracts," *Chronicle of Higher Education,* June 23, 1993, A13.

92. "Academic Freedom and Tenure," cited in n. 89, at 62. *See also* "Author of Controversial Short Stories to Leave Brigham Young," *Chronicle of Higher Education,* July 28, 1995, A17.

93. *See also* K. Haworth, "Baptist Seminary Professors Who Don't Agree That Wives Should 'Submit' May Lose Jobs," *Chronicle of Higher Education On-Line,* October 19, 1998 (faculty at Southwestern Baptist Theological Seminary expected to sign and adhere to a statement of church doctrine).

94. AAUP, "1940 Statement," cited in chap. 2, n. 4, at 3. This statement, if formally adopted by a college or university, may become part of the faculty contract with the institution. Even if not formally adopted, it may still be regarded as binding institutional custom or as "common practice" throughout the higher education community. *See* p. 19–22.

95. C. Leatherman, "Faculty Group Censures 3 Universities over Academic Freedom and Tenure Issues," *Chronicle of Higher Education,* July 26, 1998, A14.

96. Kaplin & Lee, cited in introduction, n. 2, at 168.

97. G. Niebuhr, "Catholic Bishops to Require Certification for Theologians," *New York Times,* November 18, 1999, A1; B. McMurtrie, "Bishops Approve Controversial Rules for Catholic Higher Education," *Chronicle of Higher Education,* November 26, 1999, A20; B. McMurtrie, "Vatican Backs Catholic-College Rules That Spur Fears over Academic Freedom," *Chronicle of Higher Education,* June 16, 2000, A18 (Vatican has approved national episcopal guidelines).

## 5    Faculty as Public Citizens

1. For analyses of the history of academic freedom in the United States, including faculty extra-university speech, see, e.g., Hofstadter & Metzger, cited in chap. 3, n. 5; R. Hofstadter, *Academic Freedom in the Age of the College* (Transaction Publishers: 1996); E. Schrecker, *No Ivory Tower: McCarthyism and the Universities* (Oxford University Press: 1986); Veysey, cited in chap. 4, n. 2; and M. Anderson, *Imposters in the Temple* (Hoover Institution Press: 1996). Note that even when academic freedom was less securely protected than it is today, the value of faculty autonomy was often taken seriously. Thus, in 1894, a University of Wisconsin economist was investigated—and resoundingly exonerated—by the Board of Regents for allegedly justifying labor strikes and (in an entirely nonuniversity capacity) pressuring a local printer to unionize his workplace. W. L. Hanson, ed., *Academic Freedom on Trial* (University of Wisconsin Press: 1998).

2. *Levin v. Harleston,* 770 F. Supp. 895 (S.D.N.Y. 1991), *affirmed in part and vacated in part,* 966 F.2d 85 (2nd Cir. 1992).

3. Ibid., at 911.

4. Ibid., at 925.

5. Ibid., at 918. While the result in *Harleston* is surely right, the court's analysis of the underlying free speech issues is slightly off kilter. It makes only a quick nod towards a *Pickering/Connick* determination of whether the speech in question addressed matters of public concern (the clear implication is yes), largely failing to consider whether Levin's right to express his opinions might be outweighed by City College's interest in a smoothly running institution (presumably both the trial and appellate courts would strike this balance in favor of the professor). Instead, the trial court in particular focuses on a Fourteenth Amendment due process analysis of how the college deprived Levin of liberty and property. *See* pp. 239–49.

6. 420 F.2d 499 (5th Cir. 1969).

7. Assuming, of course, that such expressive activity did not incite imminent lawless action. *Brandenburg,* cited in chap. 1, n. 60.

8. *See* pp. 135–37.

9. *See* pp. 107–8 and accompanying notes.

10. A sharper dichotomy exists for faculty at private institutions. There, while the government still cannot impose viewpoint-based restrictions on a professor's speech as a citizen, the employer college or university can limit a professor's extra-institutional speech as a condition of employment.

11. This point is treated in more detail at pp. 135–36. Faculty who wish to minimize confusion about the hat they are wearing should at the very least identify their personal views as such.

12. Pp. 114–16.

13. 434 F. Supp. 1273, 1289, 1294–1302 (D. Del. 1977).

14. 164 F.3d 221, 225–26 (5th Cir. 1998).

15. Ibid., at 226.

16. 52 F.3d 9 (2nd Cir. 1994), *cert. denied,* 516 U.S. 862 (1995).

17. Ibid., at 13, relying in large part on *Waters,* cited in chap. 4, n. 65. The court also claimed that Jeffries' academic freedom to express controversial ideas was not infringed when he was stripped of the ministerial position of chair, since he remained a tenured professor. In my view, this argument does not hold water. Removal as chair is a powerful sanction, involving considerable loss of status, which under different circumstances could impermissibly chill faculty speech.

18. Cited in chap. 3, n. 25.

19. Starsky's protected expression also included a television speech and a press release criticizing personnel actions taken against him by the Arizona Board of Regents and the board's political philosophy. While the court considered these items speech by a private citizen in a "context apart from his role as a faculty member" (*Starsky,* cited in chap. 3, n. 25, at 920), I regard them as statements about intra-university affairs made in Starsky's capacity as an institutional citizen

but at off-campus locations. However classified, they are covered by the First Amendment.

20. Ibid., at 924.

21. In *Megill v. Bd. of Regents*, 541 F.2d 1073 (5th Cir. 1976), a University of Florida faculty member was denied tenure for (among other reasons) disrupting a meeting of the local Yale Club where Florida's chancellor was speaking. The regents felt that the professor's "conduct and profanity lacked the maturity and discretion of a qualified member of the academic community" (id. at 1084), and the Fifth Circuit agreed that off-campus conduct by faculty as private citizens could "appropriately be used by the Board to evaluate the competence of a teacher without violating any First Amendment right." Ibid. I believe this holding misreads the scope of faculty freedom in extramural activities and would not be confirmed today. However, the *Megill* court did correctly note that faculty could be dismissed for cause for repeatedly making false and misleading statements in a variety of (intra-and extra-university) contexts.

22. One could make the chicken-or-egg argument that institutional stature is largely the accumulated residue of the stature of the faculty and their ideas (the balance stemming from public service, prominent alumni, and athletic triumphs). But there is no denying that colleges and universities have genuine and enduring independent stature *as institutions*.

23. AAUP, "1940 Statement," cited in chap. 2, n. 4, at 4.

24. Historian Walter Metzger recounts how AAUP negotiators "settled" for this language in no small part as a trade-off for administrative concessions on tenure in the 1940 Statement. W. Metzger, "The 1940 Statement of Principles on Academic Freedom and Tenure," in Van Alstyne, ed., cited in chap. 2, n. 12, at 53–64.

25. *Starsky*, cited in chap. 3, n. 25, at 922.

26. 523 F.2d 929 (9th Cir. 1975).

27. AAUP, "1940 Statement," cited in chap. 2, n. 4, at 6 (citing as authoritative a 1964 AAUP interpretation that, inter alia, "extramural utterances rarely bear upon the faculty member's fitness for the position").

28. P. Cytrynbaum, "Web Site Entangles NU in Free-Speech Debate," *Chicago Tribune*, December 29, 1996, 1.

29. J. Basinger, "Wayne State U. Bans Internet Use That Is Not Related to University Purposes," *Chronicle of Higher Education*, November 21, 1997, A23.

30. AAUP report, "Academic Freedom and Electronic Communications," June 1997 (copy on file with author).

31. *Urofsky*, cited in chap. 3, n. 2.

32. *R.A.V.*, cited in chap. 1, n. 59 (striking down local ordinance banning content-specific hate speech).

33. 385 U.S. 589 (1967).

34. Ibid., at 603. Note, however, that the Court stopped short of holding that

academic freedom was covered or protected by the First Amendment. This is still a source of disappointment in many quarters.

35. Ibid., at 606.

36. *Cooper,* cited in chap. 3, n. 59, at 810. As discussed at pp. 82–83, the professor's right to teach his courses from a Marxist perspective also received judicial support.

37. *Ollman,* cited in chap. 2, n. 20, at 1201–2.

38. Ibid., at 1207, 1214–15, 1217. See also *Selzer v. Fleisher,* 629 F.2d 809 (2nd Cir. 1980), *cert. denied,* 451 U.S. 970 (1981), for a possible extension of the scope of faculty freedom in extramural associations. The Second Circuit implied that a faculty member's connections to and work for the CIA were constitutionally protected ("conduct which denies a person promotion or tenure because of his private associations violates his First Amendment rights"). Ibid., at 812.

39. *See, e.g.,* Georgetown University, "Computer Systems Acceptable Use Policy," at <http://www.georgetown.edu/acs/use/>.

## 6   Faculty as Employees

1. *Sweezy,* cited in chap. 3, n. 13, at 263.

2. 621 F.2d 532, 547–48 (3rd Cir. 1980). *Zahorik v. Cornell Univ.,* 729 F.2d 85, 92–93 (2nd Cir. 1984), recognizes the uniqueness of tenure and the importance of departmental peers' views in tenure decisions.

3. But at least one prominent historian of academic freedom argues that modern faculties have in fact moved far away from a guildist model, though their rhetoric still frequently invokes this medieval ideal. W. Metzger, cited in chap. 5, n. 24 (referring, inter alia, to the "deguilding of the idea of academic freedom"), at 39.

4. *In re Dinnan,* 661 F.2d 426 (5th Cir. 1981).

5. AAUP, "1940 Statement," cited in chap. 2, n. 4, at 4. Prior to changes in federal and state age discrimination law, tenure could also be terminated under the 1940 Statement for mandatory retirement.

6. R. Wilson, "Wesleyan U. Wins Challenge of Tenure Denial, despite Testimony by Outside Experts," *Chronicle of Higher Education On-Line,* July 29, 1998.

7. *See* E. Boyer, *Scholarship Reconsidered: Priorities of the Professoriate* (Carnegie Foundation for the Advancement of Teaching: 1990), for the argument that—in addition to the traditional "scholarship of discovery"—institutions should value different kinds of intellectual endeavor such as the "scholarship of integration," the "scholarship of application," and the "scholarship of teaching."

8. 648 F.2d 61 (1st Cir. 1981), *cert. denied,* 454 U.S. 1098 (1981). *See also Scott v. Univ. of Delaware,* 601 F.2d 76 (3rd Cir. 1979), *cert. denied,* 444 U.S.

931 (1979) (Sociology Department lawfully placed new emphasis on scholarship; no discrimination when plaintiff—who had been fully apprised of such criteria—not reappointed); and *Randolph v. Bd. of Regents,* 1982 Okla. LEXIS 240 (Okla. 1982) (university can impose more rigorous standards for faculty *promotions*). When a college or university demands faculty research, its absence constitutes grounds for denial of reappointment or tenure. *Weinstein,* cited in chap. 2, n. 61, at 1097 n. 4; *Carr,* cited in chap. 3, n. 101, at 896; *Watts v. Bd. of Curators,* 495 F.2d 384 (8th Cir. 1974).

9. AAUP, "1940 Statement," cited in chap. 2, n. 4, at 3.

10. Prominent exceptions being the American Council on Education and the Association of American Universities.

11. AAUP policies should not be accorded undue legal weight. Notwithstanding the wide recognition of its pronouncements, the AAUP remains essentially a faculty advocacy group and sometime collective bargaining agent. It is often fiercely partisan (though not without good reason, historically). As the court observed in *Browzin v. Catholic Univ.,* 527 F.2d 843, 848 n. 8 (D.C. Cir. 1975), "Although the AAUP's investigations are noted for their thoroughness and scrupulous care, the reports remain the product of an organization composed of professors alone." AAUP regulations almost always impose more restraints on institutions than does applicable law (e.g., the presence of counsel and the preparation of a transcript in a faculty discharge proceeding). Accordingly, sophisticated institutions will not indiscriminately adopt AAUP directives. Nor is it well settled that AAUP standards on tenure and other matters constitute national custom and usage.

12. "1940 Statement," cited in chap. 2, n. 4, at 4, also offering guidance on how to treat faculty who move from one institution to another.

13. *See* discussion of "for cause" terminations of faculty at pp. 215–17.

14. Of course, periodic *pre*tenure performance evaluations can provide an early warning that junior faculty are not succeeding as hoped.

15. *See,* e.g., Commission on Academic Tenure in Higher Education, *Faculty Tenure* (Jossey-Bass: 1973); Van Alstyne, ed., cited in chap. 2, n. 12; T. Leap, *Tenure, Discrimination, and the Courts* (ILR Press: 1995); C. Leatherman, "More Faculty Members Question the Value of Tenure," *Chronicle of Higher Education,* October 25, 1996, A12; M. Finkin, ed., *The Case for Tenure* (Cornell University Press: 1996); R. Chait, "Thawing the Cold War over Tenure: Why Academe Needs More Employment Options," *Chronicle of Higher Education,* February 7, 1997, B4; J. P. Byrne, "Academic Freedom without Tenure?" AAHE New Pathways Working Paper Series, no. 5, American Association for Higher Education, Washington, D.C., 1997; D. Breneman, "Alternatives to Tenure for the Next Generation of Academics," AAHE New Pathways Working Paper Series, no. 14, American Association for Higher Education, Washington, D.C., 1997; J. Perley, "Tenure Remains Vital to Academic Freedom," *Chronicle of*

*Higher Education,* April 4, 1997, A48; M. Brand, "Why Tenure Is Indispensable," *Chronicle of Higher Education,* April 2, 1999, A64; and M. Finkin, "The Campaign against Tenure," 86 *Academe* 20 (May–June 2000). The preceding analysis draws heavily from a discussion of the pros and cons of tenure (especially in opposition to long-term employment contracts) in *Faculty Tenure,* at 13–16.

16. At some institutions nontenured faculty are represented on department personnel committees, but not in sufficient numbers to control votes.

17. For a somewhat novel critique of faculty performance in this area by a staunch defender of traditional prerogatives, *see* C. Nelson, "The Real Problem with Tenure Is Incompetent Faculty Hiring," *Chronicle of Higher Education,* November 14, 1997, B4.

18. *Penn Handbook,* cited in chap. 2, n. 26, "Procedures for Academic Appointments and Promotions," §II.D.1.

19. State University of New York, *Policies of the Board of Trustees 1998,* Art. XII, "Evaluation and Promotion of Academic and Professional Employees," Tit. A., §4, p. 21.

20. *See, e.g., Coats,* cited in chap. 4, n. 6; and *Colburn,* cited in chap. 4, n. 26.

21. *See, e.g., Brown v. Boston Univ.,* 891 F.2d 337 (1st Cir. 1989) (Title VII tenure denial case); and more generally, pp. 158–77.

22. *E.g.,* in *Mumford,* cited in chap. 4, n. 12, the plaintiff argued that Iowa State had not followed agreed-upon procedures in denying him tenure, thereby attempting (unsuccessfully) to bootstrap this assertion into a Fourteenth Amendment due process claim (*see* pp. 239–49 for a discussion of constitutional due process).

23. 493 U.S. 182 (1990).

24. Even more troubling, these materials would then become available to complainants (and their attorneys) through Freedom of Information Act requests. The EEOC was in effect providing free discovery for current and future plaintiffs, without any threshold determination as to the existence of a cause of action.

25. *Univ. of Pa.,* cited in n. 23, at 188–90. For a discussion of Title VII and its enforcement mechanisms, see pp. 160–67.

26. Ibid., at 195–96 (citing *Sweezy,* cited in chap. 3, n. 13), 199–200.

27. Ibid., at 199.

28. Ibid., at 197.

29. Ibid., at 202 n. 9.

30. Ibid., at 194.

31. Ibid., at 200.

32. *Dinnan,* cited in n. 4, offers another fine example of judicial skepticism about broad institutional and faculty autonomy. The Fifth Circuit warned that if academic freedom "is expanded too far it can cause other important societal

goals (such as the elimination of discrimination in employment decisions) to be frustrated." Ibid., at 430.

33. *But see* A. Schneider, "Why You Can't Trust Letters of Recommendation," *Chronicle of Higher Education,* June 30, 2000, A14, reporting that, without assurances of confidentiality (and reflecting both a fear of being sued for libel and feelings of sympathy towards candidates), some professors are less willing to write candid evaluation letters. Phone calls have been used to supplement or replace some letters.

34. "The report of my death was an exaggeration," M. Twain [S. Clemens], *Bartlett's Familiar Quotations* (1992), 528.

35. C. Leatherman, "Abolition of Tenure Rattles Faculty at College of Ozarks," *Chronicle of Higher Education,* January 26, 1994, A18; J. Selingo, "2-Year College in Arkansas Ends Tenure-Track Posts for New Faculty Members," *Chronicle of Higher Education On-Line,* May 21, 1998.

36. D. Magner, "Bennington Dismisses 20 Professors and Announces a Major Reorganization of Its Academic Structure," *Chronicle of Higher Education,* June 29, 1994, A16; L. Guernsey, "19 Professors Fired by Bennington Sue for $3.7-Million," *Chronicle of Higher Education,* May 17, 1996, A23; R. Wilson, "Bennington, after Eliminating Tenure, Attracts New Faculty Members and Students," *Chronicle of Higher Education,* January 10, 1997, A10.

37. P. Healy, "Mass. Governor Seeks to Free Some Colleges from Tenure and Most Regulations," *Chronicle of Higher Education,* March 26, 1999, A43.

38. Post-tenure reviews are discussed in more detail at pp. 202–8.

39. In 1996–97, the regents of the University of Minnesota stirred up controversy with an attempt (ultimately scaled back) to revise the university's tenure policy along these lines. *See* pp. 237–38.

40. For example, in 1993 Howard University's trustees added a provision to the faculty handbook authorizing the removal of a professor "when, in the board's judgment, the interests of the university require it." This language was wildly unpopular with faculty and was subsequently suspended. C. Leatherman, "Board of Trustees' Definition of Tenure Rankles Faculty Leaders at Howard U.," *Chronicle of Higher Education,* September 29, 1993, A15; D. Magner, "Howard Wonders Which Issues Pushed President to Leave," *Chronicle of Higher Education,* May 4, 1994, A24. *See also* pp. 208–17.

41. C. Leatherman, "Part-Timers Continue to Replace Full-Timers on College Faculties," *Chronicle of Higher Education,* January 28, 2000, A18; National Center for Education Statistics, "Fall Staff in Postsecondary Institutions, 1997" (NCES 2000-164), November 1999, table B-1.

42. *See, e.g.,* J. Berger, "After Her Ph.D., the Scavenger's Life; Trying to Turn a Patchwork of Part-Time Jobs into an Academic Career," *New York Times,* March 8, 1998, 1:35; P. Lesko, "What Scholarly Associations Should Do to Stop the Exploitation of Adjuncts," *Chronicle of Higher Education,* December 15,

1995, B3; American Association of State Colleges and Universities, *Facing Change: Building the Faculty of the Future* (1999), 44 (recommending, inter alia, that part-time faculty be "compensated equitably relative to the institution's full-time faculty" and that all non-tenure-track instructors be provided with "benefits, support services, and opportunities for career advancement and collegial participation . . . whenever feasible"); and C. Leatherman, "Part-Time Faculty Members in California Rally over Pay Disparities," *Chronicle of Higher Education On-Line,* December 13, 1999.

43. C. Leatherman, "Use of Non-Tenure-Track Faculty Members Is a Long-Term Trend, Study Finds," *Chronicle of Higher Education On-Line,* April 5, 1999.

44. R. Wilson, "Contracts Replace the Tenure Track for a Growing Number of Professors," *Chronicle of Higher Education On-Line,* June 12, 1998. The National Center for Education Statistics reported that 51% of all full-time faculty hired in 1995 were not on a tenure track. A. Schneider, "More Professors Are Working Part Time, and More Teach at 2-Year Colleges," *Chronicle of Higher Education,* March 13, 1998, A14, cited in n. 41.

45. Wilson, "Contracts Replace the Tenure Track," cited in n. 44; M. Cage, "New Fla. University to Offer Professors Alternative to Tenure," *Chronicle of Higher Education,* June 2, 1995, A15.

46. "Boston U. Management School Pays New Professors More if They Work under Contract," *Chronicle of Higher Education,* July 17, 1998, A14.

47. K. Haworth, "Faculty Members at Philadelphia Textile Raise Concern over Non-Tenure Contracts," *Chronicle of Higher Education On-Line,* May 5, 1998; Wilson, "Contracts Replace the Tenure Track," cited in n. 44.

48. D. Magner, "The Right Conditions May Lure Scholars to Jobs off the Tenure Track, Study Finds," *Chronicle of Higher Education,* April 7, 2000, A20 (Harvard University Project on Faculty Appointments data show that new and prospective faculty still strongly prefer to be on the tenure track, but also give considerable weight to geographic location and mix of research and teaching).

49. *Faculty Tenure,* cited in n. 15, at 16–19.

50. Leatherman, "Use of Non-Tenure-Track Faculty," cited in n. 43.

51. D. Magner, "North Dakota Revises Tenure Code to Allow Professors to Emphasize Teaching," *Chronicle of Higher Education,* July 12, 1996, A16.

52. With the rise of managed care, many faculty members' clinical income is dropping. Predictably, this has led to concern about tenure status being uncoupled from the maintenance of current salary levels. W. Tierney, "The End of Medical Tenure As We Know It," 85 *Academe* 38 (November–December 1999).

53. New York City Human Rights Law, cited in chap. 1, n. 17. But note that even local nondiscrimination law may be trumped by higher authorities. In late 1999 Pennsylvania passed legislation exempting state colleges from municipal ordinances mandating the provision of health care benefits to same-sex partners of employees. W. Weissert, "Pennsylvania Measure May Squelch U. of Pitts-

burgh Debate over Benefits to Gay Partners," *Chronicle of Higher Education On-Line,* November 18, 1999.

54. 42 U.S.C. §2000e et seq.

55. *See, e.g., Whiting v. Jackson State Univ.,* 616 F.2d 116 (5th Cir. 1980) (historically black institution discriminates against white professor); and D. Magner, "Men on the Firing Line," *Chronicle of Higher Education,* October 20, 1995, A17 (EEOC finds cause to sue when St. Bonaventure University lays off male faculty to preserve female faculty jobs).

56. 411 U.S. 792 (1973).

57. In technical legal terms, this is called demonstrating that the plaintiff belongs to a "protected classification" under the law. Here, the classifications are enormously broad.

58. *Texas Dept. of Community Affairs v. Burdine,* 450 U.S. 248, 254–55 (1981) (quote on 254).

59. *St. Mary's Honor Center v. Hicks,* 509 U.S. 502, 515 (1993). In *St. Mary's,* a 5-4 majority of the Supreme Court held that Title VII plaintiffs cannot prevail merely by demonstrating that the employer's stated reasons were spurious. They must still prove that the employer acted from a discriminatory motive.

60. 42 U.S.C. §2000e-2(a)(2) declares that an employer may not "limit, segregate or classify his employees or applicants for employment" in ways that foreclose opportunities on the basis of race, color, religion, sex, or national origin.

61. *See, e.g., Griggs v. Duke Power,* 401 U.S. 424 (1971) (striking down an employer's use of intelligence and aptitude tests that operated to disqualify black applicants).

62. 455 F. Supp. 1102, 1126 (D. Del. 1978), *aff'd on other grounds,* 601 F.2d 76 (3rd Cir. 1979).

63. 42 U.S.C. §2000e-2(h).

64. 42 U.S.C. §2000e-2(e)(1).

65. *See, e.g., Robino v. Iranon,* 145 F.3d 1109 (9th Cir. 1998) (gender was a bona fide occupational qualification under Title VII for several designated guard positions at a women's prison).

66. 42 U.S.C. §§2000e-1(a) and 2000e-2(e)(2). *See* p. 121.

67. If the claim was first filed with a state or local civil rights agency, the filing deadline is extended to the earlier of 300 days or 30 days after that first claim has been terminated. 42 U.S.C. §2000e-5(e)(1).

68. *See* pp. 152–54.

69. *Kunda,* cited in n. 2.

70. *Brown,* cited in n. 21.

71. Ibid., at 344 n. 6.

72. Ibid., at 349 (President Silber had called the English department a "damn matriarchy," and said to another female tenure candidate "your husband is a parachute, so why are you worried[?]").

73. Ibid., at 347.

74. 941 F.2d 154 (3rd Cir. 1991), *cert. denied,* 502 U.S. 1066 (1992).

75. Ibid., at 177–80. For another example of a court awarding promotion to full professor as a remedy in a Title VII case, see *Jew v. Univ. of Iowa,* 749 F. Supp. 946, 960–63 (S.D. Iowa 1990) (court concludes, without much discussion, that it would be unreasonable to conduct a de novo promotion review seven years later).

76. Yet if a provost trained in, say, economics can confidently evaluate the tenure file of a microbiologist, placing (as central administrators and institution-wide personnel committees do) considerable weight on assessments solicited from outside experts, cannot judges and investigators do likewise?

77. 656 F.2d 1337, 1343 (9th Cir. 1981), *cert. denied,* 459 U.S. 823 (1982).

78. 4 F. Supp. 2d 224, 239 n. 18 (S.D.N.Y. 1998).

79. C. Leatherman, "Credentials on Trial," *Chronicle of Higher Education,* February 3, 1995, A14 (describing the fallout from a sex and age discrimination suit in Vassar's biology department).

80. 42 U.S.C. §2000d.

81. Indeed, there are occasional instances of colleges that refuse all federal funding, including financial aid to students, in order to preserve their autonomy. *See, e.g.* J. Nicklin, "Hillsdale College Stands Out for Refusing Federal Money," *Chronicle of Higher Education,* March 1, 1996, A30.

82. 20 U.S.C. §1687.

83. 42 U.S.C. §2000d-3.

84. *See, e.g., United States v. Fordice,* cited in chap. 1, n. 4.

85. While a funding cut-off is legally possible, enforcement agencies are most unlikely to resort to such a drastic remedy. Instead, compliance will be achieved through more gentle pressure (including the prospect of adverse publicity), backed by the threat of litigation.

86. 20 U.S.C. §1681(a).

87. *See, e.g., Cohen v. Brown Univ.,* 879 F. Supp. 185 (D. R. I. 1995), *affirmed in part, reversed in part,* 101 F.3d 155 (1st Cir. 1996); W. Suggs, "Colleges Consider Fairness of Cutting Men's Teams to Comply with Title IX," *Chronicle of Higher Education,* February 19, 1999, A53.

88. 20 U.S.C. §1681(a)(3).

89. 20 U.S.C. §1681(a)(1).

90. 20 U.S.C. §1681(a)(6)(a).

91. 34 C.F.R. §106.61.

92. 503 U.S. 60 (1992).

93. Private causes of action under Title IX were approved in *Cannon v. Univ. of Chicago,* 441 U.S. 677 (1979).

94. 66 F.3d 751, 753 (5th Cir. 1995), *cert. denied,* 519 U.S. 947 (1996).

95. 29 U.S.C. §621 et seq.

96. 29 U.S.C. §623(f)(1).

97. *See* "Chicano-Studies Professor Wins Money, but Not Job," *Chronicle of Higher Education,* February 9, 1996, A6 (age discrimination victim gets damages in lieu of court-ordered appointment at different institution). *But see Leftwich v. Harris-Stowe College,* 702 F.2d 686 (8th Cir. 1983) (ADEA plaintiff who lost tenured post in institutional "restructuring" reinstated with tenure at new incarnation of college).

98. 710 F.2d 1091 (5th Cir. 1983).

99. 29 U.S.C. §623(f)(3).

100. One of the ADEA's few remaining exceptions authorizes mandatory retirement for appointed public officials at the "policymaking level." 29 U.S.C. §630(f). On a public college or university campus, this would probably apply to the president (*see E.E.O.C. v. Bd. of Trustees of Wayne County Community College,* 723 F.2d 509 [6th Cir. 1983]), but no one else.

101. With the end of uncapping, colleges and universities have turned to other mechanisms to achieve a healthy level of faculty turnover, thereby continually reanimating the institution's intellectual climate and (of course) saving money. Chief among these have been early retirement incentive plans. While the legality of particular plans and the tax and benefit consequences of early retirement for individual faculty are highly technical matters beyond the scope of this volume, a couple of general points about such packages are in order.

First, early retirement plans must be carefully structured to avoid discriminating against persons aged 40 or older in violation of the ADEA. However, recent amendments to that statute explicitly authorize higher education institutions to offer plans that target supplemental benefits (beyond those included in the regular retirement or severance package) to tenured faculty of specified ages. Under lawful plans, retirement incentives may now be reduced or eliminated based on the age of tenured employees who elect to participate (e.g., more generous inducements to faculty aged 55–59 than those aged 60–65). 29 U.S.C. §623(m).

Second, in crafting early retirement plans, colleges and universities should ideally be creative, offering different options for faculty members' varied interests and needs (e.g., immediate and complete retirement; commitments *to* retire completely in one or two years; scaling back over several years in accordance with a schedule). What the institution must insist upon, however, is sufficient definiteness to permit planning about staffing.

Third, employer institutions would do well to remember that, although faculty care passionately about their personal finances, the ultimate attractiveness of an early retirement package may turn on more intangible items such as whether retired faculty retain an office, a parking space, and library privileges; whether they automatically receive "emeritus" designation; and—very importantly— whether they have appropriate means of maintaining personal ties with colleagues (e.g., receipt of departmental mailings and invitations to events) and intellectual ties to their disciplines. Giving retired faculty the opportunity to teach part time may have great individual and institutional appeal. In appropriate circumstances, it allows a college or university to continue to draw on a unique resource.

102. P. 23.

103. 29 U.S.C. §794(a) (emphasis added).

104. *See* Note, *Americans with Disabilities Act of 1990: Significant Overlap with Section 504 for Colleges and Universities,* 18 J.C. & U.L. 389 (1992).

105. *See, e.g., Southeastern Community College v. Davis,* 442 U.S. 397 (1979).

106. 34 C.F.R. §104.3(k)(1). Section 503 of the act goes even further to impose affirmative action obligations on federal contractors to hire and promote the disabled. 29 U.S.C. §793.

107. 34 C.F.R. §104.12(a).

108. Note, however, that in *Southeastern Community College,* cited in n. 105, the Supreme Court read this "reasonable accommodation" requirement quite narrowly.

109. *School Bd. of Nassau County v. Arline,* 480 U.S. 273 (1987) (TB is disability under §504); S. Jaschik, "U.S. Charges University with Firing Instructor for Having AIDS," *Chronicle of Higher Education,* May 11, 1994, A30 (EEOC sues Campbell University under ADA).

110. While alcoholism qualifies as a disability, employers can still prohibit intoxication on the job and hold alcoholics to the same performance standards as other employees. Disability discrimination laws would not cover current abusers of illegal drugs.

111. 527 U.S. 471 (1999). *See also Murphy v. United Parcel Service,* 527 U.S. 516 (1999) (hypertension not a disability because plaintiff functioned normally when medicated).

112. *Sutton, Murphy,* both cited in n. 111.

113. 42 U.S.C. §12101 et seq.

114. Because its definitions of "state and local government" and places of "public accommodation" include, respectively, public and then private colleges and universities, the ADA also protects the rights of disabled students.

115. 42 U.S.C. §12111(8).

116. 42 U.S.C. §12112(b)(4).

117. 42 U.S.C. §12112(b)(5)(A).

118. *Bd. of Trustees of Univ. of Ala.,* cited in chap. 1, n. 80. Only appropriate remedial legislation under §5 of the Fourteenth Amendment can abrogate the states' sovereign immunity.

119. 30 Fed. Reg. 12319 (as amended by Executive Order 11375, 32 Fed. Reg. 14303).

120. 29 U.S.C. §206(d) (prohibits sex discrimination in compensation).

121. 42 U.S.C. §6101 et seq. (prohibits age discrimination in federally funded programs).

122.   38 U.S.C. §4212 (affirmative action for Vietnam veterans and disabled veterans from other wars).

123.   42 U.S.C. §1981 (civil rights statute ensuring citizens' right, inter alia, to make and enforce contracts, which has been interpreted to reach private discrimination).

124.   42 U.S.C. §1983 (reaches discrimination carried out "under color of" state law).

125.   Gays and lesbians are probably the largest and most vulnerable minority group lacking federal protected classification status. As noted above, though, many states and localities prohibit discrimination on the basis of sexual orientation. In addition, growing numbers of colleges and universities have *institutional* nondiscrimination policies—often covering sexual orientation as well as the standard federal categories—that afford gays and lesbians protection against unfair employment decisions or a hostile campus environment. (*See, e.g., Penn Handbook,* cited in chap. 2, n. 26, "Equal Opportunity/Affirmative Action Policy," §I.J.1, and discussion of sexual harassment, pp. 217–26.) In recent years (in response to claims that local antidiscrimination laws were being violated, or in order to be equitable and retain valued employees) a substantial number of colleges and universities have changed their benefits policies to make domestic partners of gay and lesbian employees eligible for the same health insurance and other benefits extended to spouses (*see, e.g.,* University of Chicago Benefits Policy [on file with author]). Other institutions have modified graduate student housing rules to allow same-sex couples the same rights as married couples, or sought to allow same-sex commitment ceremonies in university chapels. "Emory Offers a Narrow Way for Gay Marriages," *New York Times,* November 15, 1997, A18. At institutions and in jurisdictions lacking any such protections, though, the status of gay or lesbian employees remains tenuous. K. Mangan, "University Fires Homosexual Theater Director," *Chronicle of Higher Education,* May 19, 1995, A26 (Abilene Christian University discharges gay man).

126.   U.S. Const. Amend. XIV ("no State shall . . . deny to any person within its jurisdiction the equal protection of the laws").

127.   Kaplin & Lee, cited in introduction, n. 2, at 230–33, citing *Washington v. Davis,* 426 U.S. 229 (1976) on burden of proof.

128.   G. LaNoue & B. Lee, *Academics in Court: The Consequences of Faculty Discrimination Litigation* (University of Michigan Press: 1987), 30. Plaintiffs won 34 of 160 cases that reached the merits.

129.   Ibid., at 24, 31.

130.   Ibid., at 24; Leap, cited in n. 15, at 32. Faculty age discrimination cases are more likely to involve pay inequities with junior colleagues than tenure or job security. *See, e.g., Davidson v. Western Illinois Univ.,* 920 F.2d 441 (7th Cir. 1990) (upholding system of market-based individual pay raises).

131.   LaNoue & Lee, cited in n. 128, at 34.

132. Ibid., at 224 (median reported cost of $52,000 for plaintiffs' attorneys' fees).

133. D. Blum, "10 Years Later, Questions Abound over Minnesota Sex-Bias Settlement," *Chronicle of Higher Education,* June 13, 1990, A13.

134. LaNoue & Lee, cited in n. 128, at 224–26.

135. For the remainder of this section, the terms *minority* and *minorities* include women faculty and students in disciplines (such as physics) where they are underrepresented, as well as members of racial and ethnic minorities.

136. A. Schneider, "Union College Limits Search for 4 New Faculty Slots to Black and Hispanic Scholars," *Chronicle of Higher Education,* April 16, 1999. For reasons discussed infra, such a quota system is most likely illegal under Titles VI and VII.

137. E.g., the "Michigan Mandate," the "Madison Plan," and the University of California's "Targets of Opportunity" program.

138. Note, however, that non–state actors are still subject to claims of reverse discrimination under Titles VI, VII, IX, and other nondiscrimination statutes. If courts follow Equal Protection Clause standards and precedent in adjudicating such claims, private-sphere affirmative action will be as open to attack as its public counterpart.

139. 515 U.S. 200 (1995). *Adarand* invalidated a minority set-aside program in federal construction contracts, but the standard of review it articulates would clearly apply to affirmative action in hiring.

140. Justice Powell's opinion in *Bakke v. Regents of Univ. of California,* 438 U.S. 265, 311 (1978), found that seeking the educational benefits that flow from a diverse student (and presumably also faculty) body *was* a compelling state interest. *Bakke* was not an employment case, however, and Powell's opinion did not command a majority of the Court on all points.

141. *Wygant v. Jackson Bd. of Educ.,* 476 U.S. 267 (1986).

142. 78 F.3d 932 (5th Cir. 1996), *cert. denied,* 518 U.S. 1033 (1996).

143. *United Steelworkers v. Weber,* 443 U.S. 193, 209 (1979).

144. *But see Hill v. Ross,* 183 F.3d 586 (7th Cir. 1999), discussed infra, for a statistical argument casting doubt on the use of departmental hiring pools as a valid basis for affirmative action plans.

145. *United Steelworkers,* cited in n. 143, at 208.

146. *Bakke,* cited in n. 140.

147. They may also lack the legal standing to sue, if they have suffered no harm themselves.

148. Even institutional affirmative action plans are most unlikely to state that clear preferences will be given to minority candidates.

149. 930 P.2d 730, 735 (Nev. 1997), *cert. denied,* 523 U.S. 1004 (1998).

150. Ibid.

151. *Wilson v. State Personnel Bd.,* No. 96CS01082, slip op. (Cal. Super. Ct. Sacramento County Nov. 30, 1998).

152. P. Schmidt, "Cal. Vote to Ban Racial Preferences Sparks Lawsuits, Protests," *Chronicle of Higher Education,* November 15, 1996, A35 and "California Judge Upholds Law Allowing 2-Year Colleges to Use Hiring Preferences," *Chronicle of Higher Education,* December 11, 1998, A52.

153. *Ready v. Bd. of Regents,* No. 97-C-0310-C (W.D. Wis., July 28, 1999), *appeal dismissed,* December 27, 1999; A. Schneider, "Federal Judge Rejects Race-Based Hiring Decision at U. of Wisconsin at La Crosse," *Chronicle of Higher Education On-Line,* July 30, 1999.

154. *Hill v. Ross,* cited in n. 144. Note that despite their anti-affirmative-action outcomes, in neither of these Wisconsin cases was the campus's plan invalidated.

155. Ibid., at 591–92, quote on 592.

156. J. Selingo, "U. of Texas Ends Minority-Hiring Plan," *Chronicle of Higher Education,* January 15, 1999, A38.

157. S. Nasar, "New Breed of College All-Star; Columbia Pays Top Dollar for Economics Heavy Hitter," *New York Times,* April 8, 1998, D1; A. Schneider, "Recruiting Academic Stars: New Tactics in an Old Game," *Chronicle of Higher Education,* May 29, 1998, A12.

158. R. Wilson, "By the Numbers," *Chronicle of Higher Education,* June 30, 1995, A15 (Mercy College links salaries to enrollment for one year); K. Magnan, "Georgetown U. Kills Controversial Program for Setting Medical-Faculty Salaries," *Chronicle of Higher Education On-Line,* March 1, 1999 (plan in effect for almost two years had tied salaries to amount of grants received).

159. K. Lively, "Northwestern Professor Loses Suit over Pay," *Chronicle of Higher Education,* July 31, 1998, A9.

160. *See, e.g.,* A. Schneider, "Law and Finance Professors Are Top Earners in Academe, Survey Finds," *Chronicle of Higher Education,* May 28, 1999, A14 (results of annual survey by College and University Personnel Association).

161. 15 U.S.C. §1. For the relevance of the Sherman Act to nonprofits in general and universities in particular, *see Goldfarb v. Virginia State Bar,* 421 U.S. 773 (1975); and *NCAA v. Bd. of Regents of Univ. of Oklahoma,* 468 U.S. 85 (1984).

162. May 22, 1991, consent decree between the United States and the Ivy League institutions, §IV(I) (on file with author). The ninth institution, MIT, chose to litigate the case and ultimately prevailed (*see United States v. Brown Univ. et al.,* 5 F.3d 658 [3rd Cir. 1993]). However, the subsequent trial and judicial opinions did not address the faculty salary issue.

163. R. Hurd, A. Foster & B. Johnson, *Directory of Faculty Contracts and Bargaining Agents in Institutions of Higher Education* (National Center for the Study of Collective Bargaining in Higher Education and the Professions: 1997), v. Ninety-six percent of unionized faculty are at public institutions, with by far the largest geographic concentrations in California and New York. Ibid., at ix–x.

164. *N.L.R.B. v. Yeshiva Univ.,* 444 U.S. 672 (1980).

165. *See, e.g.,* C. Leatherman & D. Magner, "Faculty and Graduate-Student Strife over Job Issues Flares on Many Campuses," *Chronicle of Higher Education,* November 29, 1996, A12 (describing conference of students, faculty, and union activists).

166. 29 U.S.C. §151 et seq.

167. *Bayamon,* cited in chap. 4, n. 79.

168. 440 U.S. 490 (1979).

169. *Bayamon,* cited in chap. 4, n. 79, at 402. However, in 2000 the NLRB let stand a ruling by one of its regional offices that faculty at Manhattan College could unionize in part because the level of religious control over that institution fell below the protective threshold of *Catholic Bishop.* While Manhattan faculty ultimately voted not to unionize, this holding may lead to further organizing at private denominational—and secular—institutions. C. Leatherman, "NLRB Lets Stand a Decision Allowing Professors at a Private College to Unionize," *Chronicle of Higher Education,* July 7, 2000, A14; and C. Leatherman, "Union Movement at Private Colleges Awakens after a 20-Year Slumber," *Chronicle of Higher Education,* January 21, 2000, A16.

170. *Directory of Faculty Contracts and Bargaining Agents,* cited in n. 163, at 135. States allowing collective bargaining are Alabama, Alaska, Arizona, California, Connecticut, Delaware, Florida, Hawaii, Illinois, Indiana, Iowa, Kansas, Maine, Maryland, Massachusetts, Michigan, Minnesota, Missouri, Montana, Nebraska, Nevada, New Hampshire, New Jersey, New Mexico, New York, Ohio, Oregon, Pennsylvania, Rhode Island, South Dakota, Vermont, Washington, and Wisconsin.

171. Cal. Gov. Code §§3562(q) and (r). These excluded matters remain the province of academic senates and governing boards.

172. *See* NY CLS Civ S §210.

173. *Directory of Faculty Contracts and Bargaining Agents,* cited in n. 163, at vii. *See also* C. Leatherman, "AAUP Reaches Out and Takes Sides," *Chronicle of Higher Education,* June 23, 2000, A16 (AAUP's new, more activist leadership aligning itself with the union movement). (This article describes the AAUP's collective bargaining arm as having 21,700 members in over 70 units. Ibid., at A16, A19.)

174. *See, e.g.,* the identical definitions of "professional employees" eligible to form unions under California higher education labor law (Cal. Gov. Code §§3562[o]) and the NLRA (29 U.S.C. §152[12]). Because state and federal authorities often approach and resolve key legal issues about faculty unionization in the same way, the following discussion of such issues focuses on federal statute and precedent.

175. The key portions of the definition cover persons whose work is "predominantly intellectual and varied in character . . . involving the consistent exercise of discretion and judgment . . . [and] requiring knowledge of an advanced

type in a field of science or learning customarily acquired by a prolonged course of specialized intellectual instruction and study in an institution of higher learning or a hospital." 29 U.S.C. §152(12).

176. 29 U.S.C. §152(11).

177. *N.L.R.B. v. Bell Aerospace,* 416 U.S. 267, 288 (1974) (quoting *Palace Laundry Dry Cleaning Corp.,* 75 N.L.R.B. 320, 323 n. 4 [1947]).

178. D. Rabban, *Distinguishing Excluded Managers from Covered Professionals under the NLRA,* 89 Colum. L. Rev. 1775, 1822 (1989).

179. *Yeshiva,* cited in n. 164, at 688. Earlier in this chapter (pp. 143–45) we considered how academic personnel decisions balance the need for institutional versus individual faculty autonomy. Using this same conceptual lens, *Yeshiva* favors institutional over personal interests. The pursuit of the university's academic objectives—themselves forged by the faculty as a collective—trumped professors' individual freedom, such that they were not accorded the same bargaining rights as other employees.

180. Ibid., at 686. In contrast, the minority opinion argues that traditional notions of collegial governance grew obsolete as higher education became big business and that actual control over institutions has passed from faculty to professional administrators. Ibid., at 702–3 (Brennan, J., dissenting).

181. Ibid., at 686 n. 23. *See also* Rabban, cited in n. 178, at 1808 n. 140.

182. *Boston Univ. Chapter, AAUP v. N.L.R.B.,* 835 F.2d 399, 402 (1st Cir. 1987) (quoting *Yeshiva,* cited in n. 164, at 686).

183. C. Leatherman, "A Private College's Professiors Try for a Unionizing Breakthrough," *Chronicle of Higher Education,* December 15, 2000, A12. Whenever bargaining rights are granted to faculty at a private college or university, union advocates herald the demise of *Yeshiva,* as with the recent holding by an NLRB regional director that faculty at Manhattan College were not managerial employees. Leatherman, "Union Movement at Private Colleges Awakens," cited in n. 169.

184. Rabban, cited in n. 178, at 1806 n. 132, 1827.

185. *Lehnert v. Ferris Faculty Association,* 500 U.S. 507 (1991).

186. 29 U.S.C. §158(d).

187. Thus, precise steps in the tenure process might be mandatory, but not the adoption of financial or administrative policies that will surely affect awards of tenure. *See Assn. of N.J. State College Faculties v. Dungan,* 64 N.J. 338, 316 A.2d 425 (1974) (State Board policies to limit the proportion of tenured faculty [e.g., calling for institution-specific goals and post-tenure review] not mandatorily negotiable).

188. D. Rabban, *Can American Labor Law Accommodate Collective Bargaining by Professional Employees,* 99 Yale L.J. 689, 705 (1990). In criticizing the entire mandatory/permissive framework, Rabban relies on both high school and university cases.

189. *St. Clare's Hospital and Health Center,* 229 N.L.R.B. 1000, 1002 (1977), *overruled* in *Boston Medical Center Corp.,* 1999 NLRB LEXIS 821 (Nov. 26, 1999).

190. S. Smallwood, "Success and New Hurdles for T.A. Unions," *Chronicle of Higher Education,* July 6, 2001, A10 (the totals include the new California unions); C. Leatherman, "Graduate Students Gather to Learn 'Organizing 101,'" *Chronicle of Higher Education,* August 14, 1998, A10–11; C. Leatherman, "Teaching Assistants Plan Showdown over Unionization," *Chronicle of Higher Education,* November 13, 1998, A10; "Cal. Board Says T.A.'s Can Bargain Collectively," *Chronicle of Higher Education,* January 8, 1999, A16; C. Leatherman, "U. of California Opens Door to Recognition of Teaching Assistants' Union," *Chronicle of Higher Education,* March 26, 1999, A18; and C. Leatherman, "Teaching Assistants on 2 More U. of California Campuses Vote to Unionize," *Chronicle of Higher Education On-Line,* June 22, 1999.

191. *New York University,* 2000 NLRB LEXIS 748 (Oct. 31, 2000); K. Arenson, "U.S. Panel Allows Union Organizing by Postgraduates," *New York Times,* November 1, 2000, A1; S. Smallwood, "A Big Breakthrough for T.A. Unions," *Chronicle of Higher Education,* March 16, 2001, A10.

192. *The Leland Stanford Junior University,* 214 N.L.R.B. 621, 621 (1974). *See also Adelphi Univ.,* 195 N.L.R.B. 639 (1972) (research and teaching assistants are fundamentally students).

193. *St. Clare's Hospital,* cited in n. 189, at 1002.

194. C. Leatherman & D. Magner, "Faculty and Graduate-Student Strife over Job Issues Flares on Many Campuses," *Chronicle of Higher Education,* November 29, 1996, A12.

195. *Boston Medical Center,* cited in n. 189, reversing *Cedars-Sinai Medical Center,* 223 N.L.R.B. 251 (1976) and *St. Clare's Hospital,* cited in n. 189. In the public sector, interns and residents in California also just won the right to bargain collectively. K. Mangan, "California Labor Ruling Permits Doctors-in-Training to Vote on Unionization," *Chronicle of Higher Education On-Line,* November 17, 1999.

196. *Boston Medical Center,* cited in n. 189, at 44–45.

197. *New York University,* cited in n. 191, at 7.

198. Ibid., at 20.

199. The following discussion of the pros and cons of graduate student unionization draws heavily on materials and arguments developed by both sides in the ongoing debate over union recognition at Yale. Many of these items may be found at <http://www.yale.edu/opa/gradschool/gradschool.html>.

200. M. Cage, "Teaching Assistants Organize," *Chronicle of Higher Education,* May 26, 1995, A15, A16 (Kansas labor board finds graduate students are "increasingly teaching outside their area of study"); S. Sterngold, "Betwixt and Between," *New York Times Education Life Supplement,* August 1, 1999, 4A, 17

(profiling UCLA graduate student in economic geography who must teach undergraduate course in *bio*geography).

201. I would expect more support for unions among Ph.D. students in the humanities and social sciences than among students in the physical and biological sciences. Generally, the former work more independently (which could cut against a desire for collective bargaining) but have long times-to-degree and face a savage job market (which cut strongly in favor of unionization). *See, e.g.,* S. Boxer, "Professors or Proletarians? A Test for Downtrodden Academics," *New York Times,* January 16, 1999. In contrast, most "hard science" students are part of organized research groups led by senior faculty. While enjoying less freedom in the selection and pursuit of research topics (which could lead to feelings of powerlessness and support for unionization), they are less isolated or alienated, earn their doctorates faster, and foresee robust academic and nonacademic career options (all of which should reduce union sentiment). *See* W. Bowen & N. Rudenstine, *In Pursuit of the Ph.D.* (Princeton University Press: 1992) for a comprehensive analysis of doctoral student experiences.

202. T. Joseph & J. Curtiss, "Why Professors Should Support Graduate-Student Unions," *Chronicle of Higher Education,* February 21, 1997, B6.

203. T. Applequist, "Graduate Students Are Not Employees," *Chronicle of Higher Education,* April 18, 1997, B6.

204. A. Richard to S. Hockfield, August 19, 1998, about likely effects of union recognition at Yale (on file with author).

205. *See, e.g.,* C. Leatherman, "For T.A.'s, Winning the Right to Unionize Is Only Half the Battle," *Chronicle of Higher Education,* March 31, 2000, A16 (detailing lengthy and fractious contract negotiations between the University of California and its new graduate student union). The counterargument, of course, is that with more generous stipends obtained through unionization, students can complete their degrees faster. In any event, all parties should recognize that initial contract negotiations are likely to be protracted, since there is scant case law or other direct legal guidance on what constitutes bargainable "terms or conditions of employment" for graduate students.

206. Of course, as union advocates will rightly observe, safeguards are also being provided to *legitimate* claims.

207. Letter from A. Richard, cited in n. 204.

208. *See, e.g.,* M. Werner, "Former Grad Student Sues CU," *Ithaca Journal,* March 27, 1999, 1A (Cornell student alleges that faculty member on her graduate committee took credit for her work).

209. *But see* A. Schneider, "9 of 10 Professors Say Grad-Student Unions Don't Strain Advisor-Advisee Ties," *Chronicle of Higher Education On-Line,* October 22, 1999 (faculty at institutions with unions report that collective bargaining does not inhibit graduate instruction or advising).

210. Medical schools and teaching hospitals have made parallel arguments in

opposing unions of interns and residents (i.e., labor contracts and outside arbitrators should not override faculty judgments on the content, duration, and intensity of professional training). K. Mangan, "Academic Medicine Becomes a Target for Labor Organizing," *Chronicle of Higher Education*, August 6, 1999, A14.

211. Letter from A. Richard, cited in n. 204.

212. "Frequently Asked Questions," Yale Web site, cited in n. 199. This figure will be rising in the future.

213. *Yale University*, 1999 NLRB LEXIS 820 (Nov. 29,1999).

214. A. Richard to Graduate School Faculty and Students, March 29, 2000, about settlement agreement (on file with author).

215. *New York University*, No. 2-RC-22082 (NLRB Region 2 April 3, 2000) at 26.

216. *New York University*, cited in n. 191, at 7.

217. Ibid., at 10, 12.

218. Ibid., at 17, citing *Univ, of Pa.*, cited in n. 23.

219. *New York University*, cited in n. 191, at 16–17, quoting *Boston Medical Center*, cited in n. 189.

220. *New York University*, cited in n. 215, at 33.

221. Ibid. (emphasis added).

222. *New York University*, cited in n. 191, at 19.

223. *See* pp. 239–43, 248–49 for a discussion of the due process afforded professors in contract nonrenewals.

224. C. Licata & J. Morreale, "Post-Tenure Review: Policies, Practices, Precautions," AAHE New Pathways Working Paper Series, no. 12, American Association for Higher Education, Washington, D.C., 1997, 2. In 1989, only 3 of the 46 institutions comprising the Association of American Universities had post-tenure review policies. Ibid.

225. D. Magner, "Beyond Tenure," *Chronicle of Higher Education*, July 21, 1995, A13. States where one or more public colleges or universities have adopted post-tenure include Colorado, Florida, Hawaii, Iowa, Kansas, Kentucky, Minnesota, Montana, Nebraska, North Dakota, Oregon, Pennsylvania, South Carolina, Texas, Virginia, and Wisconsin.

226. AAUP, "Post-Tenure Review: An AAUP Response," June 1998 ("AAUP Post-Tenure Review"), at 3.

227. Ibid., at 7.

228. "U. of Ky. Hopes to Inspire Lazy Professors," *Chronicle of Higher Education*, April 20, 1994, A19; J. Basinger, "U. of South Carolina Starts Post-Tenure Reviews to Comply with State Law," *Chronicle of Higher Education*, May 29, 1998, A15.

229. "AAUP Post-Tenure Review," cited in n. 226, at 9.

230. Ibid., at 4.

231. Ibid., at 3.

232. Note that even faculty who are not themselves the subject of a triggered post-tenure review will be mindful that they could be next. Depending on one's point of view, this *in terrorem* effect either encourages quality performance or is needlessly debilitating.

233. "AAUP Post-Tenure Review," cited in n. 226, at 2.

234. Ibid., at 3.

235. R. Chait, "Ideas in Incubation: Three Possible Modifications to Traditional Tenure Practices," AAHE New Pathways Working Paper Series, no. 9, American Association for Higher Education, Washington, D.C., 1998, at 15.

236. Ibid., at 19.

237. Ibid.

238. Ibid., at 20.

239. AAUP, "1940 Statement," cited in chap. 2, n. 4, at 4. Indeed, from a narrow employee-relations perspective, tenure—stripped to its essentials—has been described as merely a procedural protection or "statement of formal assurance that thereafter the individual's professional security and academic freedom will not be placed in question without the observance of full academic due process." W. Van Alstyne, "Tenure: A Summary, Explanation, and 'Defense,'" *AAUP Bulletin* 57 (autumn 1971): 328, quote on 330.

240. *See* p. 170.

241. AAUP, "Statement on Procedural Standards in Faculty Dismissal Proceedings," in *Policy Documents & Reports* (AAUP: 1995) ("AAUP Standards"), at 12.

242. *Morris v. Clifford,* 903 F.2d 574, 576 (8th Cir. 1990).

243. *Riggin,* cited in chap. 1, n. 70, at 627.

244. *See, e.g.,* Cal. Ed Code §89535.

245. AAUP, "Recommended Institutional Regulations on Academic Freedom and Tenure," in *Policy Documents & Reports* (AAUP: 1995) ("AAUP RIR"), §5(a), at 26.

246. *Adamian,* cited in chap. 5, n. 26, at 932.

247. *Riggin,* cited in chap. 1 n. 70.

248. *King v. Univ. of Minnesota,* 774 F.2d 224 (8th Cir. 1985), *cert. denied,* 475 U.S. 1095 (1986); *Agarwal v. Univ. of Minnesota,* 788 F.2d 504 (8th Cir. 1986); *Jawa,* cited in chap. 3, n. 25; *Chung v. Park,* 377 F. Supp. 524 (M.D. Pa. 1974), *aff'd,* 514 F.2d 382 (3rd Cir. 1975), *cert. denied,* 423 U.S. 948 (1975); *Potemra v. Ping,* 462 F. Supp. 328 (S.D. Ohio 1978), *cert. denied,* 444 U.S. 872 (1979).

249. *Jawa,* cited in chap. 3, n. 25.

250. Ibid.

251. *King,* cited in n. 248.

252. Pp. 171–73.

253. "Professors accept their share of faculty responsibilities for the governance of their institution." AAUP, "Statement on Professional Ethics," in *Policy Documents & Reports* (AAUP: 1995) ("AAUP Ethics Statement"), at 106.

254. *Smith v. Kent State Univ.*, 696 F.2d 476 (6th Cir. 1983); *Riggin,* cited in chap. 1, n. 70; *Jawa,* cited in chap. 3, n. 25.

255. *Josberger v. Univ. of Tennessee,* 706 S.W. 2d 300 (Tenn. Ct. App. 1985).

256. *Shaw v. Bd. of Trustees,* 549 F.2d 929 (4th Cir. 1976).

257. *Jawa,* cited in chap. 3, n. 25.

258. *Bates v. Sponberg,* 547 F.2d 325 (6th Cir. 1976) (research reports); *Garrett v. Mathews,* 474 F. Supp. 594 (N.D. Ala. 1979), *aff'd,* 625 F.2d 658 (5th Cir. 1980) (publications list; tenure revocation rather than termination).

259. *King,* cited in n. 248; *Stastny,* cited in chap. 3, n. 25.

260. *Riggin,* cited in chap. 1, n. 70.

261. *Jawa,* cited in chap. 3, n. 25; *Garrett,* cited in n. 258.

262. *Jawa,* cited in chap. 3, n. 25; *Potemra,* cited in n. 248.

263. 142 F.3d 813 (5th Cir. 1998), *cert. denied,* 525 U.S. 1102 (1999).

264. 692 F. Supp. 930 (N.D. Ind. 1988), *aff'd,* 976 F.2d 735 (7th Cir. 1992). *See also Jawa,* cited in chap. 3, n. 25 (dismissal for fighting with colleagues and administrators that disrupts department); *Adamian v. Lombardi,* 608 F.2d 1224 (9th Cir. 1979), *cert. denied,* 446 U.S. 938 (1980) (termination for leading a protest that disrupts university event and creates risk of violence).

265. *King,* cited in n. 248 (absent from faculty meetings); *Garrett,* cited in n. 258 (ignoring mail).

266. *Chitwood v. Feaster,* 468 F.2d 359, 361 (4th Cir. 1972). *See also* AAUP, "AAUP Ethics Statement," cited in n. 253, at 106 ("in the exchange of criticism and ideas professors show due respect for the opinions of others").

267. T. Lovain, *Grounds for Dismissing Tenured Postsecondary Faculty for Cause,* 10 J.C. & U.L. 419 (1983–84), 427.

268. Pp. 107–16. *See also* Lovain, supra, at 430 (First Amendment does not cover "irresponsible and destructive behavior which threatens the basic educational functions of postsecondary institutions").

269. *Chitwood,* cited in n. 266, at 361(emphasis added).

270. Pp. 71–94.

271. AAUP, "AAUP Ethics Statement," cited in n. 253, at 105.

272. 13 F.3d 1413 (10th Cir. 1993). *See also Newman v. Burgin,* 930 F.2d 955 (1st Cir. 1991) (tenured faculty member publicly censured and barred from certain committees and administrative positions because of plagiarism).

273. *Agarwal,* cited in n. 248.

274. *Barszcz v. Bd. of Trustees,* 400 F. Supp. 675 (N.D. Ill. 1975), *aff'd without opinion,* 539 F.2d 715 (7th Cir. 1976), *cert. denied,* 429 U.S. 1080 (1977) (fired teacher had represented himself as holding a masters degree, including accepting a higher salary consistent with such achievement).

275. 65 Fed. Reg. 76,260–64 (2000) (finalized Dec. 6, 2000). These omnibus regulations supplant the prior system of agency-specific rules. *See, e.g.,* Department of Health and Human Services regulations requiring entities applying for research grants under the Public Health Service Act to have policies and procedures in place to investigate and report alleged or apparent misconduct involving research. 42 C.F.R. §50.101.

276. "Professors make every reasonable effort to foster honest academic conduct and to assure that their evaluations of students reflect each student's true merit." AAUP, "AAUP Ethics Statement," cited in n. 253, at 105.

277. Rutgers's dogged—and ultimately successful—defense of its action is detailed in a series of judicial opinions including *San Filippo v. Bongiovanni*, 961 F.2d 1125 (3rd Cir. 1992), *cert. denied*, 506 U.S. 908 (1992) (published grounds for dismissal not overly vague); and *San Filippo v. Bongiovanni*, 30 F.3d 424 (3rd Cir. 1994), *cert. denied*, 513 U.S. 1082 (1995) (no summary judgment on claim that plaintiff was terminated in retaliation for protected speech).

278. AAUP, "AAUP Ethics Statement," cited in n. 253, at 105.

279. 150 Cal. App. 3d 646, 197 Cal. Rptr. 856 (Cal. Ct. App. 1983).

280. *See* pp. 239–49. Institutions must strike a similar balance in student discipline cases between the need for swift action meant (at least in part) to serve an educational purpose and permitting the criminal process to run its (often-lengthy) course, with heightened and extended risk of campus disruption.

281. 757 F.2d 223, 227 (10th Cir. 1985).

282. 16 Cal. App. 3d 820, 94 Cal. Rptr. 318 (Cal. Ct. App. 1971). *But see Texton v. Hancock*, 359 So. 2d 895 (Fla. Dist. Ct. App. 1st Dist. 1978) (pattern of indiscretions by tenured professor [including blurring the lines of teacher-student authority by swearing, drinking, and talking about sex in front of students] not adequate grounds to dismiss); and 85 Lab. Arb. 687 (BNA) (1985) (faculty member not discharged for soliciting homosexual activity at highway rest stop, as such conduct was insufficiently related to his professional fitness).

283. For a lengthier discussion of sexual harassment and inappropriate romantic relationships between faculty and students, see pp. 217–26.

284. "Academic Freedom and Tenure: The Catholic University of Puerto Rico," 73 *Academe* 33 (May–June 1987).

285. 544 N.W. 2d 32 (Minn. Ct. App. 1996).

286. Ibid., at 37.

287. *Ibid. See also Marks*, cited in chap. 2, n. 150 (NYU professor fired for simultaneously working full time at Fordham).

288. 673 F.2d 266 (9th Cir. 1982) (the opinion does not clearly indicate whether the plaintiff held tenure). *See also Jawa*, cited in chap. 3, n. 25 (one basis for plaintiff's termination was making false accusations against his superiors).

289. *See* pp. 58–59.

290. The "AAUP Ethics Statement," cited in n. 253, at 106, holds that "pro-

fessors give due regard to their paramount responsibilities within their institution in determining the amount and character of work done outside it."

291. *Zahavy,* cited in n. 285, at 37. This is contrary to the AAUP's position, which would require such a link. AAUP, "AAUP RIR," cited in n. 245.

292. A. Franke, "Private Misconduct as Grounds for Dismissal," 76 *Academe* 88 (January–February 1990).

293. Thus, the AAUP's chief counsel has wondered whether "colleges and universities should tolerate a wide range of private viewpoints and behaviors with the assumption that college students are no longer of a tender or highly impressionable age." Ibid.

294. Discharged faculty were deemed both incompetent and insubordinate in *Riggin,* cited in chap. 1, n. 70, and *Jawa,* cited in chap. 3, n. 25.

295. A schema developed by John Braxton and Alan Bayer identifies four domains of faculty misconduct. *Employee misconduct* includes violations of policies or procedures applicable to all staff (e.g., no misappropriation of university resources). *Scholarly misconduct* includes plagiarism, fabricating data, failing to train or supervise students in one's lab, and the misallocation of authorship credit. *Teaching misconduct* includes violations of what Braxton and Bayer deem "inviolable norms" of condescending negativism towards students or colleagues, inattentive course planning, moral turpitude, particularistic grading, personal disregard of students, uncommunicated course details, and uncooperative cynicism, as well as breaches of the "admonitory norms" of advisement negligence, running an authoritarian classroom, inadequate communication, inadequate course design, inconvenience avoidance, instructional narrowness, insufficient syllabus, teaching secrecy, and undermining colleagues. *Service misconduct* includes acts such as not fulfilling committee assignments, not writing a promised letter of recommendation, or failing to attend a professional association meeting after agreeing to participate. Braxton and Bayer argue that while long-established rules prohibit and punish employee misconduct, and while sets of rules have been developed to cover scholarly misconduct (e.g., federal regulations on research fraud), more formal norms or rules and better enforcement of such expectations are badly needed to address teaching misconduct. They argue that service misconduct is not yet taken seriously by the academic community. J. Braxton and A. Bayer, *Faculty Misconduct in Collegiate Teaching* (Johns Hopkins University Press: 1999)

296. Kaplin & Lee, cited in introduction, n. 2, at 277.

297. *Korf v. Ball State Univ.,* 726 F.2d 1222, 1227 (7th Cir. 1984), citing *Meehan v. Macy,* 392 F.2d 822, 835 (D.C. Cir. 1968). *See also Riggin,* cited in chap. 1, n. 70, at 628 (not feasible to formulate specific standards for measuring faculty competence).

298. *San Filippo,* cited in n. 277, at 1137.

299. Ibid., at 1127. Notwithstanding this holding, state-actor colleges and

universities must always guard against faculty discipline policies that are unconstitutionally vague such that reasonable persons must guess at their meaning.

300. Ibid., at 1130.

301. C. Mooney, "33 Days of Hearings, 49 Witnesses, and an 8,000-Page Transcript," *Chronicle of Higher Education,* December 7, 1994, A20. *See also Bates,* cited in n. 258, at 328 (proceedings took approximately 60 hours over 26 sessions); and *Barszcz,* cited in n. 274, at 679 (1,000-page transcript).

302. *McConnell,* cited in chap. 3, n. 30, at 67.

303. 167 Misc. 2d 458 (Sup. Ct. 1995).

304. Pp. 248–49.

305. AAUP, "AAUP Standards," cited in n. 241, at 12.

306. *See, e.g.* the following cases upholding terminations: *Corstvet,* cited in n. 281 (faculty panels would not have terminated plaintiff); *Samaan,* cited in n. 279 (panel only recommended written reprimand); and *Josberger,* cited in n. 255 (faculty panel could not substantiate charge). *See also* K. Haworth, "East Carolina U. Fires Tenured Professor despite Recommendation of Faculty Panel," *Chronicle of Higher Education On-Line,* April 21, 1998. All of this assumes, of course, that the faculty panel has not gone off on a tangent, as sometimes happens, critiquing the text of institutional policies rather than focusing on the facts of the case.

307. AAUP, "AAUP Standards," cited in n. 241, at 12.

308. C. Mooney, "Dismissals 'for Cause,'" *Chronicle of Higher Education,* December 7, 1994, A17, A19.

309. AAUP, "AAUP Ethics Statement," cited in n. 253, at 105–6.

310. P. 169.

311. *Burlington Industries, Inc. v. Ellerth,* 524 U.S. 742, 751 (1998).

312. *Oncale v. Sundowner Offshore Services, Inc.,* 523 U.S. 75 (1998).

313. 526 U.S. 629 (1999) (educational institutions liable for student-on-student sexual harassment under Title IX).

314. It is important to note, however, that in *Burlington,* cited in n. 311, at 753, the Supreme Court cautioned that these categories, while useful in determining whether employees have in fact been on the receiving end of an adverse employment action, are not controlling on the issue of an employer's liability for harassment carried out by its supervisors.

315. *Karibian v. Columbia Univ.,* 14 F.3d 773, 778–79 (2nd Cir. 1994), *cert. denied,* 512 U.S. 1213 (1994).

316. *Lipsett v. Univ. of Puerto Rico,* 864 F.2d 881, 912 (1st Cir. 1988). *See also Alexander v. Yale Univ.,* 631 F.2d 178, 182 (2nd Cir. 1980) ("academic advancement conditioned upon submission to sexual demands constitutes sex discrimination" under Title IX).

317. *Korf,* cited in n. 297.

318. *Lipsett,* cited in n. 316.

319.  59 F.3d 446 (3rd Cir. 1995), *cert. denied,* 516 U.S. 1146 (1996).

320.  892 F. Supp. 746 (E.D. Va. 1995). The faculty member in *Kadiki* also allegedly offered the plaintiff an *A* in the course if she refrained from making a complaint against him. While the court held that this "nonsexual" conduct could not be quid pro quo harassment (id. at 752), I think such an offer is so linked to the purported sexual advances that it would violate Title IX. *See also Levitt v. Univ. of Texas at El Paso,* 759 F.2d 1224 (5th Cir. 1985), *cert. denied,* 474 U.S. 1034 (1985) (tenured faculty member dismissed for making sexual advances to his female students).

321.  There are slight—but legally inconsequential—variations in the regulatory language implementing the two main federal sex discrimination statutes. Thus, OCR's Title IX guidance materials refer to a "hostile or abusive educational environment" (62 Fed. Reg. 12033, 12038 [1997]), while the EEOC's Title VII regulations prohibit an "intimidating, hostile, or offensive working environment." 29 C.F.R. 1604.11(a). (This latter language is the etymological ancestor of the first generation of campus hate speech codes. *See, e.g., Doe v. Univ. of Michigan,* 721 F. Supp. 852 [E.D. Mich. 1989]).

322.  *Lipsett,* cited in n. 316.

323.  94 N.Y. 2d 87, 721 N.E. 2d 966 (Ct. App. N.Y. 1999). For a fuller description of the facts giving rise to this case, see R. Wilson, "Harassment Charges at Cornell U.," *Chronicle of Higher Education,* February 10, 1994, A13; and R. Wilson, "Whose Rights Are Protected?" *Chronicle of Higher Education,* September 8, 1995, A25.

324.  *Jew,* cited in n. 75.

325.  89 Wash. 2d 874, 576 P.2d 397 (Sup. Ct. Wash. 1978).

326.  *Burlington,* cited in n. 311, at 765; *Faragher v. Boca Raton,* 524 U.S. 775, 807 (1998).

327.  *McKenzie v. Illinois Dept. of Transp.,* 92 F.3d 473, 480 (7th Cir. 1996); *Hall v. Gus Construction Co.,* 842 F.2d 1010, 1015–16 (8th Cir. 1988); 29 C.F.R. 1604.11(d). *See also* Note, *Notice in Hostile Environment Discrimination Law,* 112 Harv. L. Rev. 1977, 1978 (1999) ("rule of negligence governing employer liability when co-workers create a hostile environment").

328.  *Gebser v. Lago Vista Indep. School Dist.,* 524 U.S. 274 (1998).

329.  *See, e.g.,* B. George, *Employer Liability for Sexual Harassment: The Buck Stops Where?* 34 Wake Forest L. Rev. 1, 24 (1999); and A. Franke, "The Message from the Supreme Court: Clarify Sexual-Harassment Policies," *Chronicle of Higher Education,* July 17, 1998, B6.

330.  *Campbell v. Kansas State Univ.,* 780 F. Supp. 755 (D. Kansas 1991). While *Campbell* clearly stands for the proposition that a single act may violate Title VII, a close reading of the opinion raises a question of whether the court's holding was also influenced by the fact that Kansas State conducted a perfunctory investigation of the alleged harassment even though university officials knew

that this professor had a history of making sexually inappropriate comments to support staff. Ibid., at 758.

331. 924 F.2d 872, 879 (9th Cir. 1991).

332. R. Wilson, "California Professor Found Not to Have Harassed Male Student," *Chronicle of Higher Education,* June 2, 1995, A14.

333. *Lipsett,* cited in n. 316, at 897.

334. Pp. 72–80, with particular emphasis on the *Silva* and *Cohen* cases. *See also* O'Neil, "Protecting Free Speech When the Issue Is Sexual Harassment," cited in chap. 3, n. 46, and *Booher,* cited in chap. 4, n. 15 (Northern Kentucky's sexual harassment policy—which was closely patterned on EEOC Title VII regulations—struck down for overbreadth and vagueness).

335. R. Wilson, "A Professor's Personal Teaching Style Wins Him Praise and Costs Him His Job," *Chronicle of Higher Education,* November 14, 1997, A12.

336. Indeed, the Colby professor had also been accused of other sexually harassing behavior that "invaded students' privacy in disturbing ways." His claim was rejected by the Maine Human Rights Commission before an out-of-court settlement was reached. "Colby College Settles Lawsuit over Professor's Teaching Style," *Chronicle of Higher Education,* June 26, 1998, A12.

337. *See* B. Dziech & L. Weiner, *The Lecherous Professor* (University of Illinois Press: 1990).

338. But note that the *absence* of such a policy does not *constitute* discrimination under Title IX. *Gebser,* cited in n. 328, at 293.

339. R. Wilson, "William and Mary Seeks to Shift Liability for Damages to Professor in Federal Sexual-Harassment Case," *Chronicle of Higher Education,* June 9, 1995, A20; "Judge Says College Can Be Sued for Professor's Harassment," *Chronicle of Higher Education,* July 7, 1995, A13. Academic freedom does not leave faculty unaccountable to their employer universities (pp. 208–15), and in any event does not encompass the right to commit sexual harassment.

340. *University of Iowa Faculty Handbook,* "Sexual Harassment and Consensual Relationships," §7 ("Iowa Relationship Policy"). *Cf.* the essentially precatory AAUP statement, "Consensual Relations between Faculty and Students," in AAUP, *Policy Documents & Reports* (AAUP: 1995), 174 ("In their relationships with students, members of the faculty are expected to be aware of their professional responsibilities and avoid apparent or actual conflict of interest, favoritism, or bias").

341. *Penn Handbook,* cited in chap. 2, n. 26, §VI.E, "Consensual Sexual Relations between Faculty and Students."

342. "Iowa Relationship Policy," cited in n. 340, §6(b) ("Voluntary consent by the student in such a relationship is suspect, given the fundamentally asymmetric nature of the relationship").

343. G. Elliott, *Consensual Relationships and the Constitution: A Case of Liberty Denied*, 6 Mich. J. Gender & Law 47, 51 (1999).

344. If we think it appropriate to prevent faculty from dating students, should similar restrictions be placed on senior faculty dating junior faculty? Even if the logical answer is yes, the enormous difficulty of policing such a ban, the degree to which it ignores a very common means and locus of forming personal relationships, and—above all—the absence of a felt need or obligation to protect junior faculty, as compared to students, together make such limitations highly impractical.

345. Elliott, cited in n. 343, at 51.

346. Requisite debates over a proposed policy will cast the university in a bad light, with the libertarian argument for personal choice and freedom lost in the din of public outrage or ridicule heaped upon the supposed faculty "right" to have amorous relationships with students. D. Kennedy, *Academic Freedom*, cited in chap. 4, n. 1, at 110–11.

347. Nonconsensual relationships between faculty and students would of course constitute sexual harassment.

348. C. Leatherman, "To Get Rid of a Difficult Employee, a College May Hush Up Problems in a Professor's Past," *Chronicle of Higher Education*, December 6, 1996, A14.

349. *See, e.g.,* Conn. Gen. Stat. §31-128f (1999).

350. Conversely, it has been argued that not disclosing a prior investigation or sanction for harassment will encourage repentant faculty to behave well.

351. C. Leatherman, "Ex-Student Sues Professor at U. of Pennsylvania for Sexual-Harassment," *Chronicle of Higher Education*, April 13, 1994, A16; "University of Pennsylvania Sexual-Harassment Cases Are Settled," *Chronicle of Higher Education*, June 2, 1995, A13.

352. C. Leatherman, "Ohio State Withdraws Its Job Offer to a Yale Professor Accused of Harassing a Student," *Chronicle of Higher Education*, January 10, 1997, A11.

353. Wilson, "Whose Rights Are Protected?" cited in n. 323.

354. *Jimenez v. Almodovar,* 650 F.2d 363, 369 (1st Cir. 1981).

355. *Pace v. Hymas,* 111 Idaho 581, 726 P. 2d 693 (S. Ct. Idaho 1986); *Scheuer v. Creighton Univ.,* 199 Neb. 618, 260 N.W. 2d 595 (S. Ct. Neb. 1977); *A.A.U.P. v. Bloomfield College,* 129 N.J. Super. 249, 322 A. 2d 846 (Sup. Ct. N.J. 1974), *affirmed,* 136 N.J. Super. 442, 346 A. 2d 615 (Sup. Ct. N.J. 1975); *Browzin,* cited in n. 11. Financial exigency provisions are commonly included in faculty handbooks, which are themselves incorporated into the employment contract.

356. *Graney v. Bd. of Regents,* 92 Wis. 2d 745, 757–58, 286 N.W. 2d 138, 145 (Ct. App. Wis. 1979) ("The Board of Regent's [sic] authority to terminate employees for reasons of financial exigency . . . is implied under the general powers of the board"); *Krotkoff,* cited in chap. 1, n. 68; *Steinmetz v. Bd. of Trustees,* 68

Ill. App. 3d 83, 385 N.E. 2d 745 (App. Ct. Ill. 1978) (implied power to dismiss faculty for reasons of retrenchment).

357. AAUP, "1940 Statement," cited in chap. 2, n. 4, at 4.

358. AAUP, "AAUP RIR," cited in n. 245, §4(c)(1), at 23.

359. *Krotkoff,* cited in chap. 1, n. 68, at 681. *See also* R. Ludolph, *Termination of Faculty Tenure Rights Due to Financial Exigency and Program Discontinuance,* 63 Det. L. Rev. 609, 652 (1986) (the "prevailing test" for gauging financial exigency is the "adequacy of the operating funds"). *But cf.* another commentator who argued that "expenditures which cannot be justified as necessary to the development of a sound academic program may not be considered in evaluating the institution's financial condition." Note, *The Dismissal of Tenured Faculty for Reasons of Financial Exigency,* 51 Ind. L.J. 417, 424 (1976).

360. 136 N.J. Super. 442, 346 A. 2d 615 (Sup. Ct. N.J. 1975).

361. *Scheuer,* cited in n. 355, at 630, 601. The *Scheuer* court cites *Browzin,* cited in n. 11, in support of unit-specific exigencies.

362. 117 Md. App. 662, 716, 701 A.2d 1113, 1140 (Md. Ct. Spec. App. 1997), *cert. denied,* 347 Md. 681, 702 A.2d 290 (Ct. App. Md. 1997).

363. *See* pp. 235–37.

364. *Polishook v. C.U.N.Y.,* 234 A.D. 2d 165 (S. Ct. N.Y. 1996); *Graney,* cited in n. 356; A. Johnson, *The Problems of Contraction: Legal Considerations in University Retrenchment,* 10 J. Law & Ed. 269, 285 (1981) ("It is clear that it is the trustees who must be responsible for declaring the existence of the need to reduce the college or university"). The board would retain this power even in a unionized environment. Ludolph, cited in n. 359, at 649.

365. *Pace,* cited in n. 355, at 585–86, 697–98. *See also Bignall v. North Idaho College,* 538 F.2d 243 (9th Cir. 1976); *Milbouer v. Keppler,* 644 F. Supp. 201 (D. Idaho 1986); *A.A.U.P,* cited in n. 360; and Johnson, cited in n. 364, at 279 n. 36 (all confirming that the terminating institution bears the burden of proof).

366. *Pace,* cited in n. 355, provides an example of how no exigency may be found when a university fails to pursue alternatives to breaking tenure.

367. AAUP, "AAUP RIR," cited in n. 245, §4(c)(1), at 24. Financially strapped colleges sometimes affiliate or merge with other institutions to keep the wolf from their door. However, unless faculty employment contracts or institutional policies specify faculty prerogatives under such circumstances, one cannot blithely assume that such a union voids the tenure rights of faculty from the now-recast (or defunct) college. In *Gray v. Mundelein College,* 296 Ill. App. 3d 795, 695 N.E. 2d 1379 (App. Ct. Ill. 1998), the implementation of Mundelein's "affiliation" with Loyola University left it vulnerable to breach-of-contract suits from tenured faculty who were not hired by Loyola. Mundelein had not declared a financial exigency allowing it to break tenure, nor had it provided the discharged faculty with the procedural protections that follow upon such declaration. *See also Leftwich,* cited in n. 97 (age discrimination occurred when tenure broken as

part of change in control of college). *But see Gardiner v. Tschechtelin,* 765 F. Supp. 279 (D. Md. 1991) (no unconstitutional impairment of contract when legislation shifting control of a community college to the state eliminated permanent tenure).

368. *Levitt v. Bd. of Trustees,* 376 F. Supp. 945, 950 (D. Neb. 1974) (emphasis added). *See also Bd. of Trustees v. Adams,* cited in n. 362, at 722, 1143 ("which faculty would be terminated constituted discretionary policy decisions for the administration"); *Klein v. Bd. of Higher Ed.,* 434 F. Supp. 1113 (S.D.N.Y. 1977) (quoting *Levitt*); *Refai v. Central Wash. Univ.,* 49 Wash. App. 1, 8, 742 P. 2d 137, 142 (Ct. App. Wash. 1987), *review denied,* 110 Wash. 2d 1006 (1988) ("the question of whether the termination was the best response under the circumstances is a purely administrative one"), citing T. Bolger and D. Wilmoth, *Dismissal of Tenured Faculty Members for Reasons of Financial Exigency,* 65 Marq. L. Rev. 347, 355 n. 35 (1982); and *Johnston-Taylor v. Gannon,* 1992 U.S. App. LEXIS 22052 (6th Cir. 1992), *cert. denied,* 507 U.S. 986 (1993) (ratifying criteria selected and used by dean in financial exigency termination).

369. The Constitution does not require that state-actor universities "use any particular selection process [for exigency terminations], so long as the procedure chosen is a reasonable one." *Brenna v. Southern Col. St. College,* 589 F.2d 475, 477 (10th Cir. 1978).

370. *Johnson v. Bd. of Regents,* cited in chap. 1, n. 69, at 239–40.

371. Ibid., at 240.

372. For examples of substantial faculty involvement across the chain of exigency termination decisions—which can accrue both to an institution's legal and educational benefit—*see Christensen v. Terrell,* 51 Wash. App. 621, 754 P. 2d 1009 (Ct. App. Wash. 1988); *Refai,* cited in n. 368; and S. Olswang, "Facing Financial Distress: A Case Study of the University of Washington," *Higher Education* 16 (1987): 145 (faculty and student input).

373. AAUP, "AAUP RIR," cited in n. 245, §4(c)(1), at 24.

374. R. Brown, "Financial Exigency," *AAUP Bulletin* 61 (spring 1976): 5, 8.

375. *Krotkoff,* cited in chap. 1, n. 68, at 678.

376. Pp. 239–49.

377. *Johnson v. Bd. of Regents,* cited in chap. 1, n. 69, at 239. *But see* AAUP, "AAUP RIR," cited in n. 245, §4(c)(2), at 24 (calling for discharged professors to receive an on-the-record adjudicative hearing before a faculty committee probing into a wide range of issues, including the existence of the exigency itself and the selection and application of criteria for making particular termination decisions).

378. *See* n. 11.

379. AAUP, "AAUP RIR," cited in n. 245, §4(c)(3), at 25.

380. *Brenna,* cited in n. 369. *See also* B. Lee & S. Olswang, "Legal Parameters of the Faculty Employment Relationship," in J. Smart, ed., *Higher Educa-*

tion: *Handbook of Theory and Research* (Agathon Press: 1985), at 226 ("no court has formally stated that tenured faculty must be given preference over nontenured faculty in such situations"). Of course, state civil service codes or the terms of a faculty collective bargaining agreement could so require.

381. AAUP, "AAUP RIR," cited in n. 245, §8, at 28.

382. *Klein,* cited in n. 368.

383. AAUP, "AAUP RIR," cited in n. 245, §4(c)(4), at 25.

384. *Krotkoff,* cited in chap. 1, n. 68, at 682.

385. AAUP, "AAUP RIR," cited in n. 245, §4(c)(3), at 24–25 (the only permissible exception again being hires necessary to avoid "a serious distortion in the academic program").

386. AAUP, "AAUP RIR," cited in n. 245, §4(c)(6), at 25.

387. *A.A.U.P,* cited in n. 355 (trial court opinion) (hiring 12 new faculty while simultaneously terminating 13 undercut Bloomfield's claim of exigency).

388. *Refai,* cited in n. 368, at 7, 142.

389. *See, e.g.,* D. Magner, "Administration and Faculty Are at War over How to Rescue U. of Bridgeport from Its Daunting Financial Problems," *Chronicle of Higher Education,* July 5, 1990, A25 (faculty characterize declaration of exigency as effort to skirt terms of union contract); *A.A.U.P,* cited in n. 355 (trial court opinion) (college's hiring of a dozen new faculty and its imposition of one-year terminal contracts on all remaining instructors led court to conclude that the true goal was the "abolition of tenure). Ibid., at 272, 858.

390. *See, e.g.,* University of Wisconsin System, *Board of Regents Rules,* chapter UWS 12, "Layoff of Academic Staff for Reasons of Budget or Program" ("Wisconsin Layoff Policy"); University of Washington, *University Handbook,* vol. 2, part 2, chapter 26, "Financial Emergency and Procedures for Elimination of an Academic Program" ("UWashington Procedures"); Ohio State University, *Rules of the Faculty Senate,* chapter 5, rules 3335-5-021, "Financial Exigency," and 3335-5-022, "Treatment of Tenured Faculty Members during Financial Exigency" (the latter hereafter "OSU Treatment Rules"). Note that in a collective bargaining context, an employer institution that unilaterally promulgates or amends such rules may be charged with an unfair labor practice. Ludolph, cited in n. 359, at 649.

391. *Jimenez,* cited in n. 354, at 368.

392. *See, e.g.,* S. Heller, "Despite Protests, Washington U. Stands by Decision to Close Its Once-Vaunted Sociology Department," *Chronicle of Higher Education,* March 14, 1990, A1 (arts and science faculty and dean focus their academic priorities elsewhere; tenured sociologists to be assigned to other departments); *Hamer,* cited in chap. 4, n. 22 (chancellor closes academic division because of plummeting enrollment).

393. P. Schmidt, "Sweeping Reviews Lead States to Consider Cutting Many Academic Programs," *Chronicle of Higher Education,* February 14, 1997, A33.

394. Brown, cited in n. 374, at 13.

395. AAUP, "AAUP RIR," cited in n. 245, §4(d), at 25.

396. Ibid., §4(d)(1), at 25.

397. Ludolph, cited in n. 359, at 638.

398. *E.g.*, the trustees of the State University of New York are empowered "to regulate . . . curricula and all other matters pertaining to the operation and administration of each state-operated institution in the state university" (NY CLS Educ. §355 [2][h]), and the regents of the University of California have "full powers of organization and government" of that institution (Cal. Const. Art IX, §9).

399. 767 P. 2d 746 (Colo. Ct. App. 1988). The governing board's plan was the result of "extended study by various task forces within USC." Ibid., at 747. If, as would seem likely, these task forces included faculty, attacks on the plan begin to ring hollow. Elsewhere in the state, tenured professors who lost their jobs when the University of *Northern* Colorado adopted a plan that eliminated departments and degree programs had no standing to sue under a Colorado law that vested the trustees with authority over curricula. The formal basis for this holding was that the statute in question did not address employment terminations (one wonders whether the faculty should have pursued a breach-of-contract claim instead). The practical result was that aggrieved faculty could not block the university from revamping its programs, and they were still out of their jobs. *Bennett v. Bd. of Trustees*, 782 P. 2d 1214 (Colo. Ct. App. 1989). *See also Behrend v. Ohio*, 55 Ohio App. 2d 135, 140, 379 N.E. 2d 617, 621 (Ct. App. Ohio 1977) ("The board of trustees has the jurisdiction to make the policy determination of the continued existence of the various departments within the university").

400. *See* pp. 80–92 for a detailed discussion of the respective faculty and institutional interests in, and control over, course content.

401. *Brine v. Univ. of Iowa*, 90 F.3d 271 (8th Cir. 1996), *cert. denied*, 519 U.S. 1149 (1997). Tenured dental hygiene faculty were reassigned elsewhere in the university.

402. 198 Cal. App. 3d 1084, 244 Cal. Rptr. 312 (Cal. Ct. App. 1988).

403. Ibid., at 1099, 321.

404. "UWashington Procedures," cited in n. 390, §26-41. *See also* "OSU Treatment Rules," cited in n. 390, for Ohio State's definition of "academic program" for use in a financial exigency.

405. S. Olswang, E. Cole & J. Wilson, *Program Elimination, Financial Emergency, and Student Rights*, 9 J.C. & U.L. 163, 165 (1982–83) ("when a student enrolls in a particular degree program, there is an implied contract that the student will be able to receive the degree sought if he/she successfully completes the academic requirements formulated by the institution").

406. Ibid., at 173. *See also* Johnson, cited in n. 364, at 319; and Olswang, "Facing Financial Distress," cited in n. 372 (University of Washington did not

terminate tenured faculty, in part because they would be needed for several years to teach students who were completing degrees in programs slated for elimination).

407. In one idiosyncratic case, the State University of New York at Stony Brook was actually ordered to let students enroll in first-year podiatry program classes even though it had abandoned plans to open a new podiatry school. The "specific performance" mandated here reflected highly unusual circumstances in which SUNY would not save any money if it did not offer such instruction. *Eden v. Bd. of Trustees*, 49 A.D. 2d 277, 374 N.Y.S. 2d 686 (N.Y. App. Div. 1975). Needless to say, monetary damages are a much more typical remedy.

408. *Behrend*, cited in n. 399. *But see Beukas v. Fairleigh Dickinson Univ.*, 255 N.J. Super. 552, 605 A. 2d 776 (Super. Ct. N.J. 1991), *aff'd*, 255 N.J. Super. 420 (1992) (FDU did not act unfairly or arbitrarily in closing its dental program). The *Beukas* court argued that quasi-contract theory—rather than formal contract law—offered the correct lens to analyze conflicts between institutions and students over program closures. However, the court noted that even under contract law, FDU was not liable for damages since its academic bulletin expressly reserved the right to recast or terminate programs at any time.

409. Brown, cited in n. 374, at 13.

410. *See, e.g., Browzin*, cited in n. 11 (tenured professor dismissed when the university eliminates his courses in soil mechanics and hydrology; however, the sole reason for eliminating such courses was a financial exigency in the Engineering School). The AAUP would treat a program closure "mandated by financial exigency" exactly the same as a purely financial layoff. AAUP, "AAUP RIR," cited in n. 245, §4(d) n. 7, at 25.

411. *Unterschuetz and Keppeler v. Bd. of Trustees*, 38 Wash. App. 729, 688 P. 2d 512 (Wash. Ct. App. 1984).

412. *Bd. of Trustees v. Adams*, cited in n. 362, at 714, 1139. I would argue that enrollment declines are really a subset of the financial problems that may necessitate program closures.

413. Ibid., at 665, 1115.

414. 64 Ill. App. 3d 355, 380 N.E. 2d 1089 (Ill. App. Ct. 1978). The court reached this result even though the contract gave seniority-based "bumping rights" to faculty terminated because of declining enrollment but not to faculty dismissed for program closure—language that might tempt Kendall to claim that all layoffs resulted from closures.

415. 62 Ill. App. 3d 824, 379 N.E. 2d 791 (Ill. App. Ct. 1978). An unusual feature of this case is that the faculty manual expressly allowed dismissals due to either the elimination or the curtailment of programs (and an earlier version of that manual allowed dismissals for dips in enrollment).

416. 174 W. Va. 643, 328 S.E. 2d 519 (S. Ct. App. W. Va. 1985). Despite this holding, the plaintiff successfully invoked reinstatement rights.

417. *Browzin,* cited in n. 11.

418. "Wisconsin Layoff Policy," cited in n. 390, §12.01.

419. D. Magner, "Minnesota Regents' Proposals Would Effectively Abolish Tenure, Faculty Leaders Say," *Chronicle of Higher Education,* September 20, 1996, A11; and D. Magner, "A Fierce Battle over Tenure at the U. of Minnesota Comes to a Quiet Close," *Chronicle of Higher Education,* June 20, 1997, A14.

420. S. Olswang, *Planning the Unthinkable: Issues in Institutional Reorganization and Faculty Reductions,* 9 J.C. & U.L. 431 (1983).

421. But in deploying their resources, colleges and universities must be able to take into account programmatic needs and the quality of past and projected faculty performance. Such a process "does not transform a reduction decision into an incompetency removal." Ibid., at 442.

422. AAUP, "AAUP RIR," cited in n. 245, §4(d)(2), at 25. Again, while courts will demand that employer institutions make reasonable efforts to reassign faculty, they have not mandated training in a new scholarly field.

423. Some commentators urge that institutions preserve their flexibility by expressly disclaiming adherence to AAUP faculty termination rules. Speech by T. Hustoles, National Association of College and University Attorneys Annual Conference (June 30, 1992), p. 11 (copy on file with author).

424. 946 F.2d 379 (5th Cir. 1991).

425. Ibid., at 382.

426. Ibid., at 387.

427. Ibid.

428. *Zuelsdorf v. Univ. of Alaska,* 794 P. 2d 932 (Alaska 1990) (faculty plaintiffs acquired additional year of employment when university missed deadline for sending notice of nonretention); *Johnson v. San Jacinto Jr. College,* 498 F. Supp. 555 (S.D. Texas 1980) (reassignment of faculty member violated campus's own "due process" policy as well as constitutional standards); *Skehan v. Bd. of Trustees,* 590 F.2d 470 (3rd Cir. 1978), *cert. denied,* 444 U.S. 832 (1979) (college breached a contractual obligation to give a faculty member who was not being reappointed an internal hearing on whether such action infringed academic freedom; this also violated procedural due process under the Fourteenth Amendment).

429. AAUP, "AAUP RIR," cited in n. 245, especially §§5–8, at 26–28. *See, e.g., Skehan v. Bd. of Trustees,* 669 F.2d 142, 152 (3rd Cir. 1982), *cert. denied,* 459 U.S. 1048 (1982) (college need not abide by AAUP policies it had not adopted).

430. U.S. Const. Amend. Art. XIV, §1.

431. *Bd. of Regents v. Roth,* 408 U.S. 564 (1972) (*Roth* also described the first of these notions as having one's "good name, reputation, honor, or integrity [put] at stake because of what the government is doing to him"), citing *Wisconsin v. Constantineau,* 400 U.S. 433, 437 (1971).

432. *Bunger,* cited in chap. 4, n. 26, at 991. *See also Roth,* supra, at 574 n. 13 (while a "record of nonretention in one job, taken alone, might make [the plaintiff] somewhat less attractive to some other employers [this] would hardly establish the kind of foreclosure of opportunities amounting to a deprivation of 'liberty'").

433. *Cleveland Bd. of Ed. v. Loudermill,* 470 U.S. 532, 547 n.13 (1985), citing *Bishop v. Wood,* 426 U.S. 341 (1976).

434. *Bd. of Regents v. Roth,* cited in n. 431, at 577.

435. Ibid.; and 408 U.S. 593 (1972).

436. *Bd. of Regents v. Roth,* cited in n. 431, at 573–78.

437. *Perry,* cited in n. 435, at 600–601.

438. Ibid., at 600.

439. For a case in which de facto tenure (i.e., a permanent appointment) was ultimately found, see *Soni v. Bd. of Trustees,* 513 F.2d 347 (6th Cir. 1975), *cert. denied,* 426 U.S. 919 (1976). *Cf. Edinger v. Bd. of Regents,* 906 F.2d 1136 (6th Cir. 1990) (no de facto tenure).

440. *Collins v. Marina-Martinez,* 894 F.2d 474, 480 (1st Cir. 1990) (university's "grant of tenure to [plaintiff] created a constitutionally protected property interest"); *Cotnoir v. Univ. of Maine,* 35 F.3d 6, 10 (1st Cir. 1994) ("a tenured professor enjoys a property right sufficient to invoke procedural due process").

441. *Skehan,* cited in n. 429.

442. *Bd. of Regents v. Roth,* cited in n. 431, is of course the most prominent precedent on point. *See also Bunger,* cited in chap. 4, n. 26, at 990 (nontenured professors "do not possess [a] 'legitimate claim of entitlement' to their reappointment").

443. *Johnson v. Univ. of Pittsburgh,* 435 F. Supp. 1328, 1353 (W.D. Pa. 1977).

444. Ibid., at 1369. *See also Spuler v. Pickar,* 958 F.2d 103 (5th Cir. 1992); and *Colburn,* cited in chap. 4, n. 26. *But see McClendon v. Morton,* 162 W.Va. 431, 249 S.E. 2d 919 (S. Ct. App. W. Va. 1978), in which a West Virginia appellate court declared that because the plaintiff had satisfied the objective eligibility criteria for tenure, she could not be *denied* tenure without a due process hearing on her teaching skill. This idiosyncratic holding came close to finding a property right in the *process* by which tenure decisions are made, contrary to the cases cited in n. 451. As previously noted (pp. 151–52), when tenure is denied, unsuccessful candidates often sue their employer colleges or universities under applicable federal law (e.g., First Amendment; employment discrimination statutes such as Titles VII and IX) or pursuant to state law (perhaps alleging a breach of contract in this latter context).

445. *Clark v. Whiting,* 607 F.2d 634, 641 (4th Cir. 1979) (faculty have no "property entitlement to a promotion").

446. *Maples,* cited in chap. 4, n. 14, at 1550. *See also Huang v. Bd. of Governors,* 902 F.2d 1134 (4th Cir. 1990) (interdepartmental transfer not an infringe-

ment of property); and *Farkas v. Ross-Lee,* 727 F. Supp. 1098 (W.D. Mich. 1989), *aff'd without opinion,* 891 F.2d 290 (6th Cir. 1989) (no property right to remain in a given department).

447. *Maples,* cited in chap. 4, n. 14, at 1550 n. 5. *See also Farkas,* supra (no liberty interest trammeled by transfer; court even observed that "transfers may be especially appropriate as a matter of practical internal college administration"). Ibid., at 1104. Though not legally significant, it is interesting to note that the transfer challenged in *Farkas* was quickly countermanded by the university administration.

448. *Garvie v. Jackson,* cited in chap. 4, n. 26. *Cf. Johnson v. San Jacinto,* cited in n. 428, where the court found a property interest in a midterm "demotion" (more accurately described as a shift in jobs) from college registrar back to faculty member.

449. *Mahaffey,* cited in chap. 4, n. 21. *See also Swartz v. Scruton,* 964 F.2d 607 (7th Cir. 1992) (no property interest in merit pay increase).

450. 845 F.2d 660 (6th Cir. 1988).

451. *Mumford,* cited in chap. 4, n. 12, at 759. *See also Bunger,* cited in chap. 4, n. 26, at 990–91 (plaintiff may not "construct a property interest out of procedural timber"); *Swartz,* cited in n. 449 (no property right in institutional adherence to a particular method for calculating merit increases); and *Colburn,* cited in chap. 4, n. 26.

452. "Not every disregard of its regulations by a public agency . . . gives rise to a cause of action for violation of constitutional rights. Rather, it is only when the agency's disregard of its rules results in a procedure which in itself impinges upon due process rights that a federal court should intervene." *Bates,* cited in n. 258, at 329. *See also Kilcoyne v. Morgan,* 664 F.2d 940 (4th Cir. 1981), *cert. denied,* 456 U.S. 928 (1982) (absence of a Fourteenth Amendment claim did not preclude suit for breach of promise); *Swartz,* cited in n. 449; and *Christensen,* cited in n. 372.

453. 424 U.S. 319 (1976).

454. *Newman,* cited in n. 272, at 960.

455. For a good compilation of adequate process in this setting, *see Potemra,* cited in n. 248, at 332.

456. *Fong,* cited in n. 264, at 950.

457. *Frumkin v. Bd. of Trustees,* 626 F.2d 19 (6th Cir. 1980) (no due process violation at dismissal hearing where faculty member's lawyer allowed to consult with client but not to examine witnesses or raise objections).

458. *Cleveland Bd. of Ed.,* cited in n. 433, at 546.

459. *Cotnoir,* cited in n. 440, at 14–17. *See also Calhoun v. Gaines,* 982 F.2d 1470 (10th Cir. 1992) (pretermination notice constitutionally invalid if employee not aware that his or her job is in jeopardy).

460. *McDaniels,* cited in n. 319. After exhausting intracollege appeals, the

plaintiff had a right to arbitration and to external judicial review. Ibid., at 453, 460–61.

461. Pp. 228–30.

462. *Russell et al. v. Harrison,* 562 F. Supp. 467, 469 (N. D. Miss. 1983), *rev'd on other grounds,* 736 F.2d 283 (5th Cir. 1984). *See also Browzin,* cited in n. 11, at 847 (endorsing fewer and simpler safeguards in an exigency); and *Refai,* cited in n. 368, at 16–17, 146–47.

463. *Johnson v. Bd. of Regents,* cited in chap. 1, n. 69, at 239. One federal appellate court opined even more generally that colleges and universities facing an exigency must just use "fair and reasonable standards" in selecting which faculty to terminate. *Krotkoff,* cited in chap. 1, n. 68, at 682.

464. *See, e,g., Texas Faculty Ass'n.,* cited in n. 424; *Browzin,* cited in n. 11, at 847.

465. *Texas Faculty Ass'n.,* cited in n. 424. *See* p. 239 for further discussion of this opinion.

466. The court noted that a written submission would probably be acceptable for this purpose. Ibid., at 388.

467. In this situation, these proposed safeguards were not deemed vital in order to reach informed decisions or to advance justice: "We see no need to test in an adversary fashion the veracity of witnesses or the reliability of evidence. . . . And because oral testimony would play no role or but a minimal role in such proceedings, a written record or its equivalent would be of little value." Ibid., at 389.

468. "A due process hearing is not rendered constitutionally inadequate solely because university administrators are asked to review their own decision. . . . Absent affirmative evidence of bias, the official responsible for the original termination decision may conduct the hearing on whether to retain a given faculty member." Ibid., at 388–89. *See also Bignall,* cited in n. 365, at 247 (no due process violation when hearing before board of trustees that previously mandated faculty layoffs in response to declining enrollment).

469. AAUP, "AAUP RIR," cited in n. 245, §§4(c)(2) and 4(d)(3), at 24–25.

470. *Regents of Univ. of Michigan v. Ewing,* 474 U.S. 214, 225 (1985). *Ewing* involved a student dismissal, but this principle certainly applies to faculty discipline too.

471. *See, e.g. Newman,* cited in n. 272, at 962; and *Huang,* cited in n. 446, at 1142 (both citing *Ewing* in rejecting substantive due process challenges to a faculty censure and an interdepartmental transfer, respectively).

472. *Johnson v. San Jacinto,* cited in n. 428, at 577.

473. *See, e.g., Slaughter,* cited in chap. 1, n. 50 (constitutional standards used to assess student discipline at private university).

474. Kaplin & Lee, cited in introduction, n. 2, at 298.

475. *See, e.g., Kramer v. Horton,* 128 Wis. 2d 404, 383 N.W. 2d 54 (S. Ct.

Wis. 1986), *cert. denied,* 479 U.S. 918 (1986) (faculty member must exhaust administrative remedies before pursuing due process claim in state court). *But cf. Patsy v. Bd. of Regents of Fla.,* 457 U.S. 496 (1982), where the Supreme Court held that exhaustion of state administrative remedies was not a prerequisite to bringing a civil rights suit under 42 U.S.C. §1983 in *federal* court.

## Final Observations on Faculty Law

1. *See* pp. 92–94.

2. *See* pp. 215–17 for a discussion of the practical difficulties of disciplining faculty. Faculty, of course, regularly bring suit as plaintiffs against their employer institutions—but such cases do not usually involve a professor's personal liability for a judgment (except perhaps for legal fees incurred in earlier rounds of the same dispute).

3. Since acts beyond the scope of one's authority may create personal but not employer liability, faculty and administrators (especially those who deal with extra-university parties in commercial situations) should seek clear demarcations of their authority, ideally in writing.

4. In some cases the employee will be permitted to select his or her own attorney; more commonly, the indemnifying institution will choose counsel.

5. *See, e.g., Statutes of the Trustees of the University of Pennsylvania,* Article 12, "Indemnification" (1990).

6. Hypothetically, if a penurious institution, without no or little insurance, proved unable to indemnify its employees, a court might turn to a wealthy (and legally culpable) individual defendant to satisfy a judgment. However, I have never encountered such a case.

7. Because it may be difficult to determine whether an individual was acting within the scope of employment and in good faith (especially in the tense and heated environment that surrounds the filing of a lawsuit), practical considerations of ease, timeliness, and the maintenance of employee morale may lead colleges and universities to give employees the substantial benefit of the doubt in making indemnification decisions.

8. The following discussion is premised upon ideas developed in Wright, cited in introduction, n. 1.

9. *See, e.g.,* Occupational Safety and Health Act of 1970, 29 U.S.C. §651 et seq.; Laboratory Animal Welfare Act, 7 U.S.C. §2131 et seq.

10. Wright, cited in introduction, n. 1, at 378.

11. Ibid.

# Index

AAUP. *See* American Association of University Professors (AAUP)

"AAUP Ethics Statement," 323–24n. 290

AAUP "1940 Statement of Principles on Academic Freedom and Tenure": on academic freedom, 124; on extramural behavior, 136–37; on faculty contract, 301n. 94; on tenure, 145–46, 147–48

*A.A.U.P. v. Bloomfield College,* 227

abuse of students, 72

academic freedom: AAUP "1940 Statement" and, 124, 136–37; absence of consensus and, 284n. 11; accountability and, 327n. 339; classroom behavior and treatment of students, 64–69, 72–73; collective bargaining with graduate students and, 196–97; conceptual framework for, 67–69; contract law and, 66, 102; course content, theoretical emphasis, and, 80–92; course evaluations and, 71–72; debates on, 283n. 6; deference to academic decisions and, 21–22, 64–65, 143–45; First Amendment and, 17, 66–67, 303–4n. 34; grading and, 92–94; history of protection of, 301n. 1; institutional *vs.* individual, 102–3; obtaining support for scholarship and, 31–34, 61–62, 270n. 14, 271n. 24; private institutions and, 66, 120–25; pub-lic institutions and, 65–66; scholarship and, 25; selection of research topics and, 25–30; teaching meth-ods and, 73–80

ADA. *See* Americans with Disabili-ties Act (ADA)

*Adamian v. Jacobsen,* 136–37, 209

*Adarand Constructors, Inc. v. Pena,* 178

ADEA. *See* Age Discrimination in Employment Act (ADEA)

administration, managerial role and unionization, 188, 190

affiliations and mergers, 329–30n. 367

affiliation with unions, 187–88

affirmative action: case law regard-ing, 180–81; compelling interest and, 178–79; legislative and constitutional complications to, 181–82; mandatory *vs.* voluntary programs, 178; "narrowly tailored" preferences, 179–80; overview of, 177–78; "two for one" deal, 177, 180–81

*Agarwal v. University of Minnesota,* 211

age discrimination cases, 176, 313n. 130

Age Discrimination in Employment Act (ADEA), 169–71, 175; man-datory retirement and, 311n. 100

*Ahmadieh v. St. Bd. of Agriculture,* 232–33

American Association of University Professors (AAUP): on academic freedom, 269n. 4; breaches of academic integrity and, 211; on Brigham Young University, 123; as collective bargaining agent, 188; partisanship of, 238–39, 305n. 11; post-tenure review and, 204; on program closures, 232, 238–39, 333n. 410; program reductions and, 238; termination policies of, 209, 226, 229, 230, 231. See also "AAUP Ethics Statement"; AAUP "1940 Statement of Principles on Academic Freedom and Tenure"

American Geophysical Union v. Texaco Inc., 47–48

Americans with Disabilities Act (ADA), 171, 172–73, 175, 312n. 114

antitrust laws, 6, 183–84

appellate court, 10

appointment letter, 20, 184–85, 274n. 66

Apte v. Regents of the Univ. of California, 233–34

Arizona State University, 134–35

Auburn University, 110, 115, 242

Aumiller v. University of Delaware, 132–33

Bakke v. Regents of Univ. of California, 180, 181, 314n. 140

Ball State University, 209

Banerjee v. Bd. of Trustees, 147

"baseline scenario": copyright, 39; patent, 44

Basic Books, Inc. v. Kinko's Graphics Corp., 98

Bates College, 225

Baylor University, 106–7

Bd. of Trustees of Univ. of Alabama v. Garrett, 23, 173

Bd. of Trustees v. Adams, 227, 236

Behrend v. Ohio, 235

Bennington College, 155

Bennun v. Rutgers, 165

Bishop v. Aronov, 87–89, 91, 102, 289nn. 87&100, 290n. 102

Blum v. Schlegel, 75

Blum v. Yaretsky, 14

Board of Regents v. Roth, 241

Board v. Stubblefield, 213

bona fide occupational qualification, 162, 168–69, 170, 171

Booher v. Bd. of Regents, 116, 298n. 63

Boston Medical Center, 193, 198

Boston University, 156–57, 164–65, 190, 193

Branzburg v. Hayes, 278–79n. 121

Braxton, John, 324n. 295

breach of academic integrity, 211–12. See also termination of tenure "for cause"

Brenna v. Southern Col. State College, 230

Brigham Young University, 122–24

Brown v. Boston University, 164–65, 166

Browzin v. Catholic Univ., 237

Bunger v. University of Oklahoma Board of Regents, 112

Burlington Industries, Inc. v. Ellerth, 325n. 314

Burnham v. Ianni, 297–98n. 57

Burton v. Wilmington Parking Authority, 13, 264n. 38

Byrne, J. Peter, 283n. 6

California Higher Education Employer-Employee Relations Act, 187

Campbell v. Kansas State University, 326–27n. 330

Carley v. Arizona Bd. of Regents, 78–79, 285nn. 24&25, 286n. 52

case law, 9–10

Catholic universities, 124–25
Catholic University of Puerto Rico, 213
chair position: removal from, 242, 302n. 17; unionization and, 190
Chait, Richard, 207
charitable immunity, 268n. 81
City College, 128–29, 133
City University of New York, 134
civility in classroom, 72–73
civil rights statutes, 6
*Clark v. Community for Creative Non-Violence*, 18
*Clark v. Holmes*, 86–87, 288n. 76
classroom. *See* teaching
classroom metaphors, 74–75
*Cleveland Bd. of Education v. Loudermill*, 245, 246
"close nexus" test, 12–13
*Cohen v. San Bernardino Valley College*, 76–77, 286n. 46
*Colburn v. Trustees of Indiana University*, 111–12
Colby College, 222
*Coleman v. Wagner College*, 12–13
collective bargaining: costs of, 197; extramural behavior and, 136–37; freedom in research and, 26; of graduate students, 192–200; higher education setting and, 186; mandatory subjects for, 191–92; at private institutions, 186–92; at public institutions, 187–88; states allowing, 316n. 170
College of the Ozarks, 155
Columbia University, 40
"common law" principles, 9
compelled disclosure of scholarly work: criminal investigation or trial, 53–54; published research, 51–53; unpublished research, 48–51, 54–55
Concord University School of Law, 41

Conference on Fair Use, 99–100
conferences, free speech at, 117–20
confidentiality: letters of recommendation and, 307n. 33; reports of sexual harassment and, 220–21; research sources and, 53, 54–55; tenure process and, 152–54
conflicts of commitment: consulting work, 58–59; description of, 55; electronic instruction, 41–42; policies regarding, 59; violations of, 214
conflicts of interest: description of, 55; electronic instruction, 42; institutional, 56–57; nonresearch settings, 279–80n. 141; policies regarding, 59–60, 280n. 146, 281n. 154; research projects and, 55–57, 59–60; violations of, 214
Congressional statutes, 7
*Connick v. Myers*, 131–35, 211, 293nn. 7, 8&10
consensual-relationship policies, 213, 223–24
constituencies, growth in number of, 256–57
consulting work, 58–59
content-based restrictions on speech, 17–18, 74, 266n. 60
content-neutral restrictions on speech, 17–18, 138–39, 266n. 60
continuous appointment. *See* tenure
contract law: academic freedom and, 66, 102; conflicts of interest and conflicts of commitment, 58; copyright and, 39; faculty intramural speech and, 106; freedom in research and, 26–27; importance of principles of, 19–22, 143; between institutions and faculty, 20; between institutions and students, 20–21; patent rights and, 44; personnel issues and, 250; private college or university

contract law (*continued*)
　setting, 266n. 66; scholarly work
　and, 60; support for research, 30–
　31
*Cooper v. Ross*, 82–83, 140, 287n. 63,
　304n. 36
Copyright Act of 1976, 37, 38, 39, 47,
　97
copyright blanket license, 100
Copyright Clearance Center, 292n.
　135
copyright law: adoption of copyright
　policies and, 39–43, 274n. 64; case
　law regarding, 38–39; course
　materials and, 94–101; distribu-
　tion via Internet and other tech-
　nologies and, 39–43; faculty
　indemnification and, 291n. 131;
　"fair use" doctrine and, 47–48,
　96–101, 103; overview of, 35, 36;
　ownership and, 36–39; publishers'
　stance on copyright ownership
　and, 46–47; *Williams v. Weisser*,
　273n. 52; "work made for hire,"
　36–39. *See also* Copyright Act of
　1976
Cornell University, 8, 40, 50
corporate interests and research
　funding, 32–33
*Corstvet v. Boger*, 213
Council on Government Relations,
　262n. 8
course-approval process, 81, 287n. 56
course content: faculty control of,
　80–81, 83–84, 91–92; institutional
　control of, 85–91, 288n. 72, 289n.
　87; at private sectarian institu-
　tions, 122
course evaluations, 71–72
"course packs," 95–99, 100–101
Creighton University, 227
criminal acts, 212–13
*Curran v. Catholic University*, 122
curriculum. *See* course content

custom and practice, 20, 21, 26–27,
　184–85, 266n. 68
*Cusumano*, 278–79n. 121

dating students or junior colleagues,
　limitations on, 328n. 344
*Davis v. Monroe County Bd. of Ed.*,
　218
deference to academic decisions, 21–
　22, 64–65, 143–45, 253
*Deitchmann v. E.R. Squibb & Sons,
　Inc.*, 52
departmental reviews, 207
Department of Education Office of
　Civil Rights (OCR), 168
Department of Labor Office of
　Federal Contract Compliance
　Programs, 174
deployment of resources, 334n. 421
dereliction of teaching duties, 72
*Diamond v. Chakrabarty*, 34
*DiBona v. Matthews*, 84–85, 88,
　288n. 72
disability, definition of, 171–73, 251
disability discrimination, 171–72,
　312n. 110
discipline: overview of, 200–202;
　post-tenure review, 202–8; steps
　before dismissal, 201–2. *See also*
　termination of tenure; termination
　of tenure "for cause"
disclosure of potential conflicts of
　interest and conflicts of commit-
　ment, 59
discrimination: on basis of age, 169–
　71, 175, 311n. 100; on basis of
　disability, 171–73, 312n. 110; on
　basis of race, 167–68, 175; on
　basis of sex, 176, 217–26, 326n.
　321; on basis of sexual orientation,
　251, 313n. 125; confidentiality of
　tenure process and, 153; expanded
　protections against, 251; reverse
　type, 160, 252, 314n. 138. *See also*

nondiscrimination law; Title VII
(Civil Rights Act of 1964)
disparate impact case, 161–62
disparate treatment case, 160–61
dissemination of and access to scholarly work: compelled disclosure,
48–54; copyright law and, 46–47;
former colleagues, 48; overview
of, 46
distance learning, 39–43, 61
diversity issues, 177–78, 251–52, 257
doctrine of immunity, 22–24
"dollar hook," 6, 167–68
domestic partners, 313n. 125
dossier for tenure, 146
*Dow Chemical Co. v. Allen,* 49–50
due process: applicability of, 239–40,
248–49; conduct of pretermination hearing for, 245–46, 335n.
444, 337n. 468; discharges for
financial exigency and, 228–30,
246–47; disregard of regulations
and, 336n. 452; ending term
appointment and, 246; minimal
requirements for, 248–49; overview of, 244; program closures
and, 247–48; substantive, 248;
termination of tenure "for cause"
and, 244–46
Duke University, 42
Dworkin, R., 270n. 14

early retirement plans, 311–12n. 101
Eastern Kentucky University, 78
education as local concern, 7
*Edwards v. California Univ. of Pa.,*
89, 91, 102, 289nn. 87&100
EEOC. *See* Equal Employment
Opportunity Commission
(EEOC)
*E.E.O.C. V. Univ. of Texas Health
Science Center,* 170
electronic instruction, 39–43
Eleventh Amendment: immunity
and, 23, 267n. 77, 267–68n. 78;
prohibition of suits brought
against state, 251; sovereign immunity, ADA, and, 23, 173; sovereign immunity, ADEA, and, 170–
71
elimination of department. *See*
program closures
*Ellison v. Brady,* 221
"employee status" of graduate
students, 192–200
Equal Employment Opportunity
Commission (EEOC): ADA and,
173; ADEA and, 169; tenure files
and, 152–54; Title VII and, 162–
63, 165
equal protection of the laws, 6, 175,
178–80
Essex Community College, 227
evaluation: of academic departments,
207; of faculty performance, 71–
72, 200–202; of peer research, 29;
of tenured faculty, 155, 202–7,
320n. 225
Executive Order 11246, 174
exhaustion doctrine, 249
external attacks on classroom
autonomy, 69–71
external support for research, 31–34,
61–62
extramural associations, 139–40,
304n. 38
extramural speech: case law regarding, 128–30; conceptual framework for, 130–31; Internet and,
138–39; location of, 134–35;
overview of, 127–28; peer pressure and, 135–36, 137, 141;
Pickering/Connick balancing test
of, 131–35; public-private distinction and, 140–41

"fair use" doctrine, 47–48, 96–101,
103

federal grants, 262n. 8, 310n. 81
federal regulations, 6–7
federal statutes, 6, 7, 186–87
Fifth Amendment, 6
financial exigency: AAUP recommended safeguards and, 230–31; affiliations, mergers, and, 329–30n. 367; Constitution and, 330n. 369; definition of, 226–27; determination of, 227–28; due process and, 228–30, 246–47; faculty involvement in, 229, 330n. 372; future of, 231, 252; program closures compared to, 236–37; response to, 228–29; termination of tenure for, 226–31
Finkin, Matthew, 283n. 6, 292–93n. 3
First Amendment: academic freedom and, 17, 66–67, 303–4n. 34; associational rights and, 139–40; content-based vs. content-neutral restrictions on speech, 17–18; discipline for insubordination and, 210–11; freedom of religion and, 261n. 3 (ch. 1), 300n. 81; overview of, 5–6, 16–17; Pickering/Connick analysis and, 114–17, 126, 131–35; subject matter-based vs. viewpoint-based restrictions on speech, 18–19
fixed-term academic appointments, 156–57
Fong v. Purdue University, 210
Fourteenth Amendment: due process and, 6, 240, 244, 250; equal protection and, 6, 175, 178–80; sovereign immunity and, 312n. 118
Frankfurter, Felix, 69–70, 144, 284n. 16
Franklin v. Gwinnett County Public Schools, 169
freedom in research. See research projects
freedom of association, 139–40

free speech: content-based restrictions on, 17–18, 74, 266n. 60; content-neutral restrictions on, 17–18, 138–39, 266n. 60; in intra-university matters, 107–8; "low" value vs. "high" value, 18; Pickering/Connick balancing test of, 114–17, 131–35; private institutions and, 16; subject matter-based vs. viewpoint-based restrictions on, 18–19. See also extramural speech; intramural speech
funding: conflicts of interest and, 55–57, 59–60; cut-off of, 310n. 85; federal, 262n. 8, 310n. 81; as legal hook, 6, 167–68; professional development, 206–7; for research and scholarship, 30–34, 61–62, 270n. 14, 271n. 24; as source of legal tension, 257; Title IX and, 168–69
general custom and usage, 20, 21, 26–27, 184–85, 266n. 68
governance and operations: academic freedom and, 105–6; case law regarding, 108–9; conferences and symposia, 117–20; free speech and, 107–8; overview of, 104–5, 125–26; private sectarian institutions, 120–25; protected speech, status as, 114–17; public concern, speech regarding, 109–14; public vs. private institutions, 106–7
grading policies, 92–94
graduate students: oversupply of and fixed-term contracts, 156–57; unionization of, 192–200, 319n. 205
Grayned v. Rockford, 18
Gray v. Mundelein College, 329–30n. 367
Greer v. Spock, 18
Gross v. University of Tennessee, 58–59

guild model, 144–45, 151, 158, 304n. 3

Hahnemann University, 14–15
*Hale v. Walsh*, 116, 298n. 62
*Hall v. Kutztown University*, 111
*Hamer v. Brown*, 114
handbooks, 20
*Harris v. Arizona Bd. of Regents*, 115
Harvard Law School, 41
*Hays v. Sony Corporation of America*, 38
Henderson Act, 264nn. 28&30
*Hetrick v. Martin*, 78, 79, 286n. 48, 287n. 54
*Hickingbottom v. Easley*, 111
"high" value speech, 18
*Hillis v. Stephen F. Austin University*, 65, 94
hiring: affirmative action and, 177–82; deference to faculty decisions regarding, 143–45; part-time faculty, 155–56; in private sectarian institutions, 121. *See also* nondiscrimination law
*Hooper v. Jensen*, 237
*Hoover v. Morales*, 133
*Hopwood v. State of Texas*, 179
hostile environment sexual harassment, 219
Howard University, 307n. 40

Idaho State University, 27
immunity: charitable type, 268n. 81; confusion in terms regarding, 268n. 82; of state-actor institutions, 22–24. *See also* sovereign immunity
impact of law on faculty, 258–60
incompetence, 209. *See also* termination of tenure "for cause"
indemnification of faculty, 255–56, 291n. 131, 338n. 7
*In re Dinnan*, 306–7n. 32
*In re Grand Jury Subpoena*, 53–54

*In re Mt. Sinai School of Medicine v. American Tobacco Co.*, 51–52
institutional citizenship. *See* governance and operations
institutional governance and operations. *See* governance and operations
institutional stature, 303n. 22
institutions: academic standards, establishment and enforcement of, 75–80; constituencies, growth in number of, 256–57; contractual relationship with faculty, 20; contractual relationship with students, 20–21; custom and practice of, 20, 21, 26–27, 184–85, 266n. 68; differences in, 4; land grant type, 62, 281n. 160; number of, 261n. 4 (Introduction). *See also* private institutions; private sectarian institutions; public institutions
instructional workloads, 262n. 13
insubordination, 116, 209–11. *See also* termination of tenure "for cause"
"intellectual content" in digital age, 99–100, 103
intellectual property law: copyright law, 35, 36–43; gaps in institutional policies and, 45–46; overview of, 34–36; patent law, 35–36, 43–46; trademark, 272n. 36
intercollegiate athletics, 6, 7, 168
Internet: copyright law and, 39–43; extramural speech and, 138–39
intramural speech: analytical framework, 107; conferences and symposia, 117–20; on matter of public concern, 107–13; Pickering/Connick balancing test of, 114–17; at private institutions, 106–7; at private sectarian institutions, 120–25
Iowa State, 110–11

Ithaca, New York, 8
Ivey v. Univ. of Alaska, 214

Jalal v. Columbia University, 166
Jawa v. Fayetteville State Univ., 92,
    324n. 294
Jeffries v. Harleston, 133–34
Jew v. Univ. of Iowa, 219
Jimenez v. Almodovar, 231–32
Johnson, Lyndon, 174
Johnson v. Bd. of Regents, 21, 228–
    29, 230, 246
Johnson v. Lincoln Univ., 109–10
Johnson v. San Jacinto Junior
    College, 248
Johnson v. Univ. of Pittsburgh, 242
judiciary: case law and, 9–10; com-
    mon academic practice and, 266n.
    68; deference to academic deci-
    sions by, 21–22, 64–65, 143–45;
    organization and operation of, 9–
    10; overlapping jurisdictions of,
    159
junior colleagues: consensual sex
    with, 223–24; dating, 328n. 344;
    intellectual influence over, 149–50

Kadiki v. Virginia Commonwealth
    Univ., 218–19, 326n. 320
Kansas State University, 326–27n.
    330
Kaplan v. Johnson, 43, 276n. 89
Kaplin, William, 249
Kaufman v. Board of Trustees, 58
Keen v. Penson, 72–73, 94
Kent State University, 70
Keyishian v. Board of Regents, 17,
    139–40
Killinger v. Samford Univ., 122
Kimel v. Florida Board of Regents,
    23, 170–71
Klinge v. Ithaca College, 216
knowledge, specialization of, 60–61
Korf v. Ball State Univ., 218
Kovacs v. Cooper, 18

Krotkoff v. Goucher College, 227,
    229, 230
Kunda v. Muhlenberg, 144, 163–64
Kurtz v. Vickrey, 112–13

labor law, 185–200
Lakoski v. Univ. of Texas Medical
    Branch, 169
land grant colleges, 62, 281n. 160
Leadbetter v. Rose, 22
Lee, Barbara, 249
legal considerations: consequences of
    discrimination litigation, 174–77;
    impact of, 1, 258–60; overlapping
    jurisdictions, 159; tension, sources
    of, 256–58
Lehman v. Bd. of Trustees of
    Whitman College, 219
Levin v. Harleston, 128–29, 133, 134,
    301n. 2
liberty interests, 240, 241–43
Lipsett v. Univ. of Puerto Rico, 218,
    219
local law, 8–9, 159, 308–9n. 53
Lovelace v. Southeastern Mass.
    Univ., 79, 92
"low" value speech, 18
Lynn v. Regents of Univ. of Cali-
    fornia, 166

Maas v. Cornell Univ., 219
Maguire v. Marquette Univ., 121
Mahaffey v. Kansas Bd. of Regents,
    243
Mahoney v. Hankin, 75
managerial role and unionization,
    188, 190
mandatory retirement, 170
Maples v. Martin, 110, 115, 242
Marks v. New York University, 58
Martin v. Parrish, 72
Matthews v. Eldridge, 244
McClendon v. Morton, 335n. 444
McConnell v. Howard University, 73,
    216

*McDaniels v. Flick,* 218, 245–46
*McDonnell Douglas Corp. v. Green,*
160
*McElearney v. Univ. of Illinois,* 31
*Megill v. Bd. of Regents,* 303n. 21
membership in controversial
organizations, 139–40, 304n. 38
Metzger, W., 304n. 3
Microsoft Corporation, 50–51
Midland College, 72
Miller, Arthur, 41–42
minority, definition of, 314n. 135
Monsanto Corporation, 59–60
moral turpitude, 212–14, 217–26,
300n. 84. *See also* termination of
tenure "for cause"
*Mumford v. Godfried,* 306n. 22

*Nardi v. Stevens Institute of Tech-*
*nology,* 31
National Conference of Catholic
Bishops, 125
National Labor Relations Act
(NLRA), 186–87
National Labor Relations Board
(NLRB), 186, 200
*Newman v. Burgin,* 244
New York University, 40, 98, 192,
198–99
*New York University,* 193, 199
NLRA. *See* National Labor Relations
Act (NLRA)
NLRB. *See* National Labor Relations
Board (NLRB)
*N.L.R.B. v. Catholic Bishop of*
*Chicago,* 186–87
*N.L.R.B. v. Yeshiva University,* 189,
190, 317n. 179
noncompliance with employment
contract, 210
nondiscrimination law: affirmative
action and, 178; Americans with
Disabilities Act, 172–73; conse-
quences of litigation, 174–77;
Executive Order 11246, 174;

local, 159, 308–9n. 53; overview
of, 158–60, 175; Section 504, 171–
72; Title VI, 167–68; Title VII,
160–67; Title IX, 168–69
non-tenure-track jobs, 155–57
North Dakota University System, 158
Northern Illinois University, 86–87
Northwestern University, 138, 183

objectivity in scholarship, 28–30
Odessa College, 241
Office of Civil Rights, 168
Office of Federal Contract Compli-
ance Programs, 174
Office of Science and Technology
Policy, 212
Ohio State University, 225
Ohio University, 235
*Ollman v. Toll,* 30, 140
ownership: of course outlines or
teaching notes, 94–95; of scholarly
work, 34–45. *See also* copyright
law; patent law

*Parate v. Isibor,* 93–94, 287n. 54
part-time faculty, 155–56
patent law: adoption of patent
policies, 44–46; employers and,
275n. 85, 276n. 87; overview of,
35–36, 43–46; shop rights and, 43,
276n. 90; types of patents, 272n.
40
pedagogical techniques and styles,
73–80
peer pressure: behavior change and,
207–8, 217; extramural behavior
and, 135–36, 137, 141; selection
of research topics and, 28, 150;
sexual relationships with students
or junior colleagues and, 224
peer review: guild model and, 144–
45, 151, 158, 304n. 3; in hiring,
promotion, and tenure decisions,
143–47; of scholarship, 28–30, 32;
of teaching methods, 75

performance standards, 200–202
permission to use copyrighted works, 100
perquisites, loss of, 243
*Perry v. Sindermann,* 241, 242
personal grievances, 111–14
personal immunity, 23
personal liability risk, 254–56
personal liability risk of administration, 254–56
personnel decisions: affirmative action, 177–82; key concepts in, 250; procedural protections for faculty in, 239–49. *See also* discipline; nondiscrimination law; tenure
Peru State College, 228
Ph.D. students, 156–57, 192–200, 319n. 201
Philadelphia College of Textiles and Science, 157
photocopying for educational uses, 95–99, 100–101
*Piarowski v. Illinois Community College Dist.,* 282n. 2
*Pickering v. Board of Education,* 114–17, 126, 131–35, 211, 293n. 10, 297n. 47, 297–98n. 57
plagiarism, 211
policies: on acceptable use of computing facilities, 141–42; adherence to, 243; on conflicts of commitment and conflicts of interest, 57–60, 280n. 146, 281n. 154; on consensual relationships, 213, 223–24; on copyright law, 39–43, 274n. 64; due process and, 336n. 452; on grading, 92–94; on patent law, 44–46; on research support, 32–34; on sexual harassment, 222; significance of, 21, 248–49; on termination "for cause," 208–9, 215–17
political organizations, 139–40
political views: academic appoint-

ments and, 29–30; in classroom, 82–86
post-tenure review: adoption of, 207; blanket type, 203–5; faculty development funds and, 206–7; fear about, 206; focused type, 205; prevalence of, 155, 202–3, 320nn. 224&225; *in terrorem* effect of, 321n. 232
Powell, Justice, 314n. 140
pretenure performance evaluation, 202, 305n. 14
preventive law, 3
prima facie case under Title VII, 160–61
Princeton University, 16
private institutions: academic freedom and, 66; charitable immunity and, 268n. 81; collective bargaining and, 186–92; control of private faculty behavior at nonsectarian, 300n. 81; extra-institutional speech restrictions and, 302n. 10; faculty intramural speech and, 106–7; U.S. Constitution and, 11, 15–16
private sectarian institutions: academic freedom at, 120–25; Catholic universities, 124–25; collective bargaining and, 186–87, 316n. 169; discharge "for cause" from, 300n. 84; faith-based requirements for faculty in, 299n. 77; First Amendment and, 261n. 3 (ch. 1), 300n. 81
procedural protections in personnel decisions: due process and, 244–49; liberty or property interests and, 240–41; overview of, 239–40
program, definition of, 234–35
program closures: AAUP and, 232, 238–39, 333n. 410; on academic grounds, 231–33, 235–37; authority to make decision regarding, 232–34; case law

regarding, 332n. 399, 333n. 408;
due process and, 239, 247–48;
financial exigency compared to,
235–37; involvement of faculty in,
233, 234; liability to students after,
235; mixed motives for, 235–36;
safeguards afforded faculty, 238–
39; termination of tenure for,
231–39
program reductions, 237, 238
program restructuring, 237–38, 332n.
399
promotion, denial of, 242
property interests, 240–43
protected speech, status as, 114–17,
126, 131–35
public concern, speech regarding,
109–14, 131, 293nn. 7&8
"public function" test, 13, 264nn.
31& 32
public institutions: academic
freedom and, 65–66; collective
bargaining at, 187–88; due
process in personnel decisions,
240–49; faculty extramural speech
at, 131–35; faculty intramural
speech at, 107–17; U.S. Constitution and, 11–15
publicity, 135–36
publishers and "course packs," 95–
99, 100–101

quid pro quo sexual harassment,
218–19

Rampey v. Allen, 114
"reasonable accommodation," 171
reduction of programs, 237–38
religiously affiliated institutions. See
private sectarian institutions
religious views in classroom, 87–89
Rendell-Baker v. Kohn, 13, 264n. 38
reprehensible personal conduct,
212–14
research projects: academic freedom

and, 25–26, 68; attacks on discipline and, 29–30; commercialization of, 61; compelled disclosure
of data, 48–54; conflicts of interest, 55–57, 59–60; external support for, 31–34, 61–62, 270n. 14,
271n. 24; fraud or misconduct in,
211–12; internal support for, 30–
31; peer pressure and, 28–30;
quality of, 28–29; selection of
topics, 25–30
restructuring of programs, 237–38,
331–32n. 399
retirement: early retirement plans,
311–12n. 101; mandatory, 170
reverse discrimination, 160, 252,
314n. 138
Riggin v. Bd. of Trustees of Ball State
Univ., 81, 209, 285n. 25, 287n. 57,
324n. 294
Rosenberger v. Rector and Visitors of
University of Virginia, 18–19
Rose v. Elmhurst College, 237
royalties, 44–45, 61
Rust v. Sullivan, 19
Rutgers, 212, 215, 322–23n. 277
Rymer v. Kendall College, 236

salary, 182–84
Samaan v. Trustees, 212
Samad v. Jenkins, 243
San Filippo v. Bongiovanni, 215
San Francisco State, 89–90
Scallet v. Rosenblum, 90–91
Scarce v. United States, 53
Schier v. Temple University, 14–15
Scott v. Univ. of Delaware, 161–62
sectarian institutions. See private
sectarian institutions
Section 504 (Rehabilitation Act of
1973), 171–72, 175
self-regulation. See peer pressure
Selzer v. Fleisher, 304n. 38
sex discrimination: in federal
statutes, 326n. 321; sexual

sex discrimination (*continued*)
harassment, 73–78, 217–26, 251,
326–27n. 330. *See also* Title VII
(Civil Rights Act of 1964); Title IX
(Education Amendments of 1972)
sexual harassment: confidentiality of
reports of, 220–21; definitions of,
221, 251; movement of professor
to another school after, 224–26;
policies regarding, 222; single act
and, 326–27n. 330; teaching styles
and, 73–78, 222; termination of
faculty for, 213, 217–26; types of,
218–19; vicarious liability of
employers for, 220
sexual orientation, discrimination on
basis of, 251, 313n. 125
sexual relationship: with junior
colleagues, 223–24; with students,
213, 223–24
Sherman Antitrust Act, 183–84
"shop right," 43, 276n. 90
*Silva v. University of New Hamp-
shire,* 74–75, 77, 286n. 35
*Sinott v. Skagit Valley College,* 293–
94n. 14, 298–99n. 66
Smith College, 147
sovereign immunity: ADA and, 23,
173; ADEA and, 170–71; Fourteenth Amendment and, 312n.
118; limitations on, 23–24; original
justification for, 267n. 73; state-
actor institutions and, 22–24;
successful assertions of, 267n. 76
*Speck v. North Carolina Dairy
Foundation,* 276n. 87
speech. *See* extramural speech; free
speech; intramural speech
Stanford University, 40, 44, 45, 277n.
102
*Starsky v. Williams,* 134–35, 136,
296n. 25, 302–3n. 19
state actor: "close nexus" test, 12–13;
description of, 5, 11; immunity
and, 22–24; "public function" test,

13, 264nn. 31&32; status as, 11–
12, 15–16; "symbiotic relationship" test, 13–15; threshold
question, 15
state constitutions, 7, 16
state regulations, 8
state statutes, 7–8, 187
State University of New York, 118,
139–40, 333n. 407
*State v. Schmid,* 16
*Stone v. Dartmouth College,* 15
strikes, 187
students: consensual sex with, 213,
223–24; contractual relationship
between institutions and, 20–21;
discipline cases, 323n. 280;
grades, 93, 290n. 108; liability to
with degree program termination,
235; Ph.D. level, 156–57, 195,
319n. 201; at private sectarian
institutions, 121; Section 504 and,
171; sexual harassment and, 217–
26; Title IX and, 168–69; unionization of, 192–200, 319n. 205
subject matter-based restrictions on
free speech, 18–19
substantive due process, 248
supervisory role and unionization,
188–89
support. *See* funding
supreme court, 10
*Sutton v. United Air Lines,* 172
*Sweezy v. New Hampshire,* 69–70,
84, 85, 144
"symbiotic relationship" test, 13–15
symposia, free speech at, 117–20

teaching: academic freedom and, 64–
69; breach of integrity in, 212;
classroom behavior and treatment
of students, 72–73; conferences
and symposia as expanded version
of, 118–20; copyright law and
course materials, 94–101; course
content and theoretical emphasis,

80–92, 122–24; course evaluation requirements, 71–72; external attacks on classroom autonomy, 69–71; grading policies, 92–94; instructional workloads, 262n. 13; methods of, 73–80; overview of, 63–64; at private sectarian institutions, 121–22

teaching assistants. *See* graduate students

technological change, 39–43, 61, 257

Temple University, 14–15

tenure: alternatives to, 154–58, 250–51; award of under Title VII, 163–65, 166–67; benefits of, 154–55; confidentiality of review process, 152–54; criteria for, 147; definition of, 145–46; denials of, 151–52, 242, 335n. 444; discipline-driven variations in, 147; guild model and, 151; liberty or property interests and, 241–42; narrow employee-relations perspective of, 321n. 239; probationary period before, 147–48, 202; process of awarding, 146–48; research and, 304–5n. 8; systems of, 145–52; views of, 148–51. *See also* termination of tenure; termination of tenure "for cause"

tenure track, percent of faculty on, 308n. 44

term contracts: ending or nonrenewal of, 241–42, 246; overview of, 156–57

termination of department or program. *See* program closures

termination of tenure: for financial exigency, 226–31, 246–47; for program elimination, 231–37, 247; for program reduction, 237, 238; for program restructuring, 237–38

termination of tenure "for cause": AAUP and, 148; breach of academic integrity, 211–12; due process and, 244–46; incompetence, 209; insubordination, 209–11; moral turpitude or reprehensible personal conduct, 212–14; multiple categories of, 214–15; policies regarding, 208–9, 215; practical and political hurdles to, 215–16; procedures for, 216–17; sexual harassment, 217–26

terms of employment: nonunion setting, 184–85; overview of, 182–84. *See also* tenure; term contracts; unionization

Texas A&M University, 28, 133

*Texas Faculty Ass'n. v. University of Texas at Dallas*, 239, 247

*Texas v. Walker*, 210

theoretical perspective in classroom, 82–90, 122–24

Thomson, J., 270n. 12

Title VI (Civil Rights Act of 1964), 167–68, 175

Title VII (Civil Rights Act of 1964): award of tenure as damages under, 163–65, 166–67; bona fide occupational qualification, 162; disparate impact case, 161–62; disparate treatment case, 160–61; EEOC and, 162–63, 165; language of sex discrimination statutes, 326n. 321; overview of, 160, 175; prima facie case under, 160–61; private sectarian institutions and, 121, 162; proving discriminatory motive, 309n. 59; sexual harassment and, 217–18, 220–22

Title IX (Education Amendments of 1972): bona fide occupational qualification, 168–69; funding and, 168–69; language of sex discrimination statutes, 326n. 321; overview of, 6, 168–69, 175; regulations, 7, 262n. 7; sexual harassment and, 217–18, 220–22

trademark, 272n. 36

transfer of faculty between departments, 242
trial court, 10
*Trister v. University of Mississippi,* 129–30

UCLA, 273n. 52
UNext.com, 40
unionization: eligibility to unionize, 188–91; future of, 252; of graduate students, 192–200, 319nn. 201&205; overview of, 185–88; at private institutions, 186–87, 316n. 169; at public institutions, 187–88. *See also* collective bargaining
*Univ. and Comm. College System of Nevada v. Farmer,* 180–81
*Universidad Central de Bayamon v. N.L.R.B.,* 186–87
University of Alabama, 23, 87–89, 173
University of Arkansas at Little Rock, 82–83
University of California, 192
University of Central Arkansas, 296n. 25
University of Chicago, 40, 42, 59, 275nn. 81&82, 281n. 154
University of Colorado, 27, 71–72
University of Florida, 44, 303n. 21
University of Iowa, 223, 233
University of Kansas, 215–16
University of Maryland, 140
University of Minnesota, 176, 237–38
University of Montevallo, 112–13
University of Nevada at Reno, 136–37
University of North Dakota, 208–9
University of Pennsylvania, 223, 225, 263n. 21, 265n. 49
*University of Pennsylvania v. Equal Employment Opportunity Commission,* 152–54
University of Pittsburgh, 265n. 42

University of Puerto Rico, 231–32
University of Southern Colorado, 232–33
University of Utah, 211
University of Virginia, 90–91
University of Washington, 234–35
University of Wisconsin System, 181, 228–29, 237, 246
*Urofsky v. Gilmore,* 138–39, 282n. 2, 283–84n. 8
U.S. Commerce Department Conference on Fair Use, 99–100
U.S. Constitution: academic freedom and, 67; due process in employee discipline, 239–49; overview of, 5–6; purview of, 11. *See also* specific amendments
U.S. Supreme Court, 10, 152–54

Van Alstyne, W., 283n. 6
*Vanderhurst v. Colorado Mountain College District,* 95
Veblen, Thorstein, 62
viewpoint-based restrictions on free speech, 18–19, 83, 89
Washington University, 59–60
*Weinstein v. University of Illinois,* 38
Wesleyan University, 146
Westmark Community College, 155
*White v. Davis,* 70
*Williams v. Weisser,* 273n. 52
Wisconsin State University-Oshkosh, 241
"work made for hire," 36–39
Wright State University, 90

Yale University, 193, 197–98
Yeshiva University, 185, 189, 190
Yudof, Mark, 283n. 6
*Yu v. Peterson,* 211

*Zahavy v. Univ. of Minnesota,* 214
*Zahorik v. Cornell Univ.,* 304n. 1
"zero-based salary" plan, 183

AcX-1579
19.95
1-15-02

DISCARD

VCTC Library
Hartness Library
Vermont Technical College
Randolph Center, VT 05061